EVER FORWARD!

The story of one of the nation's oldest
and most historic military units

Theodore G. Shuey, Jr.

Lot's Wife Publishing
Staunton, Virginia
September 2008

Cover design by Jennifer Wood Monroe
Cover illustration by Kyle Carroll
Interior layout by Nancy Sorrells
Interior maps and illustrations by Anna Davis

ISBN Number: 9781934368084 (softcover)
ISBN Number: 9781934368091 (hardcover)

Library of Congress Control Number: 2008934485

Lot's Wife Publishing
P.O. Box 1844
Staunton, VA 24402
www.lotswifepublishing.com

To my parents, Dr. Theodore George and Mary Ellen Long Shuey, without whose emphasis on education I would never have enjoyed such a wonderful career and certainly not been able to write *Ever Forward*.

Contents

List of Illustrations   vii

Foreword by John O. Marsh, Jr.   xi

Preface   xiii

Introduction   xv

Acknowledgments   xvii

Into the Valley   1

The Tradition Begins   13

More Indian Wars   26

Dunmore's War & Point Pleasant   39

The American Revolution   50

The Building of a Nation   67

The Foundation of the Stone Wall   76

The Valley Campaign   90

The Peninsula to Appomattox   109

Reconstruction, Reorganization, & Over There   143

Great Depression & War Again   156

Omaha Beach to St. Lô   179

Vire to the Elbe   203

Reorganization & the Cold War   222

29 Let's Go Again   241

Peacekeeping, 9-11, & the War on Terrorism   256

Abbreviations, Code names, and Glossary   270

Appendix A: Official Statement of Lineage & Battle Honors
                                                        276

Appendix B: Commanders of the Regiment   280

Appendix C: Works cited   284

Index   294

About the author   311

List of illustrations

Chapter 1:   2   *1-1: Regions of Virginia*
              3   *1-2: Virginia's Valley Region*
              4   *1-3: Indian tribe locations*
              5   *1-4: The Warriors Path*
              6   *1-5: Early Exploration into Virginia's Valleys*
              8   *1-6: The Great Road*
              9   *1-7: Blockhouse*
             10   *1-8: Stockade*
             10   *1-9: Fort*
             11   *1-10: The lands of Augusta County*

Chapter 2:   17   *2-1: Augusta Militia – "The Tradition Begins" - 1742*
             21   *2-2: Washington's Expedition, Winter 1753*
             23   *2-3: Photograph of Fort Necessity*
             25   *2-4: George Washington's route toward Fort Duquesne*

Chapter 3:   27   *3-1: Braddock's Expedition*
             29   *3-2: Site of Braddock's Defeat*
             31   *3-3: Big Sandy Expedition*
             33   *3-4: Virginia's Frontier Forts, 1756*
             35   *3-5: Forbes' Route to Capture Fort Duquesne, 1758*
             38   *3-6: Division of Botetourt County from Augusta*

Chapter 4:   40   *4-1: Dunmore's Expedition against the Shawnees – 1774*
             41   *4-2: Day by Day from Fort Savannah to Point Pleasant*
             42   *4-3: Colonel Fleming's Order of March Sketch -1774*
             44   *4-4: Sketch of the Battle Drawn by Steven R. Kidd*
             45   *4-5: The Battle of Point Pleasant – October 10, 1774*
             47   *4-6: Route to Chillicothe*
             49   *4-7: Photograph of author with DAR & SAR representatives at the 225th anniversary of the battle on October 10, 1999*

Chapter 5:   53   *5-1: Gwynn's Island & Great Bridge*
             54   *5-2: Virginia's Western Counties - 1776*
             57   *5-3: The Battle of King's Mountain, October 7, 1780*

	59	5-4: *Over Mountain Men Route – 1780*
	60	5-5: *Battle of Cowpens, January 17, 1781*
	62	5-6: *Battle of Guilford Courthouse, March 15, 1781*
	64	5-7: *The Southern Campaign and Tarleton's Raid Route*
	65	5-8: *Seige of Yorktown*
Chapter 6:	68	6-1: *Western Forts*
	71	6-2: *War - 1812*
	75	6-3: *West Augusta Regiment Officers*
Chapter 7:	77	7-1: *Augusta County 5th Regiment Communities - 1861*
	79	7-2: *Stonewall Brigade Communities*
	81	7-3: *Jackson's Brigade in the Lower Valley*
	83	7-4: *The Route to Manassas*
	85	7-5: *Jackson ". . . standing like a stone wall"*
	86	7-6: *First Brigade at First Manassas, July 21, 1861*
Chapter 8:	91	8-1: *Jackson threatens western Maryland*
	95	8-2: *Battle of Kernstown, March 23, 1862*
	100	8-3: *McDowell and Franklin*
	101	8-4: *McDowell to Winchester, Spring 1862*
	103	8-5: *Battle of Winchester – May 25, 1862*
	105	8-6: *Battle of Cross Keys – June 8, 1862*
	106	8-7: *Battle of Port Republic – June 9, 1862*
	107	8-8: *The Valley Campaign Map*
Chapter 9:	110	9-1: *First Brigade Route to Peninsula – June 1862*
	111	9-2: *First Brigade in the Seven Days Campaign*
	114	9-3: *First Brigade at Cedar Mountain, August 9, 1862*
	115	9-4: *Groveton – August 28, 1862*
	117	9-5: *The Route to 2nd Manassas*
	118	9-6: *Second Manassas – August 29-30, 1862*
	120	9-7: *Route to Antietam – September 1862*
	121	9-8: *Antietam – September 17, 1862*
	123	9-9: *Fredericksburg – December 13, 1862*
	125	9-10: *Chancellorsville – May 2, 1863*
	128	9-11: *Route to Gettysburg*
	130	9-12: *Brigade position at Gettysburg, July 3, 1863*
	132	9-13: *Mine Run – November 27, 1863*
	134	9-14: *The Wilderness – May 5, 1864*
	136	9-15: *Bloody Angle – May 12, 1864*
	137	9-16: *Headed to Washington – Summer 1864*
	139	9-17: *Defeat, Retreat, and Appomattox*

Chapter 10:   148   **10-1: Original stitched 29th patch**
               149   **10-2: Route to the Front**
               151   **10-3: Alsace Map**
               152   **10-4: Meuse-Argonne Map**
               153   **10-5: Regimental Crest**
               154   **10-6: Seal of Virginia**

Chapter 11:   159   **11-1: 116th Infantry Regiment Company locations**
               168   **11-2: Fort Meade to Camp Blanding**
               171   **11-3: Greenock Harbor to Tidworth Barracks**
               172   **11-4: Tidworth Barracks Photograph**
               173   **11-5: Another View of Tidworth Barracks**
               177   **11-6: General Dwight D. Eisenhower visits the officers of the 116th Regiment as they prepare for D-Day.**

Chapter 12:   183   **12-1-1: Omaha Beach at low tide looking west**
               183   **12-1-2: Omaha Beach at low tide looking east**
               183   **12-2: Omaha Beach – High Tide Photograph**
               185   **12-3: Part of WN71 showing a concrete pillbox – Vierville Draw**
               186   **12-4: 116th Landings on Omaha Beach**
               188   **12-5: The 116th breaks out from Omaha Beach**
               189   **12-6: Sergeant John Polyniak, COL Ted Shuey, SFC Terry Howard**
               193   **12-7: Hedgerows of France**
               194   **12-8: Peregoy memorial marker in Couvains, France and his final resting place at Colleville-sur-Mer in the American Cemetery**
               195   **12-9: Omaha Beach to St. Lô**
               197   **12-10: Attack on St. Lô Map**
               201   **12-11: Resting place of the "Major of St. Lô"**
               202   **12-12: Thomas D. Howie Memorial in St. Lô**

Chapter 13:   204   **13-1: Advance to Vire**
               207   **13-2: 116th Movement to Brest**
               208   **13-3: Attack to Brest**
               210   **13-4: 116th Movement to the Front - Vise**
               212   **13-5: Attack to the Roer River**
               216   **13-6: Delbert Cartoon and Julich banner Photographs**
               218   **13-7: Julich to Dortmund**
               219   **13-8: Last WWII locations of the 116th**
               220   **13-9: WWI and WWII movements of the 116th Regiment**

Chapter 14:   225   **14-1: Typical Training Activities – Summer Camp 1950s**
               227   **14-2: MG Paul Booth, COL Mifflin Clowe, BG Archibald Sproul**
               230   **14-3: Monticello Guard retiring the Colors at the 1st Muster – November 18, 1967**
               234   **14-4: 116th Separate patch**
               236   **14-5: Sennybridge Training area, South Wales photo**
               238   **14-6: CPT Harman & MG McCaddin; CPT Harman & LTC of the Royal Guard Photograph**

Chapter 15:   241   **15-1: Captains Castles and Marsh test the .30 caliber machine gun**
               250   **15-2: Desert Panthers**
               251   **15-3: "Freedom Isn't Free" – Painting by James Dietz Photograph**
               253   **15-4: MG Thackston with Division and Brigade leaders, welcome 1SG Dancy and C Company back to Ft. Benning**

Chapter 16:   258   **16-1: Noble Eagle – Airport Duty**
               259   **16-2: GTMO Duty**
               260   **16-3: Task Force Normandy Area of Operation**
               261   **16-4: "On Patrol – Task Force Normandy" Painting by James Dietz Photograph**
               262   **16-5: Task Force Normandy returns home**
               263   **16-6: 1/116th Red Dragons accept TOA as part of TF Falcon – December 2006**
               266   **16-7: Hurricane Katrina relief efforts**
               267   **16-8: Task Force Stonewall on Duty**
               268   **16-9: Training at Camp Shelby, Mississippi; Boarding aircraft for Iraq Photographs**
               268   **16-10: SSG Amy Wenger and GEN Petraus**
               269   **16-11: JASG-C Command Directorate in the Green Zone at Baghdad**

Foreword

The invasion of Normandy by Allied forces in June of 1944 ranks among the great battles of the ancient and modern world. Its fame will only grow. The invasion's success hinged on that area of the French coast designated "Omaha." By the end of the Longest Day, it would be called "Bloody Omaha."

Only one National Guard unit had been chosen to be in the first wave of invasion forces on Normandy. The 116th Infantry Regiment of the Virginia Guard, better known as the Stonewall Brigade, a tribute earned by service under its illustrious commander in the Civil War. Its reputation for distinguished service also included the French and Indian War (commanded by Washington), the Revolutionary War, and at the Meuse–Argonne in World War I.

This highly distinguished record of combat service was no doubt a factor that caused the military high command to put the 116th into the epicenter of violent combat with a battalion of Rangers, and elements of the First Division. The soldiers found themselves confronted with German troops seasoned by combat on the Eastern Front and inserted without awareness of Allied intelligence resources. Nonetheless, the Stonewallers fought and clawed across the beach, and, by day's end took the high ground, unaware that General Bradley gave serious consideration to withdrawing Omaha sector forces because of the violent resistance that threatened invasion success. When the Regiment sailed for France that fateful day, it numbered more 3,100 officers and men. From D-Day to V-E Day its numbers turned over three times

The Stonewall Brigade is not just the story of a National Guard unit; rather it is a fine historical account of the saga of the militia in our nation's experience. It weaves together the history of the Militia on the early frontier, and in the westward movement of our country. Using one of America's most fabled military units as its centerpiece, the book demonstrates the importance of the National Guard in times of war and peace. The writer skillfully moves into modern times and the war on terrorism. The role that the National Guard and its soldiers are playing in performing their mission, often in successive deployments to dangerous areas and harsh environments, is detailed in these pages.

The author, Ted Shuey, writes from a background of labor and love. A native of the Shenandoah Valley, home of the Brigade, he served as a public school teacher, and coach. He majored in history in college. Importantly, for years he marched in the ranks of the 116th, and his last military assignment was Commander of the Stonewall Brigade. He retired from the Virginia Guard with the rank of Brigadier General.

The Stonewall Brigade is written in an interesting and readable style. It is based on extensive research, and paints with a broad brush historically. It is a must read for the military historian, but has a far broader appeal because of its lessons and insights. The Stonewall Brigade should be on the bookshelves of every high school library, but deserves a far broader readership by all those who want to know more about the National Guard. It is a story in which not only Virginians, but also all Americans can take special pride.

John O. Marsh, Jr.
Former Secretary of the Army
U.S. Congressman from Virginia
Distinguished Professor, George Mason
University School of Law
30 June 2008

Preface

The story of the 116th Infantry has to be one of the greatest American history stories _never_ told. It captures the American dream, tracing the evolution of a frontier culture into the most powerful country in the world. It is the story of simple people willing to sacrifice all to preserve the freedom they loved. It is a story of settlers who defended their homes against warring Indians, then the French and powerful British, before surviving the destruction wrought by a tragic Civil War and crossing the ocean time and time again to secure the peace and freedom they enjoyed for less fortunate people in foreign lands.

The heroes of the 116th Infantry are not the soldiers alone, but also their families who sacrificed equally in the struggles of a growing America. Their strength is in their diversity. The "Stonewallers" as they became known during the Civil War, have always valued their religious freedom, independence, and peace. They never sought any glory or recognition, only the reward of being able to pass on to another generation the torch of freedom, which they have fought to keep burning for over 250 years.

It is fitting that today three of the main travel corridors in Virginia commemorate the service and sacrifice of the Augusta Militia and the 116th Infantry. Interstate 81 honors John Lewis as it goes north down the Valley from Staunton; while going south, it is named for his son, Andrew Lewis. On the east side of the Blue Ridge Mountains is U.S. Route 29 that carries the name of 29th Division Highway, remembering the 116th's heroes of Omaha Beach, while west of the Blue Ridge the old Valley Pike, U.S. Route 11, bears the name 116th Infantry Highway. Lest we forget!

Introduction

This work is intended to capture the complete history of the Augusta Militia, recognized as America's Stonewall Brigade, and today's 116th Infantry Brigade Combat Team. It traces the unit's foundation from its pioneer founders to the current members serving in Operation Iraqi Freedom. The maps and details are provided to allow readers in general, but especially today's Stonewallers, the opportunity to walk the ground where the members of this organization made history. Their legacy of service and sacrifice is certainly worthy of being captured for posterity.

The 116th Infantry Regiment was organized in 1742 and has distinguished itself through its continuous service to its communities, the Commonwealth of Virginia, and the United States. It is America's seventh oldest military organization and has maintained a tradition of excellence in service during four centuries. Its history begins with the Indian Wars of the 1700s and includes the service of many of its current members as a part of Task Force Noble Eagle, Operation Enduring Freedom, and Operation Iraqi Freedom. The unit has been recognized by the Commonwealth of Virginia for its role in six military campaigns before the Army was founded in 1775. Since its founding, the Army has authorized the colors of the 116th Infantry to carry forty campaign streamers earned for service during conflicts throughout America and around the world, with more to be added.

Though taking their place in military history, the unit simultaneously made monumental contributions in protecting lives and property throughout Virginia while serving in its traditional state National Guard mission. This mission has been expanded to include support to other states with communities needing assistance such as the Mississippi Gulf Coast after Hurricane Katrina. To understand the spirit and courage that epitomizes this military organization, it is first necessary to go back in time and examine the foundation of this historic unit. It is also important to understand the fighting spirit and commitment to selfless service, which has been the hallmark of members of the 116th Infantry.

The history of the United States is marbled with the sacrifices of military organizations on battle grounds throughout this country and the world. No unit, however, is more readily recognized in the United States Army than the 116th Infantry Regiment. It was initially the "Augusta Militia" of Virginia, but it remains best known as the "Stonewall Brigade" for its exploits during the Civil War and for being selected as the only National Guard unit to be a part of the initial landing at Omaha Beach on D-Day in World War II. This book is an attempt to capture, for the first time, the organization's 265 years of service and its contribution to its home communities in western Virginia, the Commonwealth, and the nation. Its publication just happens to coincide with the 400th year since landings of America's original citizen soldiers in 1607, the first settlers at Jamestown.

It is a great honor to command any military organization, but the honor of commanding the historic unit known today as the 116th Infantry Brigade Combat Team is almost impossible to describe. Wherever my military travels took me in that capacity, the distinctive regimental unit Crest and my green tabs would frequently result in someone saying, "So you command the Stonewall Brigade?" It was during 1999 that I made the commitment to write this book after a number of visits to some of the historic places in the Brigade's history. I will never forget the children of Normandy, France, waving the American flag as I visited there with a number of other National Guard commanders and veterans on the historic fifty-fifth anniversary of the liberation of France. I was equally moved less than a month later to stand before the monuments at Point Pleasant, West Virginia, and receive wreath after wreath from the Daughters and Sons of the American Revolution and place them on the tomb of heroes who died during this, the first battle for American independence.

Ever Forward!

Theodore G. Shuey, Jr.
1 August 2008

Acknowledgments

Having always enjoyed history made writing this book a labor of love, but I was amazed at how much I learned in the process. As a native of Augusta County, Virginia, and living now in the city of Staunton, the records of the Augusta Regiment were easily accessible. In working through the numerous files and artifacts in the 116th Infantry Regiment museum and archives, I stumbled across a manuscript written by Major Reese T. Grubert in 1955. This document was invaluable as an outline of the unit's early history and was apparently used by Major Grubert, a prominent attorney in Staunton, to obtain the appropriate citations for the unit from the Army's Center of Military History and Department of Heraldry.

My visit to the Wisconsin Historical Society to view the original records of the Regiment preserved in the Lyman C. Draper collection housed there and the personal help that I received from Director Richard Pifer were tremendous. Dr. Waite Rawls and the Museum of the Confederacy provided exceptional insight into the Civil War period. The assistance of my good friend and fellow historian, Craig Nannos, currently serving at the Army War College, was invaluable as was the review and support by National Guard historian Colonel Les Melnyk.

I did not go into great detail on the Brigade during the Civil War since there have been so many books published covering this period. Particularly noteworthy are the two works of Dr. James I. Robertson, Jr., of Virginia Tech. His book, *The Stonewall Brigade*, published by the Louisiana State University Press in 1963, stands alone in capturing this unit's history throughout the Civil War. His more recent biography, *Stonewall Jackson*, published in 1997, is a thorough and comprehensive study of this outstanding military commander.

There are a number of excellent works on the 29th Division in World War I and II that provide excellent insight into the 116th Infantry during those wars. *Omaha Beach* and *Beyond the Beachhead* by Joseph Balkoski of Baltimore, Maryland, provide an in-depth study of the unit in World War II. Joe is clearly an expert on WW II, and I have had the pleasure of accompanying him on a staff ride to Normandy in 1999 while serving as the Brigade Commander. I was honored to have served as an escort for D-Day veteran John Polyniak and walked Omaha Beach with him on that first visit there. I am also blessed to have enlisted in the National Guard and served with numerous WW II veterans during my early career. I have learned a great deal from visits with the veterans from the Shenandoah Valley, including the late retired former commander of the 29th Division and a Company Commander on D-Day, MG (Ret.) Archibald Sproul of Staunton.

Much of the recent history of the 116th simply entailed a review of notes and personal memos from my time as a Company Commander, Battalion Commander, and finally as the Brigade Commander. I have had the privilege of serving with many of the current members of this great unit, especially those currently serving in Iraq with Operation Iraqi Freedom. These are the newest combat veterans descending from the original Augusta Militia as the tradition continues! There are many more chapters to be written as the 116th IBCT is called to serve in the remainder of the twenty-first century and beyond. *Ever Forward!* is simply an attempt to capture the first 250 years of the service and sacrifice of the thousands of soldiers and their families who have been a part of America's Stonewall Brigade.

I am forever indebted to my associate Anna Diehl Davis who did much of the sketching, editing, scanning, and organizing necessary to make this book a reality. A special thanks also to artist Kyle Carroll for producing the historical painting used for the book cover. I cannot say enough about the hard work of my publisher, Lot's Wife, and especially Nancy Sorrells. Last, but certainly not least, I want to thank my wife Elizabeth, whose uncle Bernard was a D-Day veteran from K Company/116th Regiment. She has been my travel partner, editor, and chief critic through this long process. We have visited every site, every battlefield, and all the communities that comprised the history of the 116th. It has been a labor of love for both of us and the experience of a lifetime.

Theodore G. Shuey, Jr.
1 August 2008

-One-

Into the Valley

Beginning with the first successful settlement in America established at Jamestown, Virginia, in 1607, it was incumbent upon every male to be willing to take up arms on a moment's notice to defend his life and property. As more and more immigrants came to the New World, this requirement to serve as a member of the colony's defense and be prepared to respond quickly to any threat, never lessened. In fact, the need actually increased as the young colony began its gradual western expansion exploring new territory and infringing deeper into the land of the Indians. In order to understand the foundations of the 116th Infantry Regiment, "America's Stonewall Brigade," it is important to appreciate the land settled by its first members, the early enemies they faced there, and the makeup of the settlers themselves. We begin then, with a look at **The Land**, **The Indians**, **The Explorers**, and **The Settlers**.

The Land

Initially, the settling of Virginia was limited to the rich land along large rivers leading into the Chesapeake Bay. There were no roads, so the rivers connected the settlements and became the lines of communication within the new colony. Boats were used to ferry the English settlers and their supplies. The activity of the early settlers was restricted to the area of Virginia located below the "fall line," or below the falls of the major rivers. (See Illustration 1-1) This area became known as the Tidewater region, since the rivers were influenced by the tides and were easily navigable. It was not long, though, before the prime land in the Tidewater began to disappear and the settlers looked west to the Piedmont region of Virginia.

Piedmont means "at the foot of the mountains," and this region represents about one third of present-day Virginia. The area was heavily wooded in colonial times and required much work to clear fields for farming. The western boundary of the Piedmont was marked by a large, rugged, "blue-looking" mountain range, soon to become known as the Blue Ridge Mountains. The range created a natural dividing line between the colony in eastern Virginia and the western frontier. For centuries, buffalo had crossed these mountains at several locations in order to graze in the

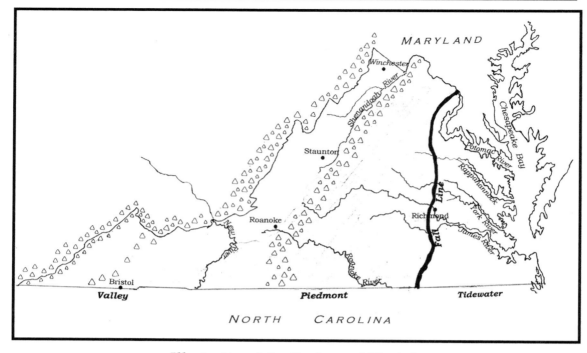

Illustration 1-1: Regions of Virginia

Piedmont and Tidewater regions. As the English settlers in Virginia tried to find routes across this challenging obstacle, they were forced to follow the trails used by the buffalo, but crossings were very slow and difficult.

The Valley of Virginia begins in the north at the Potomac River and runs southwest for over 300 miles to Bristol and the Tennessee state line. The northern portion is known as the Shenandoah Valley after the Algonquian Indian word, which means "Daughter of the Stars." It is bordered on the east by the Blue Ridge Mountains and on the west with the Allegheny Mountain range, ending near Steeles Tavern at the headwaters of the Shenandoah River. The Shenandoah flows north some 150 miles, emptying into the Potomac River at Harpers Ferry. This creates an interesting phenomenon since going south is moving "up the Shenandoah Valley," while going north is moving "down the Shenandoah Valley." The rivers in the central part of the Valley of Virginia flow either into the James River, which slips through the Blue Ridge Mountains and empties into the Chesapeake Bay, or into the Roanoke River that flows southeastward, crossing into North Carolina and emptying into Albemarle Sound. This central part of the Valley of Virginia is known as the Roanoke Valley, while the area to the south is the New River Valley which is drained by the New River as it flows north into present-day West Virginia, eventually emptying into the Ohio River. The Holston, Clinch, and Powell Valleys comprise the southernmost part of the Valley of Virginia, and their namesake rivers flow south into the Tennessee River. Another key piece of terrain in this area is the Cumberland Gap, which became the main route for the settlers moving west beyond the Allegheny Mountains. (See Illustration 1-2)

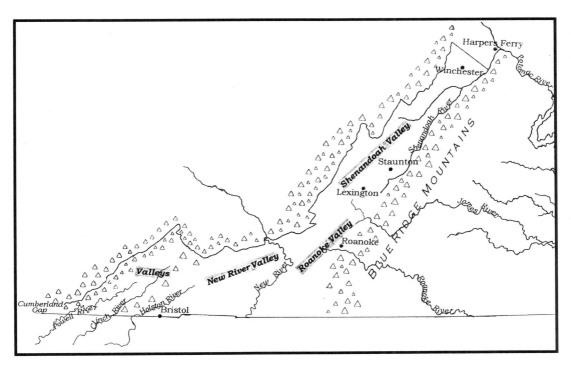

Illustration 1-2: Virginia's Valley Region

The original inhabitants of the Valley of Virginia were, of course, Indians. They were descendants of the Mongoloid tribes who probably entered North America using the Bering Strait between Siberia and Alaska over forty thousand years ago. They moved across the continent to the Atlantic Ocean, entering the lands of Virginia around ten thousand years ago. As settlers began moving west, the Indians were forced to move ahead of them. The Delaware Indians moved west from the area that later became a state named for them, through present-day Pennsylvania and into the Ohio Valley. The Wyandots and Miamis tribes were driven south into the Ohio region by the French. The Shawnees moved there from the south at the invitation of the Miamis who wanted them as a buffer from the white settlements. (See Illustration 1-3)

The tribes known as the Six Nations consisted of the five Iroquois tribes: the Mohawks, the Oneidas, the Onandagas, the Cayugas, and the Senecas, plus the Tuscaroras. This group of tribes and the other Indians inhabiting the Ohio Valley were in constant conflict with the Cherokees who lived to the south in what is now Tennessee. The area between the Ohio and Tennessee Valleys, present-day Kentucky, was reserved for hunting and was abundant in game. There were deer, elk, beaver, bear, and even buffalo to provide valuable pelts and food. These valuable hunting areas in the Valley of Virginia and spreading west into Kentucky were a region of constant conflict among the Indian tribes. The struggles in this area would only increase with the coming of the settlers.

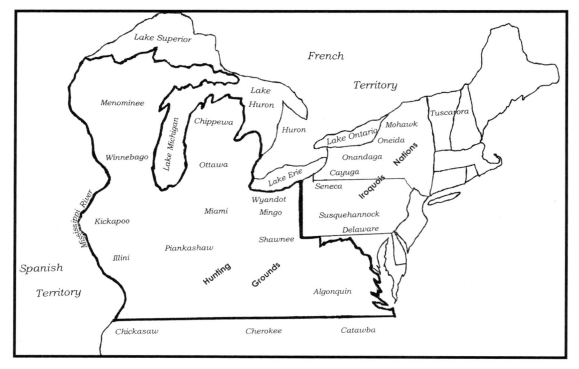

Illustration 1-3: Indian tribe locations

It is quite interesting that early settlers made little note of any permanent Indian presence in the Valley of Virginia or the Kentucky region. Indian tribes moved through the region on hunting expeditions from their base in the Ohio River Valley, as did the Iroquois from New York, the Cherokees from Tennessee, and the Catawbas from the Carolinas and Georgia. The primary route for the movement of the Indians would become known as the "Great Warrior Path." (See Illustration 1-4) Indian hunting parties regularly frequented the Shenandoah Valley as the white settlers began their migration into the region in the 1730s and early 1740s. The Indians entering Augusta County usually crossed the Ohio River and proceeded down the Kanawha River to the mouth of the Greenbrier River, then to present-day Lewisburg and White Sulphur Springs, West Virginia, and then slipped through the mountains and passed through what is today the communities of Covington, Clifton Forge, Millboro, Goshen, Buffalo Gap, and Churchville.

The Explorers

Virginia was, of course, under British authority and governed by a lieutenant governor sent from England. An early lieutenant governor, Sir William Berkeley, commissioned one of the first recorded excursions to the distant Blue Ridge Mountains. German-born John Lederer conducted the expedition. Accompanied by three Indian guides, he climbed to the crest of the mountains in March of 1670 in a location believed to be in present Madison County. Shortly thereafter, wealthy landowner Colonel

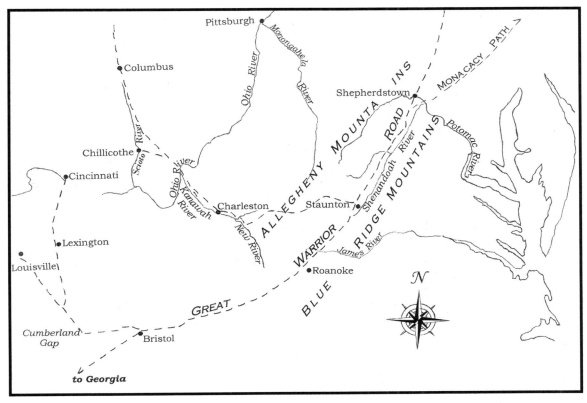

Illustration 1-4: The Warriors Paths

Abraham Wood commissioned Thomas Batts and Robert Fallam to explore lands to the west. Departing the trading center at Fort Henry, located where Petersburg, Virginia, now stands, they crossed the Blue Ridge Mountains in 1671 and entered into what is known as the Roanoke Valley area of the Valley of Virginia. The small party moved down to the New River on September 13, where they burned initials into a number of trees in the area of what is now Narrows in Giles County, Virginia. By this act, they laid claim to the surrounding area and all lands to the west for King Charles II, thus creating the first record of white men *west* of the Blue Ridge Mountains. Virginia Historical Highway Marker KG-19 marks the spot on Route 460, three miles east of Pearisburg. Another German speaking visitor to Virginia, Franz Michel, created the first map of the Shenandoah Valley in 1702, looking up the valley to the south from Maryland.

Interested in the unexplored western territory, in potential mineral extraction opportunities, and needing to lay claim to this region ahead of the French, Lieutenant Governor Alexander Spotswood personally led the first major organized visit to the region in August of 1716. (See Illustration 1-5) He rode west from Williamsburg with a troop of about fifty horsemen, including some gentlemen, a company of rangers, and four Meherrin Indian guides. They stopped at the Fort Germanna settlement on the Rapidan River northwest of present-day Orange County to shoe their horses en route west. Although it was long believed that they ascended the Blue Ridge at Swift Run Gap east of Elkton, where Virginia Historical Highway Marker D-10 marks the spot, current research suggests that the actual site was north of this in present-day Madison County. Descending the western slope of the mountain, they came upon a winding river and on reaching the western bank, buried a bottle claiming the land for King George of England. Using a variety of alcoholic beverages Spotswood had insisted on bringing, the group toasted the momentous occasion and fired a number of volleys with their long rifles in celebration. The way west was officially open.

The expedition had taken about four weeks and covered 438 miles. Later legend claimed that upon his return to Williamsburg, Spotswood established the order of "The Knights of the Golden Horseshoe," to honor the party he had taken to the Shenandoah Valley. He is said to have presented each member with a gold horseshoe, studded with diamonds to represent nails and inscribed *"Sic jurat transcendere montes"* or "Thus he swears to cross the mountains." Not a shred of contemporary evidence to prove this has ever been found. Nonetheless, the spirit of the expedition spread throughout Virginia. Stories circulated of a fertile, beautiful valley abundant in game and other wildlife, including buffalo, bear, deer, wolf, and fox. Both farmers and trappers became keenly interested in the newly discovered western region of Virginia and its potential value.

One of the most western regions of Augusta County was first mapped by Dr. Thomas Walker between March and May of 1750. He was appointed by John Lewis,

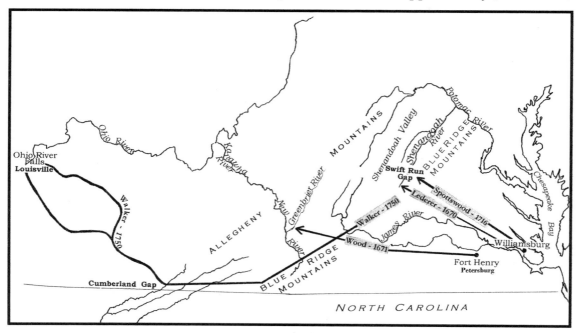

Illustration 1-5: Early Exploration into Virginia's Valleys

the head of the Loyal Company, to explore this wilderness region west of the Clinch River. Walker had accompanied Colonel James Patton to the Clinch River area to survey a grant of 100,000 acres awarded to the Augusta Militia commander by the Virginia Council in 1745.

The Settlers

Although the first settlers of the Shenandoah Valley came from a variety of backgrounds and from several European nationalities or ethnic groups, most had been small farmers in their lands of origin. It was their desire to better their economic circumstances and create a future opportunity to build a better life for themselves and their children. It was their confidence that the British could provide security in the North American colonies, and especially in Virginia, that caused them to settle here. In spite of the widespread popular belief that most settlers came to escape religious persecution, this was a primary motivating force for only a few minority groups such as German Anabaptists or French Huguenots. Other factors that motivated the migration included extreme weather conditions, crop failures, near famine situations, sharply raised rents, and the chaos of military invasion in their homelands.

The first wave of Germans and later Scotch-Irish to reach America entered Pennsylvania. Here they obtained land for farms, but Penn family policies, high prices, and frontier conditions with Indians made it difficult to secure farmland in Pennsylvania by the 1730s. This occurred just as the children of the German and Scotch-Irish immigrants were reaching maturity and hoping to establish families and acquire farms. Their desire for inexpensive land coincided with the policies of the colonial Virginia government under Lieutenant Governor William Gooch, who hoped to expand settlement into the Shenandoah Valley to further British imperial aims and to provide a buffer against the Indians and against French expansion in the interior and especially in the Ohio Valley. In addition, Lord Thomas Fairfax, who had a large private grant of millions of acres in the Northern Neck extending between the Potomac and Rappahannock Rivers from the Chesapeake Bay west to their first headwaters in the Blue Ridge and Allegheny mountains, was also seeking settlers for his land. Lord Fairfax's land included the northern or Lower Shenandoah Valley. An ambitious Tidewater Virginia land speculator who acquired a large grant in the Valley was William Beverley. His grant, issued by Governor Gooch on September 6, 1736, consisted of 118,491 acres in present-day Augusta County that would become known as "Beverley Manor."

The Blue Ridge Mountains had presented a major obstacle for the English settlers moving west from eastern Virginia. Consequently, it was Scotch-Irish and Germans in Pennsylvania, confronted by hostile Indians and by the Allegheny Mountains, who had easier access to the Valley through its extension into south central Pennsylvania. The first of these sturdy pioneers came into the Valley by way of packhorses along buffalo paths or trails cut long ago by Native American hunting parties. The principal trail wound through Lancaster, York, Gettysburg, Harpers Ferry,

Winchester, Staunton, and other points southwest. In time, it was wide enough to accommodate covered road wagons and was often called the Great Road. Today, Route 11 and Interstate 81 generally follow the route of the Great Road through the Valley.

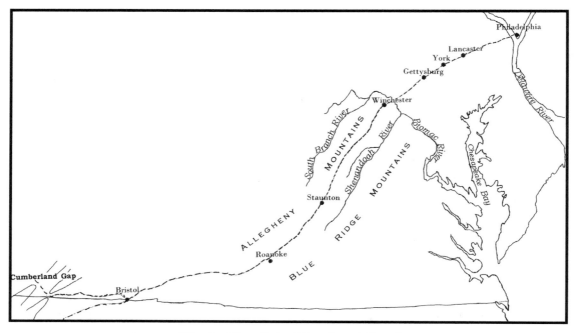

Illustration 1-6: The Great Road

With the exception of a few small villages, the Valley had been abandoned as a place of settlement by the Indians long before the Europeans arrived there. This greatly facilitated settlement, as native peoples did not have to be displaced or fought. Early settlers saw mainly Indian hunting parties traveling between the Carolinas and Pennsylvania. Not until the outbreak of the French and Indian War in 1754, some twenty years after the first settlers arrived, did Indian raiding parties become a threat and an occasional reality.

The early settlers found many open areas as a result of the fires set by the Indians in order to improve hunting. Buffalo sought open grazing land and avoided forested areas, so the Indians burned off brush and young trees to encourage grass and attract herds of buffalo and deer. These open lands made desirable farms and pastures for the European settlers, close to water sources, near abundant timber from which to construct their cabins, and with rich, fertile land to farm.

One of the first settlers to take advantage of the opportunity to move into the Valley of Virginia was the Scotch-Irishman, John Lewis. He was of French Huguenot descent, but had grown up in County Donegal in the north of Ireland as part of a prominent family. After he killed a landlord in self-defense, Lewis felt obliged to flee Ireland and settled in Pennsylvania. Joined there later by his family, he moved south into the lower Shenandoah Valley along with sixteen other families led by Joist Hite in the summer of 1732. The group settled just south of present-day Winchester on a portion of the 40,000-acre tract given to Isaac Vanmeter by Governor Gooch. Lewis, wanting to establish a settlement of his own, proceeded further south up the Valley and settled on the Beverley Manor tract. These were the first white inhabitants in this area. This location would become the heart of present-day Augusta County and the home of the Augusta Militia, the forerunner of the historic Augusta Regiment, later the Stonewall Brigade and today's 116th Infantry Regiment Combat Team.

The early settlers built log cabins and often constructed these homes as a fortress for protection against the Indians. As settlements sprang up west of the Blue Ridge Mountains, a line of "unorganized" defenses evolved. Later, there were three primary types of defensive structures built in the Valley of Virginia: the blockhouse, the stockade, and the fort.

Blockhouses were square two story log buildings, with the second floor extending eighteen to twenty-four inches beyond the first to make entry more difficult. Portholes were cut to allow the occupants to fire at an enemy approaching from any direction. Some blockhouses also served as cabins but most were constructed strictly for protection against Indian attacks. Placed on high ground and filled with good riflemen this structure served as a formidable defensive position.

The stockade consisted of sharpened palisades buried three to four feet in the ground and extending twelve to eighteen feet above the ground. Normally square or

Illustration 1-7: A Blockhouse

rectangular in structure, a stockade could sometimes be as large as an acre in size. Riflemen were positioned on a catwalk inside the wall some four to five feet below the point of the palisade to fire on any attacking enemy. Occasionally blockhouses were placed on the corners of the stockade to provide additional security. There were living areas inside stockades and corrals to hold horses and livestock.

1-8: A Stockade

The fort was a creation of European military forces and clearly provided the best and strongest defense. It consisted of an outer wall constructed with heavy palisades separated from an inner wall with dirt and rock, resulting in a solid, bulletproof barrier. A fort was normally square in form and surrounded by a deep ditch to further impede attackers. Inside were found cabins, barracks, supply houses, and stables. Water was usually supplied by a well sunk inside the fort.

The Shenandoah Valley of Virginia initially was the western part of Essex County. Spotsylvania County was formed from Essex in 1720, and its western region became

Illustration 1-9: A Fort

Orange County in 1734. As the number of inhabitants in the region grew, the need for civil government in the area west of the Blue Ridge resulted in the House of Burgesses approving the establishment of two new counties, Augusta and Frederick. Frederick County was named for Frederick, Prince of Wales. Augusta County was named for Princess Augusta of Saxe-Gotha, his wife. Their son was the future King George III. These two counties were officially divided in 1746 by the Fairfax Line.

The territory of Augusta County would be defined initially as all lands extending from the top of the "Blue Ridge on the East, to the Mississippi River in the West." The northern boundary would later be identified as the area northwest of the Ohio River, while the southern boundary was the dividing line with North Carolina. This area encompasses the present-day states of West Virginia, Kentucky, Ohio, Indiana, Illinois, Michigan, Wisconsin, and western Pennsylvania. It is difficult to imagine an area this large being considered only one county. A major issue, however, was that these western territories had been previously claimed by France as a part of "New France."

As John Lewis moved into the Valley, he was seeking that perfect spot suitable for his family's future. He finally pitched his tent on a small stream, soon known as Lewis Creek, calling the site "Bellefonte" because of its beauty. On February 21, 1738, William Beverley sold to John Lewis 2,071 acres of his "Beverley Manor for fourteen pounds. Known to early settlers as "Lord of the Hills," Lewis was blessed with five

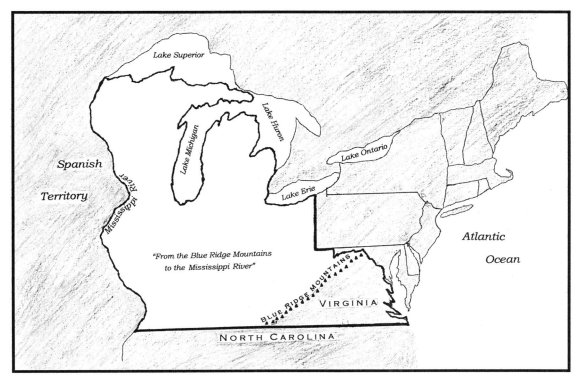

Illustration 1-10: The original lands of Augusta County

strong sons, Thomas, Samuel, Andrew, and William, all born in Ireland, and Charles, born at Bellefonte, to help him establish the settlement. The Lewises used trees and stones to build one of the first structures in the area, a half-stone house and half fortress that would become known as Fort Lewis. They were instrumental in survey-ing the county land and generally assisting in the settlement of the area. These initial settlers named the two nearby hills Betsy Bell and Mary Gray because they resembled hills in Ireland, their former homeland, which bore those names.

As county founder and father, John Lewis was chosen as one of the county magistrates and later honorary colonel of the militia. He was instrumental in open-ing roads over the mountains to connect the settlement with the Tidewater region and the seat of the colony's government. He insisted on the building of the first courthouse in the area and was generally responsible for insuring good order west of the Blue Ridge Mountains.

Fort Lewis became the welcome center for the Valley of Virginia. Settlers travel-ing into Augusta County on the Great Road or coming through the pass in the Blue Ridge Mountains at Rockfish Gap, where Route 250 and Interstate 64 now cross, were frequently hosted and entertained by the Lewis family. The first sermon in the Valley was delivered in their home in 1739. Passersby noted that they were wel-comed by the Lewis family and were always impressed with their hospitality. One visitor was Benjamin Borden, who was issued a tract of land by Governor Gooch on November 6, 1739, for 92,100 acres south of Beverley Manor, a portion of which would later become part of northern Rockbridge County. Ephraim McDowell was the first settler in that grant, and the McDowell family members would play an important role in the early history of the Augusta Militia.

-Two-

The Tradition

Begins

A s the settlement in Augusta County grew, the necessity for order and government became apparent. John Lewis was clearly instrumental in this effort, leading the way in organizing the structure of the county to include the founding of a militia regiment. In colonial Virginia, all government began at the county level. Following the pattern established throughout the colonies, each county organized a regiment for the protection of the settlers residing there. The term "citizen-soldier" originated during these early days of America where potential danger lurked behind every tree or over the next hill. The ability to respond quickly and selflessly later resulted in the term "Minuteman," which became popular during the Revolutionary War. The citizen-soldiers had to maintain their homes and farms, but also be ready to respond to any threat to their settlements. This willingness to volunteer for military service was necessary for the survival of the early settlers, but it later became a tradition that has been crucial for the survival of the nation. Serving as a citizen-soldier required all males, no matter what their profession, to leave their jobs and families and respond to the greater needs of their communities, their state, and later, their country.

The organization of a militia can be traced back to Anglo-Saxon England. The term militia originated with the Latin word *miles*, which meant soldier. Militia came to mean military service to the English, epitomized by the Elizabethan mobilization of citizens to defend England from attack by the Spanish Armada in 1588. This concept, which came to America with the first settlers, implied a duty to perform in a military organization to insure the security of a settlement. The House of Burgesses of the Virginia Colony in 1624 formally established a militia as a result of a growing Indian threat. On April 30, 1652, the Burgesses further organized the militia, directing each county to establish a regiment comprised of eight to ten companies of fifty soldiers each, commanded by a Captain. A Colonel would command the regiment.

On November 3, 1741, the first settlers of Augusta County met at Beverley's Mill Place, later known as Staunton, to discuss a governing organization for the central Shenandoah Valley. Staunton would later formally become the seat of government

for Augusta County in 1745. It was named for Lady Rebecca Staunton who was the wife of Governor Sir William Gooch. The basic government of the day was patterned after those of rural England and consisted of justices, sometimes called magistrates, who sat on the county court. The justices were responsible for establishing taxes and administering the funds for improvements needed in the county, such as roads and forts. The court met once a month, so day-to-day operations were conducted by several officials, who were appointed by the governor, based on recommendations from the county court. The job of county sheriff was very important, and James Patton was the first to serve in this position in Augusta County. He executed the decisions of the court, assisting in tax collection and law enforcement. A clerk maintained the county's legal records, and a county lieutenant commanded the militia.

This initial meeting in Staunton also resulted in the formation of the "Augusta Militia." Unit leaders were later selected, to include James Patton, who qualified to be the first "Lieutenant Colonel" and was officially appointed by these orders:

> I, William Gooch Esq. His Majesty's Lieutenant Governor and Commander in Chief of the Colony & Dominion of Virginia
> To James Patton, gentleman
> By Virtue of the Power and authority to me given as Commander and Chief of this Colony; I do hereby command and appoint you the said James Patton—Lieutenant Colonel of his Majesty's Militia in the County of Augusta—where William Beverley, Esq. is the County Lieutenant you are therefore Carefully and Diligently to perform the Duty of Lieutenant Colonel by Duty of Exercising and Disciplining the soldiers under your command and by seeing that they be provided with arms and ammunition as the law requires, and I do hereby command them to obey you as their Lieutenant Colonel and you are to follow all such Orders and Directons from time to time as you shall receive from Me or any other your Commanding Officer according to the Rules and Discipline of war.
> Given under My Hand and the Seal of the Colony at Williamsburg this 24th day of April in the 15th year of His Majesty's Reign amog Lord 1742
> William Gooch
> William Beverley Esq County Leveleor
> James Patton Colonel

Patton, like John Lewis, was a native of Ulster in the north of Ireland, and had served in the British Royal Navy. He was very enterprising, having captained his own ship and crossed the Atlantic Ocean some twenty-five times, ferrying settlers and supplies to the new world. He was well respected in Augusta County and a good friend of John Lewis to whom he was distantly related through his mother's family. During an organizational meeting of the Augusta Militia on June 24, 1742, John Buchanan, John Smith, Samuel Gay, James Cathray, and John Christian qualified as captains, and John Moffett and William Evans as lieutenants.

Captains of the militia were generally civilians who were selected to muster all eligible male citizens, "musterables," within a given area. The captains initially "listed" all free white males between the ages of twenty-one and sixty. Listing meant that any male residing in Augusta County, or a male entering the settlement who met the criteria described, had to place his name on the rolls of the captain responsible for the company where he settled. In essence, almost every male settler in the region fit the profile and was required to be listed and to serve as needed. Serving in the militia was considered a duty, a necessity of residing in a dangerous, unsettled land.

The Augusta County regiment was initially mustered on September 3, 1742. It followed the county regimental model adapted from the British. This regimental organization was modified to include ten or more companies. The Augusta organization initially consisted of twelve rifle companies of fifty men each. The leadership of the regiment, only the seventh to be formed in colonial America, consisted of:

Lieutenant Colonel James Patton - Commander
Company Commanders

Captain John Smith, Number One	Captain Peter Scholl, Number Seven
Captain Andrew Lewis, Number Two	Captain James Gill, Number Eight
Captain John Buchanan, Number Three	Captain John Willson, Number Nine
Captain James Cathrey, Number Four	Captain Hugh Thompson, Number Ten
Captain John Christian, Number Five	Captain George Robinson, Number Eleven
Captain Samuel Gay, Number Six	Captain John McDowell, Number Twelve

In addition to a captain commanding, each Augusta Militia Company had a lieutenant, an ensign, and two sergeants. During muster, the equipment of each soldier was inspected to include his flintlock rifle, cartridge box, sword or bayonet, powder and shot.

The day following the muster, a court-martial was always conducted to identify those who had been listed but failed to muster, to appoint officers and sergeants, and to deal with other regimental business. The colonel of Augusta County, William Beverley, presided, along with the lieutenant colonel and the captains of the Regiment. The court-martial levied fines for the listed who did not muster, now known as "delinquents," listened to appeals made by those requesting not to serve, tried unit members for offenses, planned for future musters, and organized work parties for construction projects that needed to be completed. You did not have to muster if you could prove you had "infirmities and were not capable of militia service" or were not eligible because of your age. The business of the early Augusta Militia court-martials also included placing a bounty on wolves and paying militia members who killed one "within ten miles of any inhabitant." The bounty was five shillings for an old wolf and two shillings and six pence for killing a young wolf.

The regiment fell in under the British flag, with all members responsible for bringing their own weapons and equipment, which included a long rifle with shot bag, tomahawk, long knife (where the Indian reference to "Long Knives" originated), and a Bible. The basic uniform was a hunting shirt, Indian leggings, and moccasins. In other words, the settlers accepted the local Indian dress as their first military uniform. It was quite practical for the conditions found in this frontier region and clearly time tested. This basic set-up served the Augusta Militia until the outbreak of the Revolutionary War. During the Indian Wars, while serving as part of the First Virginia Regiment and part of the British Army, members of the militia donned uniforms, but they generally returned to the comfort of their frontier garb when in the backcountry.

The militia companies met and conducted drill monthly under the direction of their Captains. This concept allowed the settlers to assemble in their local area, often at a church, to reduce travel time and inconvenience and hasten assembly. Wives frequently accompanied the militia members; drill became an opportunity to meet new settler families and keep up with the news from the other settlements, colonies, and Europe. The Augusta Militia companies drilled locally throughout the year, but each September assembled in Staunton, after the crops had been harvested, for a regimental muster of all companies for a large scale drill and a court-martial.

The Augusta Militia was mustered again on September 15, 1742, as a result of Indian hunting parties moving though the Shenandoah Valley. Its first real engagement, though, came in December with the eruption of the first Indian war in the Valley. A group of over thirty Delaware Indians came into Augusta County, heavily armed and indicating that they were going to attack their enemy, the Catawbas. The visitors were entertained by Captain John McDowell, and then moved to North River where they established camp for the next week. They were peaceful enough initially, but soon began wandering through the settlement and taking whatever they wanted and killing horses and cattle indiscriminately. Several settlers complained to Colonel Patton, who ordered the Twelfth Company of the regiment under the command of Captain McDowell, to escort the Indians from the settlement. As the militia company was moving the Delawares out of the area, one of the Indians slipped off into the woods and was fired upon by a member of the militia. A state of confusion erupted, and the remaining Indians attacked McDowell and his men.

This confrontation on December 12, 1742, occurred in the vicinity of Balcony Falls on the James River near the mouth of the Maury River, in what is now Rockbridge County, where the militia company was based. Captain McDowell and seven of his men were killed before the Indians retreated into the Blue Ridge Mountains, leaving seventeen of their number dead on the field. (See Illustration 2-1) The young captain was buried with his soldiers in what has become known as the McDowell burial ground on Route 11, eight miles north of Lexington, marked by Virginia Historical Marker A 43. This action began the first Indian war in Augusta County, which raged for the next eighteen months. When the Augusta Regiment next mustered on September 14, 1743, John Lewis and John Buchanan were listed as colonels, along with James Patton. In addition to the "Companies of Foot," there were five "Companies of Horse" added to the Regiment. The Horse Companies were commanded by Captains Daniel McNair, George Anderson, Daniel Harrison, John Brown, and Alex Dunlap.

William Beverley, serving as County Lieutenant, and Thomas Lee, representing the

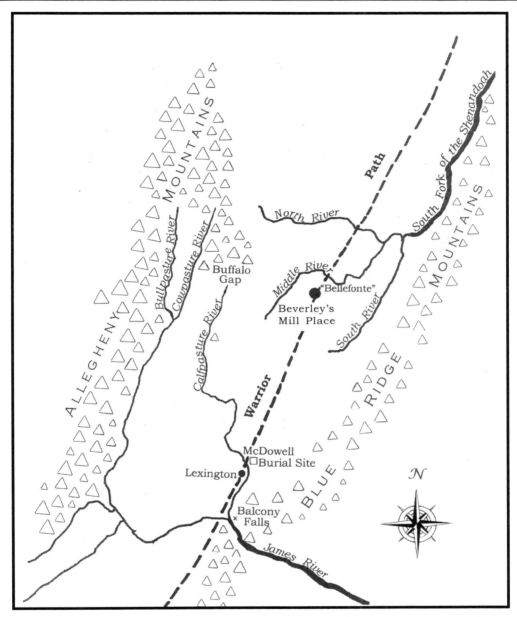

Illustration 2-1: Augusta Militia – "The Tradition Begins" - 1742

Colony of Virginia, met in Lancaster, Pennsylvania, early in the summer of 1744, with the Chiefs of the six United Indian Nations to conclude a peace treaty. After much deliberation, for payment amounting to four hundred pounds worth of gold and goods, the Indians agreed to concede all lands east of the Allegheny Mountains to Great Britain. The resulting Treaty of Lancaster, signed on July 2, opened up many of the western regions of Augusta County for settlement and provided additional trading opportunities with the Indians. Settlers coming into the Shenandoah Valley felt that they were now safe to build their cabins and plant their fields.

The Treaty of Lancaster only temporarily reduced the Indian threat to the settlement, but it contributed significantly to the decline of relations with the French. The western region of Virginia beyond the Allegheny Mountains became a pawn in a very large game being played between England and France for control of the region. England had laid claim to the land, but the French, pushing down from the north, quickly became a threat to this claim. Both sides used the Indians against the other in an attempt to block further colonization. The settlers and traders from the two countries coming into the region ultimately became the innocent victims of this political tug-of-war. The Virginia settlers in general, and the militia specifically, would have to pay a high price for the western lands in the area where the English and French claims met. This was a period of great instability and unrest in the region.

Early in 1748, Colonel Patton and Captain John Buchanan, commanding the Third Company of the Regiment, led an exploration of the lands to the south. They discovered an opening in the Allegheny Mountains that they named the Cumberland Gap, in honor of the Duke of Cumberland. This foray into the frontier regions in southern Augusta County would be invaluable to mapping the future western expansion of the colony. Both leaders found the area to their liking and would move to this area in later years. A town named Pattonsville would be established on the eastern side of the James River, opposite the community of Buchanan, still in existence today. The surviving town lies just north of Roanoke and was on the Great Road, now Route 11.

Occupying the land, not fighting, was the real key to settling the frontier. In 1748, the same year that Patton explored southwest Virginia, the Ohio Company was formed with a number of notable participants, including George and Lawrence Washington. The land company was granted 500,000 acres along what is now the Ohio River. This incursion into the Ohio Valley would be the beginning of the struggle between England and France in this New World. The French had come into what is now Canada and were moving south, as the English were moving west. A young George Washington, who would begin to take his place in history as he surveyed the land given to the Ohio Company, became involved in the western expansion of Virginia, and developed a relationship with the key leaders of the Augusta Militia.

In 1749, the Greenbrier Land Company was formed with John Lewis and his sons, Andrew and Charles, as stockholders. Andrew Lewis was appointed to survey a tract of 100,000 acres located generally west of what is today Lewisburg, West Virginia. Also in 1749, the new Lieutenant Governor of Virginia, Robert Dinwiddie, granted John Lewis and other land speculators 800,000 acres in the name of the newly formed Loyal Company. The paths of Washington, Patton, and Lewis would cross as they worked to establish settlements in the western region of Virginia, most of which today are in the state of West Virginia.

In 1752, Virginia's Lieutenant Governor, by letter, reappointed Colonel Patton to command the Augusta Militia:

Robert Dinwiddie, Esq; His Majesty's Lieutenant-Governor, and Commander in Chief of the Colony and Dominion of Virginia

By Virtue of the Authority and Power to me given by His Majesty, as Commander in Chief of this His Colony and Dominion, I, reposing special Trust and Confidence in your Loyalty, Courage, and Conduct, do hereby constitute and appoint you the said James Patton to be Lieutenant of the County of Augusta and Chief Commander of all his Majesty's Militia, Horse and Foot, in the said County of Augusta And I do give unto you, full Power and Authority, to Command, Levy, Arm, and Muster, all Persons which are or shall be liabel to be levied and lifted in the said county. You are therefore carefully and diligently to discharge the Duty of Lieutenant and Chief Commander of the Militia, by doing and performing all, and all Manner of Things thereunto belonging, particularly by taking Care that the said Militia be well provided with Arms and Ammunition as the law of this Colony directs: And that all Officers and Soldiers be duly exercised and kept in good Order and Discipline. And in Case of any sudden Disturbance or Invasion, I do likewise impower you to raise, order and march, all, or such Part of the said Militia as to you shall seem meet, for resisting and subduing the Enemy: And I do hereby command all the Officers and Soldiers of his Majesty's Militia, in the said County, to obey you as their Lieutenant, or Chief Commander, and you are to observe and follow such Orders and Directions, from Time to Time as you shall receive from me, or the Commander in Chief of this Colony for the Time being, or from any other your Superior Officer, according to the Rules and Discipline of War. GIVEN under my Hand, and the Seal of the Colony, at Williamsburg, the 16th Day of July in the 26th Year of his Majesty's Reign, Annoque Domini 1752.
Robt Dinwiddie

The Second Indian War erupted in 1753, when conflicts broke out between English settlers and the French traders along the Ohio River, in an area that was then part of Augusta County. The violence escalated, embroiling the entire settlement in what became known as the French and Indian War. Indian raiding parties appeared in numerous settlements, requiring the response of the Augusta Militia. The citizen soldiers mustered frequently to assist the troops of the organized Virginia Regiment already responsible for patrolling the frontier and disrupting Indian raiding parties. It was in this capacity that the regiment first came to serve under a young Major George Washington.

Word reached the Virginia capital in Williamsburg in the fall of 1753 that the French were moving into the Ohio Valley and often killing or taking captive the English settlers who had moved into western Augusta County and the frontier area claimed by England. Major Washington, the Adjutant of the Southern Military District of Virginia, was sent by Lieutenant Governor Dinwiddie in the winter of 1753 with a warning to the commander of the French garrison at Fort Le Boeuf on French Creek, just south of Lake Erie. Dinwiddie demanded that the French immediately cease any interference with the English settlements along the Ohio River and make a "peaceable departure" from this region claimed by the English. French claims in the

New World were identified as the region north of the Great Lakes that would become known as New France.

On November 15, Major Washington, accompanied by seven others including Christopher Gist, who had previously explored the Ohio Valley, left Williamsburg, moving north by northwest through Winchester to Wills Creek (later to become Cumberland, Maryland) and over the Appalachian Mountains. They passed though an open area called "the Great Meadows," which would play a significant role in future English military movement into the region. It is located on what would become America's "National Road" begun in 1811 to connect the eastern seaboard with the lands west of the mountains. The route extends from Baltimore, Maryland, to Vandalia, Illinois, following what is today Route 40. The Meadows site is in Pennsylvania, just north of the Maryland state line, about ten miles southeast of present-day Uniontown.

Washington's small party passed the site where the Monongahela and Allegheny Rivers converge to form the Ohio River. This strategic location became known as "The Forks," where Pittsburgh now stands. This site would become the flash point of the French and English expansion into the area. They followed the Ohio River north, where they found the French garrison at Logstown, the site of present-day Ambridge, Pennsylvania. The name "Logstown" came from the piles of logs and debris that had accumulated on the banks of the river after heavy flooding. One of the largest Indian villages in the area was located here. The English first visited the location in April 1748, when George Croghan came to meet with the Indian leaders and invite them to a conference in Lancaster, with the purpose of seeking continued peace as the settlements moved west. Representatives of both England and France would come here over the next few years, laying claim to the area, but the French were the first to construct a fort on the site.

After resting, Washington's party continued its journey on December 1. They spent the night within the French garrison at Venango, now Franklin, Pennsylvania. From this point they were guided by French Captain La Force to their destination at Fort Le Boeuf, where Washington delivered the Virginia Governor's message. The French commander's reply was a note to Dinwiddie stating, "As to the summons you send me to retire, I do not think myself obliged to obey it." Washington completed the difficult journey back to Williamsburg under challenging winter conditions, delivering the French response on January 16, 1754. Having the French position "in writing" and learning of the general French buildup within the western region of Augusta County, Dinwiddie determined it was necessary to build a line of forts along the Ohio River to protect the settlers moving there, and sent a force against the French in the region. He commissioned Captain William Trent to work with Christopher Gist to construct a fort at The Forks. The outpost would be known as Fort Prince George. He further determined it necessary to build a road into the area and sent a military force to demand the immediate French withdrawal from the Ohio Valley.

The clearing for the fort was just getting started when Ensign Edward Ward arrived with more workmen to assist in the project. It did not take long for word of the activity to reach the French, and on April 17, five hundred French troops arrived and demanded that the English depart. The small group of workers had no choice but to withdraw and leave their project only partially completed. The French immediately took over the project and began to build their own fort, which they named Fort Duquesne for Marquis Duquesne de Meneval, the Governor General of Canada. This site is now Point State Park in downtown Pittsburgh, Pennsylvania.

Even before the English workers were driven from The Forks, Lieutenant Governor Dinwiddie called for the formation of a military unit to retrace the tracks of

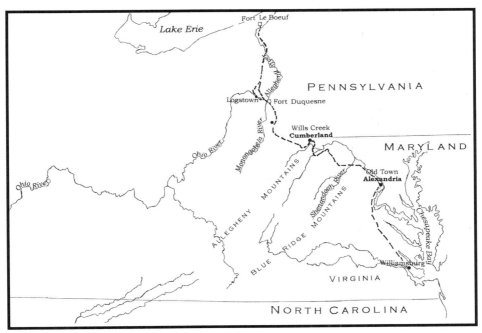

Illustration 2-2: Washington's Expedition, Winter of 1753

Washington and demand that the French withdraw from the Ohio River Valley. He notified Colonel Patton to "draw out" the Augusta Militia as part of the force he was assembling under Major Washington and dispatching to the junction of the Allegheny and Monongahela Rivers. A similar notice was sent to Lord Fairfax in Frederick County, the only other county located in the Shenandoah Valley at the time. This force, which was organized in Alexandria, was named "The Virginia Regiment," the first volunteer force raised in Virginia that was equipped and funded by public money.

Dinwiddie's plan initially was delayed, however, because a provision in the militia law prohibited the sending of militia units outside the colony, and the forks of the Ohio were considered by many to be outside the boundaries of Virginia. Despite this concern, the First Virginia Regiment was formed. Six companies comprised the regiment, two of which came from the Shenandoah Valley, one commanded by Captain Andrew Lewis of Augusta County and the second commanded by Captain Adam

Stephen of Frederick County. The force was initially in two parts. The lead element, commanded by recently promoted Lieutenant Colonel George Washington, left Alexandria on April 12, 1754. Washington was second in command to Colonel Joshua Frye, who led the second element that started in the Shenandoah Valley. The forces were to unite at Great Meadows, in what is now southwestern Pennsylvania.

Lieutenant Colonel Washington, with his Indian guides, was well served by his previous experience in the area and made steady progress west. On May 28, Christopher Gist, who had a farm in the area, informed him that a French force of about fifty soldiers, commanded by Ensign Joseph Coulon de Villiers de Jumonville, was camped just to the north. Washington took a detachment of about seventy-five men from his force and moved to confront what he perceived as a threat to his intentions. The next day the small group of Virginians and Indians surprised the unsuspecting French as they were having breakfast. The resting French, without sentries out, finally spotted the element approaching and ran for their musket stacks. It was too late, though, and Washington's force responded with well-aimed shots fired from their protected positions in the surrounding rocks and trees. In the brief encounter, ten Frenchmen, including their commander, were killed and mutilated by the Indians before Colonel Washington could call a halt to the attack. The surviving French insisted that they were on a peaceful mission, carrying a message for the Virginia governor. Clearly, the situation had gotten out of hand and Lieutenant Governor Dinwiddie, who had directed the Regiment "to be on the defensive," was not pleased when news of the attack reached Williamsburg. Washington was dismayed with the turn of events, but insisted he had acted appropriately under the circumstances.

On June 9, the militia companies commanded by Captains Andrew Lewis and Robert Stobo arrived from Winchester with the news that Colonel Frye had died from injuries received when he was thrown from his horse on May 31 during the dangerous Allegheny Mountain crossing. There was also the news that the Governor had promoted Washington temporarily to the rank of full colonel and ordered him to take command of the Regiment. He now assumed command of the entire force including the units from the Augusta Militia. It is interesting to note that the company from Augusta County was not present during the first confrontation between the French and the English, but from this point forward it would play a critical role serving with Washington in the struggle to gain control of America's frontier region.

Washington learned the French were moving against him and began consolidating his little army and preparing for the inevitable attack. He directed the building of a hastily thrown together structure, which can best be described as a stockade. A square trench roughly two-and-a-half feet deep was hastily dug around the round log fort. Swivel guns, small light cannons effective at close range when loaded with scatter shot, were placed on top of the earthen entrenchment. The defensive position was in the middle of Great Meadows, a lush grass-covered opening in the middle of a heavily wooded area comprised of large oak trees. The meadow was about two miles long and averaged two hundred and fifty yards in width. The position became known as a "fort of necessity" or Fort Necessity.

Colonel Washington, sensing the impending danger, requested reinforcements from Lieutenant Governor Dinwiddie. The response from Williamsburg brought his force to almost four hundred soldiers when they arrived. A superior French force, comprised of seven hundred and fifty French and Indians, commanded by Captain Louis Coulon de Villiers, was sent from its base at Fort Duquesne, and arrived at Fort Necessity on July 3. The Virginians were surrounded in their partially completed fort, outmanned and outgunned. The fighting started around ten o'clock in the morning and continued through the day. During nine hours of fighting, the casualties in Washington's small force of defenders mounted steadily. The French directed tremendous volumes of fire into the stockade from the protection of their positions in the forest, which ringed the small outpost. All of the horses and cattle which were part of the expedition where killed as the day wore on. With little ammunition left and their powder wet from the

Illustration 2-3: Two views of a recreated Fort Necessity

heavy rains during the day, it was apparent the militia had no chance of defending the small post against the well-supplied enemy.

The French commander, clearly recognizing the hopeless plight of the Virginians, offered surrender terms, which Washington considered honorable and accepted late that evening. Captain de Villiers revealed that his attack was a result of the brutal deaths of his brother Jumonville, and other French soldiers during Colonel Washington's unprovoked attack in late May. He indicated the French were not looking for a war over the region. Under the arrangement, Washington's expedition was allowed to withdraw with its arms and colors, leaving the French clearly in control. At 10 o'clock the next morning, July 4, 1754, Washington's force began a retreat. It was a long, difficult march home for the Virginia Regiment and a warning of what was to come. Washington's casualties included thirty-one killed, thirteen from the Augusta Militia, fifty-four wounded, including Captain Lewis who was struck twice from enemy fire. Only 165 of the original 293 defenders were suitable for duty when the force reached Wills Creek on July 9, less than a week after the engagement. As soon as Colonel Washington's force departed Fort Necessity, the French pulled up and burned the timbers in the round wall, having lost only two French soldiers in the engagement.

Lieutenant Colonel (Retired) Thompson Smith, who served full-time in the Virginia Army National Guard after the Korean War, remembers that in 1954, members of the Virginia Guard participated in the 200th Anniversary of the Battle of Fort Necessity. They formed up in Alexandria and followed, by bus, as best they could, the route taken by Washington and the Virginia Regiment. The unit, welcomed by the citizens of Pennsylvania, spent the night in Uniontown before participating in the ceremony on July 3. The unit formed on the ground where the Virginians had stood two hundred years earlier and former Army Chief of Staff General (Retired) George C. Marshall inspected their ranks. The Great Meadows, including the site of Fort Necessity, was purchased by George Washington in 1770 for 30 pistols or about $120 at the time. The site eventually became part of the National Park Service in 1933. The department excavated and restored the fort in 1953 for the Bicentennial Celebration. Every year on July 3, the park service hosts a special event to commemorate the fight at Great Meadows located on Route 40, one mile northwest of Farmington in Fayette County, Pennsylvania. The park service staff there provides excellent information on the various historical sites in the area including General Braddock's Grave and Jumonville Glen nearby.

After returning from the defeat at Fort Necessity, Captain Lewis and members of the Virginia Regiment were dispatched by Lieutenant Governor Dinwiddie to construct a fort in the area west of Beverley's Mill Place (present-day Staunton) to protect the settlers in the Valley from small parties of Indians that might try to raid the area. On October 6, the militia moved to an undetermined location, either near Greenbrier or possibly the area of Fort Lewis near present-day Salem, Virginia. On February 12, 1755, the governor notified Lewis to leave a small force to hold the fort, and to move down the Valley to Winchester

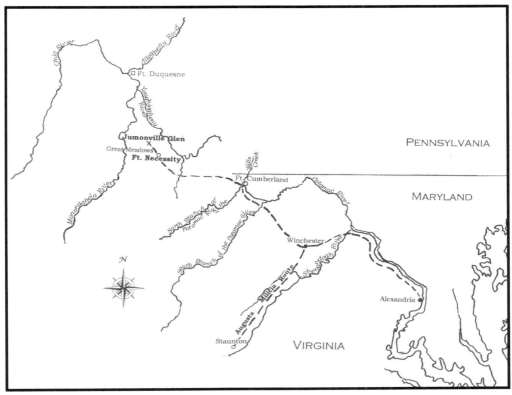

Illustration 2-4: George Washington's route toward Fort Duquesne

and join an army, which was being organized for another attack against Fort Duquesne. Lieutenant William Wright was left in charge of the small unit, with additional instructions from Lieutenant Governor Dinwiddie to call upon Colonel Patton and the remainder of the Augusta Militia for assistance if he detected any threat to the region.

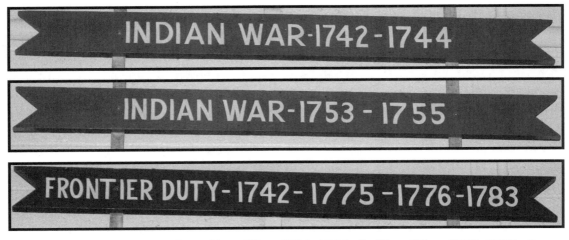

Battle streamers earned: Indian War 1742-1744, Indian War 1753-1755, Frontier Duty 1742-1775-1776-1783

-Three-

More Indian Wars

The Second Indian War flowed over into the French and Indian War when Lieutenant Governor Dinwiddie and the English finally realized the seriousness of the French intentions in the Ohio River Valley. It was becoming clear that it would require more than the colonial militia to drive the French from the western regions claimed by the English. It would take almost a year, though, for the British to organize an expedition of their "regulars," under the command of sixty-year-old Major General Edward Braddock, to assist the Virginians. The British force was comprised of the "Irish Regiments" consisting of the 44th Regiment, commanded by Colonel Sir Peter Halkett, and the 48th Regiment, commanded by Colonel Thomas Dunbar. The two "regiments of foot" crossed the Atlantic in March 1755, proceeded up the Chesapeake Bay, and then followed the Potomac River to Alexandria, Virginia. *These Regiments represented the first presence of the British Army in Virginia.* Since 1607, the militia had provided the only security for the settlers moving west.

The British troops camped there for almost a month while provisions were gathered and recruits enlisted to bring each regiment to a full strength of seven hundred on April 5. The regiments then moved west on parallel routes initially, with a linkup planned for the junction of Will's Creek and the North Branch River, where Fort Cumberland was located. Their route west became known as Braddock's Road and can be traced from the monument on Commonwealth Avenue in Alexandria, west through the city limits to Winchester, Virginia, and Cumberland, Maryland.

Upon arriving at Alexandria, General Braddock had called for a council of war, hosting the governors of Massachusetts, Maryland, New York, North Carolina, Pennsylvania, and, of course, Lieutenant Governor Dinwiddie of Virginia. The leaders approved an entire strategy for the defeat of the French in the west, plus planned manning and funding for the military expeditions. Braddock then departed Alexandria for Frederick, Maryland, where he met with other colonial leaders, including Benjamin Franklin of Pennsylvania and young George Washington of Virginia. He received only limited additional funding for his expedition, but did receive twelve companies of militia to supplement his British regiments. The addition of the militia units, totaling four hundred and fifty Virginians, including the Augusta Militia, brought his force to almost two thousand officers and soldiers. During this meeting, he solicited the assistance of Lieutenant Colonel Washington to accompany him on the expedition and serve as his aide.

General Braddock then departed south across the Potomac at Shepherdstown, and moved to Winchester, following the road opened by Halkett's Irish Regiment. His main army had left Alexandria and proceeded west along what is today known as "Braddock Road" and a portion now is designated Route 50. He caught up to the balance of his expedition at Fort Cumberland on the last day of May. Braddock was an experienced commander who believed in strict discipline in all maneuvers. The British drill and ceremonies captivated members of the militia units, but many were concerned with how effectively these regulars would fight in the rugged terrain of western Virginia. After organizing and briefly drilling his little army, General Braddock ordered the arduous march west to Fort Duquesne on June 7, 1755. His plan was to cross the difficult mountain ranges and surprise the French fortress at Fort Duquesne, on the forks of the Ohio and Monongahela Rivers where the Virginians had first built

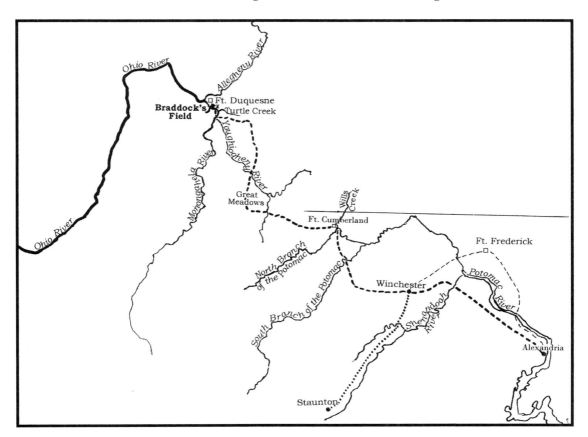

Illustration 3-1: Braddock's Expedition to Fort Duquesne

a fort. He sought to drive the French out of the Ohio River Valley in western Augusta County and force them north, as part of a larger war plan developed at Alexandria, which included attacks on Niagara and Crown Point. The large force, including its wagons of provisions and heavy guns, moved slowly through the wooded mountainous terrain.

General Braddock's army was successful in its first crossing of the Monongahela River, but in attempting a second crossing several days later on July 9, just a few miles from Fort Duquesne, they ran directly into a force comprised of French and Indians just after crossing Turtle Creek. This was a classic meeting engagement with neither side having scouted the other. The French force rushing south to protect the fort ran headlong into the British. The French commander, Captain Daniel de Beaujeu, was killed in the initial exchange between the two armies. The French force, particularly the Indian warriors, reacted quickly to the situation and took cover in the woods around Braddock's army. Although outnumbered, the French held the advantage of the defense and were able to bring fire on the British from three sides. They better understood fighting in the wooded frontier and were able to defeat the British in only two hours.

General Braddock had four horses shot from under him as he tried to rally his men, but ultimately he was wounded and died about four days later as his army retreated. Sixty-three officers and over nine hundred British soldiers and militia became casualties in the affair. The French lost sixteen men, while the Indians lost twenty-seven of their number. The experience of Lieutenant Colonel Washington and the militia allowed the remnants of the expedition to retreat to Fort Cumberland, again leaving the French in control of the western regions of Virginia. It would take the British three more years to build a force capable of returning to Fort Duquesne. In the meantime, the dispute in America spread to Europe where the Seven Years War erupted between England and France. The site of General Braddock's defeat can be found on U.S. Highway 30 in Allegheny County, just south of Exit 10 off I-376 in southwestern Pennsylvania.

The defeat of General Braddock came almost exactly one year after the surrender of Fort Necessity. Colonel Dunbar, who succeeded Braddock in command, withdrew the British force all the way to Philadelphia. If he had chosen to defend Fort Cumberland, the threat to the English settlers would have been greatly reduced, but his complete withdrawal left the French in sole possession of the Ohio Valley and poised to threaten the settlers in the Shenandoah Valley of Virginia. A dangerous frontier developed in the region between the French and English, where groups of French and Indians roamed and raided at will. From Braddock's defeat, until the fall of 1758, the Augusta Militia stood as the only line of defense between the settlers in western Virginia and the Indian threat. On August 14, Lieutenant Governor Dinwiddie again appointed now twenty-three year old George Washington as Colonel, commander of the Virginia Regiment, and commander-in-chief of all military forces in Virginia.

The defeat of the force under General Braddock was just one of the events that greatly concerned the settlers of Augusta County in the summer of 1755. While a por-

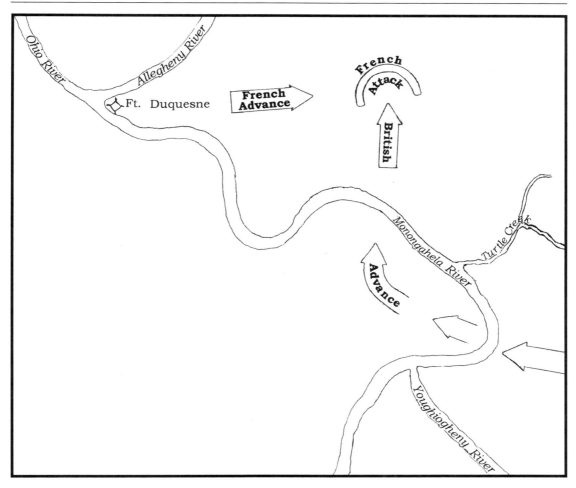

Illustration 3-2: Site of Braddock's Defeat

tion of the Augusta Regiment was serving with the Braddock Expedition, and other members were manning forts along the frontier, Lieutenant Governor Dinwiddie dispatched its commander, Colonel Patton, to inspect the companies located in the back country of western Augusta County. Patton was carrying powder and lead for the units and stopped on July 30 at the home of William Ingles in Draper's Meadows near present-day Blacksburg, Virginia. During his visit, an Indian raiding party entered the settlement practically undetected until they surprised Colonel Patton, who killed two of them before being killed himself by a third. The remaining Indians wrecked the settlement and escaped, taking five hostages, including Mrs. Mary Draper Ingles and her two children, four-year-old Thomas and George, who was only two. Militia efforts to recover the hostages failed, and the story of the courage of Mary Ingles, who gave birth to a daughter just three days after her capture, has become part of the lore of this frontier period. An excellent account of her struggle can be found in the novel, *Follow the River*, by James Alexander Thom.

The Augusta Militia's Regimental Historian during the post World War II era,

Major Reese T. Grubert, relates that "Colonel Patton had the muster rolls of the regiment with him at the time and after his death these rolls remained in the possession of Captain John Draper." Draper retained them until his death, and the records eventually became the property of a descendent, Dr. Lyman C. Draper, the founder of the Wisconsin Historical Society. The original regimental muster rolls of the Augusta militia are still the property of this organization today, but available on microfiche at university and historical libraries throughout Virginia.

On August 11, Lieutenant Governor Dinwiddie sent a letter to Captain Andrew Lewis, ordering him to assume command of the Augusta Militia as its second Colonel. This was a time of alarm in Augusta County as described by the Reverend John Craig, the first minister in the area, indicating that "When General Braddock was defeated and killed, our country was laid open to the enemy, our people were in dreadful confusion and discouraged to the highest degree." On numerous occasions during this period the militia was called out to repel Indian raiding parties and chase them from the region or conduct expeditions to recover hostages and property. In addition, the death of Colonel Patton and the capture of Mary Draper Ingles continued to stir the emotions on the western frontier.

Upon taking command of the regiment, now Colonel Lewis petitioned Lieutenant Governor Dinwiddie to allow a retaliatory expedition against the Indians and another attempt to free Mary Ingles. The request was opposed by Colonel Washington, but Dinwiddie finally relented and authorized an ill-fated venture that would become known as the "Big Sandy" Expedition. The Governor was displeased that the militia had allowed the Indians to escape with their hostages, and clearly sought some form of retaliation. Additionally, when news of the Indians at Draper Meadows reached the settlers beyond the Shenandoah Valley, many abandoned their new homes and withdrew east across the Blue Ridge Mountains for fear of further Indian attacks. Dinwiddie knew something had to be done to restore the confidence of the settlers in western Virginia and show them that their government could provide the security they needed.

This expedition was one of the few offensive focused responses to the ongoing Indian threats in the region. Organized and led by Colonel Lewis, the force assembled at Fort Frederick, near the Draper settlement and today's town of Radford, in late winter. There were over two hundred members of the Augusta Militia, plus over one hundred Cherokee Indian warriors, many serving as guides. The group got underway on February 18, 1756, proceeding initially down the north fork of the Holston River, before turning west. The soldiers were to be paid one shilling per day and were to be well supplied for the expedition, but the force was terribly undermanned and set out lacking adequate provisions. There were continuous winter rainstorms, flooding the rivers the expedition had to cross as it pursued the Indians into the Ohio River Valley. Otis K. Rice and Stephen W. Brown in their *West Virginia A History*, describe some of the difficulties encountered by the expedition.

On February 29, the men crossed the flooded Big Sandy sixty-six times within fifteen miles and had to abandon several pack horses. By March 3, rations had to be reduced to one-half pound of flour per man and whatever game could be killed.

The winter conditions, exhaustion, and lack of supplies dashed the morale of the force after thirty days, resulting in numerous desertions.

The expedition moved up the Big Sandy River, that today forms the boundary between Kentucky and West Virginia, only to find the Indians had withdrawn far-

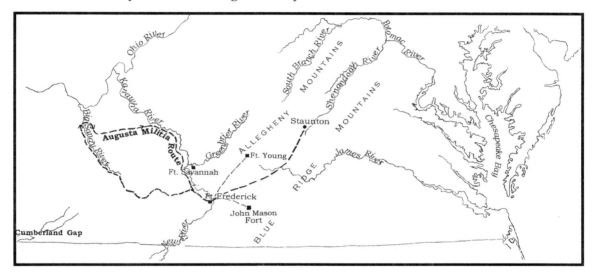

Illustration 3-3: Big Sandy Expedition

ther north above the Ohio River. Before they could re-supply and continue their pursuit, word reached them from the governor ordering their immediate return. Though regretting the order, few lacked the will to pursue their enemy any further. They began their return to the Shenandoah Valley, a trek of over three hundred miles. Several members of the expedition perished before they could return to the security of the valley. Mary Draper Ingles would, of course, eventually escape her captors at their camp near present-day Cincinnati, Ohio, and return to her home at Draper's Meadow, now part of the campus of Virginia Tech at Blacksburg.

Lieutenant Governor Dinwiddie was displeased with the failure of the Big Sandy Expedition, but appreciated the courage the Militia displayed. On April 24 he would order them back to the frontier to construct a fort in the south for the Cherokee Indians. The fort was to afford protection to the families of Cherokees who had accompanied the Augusta Militia on the Big Sandy Expedition and now volunteered to assist Washington and the Virginians in the fight against the French and Indians. A new struggle between the British and French was about to erupt into a major conflict. Colonel Lewis and a group of militia moved south to the land of the Cherokees and began constructing the fort on the Tennessee River. This initiative by Dinwiddie ultimately failed as few Cherokees actually came forward to fulfill their end of the bargain when the fort was completed. The work was completed in about six months, and the outpost became known as Fort Loudoun. It was located thirty miles southeast of today's Knoxville on the Tennessee River, below its junction with the Clinch River flowing south from Virginia.

The struggle between the British and French would become known as the French and Indian War. Although many historians trace the beginning of that war to the brief initial encounter between then Lieutenant Colonel Washington and the small force under Ensign Coulon de Jumonville on May 28, 1754, war was not formally declared for almost two years. On May 18, 1756, the British declared war on France, with the French reciprocating the next day on May 19. For the settlers in western Virginia, however, theirs was always a struggle for survival, and the Augusta Militia was their only consistent source of protection. Time and time again during this period, the militia was called upon to protect the settlements from the Blue Ridge Mountains to the Ohio River Valley. The citizen soldiers could always be counted on.

It should be noted that while Lewis was constructing Fort Loudoun, the Indian threat to the Valley resulted in a council of war, which met at the Augusta County Court House on July 27, 1756. Attending were Colonel John Buchanan acting as Regimental commander, Colonel David Stewart, Major John Brown, and Captains Joseph Culton, Robert Scott, Patrick Martin, William Christian, Robert Breckenridge, James Lockart, Israel Christian, Samuel Stalnicker, and Thomas Armstrong. The Regiment, supporting the Colony's assembly that had passed a frontier defense act in March, determined it necessary to build a line of fourteen forts covering two hundred and fifty miles. The line of forts would require six hundred and eighty men to man them, and would stretch from Mason's Fort in the south to Dinwiddie in the north. The line of forts can be seen in Illustration 3-4.

There were multiple attempts to construct this new line of defense. For example, Militia constructed "Ranger Stockades" were started immediately, resulting in Fort Dinwiddie, Seybert, Upper Tract, and Dickinson's Fort. Settlers banded together to help the militia build Hugh Mann's Mill Fort (Fort Upper Tract or Dunlap's Fort), Fort William, and Fort Young.

The forts were completed just in time, as the French sent their Indian allies to attack the English settlements in the disputed western frontier. In May of 1758, a horrible Indian massacre occurred at one of these new outposts. A party of Shawnees came into what is today Pendleton County on Route 33 in West Virginia, just across the Allegheny Mountains from Harrisonburg in Rockingham County, Virginia. Over thirty residents of the little valley rushed to the protection of newly constructed Fort Seybert. There they could probably have held out until the Augusta Militia came to their rescue, but after a short siege, the Indians offered not to harm the defenders if they surrendered. Accepting the promise, the gates were opened, but unfortunately

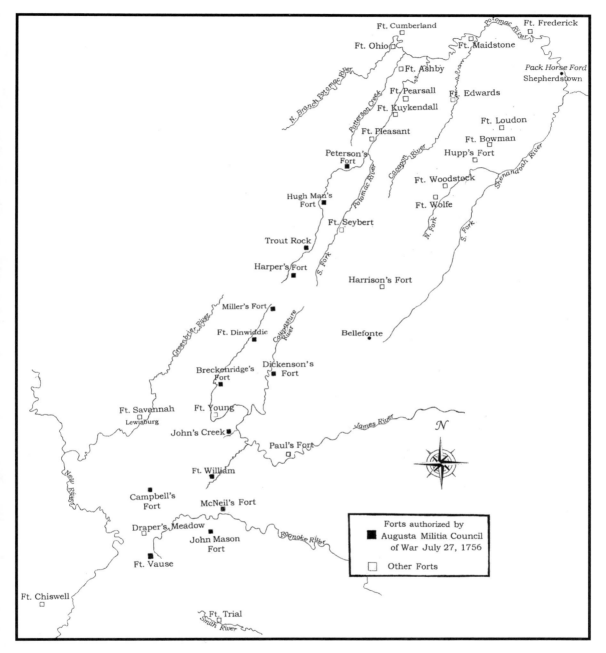

Illustration 3-4: Virginia's Frontier Forts, 1756

the Indians did not keep their word. All but seven of the settlers were killed and the survivors taken into captivity. The raiding party then moved to the northwest along today's Route 220 to the site of another outpost, Fort Upper Tract. There Captain Dunlap and twenty-one defenders were killed and the stockade burned to the ground. Both sites are easily identified today by West Virginia historical markers.

The source of the Indian problem could clearly be traced to their base of supplies at Fort Duquesne. In May of 1758, British General John Forbes, who had been a part of a number of unsuccessful attacks on French positions in Canada between 1756 and 1757, was called upon to organize an expedition to take Fort Duquesne. Although Forbes planned the attack, poor health prevented him from taking an active role in the expedition. Field command of the force being assembled was given to Colonel Henry Bouquet. His plan chose not to follow the path taken by the failed Braddock expedition, thus requiring the construction of a new, large road that became known as Forbes Road, farther north. (See Illustration 3-5) This was necessary to move the cannon and supplies that would be required for a successful attack. Colonel Lewis and the Augusta Militia were ordered to Winchester to serve again with Colonel George Washington as part of the First Virginia Regiment. They arrived on July 2 and moved on to Fort Cumberland in September. The force then moved west to within fifty miles of Fort Duquesne where Bouquet ordered British Major James Grant to conduct a reconnaissance in force to move to the post and gain whatever intelligence they could before the main body was brought up for the attack. Colonel Lewis and some members of the Augusta Militia were part of the reconnaissance force, but served as its rear guard. On September 14, the force under Grant apparently moved too close to the fort, for the gates swung open, and an overwhelming group of French and Indians attacked the British.

Hearing the noise from the fighting, Lewis left a small force under Captain Thomas Bullitt in reserve and moved to assist Major Grant's men. He arrived too late to turn the tide of battle, and after a fierce hand-to-hand struggle, surrendered, along with Grant and a majority of the surviving force. The victorious French and Indians then moved against Captain Bullitt and the remaining Virginians, but were driven off after a sharp fight. The remaining force then withdrew, leaving twenty-one officers and two hundred and seventy-five soldiers behind as casualties or prisoners. Colonel Lewis was sent to Quebec, where, according to an account by his niece, he remained a prisoner of war for three years. Learning of the "Braddock like" surprise defeat of Grant, Colonel Bouquet moved with his main force to attack Fort Duquesne. The French, knowing they were outnumbered and out-gunned by the larger British force, responded by setting fire to the fort on November 24 and withdrawing down the Ohio River in boats. The Indian allies of the French, believing they could have beaten the red coats, but not the *Ashalecoans* or Great Knives as the frontier-hardened Virginians were known, deserted in large numbers.

Colonel George Washington marched into a burning Fort Duquesne where he planted a British flag. With French domination of the Ohio Valley finally broken, the fort was rebuilt and the name changed to Fort Pitt in honor of William Pitt, the British Earl of Chatham, who was very well thought of in the colony. Once again, the Augusta Militia returned to their homes in the Valley of Virginia. The French and Indian War would continue, but the threat to the Augusta settlement had been greatly reduced by the destruction of the French base of operations at Fort Duquesne.

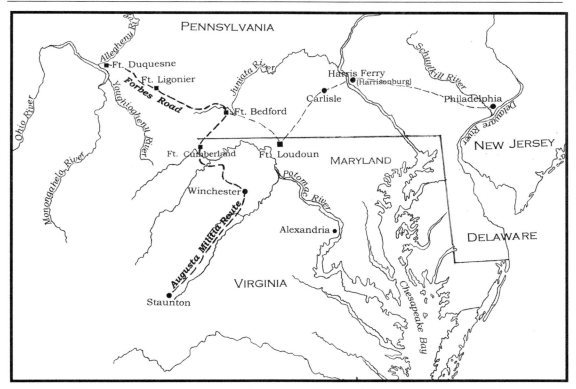

Illustration 3-5: Forbes' Route to Capture Ft. Duquesne - 1758

On February 1, 1762, Augusta County was saddened as its residents learned of the death of the county father, John Lewis, at the age of eighty-four. However, from his final resting place on a hill above Bellefonte, the view was one of a safer, peaceful, and prospering community, due in no small part to the vigilance and sacrifice of the Augusta Militia.

There was great hope by the settlers of the Virginia frontier that the Treaty of Paris, which officially concluded the French and Indian War in 1763, would also bring peace with the Indians. England now possessed the rights to the Ohio Valley and all the land east of the Mississippi River. Security of this region fell primarily to the Augusta Militia since Augusta County was Virginia's western most county. This period then became known within the regiment as the Frontier Indian War of 1763-64. Indian raiding parties shattered this hope quickly, though, after a number of incursions, some penetrating deep into the Valley of Virginia.

The Indian threat in the region consisted of the Five Nations, referred to by the French as the Iroquois. They united with the Shawnees after the defeat of the French, and eventually all of the Indian tribes in the west were united against the settlers. The Indians were determined to stop the whites from any farther movement west across the mountains to establish settlements in the Ohio River Valley and beyond.

Parties of the united western Indians routinely entered the Valley of Virginia from the west on their way to attack enemy tribes, particularly the Cherokees to the south.

Often they would enter peacefully, but then turn hostile on their return trip, attacking Virginia settlements. Early in 1763, one of the first Indian raids after the Treaty of Paris was on Kerr's Creek, in what is now part of Rockbridge County, Virginia. A party of Shawnees entered the area after raiding a Cherokee camp and began burning homes and killing settlers. Captain Moffett hastily gathered his company of the Augusta Militia to respond, but was ambushed by the raiding party as he pursued the attackers. As a result, many of the militia were killed or wounded. The Indians continued their destruction until another company of the Regiment caught up to them at Back Creek. After a close fight in which many were killed on both sides, the Indians were finally defeated and left the area. Captain Dickinson and Thomas Young, the grandfather of Colonel D. S. Young of Staunton, were among the Militia members killed. The company freed several hostages and brought back a number of settlers' scalps, many of which could be recognized from the length and color of the hair, and properly buried them.

In June of 1764, an Indian raiding party came close to the site of the present-day town of Woodstock, Virginia, and Fort Wolfe, a small home fortress constructed by Major Robert White. Alerted that the Indians had entered that part of the Valley, many families left their homes to take refuge in the fort. One group trying to reach the fort consisted of the Thomas, Jones, and Clouser families. The party was overtaken by the Indians who killed the men and took twenty-two women captive. Mrs. Thomas escaped to tell the tale, but the other women and children were taken to Indian camps where they remained for about six months before being released. Near Strasburg, Virginia, in the same year, a raiding party killed settler George Miller and his family. The same group moved on to kill John Dellinger and take his wife Rachel and her infant child as prisoners. In this case, the local militia was successful in overtaking the raiding party, killing one Indian and recovering Mrs. Dellinger and her child.

The last Indian raid in the present-day Augusta County occurred in 1764 when John Trimble was killed on his farm between Churchville and Staunton near the Middle River. Virginia Historical marker W-79 located three miles west of Staunton on Route 250 records the event. A Shawnee war party entered the Valley through Buffalo Gap and divided into three smaller groups to plunder area farms. One party initially murdered Alexander Crawford and his wife before falling upon Trimble on his way to plow, killing him and taking prisoner his eight-year-old son, a half-sister, a Negro boy named Adam, and Mrs. Estill. It is believed that Mr. Estill was wounded and escaped as did Mrs. Trimble and other family members. By coincidence, Mrs. Estill's brother was Captain George Moffett of the Augusta Militia. Upon learning of the incident, he immediately gathered a group of militiamen and pursued the Indians to an encampment near present-day White Sulphur Springs, West Virginia. The militia attacked after dark, killing and wounding a number of the Indians and recovering all of the hostages and the plunder.

During this period, two companies of the Augusta Militia, each consisting of one hundred men, commanded by Captains Charles Lewis and John McClanahan, were serving in western Virginia under British Colonel Bouquet. They were part of an expedition that resulted in the defeat of the Shawnees and Delawares, who agreed to a peace treaty on November 9, 1764, which provided for the release of all Virginians taken prisoner by the Indians. Of the two hundred and six surviving whites, ninety, thirty-two men and fifty-eight women and children, were from Virginia.

The last Indian incursion in the Valley occurred in August of 1766 when a raiding party murdered the Roads family, who had settled on the South Fork of the Shenandoah River near what was to become known as Bloody Ford. The militia was unsuccessful in recovering any of the settlers taken hostage. All were killed by the Indians during their escape west, except for one boy who was not released until almost three years later.

The atrocities during this period were not limited to the Indians. There were a number of occasions when the settlers turned on peaceful Indians visiting the Valley. As Benjamin Franklin once indicated, "Our frontier people are yet greater barbarians than the Indians and continue to murder them in time of peace." This quote is supported by a letter from Fort Loudoun in 1768 providing the following account, "The last news we have had here is the killing of nine Shawnee Indians in Augusta County, Va., who were passing this way to the Cherokee Nation, to war against them, and had obtained a pass from Colonel Lewis, of that county. Yet, notwithstanding, a number of county people met them a few miles from Colonel Lewis' and killed nine, there being but ten in the Company." On numerous occasions, the settlers attacked peaceful Indians passing through the Valley without provocation. During the period between 1766 and 1774, there was generally peaceful coexistence despite some minor Indian incursions and limited violence.

Samuel Kercheval's, *A History of the Valley of Virginia*, is an excellent source of *"Indian Incursions and Massacres"* as he calls them. He states "From the termination of hostilities in 1766, until the commencement of Dunmore's War in 1774, the people of the Valley enjoyed uninterrupted peace and tranquility, and the country settled and increased with great rapidity."

During this period, however, a new storm was building on the horizon as the colonists began to resent being ruled by a power in another part of the world. The settlers were becoming frustrated by the lack of understanding or concern the British government exhibited for issues that were critical to the Virginia Colony. In May, 1774, British Prime Minister, Lord North introduced a resolution in Parliament proposing to provide the Indian nations with ammunition, arms, and tomahawks. The great friend of the colony, William Pitt, opposed the resolution and told Parliament that "if the North resolution prevailed it would not only lose the hearts of the American Colonists, but the Colonies as well." Despite Pitt's objection, the North Resolution passed, infuriating all the colonies. The resulting sparks of discontent contributed significantly to the calling of the First Continental Congress, which convened in September, 1774, at Philadelphia.

One major event that occurred during this period came on January 31, 1770, when Augusta County was divided practically in half to create the new county of Botetourt. The Virginia General Assembly had sent a party of surveyors to the western base of the Blue Ridge Mountains to determine the dividing point. A large Spanish oak tree was found and marked on the north side with the letters "AC" for Augusta County, and on the south side by the letters "BC" for Botetourt County. A 55 degree azimuth was then shot to the northwest to establish the line that would create Botetourt County from Augusta County. This line passed just north of the junction of the Kanawha and Ohio Rivers and proceeded west to the southern tip of Lake Michigan and beyond. Later, Fincastle County would be established from Botetourt, its name changed to Kentucky County and eventually becoming the state of Kentucky.

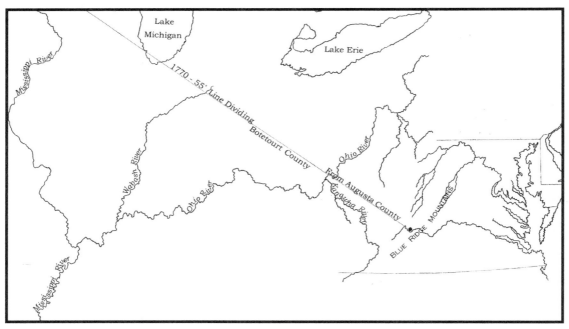

Illustration 3-6: Division of Botetourt County from Augusta

Battle streamers earned: French and Indian War, Indian War 1763-1764

-Four-

Dunmore's War
& Point Pleasant

Virginia's Governor Robert Dunmore had visited Fort Pitt in 1763, and had seen first hand the determination of the settlers moving west. As a staunch British loy-alist, he no doubt recognized this movement as an opportunity to arm and incite Indian tribes in order to distract the Virginia colony from participating in the unrest against English rule, which was gaining momentum in the northern colonies or the area becoming known as New England. If the Indian threat were made real, the Virginians would need to remain focused on self-preservation, before considering any move for independence. As discussed earlier, atrocities occurred on both sides as the frontier was being settled. In early 1774, one such incident in western Augusta County, involved the killing of the family of the Cayuga Indian Chief Logan by a group of white settlers. This unprovoked slaughter resulted in a general Indian uprising that spread death and destruction throughout the frontier settlements in the Ohio River Valley.

The new conflict would become known as Dunmore's War. Responding to the attacks, the Virginia governor developed a plan to stop the Indians by using a two-pronged attack with two divisions moving on the Indian villages, one approaching from the north and one from the south. He would lead the northern division, mostly British, from Williamsburg via Fort Pitt to the fort at Point Pleasant, while a militia force under General Andrew Lewis would move from the south. (See Illustration 4-1) Lewis was ordered to call out 650 members of the Augusta County Regiment under the command of his brother, Colonel Charles Lewis. They mustered in Staunton at Sampson Mathew's Ordinary and Pub for libation before proceeding south to join the rest of the division. The newly formed Botetourt Regiment consisting of some 450 men commanded by Colonel William Fleming, a former member of the Augusta Regiment, was also mustered into service and moved to join General Lewis.

Botetourt County was named for Virginia's then governor-in-residence, Norborne Berkeley, Lord Baron de Botetourt. The county seat became known as Fincastle after Botetourt's country home in England. Botetourt County originally included everything in southwestern Virginia and west to present-day Kentucky. The county of

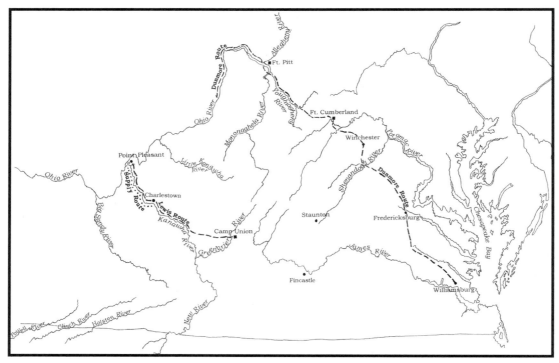

Illustration 4-1: Dunmore's Expedition against the Shawnees - 1774

Kentucky was formed from Botetourt County in 1772, substantially reducing its size. The militia from this area was initially part of the Augusta Regiment and would return to serve as part of its original organization from time to time as later chapters will detail. In 1774, though, the Botetourt Regiment and members of the small Kentucky County Militia would serve side by side with the Augusta Regiment in one of the most critical battles in American history.

General Lewis assembled his "Southern Division" at the site of Fort Savannah, designating it Camp Union, present-day Lewisburg, West Virginia. In addition to the Augusta and Botetourt Regiments, Lewis' force consisted of the Fincastle Battalion of Colonel William Christian with three hundred and fifty men, plus separate companies of the Culpeper County Volunteers commanded by Colonel John Field, one hundred and forty men, the Dunmore County Volunteers led by Captain Thomas Slaughter, forty men, the Bedford County Riflemen under Captain Thomas Bedford with forty-four men, and Captain James Harrod, with twenty-seven Kentucky pioneers. The total forces consisting of sixteen hundred officers and men began their movement west against the Indians on September 11, 1774. There were no roads in the region, so the soldiers, 400 packhorses, a herd of 108 beef cattle, and 54,000 pounds of flour, went west along narrow paths. (See Illustration 4-2)

On September 23, the southern division established a camp near where the Elk River joins the Kanawha River, just east of present-day Charleston, West Virginia. Here

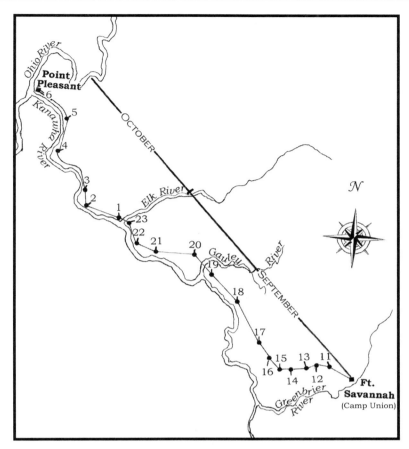

Illustration 4-2. Day by day from Fort Savannah to Point Pleasant

Colonel Charles Lewis and members of the Augusta Militia constructed twenty-seven rafts to assist in moving supplies, particularly flour, farther down the Kanawha River. The soldiers broke camp on September 30, crossing the Elk River and proceeding along the Kanawha in a formation designed by Colonel William Fleming commanding the Botetourt County militia. The formation was clearly a result of previous militia experience while conducting moves against the Indians. The force moved some one hundred and sixty miles in nineteen days, an average of eight-and-a-half miles per day using the structure found in Illustration 4-3.

Governor Dunmore took personal charge of a second, larger force, the "Northern Division," which was to take a northern route to Fort Pitt and down the Ohio River. Instead of moving to link up with Lewis as he had previously arranged, however, Dunmore crossed the Ohio River and proceeded west along the Hocking River toward the Indian villages at Chillicothe, leaving Lewis and the militia regiments to the south unsupported. In his *History of Augusta County, Virginia*, J. Lewis Peyton reveals that

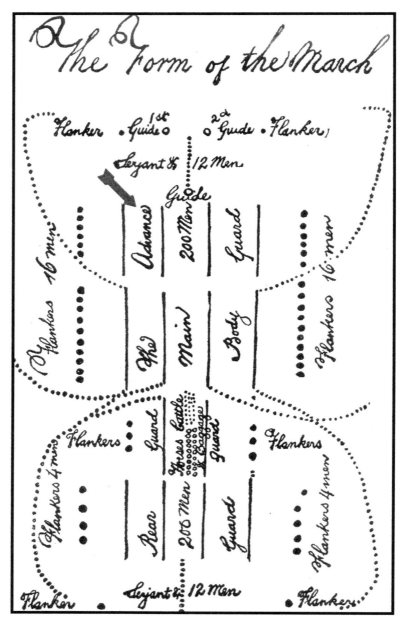

4-3. Colonel Fleming's Order of March sketch

On the 9th of October, three white couriers, who had previously lived among the Indians as traders, arrived in Lewis' camp, bearing dispatches from Dunmore, to inform Lewis that he, Dunmore, had changed the plan of campaign, and would not attempt to join Lewis at Point Pleasant, and ordering Lewis to march directly to the Indian towns on the Scioto, where Dunmore would join him. It is believed that this order was given with the base hope that Lewis' command would encounter an overwhelming savage force and be destroyed.

It is also interesting to note that there were numerous accounts of Dunmore meeting with Indian leaders as he journeyed down the Ohio River. Virginia historian Charles Campbell, for example, indicates that

> It is known that Blue Jacket, a Shawnee chief, visited Lord Dunmore's camp on the 9th, the day before the battle, and went straight from there to Point Pleasant, and that some of the Indians went to confer with Dunmore immediately after the battle; that Dunmore on the day of the battle remarked, 'Lewis is probably having hot work about this time.

It is understandable, then, that history suspects some treachery on Dunmore's part in the affair that was about to unfold at Point Pleasant, during the same time frame that Virginians were assembled in Philadelphia with representatives of the other colonies to draft petitions of relief from English rule. Virgil A. Lewis, in *Hardesty's Historical and Geographical Encyclopedia, Including Mason County, W. Va.*, states

> It is a well known fact that the emissaries of Great Britain were then inciting the Indians to hostilities against the frontier for the purpose of distracting attention, and thus preventing consummation of the Union which was being formed to resist their armed oppressor. It is well known that Lord Dunmore was an enemy of the colonists, and hence his efforts to induce the Indians to cooperate with the English and thus reduce Virginia to subjection.

Had General Lewis and the Virginia Militia regiments been destroyed, the entire western region would have erupted in a war, requiring a massive militia mobilization, leaving little capability to support any moves for independence. The colonies would be split in two, with British forces welcomed in Virginia under the auspices of assisting in defeating the Indians in the western frontier.

General Lewis knew the Indians had united to form a large force commanded by the Shawnee Chief Keigh-Tugh-Qua, known to the settlers as "Cornstalk." He established his camp on the eastern side of the Ohio River and its confluence with the Kanawha. The view to the west across the rivers was pleasant, so the location became known as "Point Pleasant." Here he was to await orders from Dunmore before crossing to locate and attack the Indians.

Before sunrise on the morning of October 10, 1774, two hunting parties slipped out of the militia camp to hunt for game. One group, Joseph Hughey and James Mooney, were hunting deer to supplement the camp's rations. Another group consisting of Valentine Sevier and James Robertson went out looking for a turkey to make a stew for Captain James Shelby who was sick. Moving north along the Ohio, Hughey and Mooney stumbled upon the lead element of a large Indian force moving south to attack the Virginians. Two shots immediately rang out, one killing Hughey and making him the first casualty of the soon-to-be Battle of Point Pleasant. The second shot missed Mooney, who raced back to warn the sleeping men of the Southern Division. The shots awakened the camp, causing soldiers to stir from under their blankets or out of their tents as Mooney raced up to Andrew Lewis, shouting there were "four acres of Indians out there." Moments later, Sevier and Robertson ran back into camp confirming the news.

General Lewis calmly lit his pipe, thinking the story to be exaggerated, but decided to order the drums to beat the "call to battle." He believed the Indians to be only a small scouting party and ordered his brother, Colonel Charles Lewis and 150 of his Augusta Militia forward to repulse the intruders. Colonel Charles Lewis was extremely proud of being one of the few colonists to have received a commission in the British Army and always insisted on wearing a scarlet waistcoat that he had earned serving in his majesty's service under Colonel Bouquet. As the company-sized formation reconnoitered forward in the early morning light, they almost immediately came under attack from hundreds of Indians advancing to their camp. Lewis' waistcoat contributed to his becoming an early casualty of the battle as he stood in the open in front of his men, shouting for his men to "Form a line. Form a line." Mortally wounded, he would walk back to his tent where he died on his cot around noon.

The Augusta Regiment wavered with the loss of its commander, but held on in a desperate hand-to-hand struggle until General Lewis ordered Colonel William Fleming and his Botetourt Regiment forward. Colonel Fleming had much experience in the Augusta Regiment because he had once lived in Staunton and served with the Regiment. Fleming's men fought well, but the superior Indian force continued to threaten to overrun the Virginians. General Lewis was forced to commit his entire reserve to the fight, which finally stopped Cornstalk's pressure from pushing the militia into the river to their rear; it was almost noon.

In the hours that followed, the two armies fought a savage, often hand-to-hand, fight with the lines moving forward and then back with neither side giving way. Late

Illustration 4-4 Sketch of the battle drawn by Steven R. Kidd

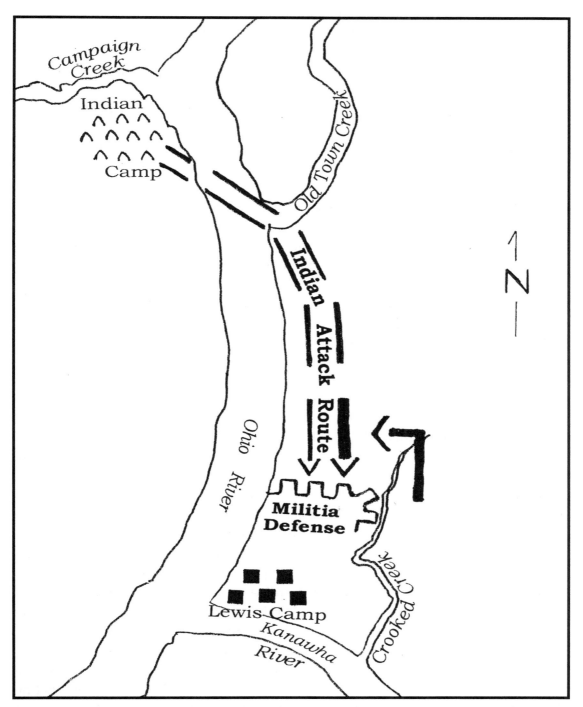

Illustration 4-5: The Battle of Point Pleasant – October 10, 1774

in the day, in a maneuver to outflank the Indians, Lewis dispatched the companies of Captains Mathews, Shelby, and Stuart to slip down Crooked Creek and attack the left side of the enemy positions. The Indians took this as an attack by reinforcements and began their gradual withdrawal. By four o'clock they were in full retreat, escaping across the Ohio River. The retreating Indians took as many of their dead as they could and tossed the rest into the Ohio River to prevent the militia from scalping them; still, seventeen scalps were taken after the battle. It is believed the Indian losses exceeded three hundred, compared to eighty-one Virginians. The retreating enemy left behind the seventy-eight canoes they had used to cross the Ohio River, plus twenty-seven tomahawks, twenty-three guns, and numerous war clubs.

As the battle started, Lewis immediately recognized that he had underestimated his enemy and sent for Colonel Christian and his force that was coming up river with supplies. Christian's fresh troops reached Lewis just before midnight and joined in the planning for the destruction of the Indian confederation for their savage attack. The next day, Lewis ordered his men to bury the dead and begin constructing a stockade, which would become known as Camp Blair, to protect the wounded. Over the next few days, the soldiers were re-supplied, each man receiving a pound and a half of lead balls and a half pound of powder. Sixty pack horses were prepared to carry a ten day supply of flour across the Ohio River, along with over a hundred head of beef. Lewis had learned from his logistical problems in the Big Sandy Expedition and wanted to insure adequate supplies for the attack west. On October 17, he crossed the Ohio River with a force of 1,150 Virginians bent on revenge. Colonel Fleming was left at Camp Blair, later to become known as Fort Randolph, with two hundred and seventy-eight soldiers, many wounded. Lewis's instructions to Fleming were clear, "Your principal duty will be to secure this camp from the attack of the enemy should any appear and make the works that are so far carried on as complete as you can."

To the north, Dunmore and his force were making steady progress to the Indian camps in the Scioto River Valley. (See Illustration 4-6) He halted short of the Indian villages and established a camp, when a messenger from Chief Cornstalk arrived, pleading for peace. Realizing hostilities would soon be ended, Dunmore sent word to Lewis to stop his advance. When the Virginians failed to halt, he again sent orders for Lewis to stop his advance and return home. Both times Lewis refused the order and continued to march west, <u>the first such defiance of an English superior's military order in the history of the colony</u>. It was not until Dunmore rode out and met with the Virginians and personally ordered Lewis to stop, that he did so. The governor had with him the friendly Indian, Chief White Eyes, and other Indian leaders confirming they wanted no more fighting with the Long Knives, as they called the Virginians. The negotiations, which Lewis refused to attend, resulted in the Treaty of Camp Charlotte, named for the wife of King George III, which once again brought peace to the region. The Indian threat to Virginia was ended, but the Battle of Point Pleasant and General Lewis' defiance afterward contributed to the battle being referred to by many as the "First Battle of the American Revolution."

Colonel John Stuart, who participated in the battle and later served as the first clerk of Greenbrier County, West Virginia, stated "The battle of Point Pleasant was in fact the beginning of the Revolutionary War, that obtained for our country the liberty and independence enjoyed by the United States, for it is well known that the Indians were influenced by the British to commence the war to terrify and confound the

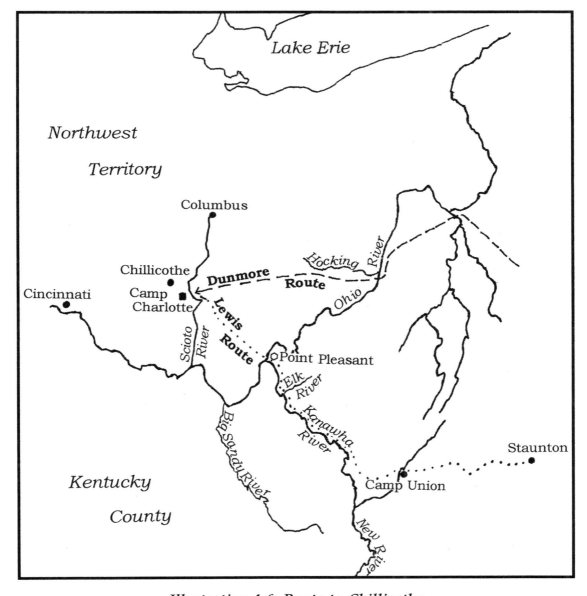

Illustration 4-6: Route to Chillicothe

people, before they commenced hostilities themselves the following year at Lexington. It was thought by British politicians that to incite an Indian war would prevent a combination of the colonies for opposing parliamentary measures to tax Americans. The blood therefore spilt upon this memorable battle field will long be remembered by the good people of Virginia and the United States with gratitude." Virgil A. Lewis concludes, "The Battle of Point Pleasant stands out conspicuously between the great constructive periods of American history. It is the greatest event of the colonial period and stands just at its close. With it the Revolutionary period begins." The 60th United States Congress convening in May, 1908, officially recognized, by unanimous vote, the Battle of Point Pleasant as "the battle of the Revolution." Additionally, funding was voted for a monument on the site.

The Virginians under Lewis returned to Point Pleasant, buried their dead, and completed the three-hundred-mile trip home with their wounded. Like the Big Sandy Expedition, the militia had failed to destroy the Indian threat. This would result in continuing hostilities in the years ahead and serve as a distraction to the western settlers as they tried to support the fight for American independence. *The Battle of Point Pleasant was the first time the Augusta Militia engaged in battle as an independent force.* There were no British leaders or soldiers in Dunmore's Southern Division, only American militia. Theodore Roosevelt in his *Winning of the West,* states, "It may be doubted if a braver or physically finer set of men ever got together in this continent." In support of this, six of the militia soldiers at Point Pleasant would become United States Congressmen, three would be U.S. Senators, four would become state governors, and six would rise to the rank of General. These experienced veterans would play a major role in the upcoming war for independence and the creation of a new nation.

The heroic effort of the militia at Point Pleasant is remembered today thanks to the tireless effort and dedication of the Colonel Charles Lewis Chapter of the National Society of the Daughters of the American Revolution. Every year near the anniversary of the battle, re-enactors, local school children, government leaders, and of course, current members of the 116th Infantry Brigade assemble at Tu-Endie-Wei Park in Point Pleasant, West Virginia, to remember the first battle of the American Revolution. Buried in the magazine are Colonel Charles Lewis, Colonel John Field, Captain John Murray, Captain Robert McClennahan, Captain Samuel Wilson, Lieutenant Hugh Allen, John Frogg, George Cameron, and other members of the militia who had made the supreme sacrifice. Their courage and the courage of all the veterans of the Battle of Point Pleasant is remembered in a moving ceremony where chapters of the Daughters of the American Revolution and the Sons of the American Revolution come from across the country to place wreaths in their memory. It was here that over thirty years after its first muster, the Augusta Militia, one day to be named the 116th Infantry Regiment, came of age. Utilizing the skill and experience they had gained in settling the rugged American frontier, these soldiers wrote their names indelibly into the pages of the history of America. Their sacrifice at the Battle of Point Pleasant in 1774 epitomizes the courage and sacrifices the militia exhibited throughout the emergence of this great nation.

Illustration 4-7: Photograph of the author with DAR and SAR representatives at the 225th anniversary of the battle on October 10, 1999

Battle streamer earned: Dunmore War (Battle of Point Pleasant)

Five

The American Revolution

With the threat of the Indian nations ended and Dunmore's War behind them, the militia returned to their homes and farms in the Valley of Virginia. They were greeted immediately with the news of events that threatened the relationship between the colonies and England. For ten years, settlers in the Valley and the lands to the west had followed the news of the Crown's efforts to invoke taxation on the colonies in order to recoup the expenses incurred in driving the French from the English colonies. Beginning with the Stamp Act in 1765, requiring stamps to be purchased and placed on all newspapers and documents generated in the America colonies, and the Townshend Acts of 1767, imposing a tax on paper, white lead, glass, and tea, the settlers of western Virginia followed the gathering storm clouds.

While the hotbeds of the controversy were centered in the seats of government in Williamsburg or Boston, the western settlements followed the events with great interest and sympathy for their fellow colonists. There was little doubt when the first shots rang out on the green at Lexington, Massachusetts, starting the Revolutionary War on April 19, 1775, how the Valley militia would respond, especially considering the conduct of English Governor Dunmore during the expedition to Point Pleasant and the Ohio River. The year 1775 also saw extensive exploration by Daniel Boone and others into western Virginia and particularly Kentucky County.

In Virginia, the actions of Governor Dunmore had stirred patriotic fervor against the Royal Governor. As early as 1773, Dunmore attempted to control Virginians and quell their growing opposition to English rule. When the elected members of the Virginia General Assembly, formerly known as th House of Burgesses, failed to follow his guidance, he disbanded them. The governor further agitated Virginians when on April 21, 1775 he took control of the colony's supply of gunpowder in Williamsburg and moved it to a British warship, the *HMS Magdalen* anchored in the York River. In response, Patrick Henry called out Virginia's Second Regiment which included companies of the Augusta Militia. Patrick Henry became another of the great Virginians to command the Valley soldiers as they moved to Williamsburg, forcing Governor Dunmore to flee his palace there on May 12, 1775, and take refuge on the *HMS Fowey* also anchored off Yorktown.

Dunmore proclaimed he would continue to govern Virginia from this position of safety, but used the opportunity to organize friends of the English King, arm slaves in the Tidewater, and encourage them to rise up against the Virginians. Additionally, he encouraged Indian uprisings in the west, threatening the Shenandoah Valley and the Virginia frontier. The situation worsened when he issued a proclamation to servants and slaves making them "free that are able and willing to bear arms, they joining His Majesty's Troops."

The Revolutionary War did present somewhat of a dilemma for the members of the Western District of Virginia Militia units. They were from frontier counties and many believed they did not have fair representation in Virginia's government. Still, the majority of the Valley citizens favored revolution, clearly wanting to defeat the British, win independence, and create a new country. The practical difficulty they also faced, however, was the very real and continuing Indian threat to their homes and communities.

The colonies had previously organized and convened a Continental Congress in an attempt to resolve the conflicts with the Crown, but now their task was to organize a new government and build an army to fight the British. They chose George Washington to serve as their first military commander-in-chief on June 15, 1775, and he immediately faced the difficult task of organizing and training the first American army. General Washington and the new Congress realized that to defeat the British they would need to organize a standing military force. The result was called the Continental Army, and its soldiers would be paid and equipped from funds generated by the new government. A large number of Augusta Militia members were quick to volunteer for service in America's first army and serve for the next five years as members of the Continental Line. Many of these young volunteers had gained valuable combat experience during the Indian Wars and at the Battle of Point Pleasant.

In the northern portion of the Valley, or lower Valley, where the Indian threat was minimal, Colonel Daniel Morgan of Winchester was quick to respond to the call from the Continental Congress for two rifle companies from Virginia. Morgan, along with frontiersman George Rogers Clark, had been in Dunmore's northern division in 1774 where he met Andrew Lewis and the Augusta Militia. He was quick to answer Washington's call and organized one company in July of 1775, and according to David McCullough in his book, *1776*, "marched on a 'bee-line' for Boston, covering six hundred miles in three weeks, or an average of thirty miles a day in the heat of summer." This effort would continue the history of the Valley soldiers being known as "foot cavalry," a tradition that remains today. Also in response to the "Virginia Colony's" first convention, Captain Daniel Stephenson raised a second company at Morgan's Spring, in what is now West Virginia. This company also initially moved to Boston to support General Washington, arriving in only twenty-four days. Washington was so pleased to see the militia that he rode to greet them and then dismounted to shake the hand of each and every volunteer.

On December 9, 1775, a militia force with members from the Augusta Militia, including Captain William Campbell's Company Number 7 and Captain George Gibson's Company Number 8, defeated Governor Dunmore's forces under British Captain Forgyce, attempting a frontal attack across the causeway at Great Bridge, Virginia. Captain Forgyce fell with fourteen bullet wounds as the militia marksmen fired volley after volley into the British attackers. The important sites involved in the battle are identified by VA Historical markers K-275 on Route 17, three miles south of Portsmouth, KY-4 on Route 170, and KY-5 on Route 168 both in Chesapeake. The loss forced Dunmore and his British fleet to retreat to Norfolk. Before leaving Hampton Roads, however, he burned Norfolk to the ground. The county in the Valley of Virginia previously named for him was renamed "Shenandoah."

Also in December of 1775, a court-martial in Augusta County met to organize two more companies to serve in the Continental Army for a two-year term beginning on April 10, 1776. During the Revolutionary War, Augusta County alone would provide roughly 2,500 volunteers for the Continental Line and militia duty. Both forces were absolutely critical in the fight for independence, but their competitive existence resulted in a controversy that continues even today. There were those who feared a standing military force as a result of their oppression in the homeland they had fled to come to America. An equally strong opposing position made the case for a well equipped and efficiently trained force prepared to react quickly to any threat to the new country.

Colonel Morgan's command later would move north, with then American General Benedict Arnold, to attack Quebec in late December. Upon Arnold's wounding, Morgan would take command of the expedition, only to be wounded himself and taken prisoner by the superior British force defending Quebec. The war was not over for Morgan, however, and his leadership was again called upon when the Augusta Militia responded to a direct threat to their beloved Shenandoah Valley. On this later occasion, a British force was moving north through the Carolinas with little resistance. Morgan and the Augusta Militia would mobilize to end that threat.

One of General Washington's first selections to command was Brigadier General Andrew Lewis, who was given charge of all the Continental forces in Virginia. On May 16, 1776, during the Fifth Virginia Convention, the newly formed troops were paraded before the assembly and their new commander. Shortly thereafter, Lewis departed for Gwynn's Island, just off the Gloucester Shore on the Piankatank River. Taking command of the Americans, or "crickets" as Dunmore had nicknamed them, Lewis immediately devised a plan to run the British governor from the shores of Virginia once and for all.

At eight o'clock on the morning of July 9, Lewis personally lit the match and fired an eighteen pounder into the British warship *HMS Dunmore*. This opening shot was followed by other American field pieces. One by one the British warships slipped their lines and withdrew under the cannonade, leaving a small force on the island itself. That night all of the boats in the area were gathered up, and the next morning an American force of two hundred slipped across the narrow waterway and captured what was by then a deserted Gwynn's Island. They were led by Captain Tho-

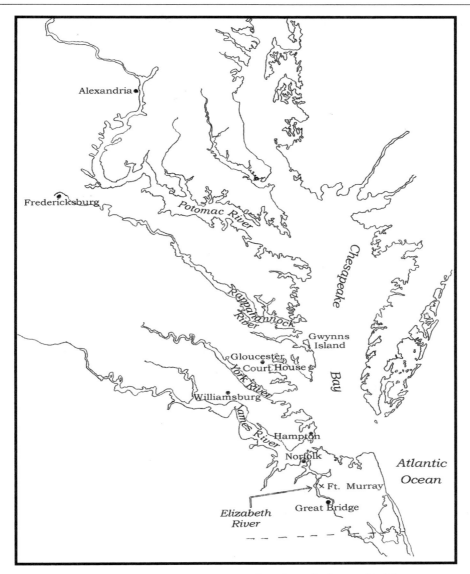

Illustration 5-1: Gwynn's Island and Great Bridge

mas Posey, formally of the Augusta Militia, but now leading the 7th Virginia Regiment and part of the Culpeper Militia that were present. Dunmore and his fleet now were forced to leave Virginia's shores, with part of the force moving south to St. Augustine, Florida, while the balance moved north to New York. The last British governor was gone, never to return. Virginia Historical marker NW-3 identifies the site. Dunmore would one day become the Governor of Jamaica.

John Randolph liked the name "Minute Men" to identify the militia volunteers who protected Virginia's frontiers during the Revolutionary War. He said, ". . .were raised in a minute, armed in a minute, fought in a minute, and vanquished the enemy in a minute." These volunteers, responsible for providing their own guns and tomahawks would be known as the "unorganized militia," in which every able-bodied man was required to serve. They should not be confused with the organized militia. The distinction is very important and has much to do with the way the different organizations performed during the Revolutionary War. The companies serving in the Continental Army were part of the national force; the companies serving in the organized militia were the Commonwealth of Virginia's military force that would support the Continental Army and serve as the state's defenders similar to our National Guard of today, while an unorganized militia served primarily in local emergencies such as Indian raids.

In October of 1776, the newly formed "General Assembly" of Virginia voted to divide Augusta County once again, this time at the Allegheny Mountains and name everything west of the range the District of West Augusta. Effective January 1, 1777, the legislature further divided the District of West Augusta by creating three new counties: Youghiogheny, Monongahela, and Ohio. Augusta County was again greatly reduced in size, and further reductions would come with the establishment of Greenbrier, Rockingham, and Rockbridge Counties by the Virginia General Assembly meeting in October, 1777. Although the territory of Augusta County had been diminished, it would continue to play a major role in the security of Virginia's, and later the new nation's, western settlements. The Augusta Militia had provided, and would continue to provide until the turn of a new century, the protection for the settlements reaching as far west as the Mississippi River.

In this regard, throughout the Revolutionary War, the Augusta Militia was called out to respond to Indian incursions primarily in the District of West Augusta. The British enlisted the Indians to assist them in defeating the colonials, promising them the return of their lands at the end of the war. This was great incentive for the Indian tribes that had long resented the continuous establishment of settlements west of the Allegheny Mountains and into the Ohio River Valley. The British provided the Indians

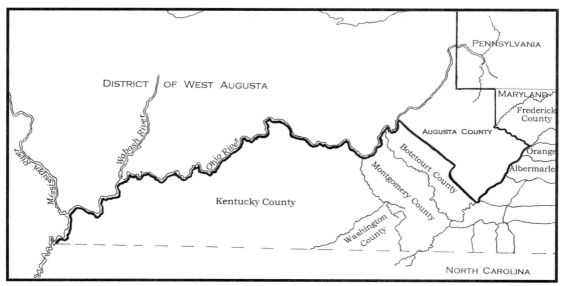

Illustration 5-2: Virginia's Western Counties - 1776

with arms, ammunition, and advisors, mostly Loyalists, to help them better understand how the Americans were organized and fought. The result was a continuous attack on settlements across the Virginia frontier. At the outset of war, for example, Captain Mathew Arbuckle was dispatched to rebuild Fort Blair at Point Pleasant on the Ohio River. The fort had been destroyed by the Indians and after rebuilding it, it was renamed Fort Randolph. Defenses were also established at the junction of the Elk and Kanawha Rivers where Charleston now stands. Initially, known as Fort Clendenin, it would later be named Fort Lee for Virginia's Governor at the time, Henry Lee. The Augusta Militia was back in the business of protecting Virginia's frontier region.

The last court in Augusta County under Crown rule was held on May 1, 1776, and when the next court was held on July 16, 1776, it was conducted under the authority of the new Commonwealth of Virginia. Colonel Abraham Smith assisted by Colonel Alex Thompson and Lieutenant Colonel John Dickenson commanded the Augusta Regiment. There were twenty-eight companies in the regiment, consisting of both foot soldiers (today's infantry) and cavalry. Captains William Christian and John Lyle commanded two companies that joined the American army as part of the 2nd Regiment. Augusta County would later provide troops for the tenth, eleventh, twelfth and thirteenth Virginia Regiments that saw service in the Revolutionary War.

The first call for militia to stop Indian incursions came in 1776, and the Augusta Militia responded with the companies of Captains Lyle and Christian mustering in Lexington, Virginia, and moving south to the Holston River. This was to block movement by the Cherokees into the Valley. In March of 1777, Captain Kincaid's Company was called to Fort Pitt, while Captain Lockridge's Company went west into what is now Pocahontas County, West Virginia, in response to another Indian raiding party. In September, Captain Thomas Smith's Company joined other militia units moving into the Greenbriar region and then on to a defensive position at Point Pleasant along the Ohio River. This company returned to the Valley in December.

On September 1, 1777, Fort Henry, named for Virginia's first Governor, Patrick Henry, was attacked by Indians and Tories (Loyalists). This outpost was established west of Fort Pitt, in what is today Wheeling, West Virginia, along U.S. Routes 40 and 250 on the Ohio River. On that day, a force of three hundred attacked the fort, initially killing one of two men working livestock outside the walls of the fort. The attackers were at first thought to be only a small group, so Captain Mason with fourteen defenders left to drive off the Indians. They immediately fell into an ambush, as did another party led by Captain Joseph Ogle that was sent to their rescue. In all, twenty defenders were killed or wounded before the survivors retreated inside the walls of Fort Henry. The siege was short lived, however, as riders from within the fort escaped to bring back additional militia forces.

Throughout 1777, the year that would become known as the year of the "Bloody Sevens," conflicts with the Indians continued to increase. Virginia's western county of Kentucky, though scarcely inhabited with only 250 settlers, became another battleground with the Indians. On December 29, 1777, the Shawnees attacked Fort

McClelland, roughly thirty miles from present day Georgetown, Kentucky. One of the heroes of this siege would be then Major George Rogers Clark, who led a relief force of militia from the District of Western Virginia to the fort. Clark was born in Albemarle County, just over the Blue Ridge Mountains from Augusta, but had moved west to help open up Virginia's frontier. Arriving in early 1778, he found John McClelland and Charles White mortally wounded. He removed the survivors to the safety of a much stronger settlement at Harrodsburg. Clark was only twenty-four years of age, but destined to become a leading figure in securing the Western District.

The year 1778 saw numerous attacks on the settlements in western Virginia, particularly in Kentucky County. The fort at Boonesborough, one of the westernmost settlements, was constantly being attacked. One siege lasted from September 9 until September 20. It was at this outpost that Daniel Boone was severely wounded in hand-to-hand fighting with the Indians. He was carried to the safety of the fort by Simon Kenton. During this year, Major Clark began gathering volunteers and initiated offensive operations further west by attacking British outposts toward the Mississippi River. He even took the British post at Vincennes on the Wabash River.

The fortress at Vincennes proved easier to capture than to hold. In December, the Virginians had no choice but to surrender the post to a superior British force, but in February of 1779, Clark retook the post and ended forever the British presence on the Mississippi River and its tributaries. He now eyed the British strong point at Detroit. The Augusta Militia Companies of Captains McCutchen and Thompson were stationed at Fort Pitt throughout this period, to guard against any breakthrough in the frontier outposts developing further to the west.

As indicated, the Valley of Virginia and Augusta County supported the fight for independence by sending men to serve in the Continental Line and the organized militia, but when the war came to the south, even the unorganized militia responded. The British strategy under General Sir Henry Clinton, who was given command of all the British forces in North America in March of 1778, was to divide the colonies. He intended to continue to pressure General Washington in the north while sending a force south to capture the ports of Savannah and Charles Town (today's Charleston) in South Carolina, and use them as a base to move north. Initially the plan worked well, as the ports were captured by the spring of 1780, and Camden, South Carolina, fell in August of that year. The British were well on their way to sweeping through the south. During these victories, Lieutenant General (Earl, Lord) Charles Cornwallis emerged as the prominent British commander.

After Camden, Cornwallis' strategy in early 1780 was to sweep though the Carolinas and into Virginia. He dispatched loyalist Major Patrick Ferguson to march through the mountains, laying waste to the land of the revolutionaries. This charge brought a response from the western Virginia Militia poised to resist any incursion into its territory. Current and former leaders of the Augusta Militia including Isaac Shelby, William Campbell, and John Sevier, to name just a few, answered the call. Campbell alone brought over four hundred Virginians. On October 7, 1780, the militia fell upon Ferguson and his forces encamped on Kings Mountain, South Carolina, and went about destroying them. This was terrain well suited to the men from the mountains and valleys of western Virginia, and they made short work of their 1,100 British and Loyalist enemies. The key blow was struck by the forces of Shelby, Sevier, and Campbell with the balance of the American units positioned to block any British retreat. Ferguson's force was surrounded and trapped. At day's end, 156 of the enemy, including Ferguson, lay dead, with an equal number wounded and the remainder captured. The results bolstered the sagging morale of the entire American military and caused Cornwallis to rethink his strategy as he awaited reinforcements.

It should be acknowledged that the militia committed numerous atrocities following this battle. They remembered what became known as the Slaughter at Waxhaws on May 29, 1780, when a cavalry force commanded by a young Colonel Banastre Tarleton killed 113 Virginia Continental soldiers retreating from the British victory at Camden, forever earning him the name of "Bloody Ban." His men killed and wounded without mercy the surrendering Continentals, thus establishing "Tarleton's Quarter" and the cry of "Bloody Tarleton." Following the Battle of Kings Mountain, as Tories presented white flags, they were shot down as they called "Quarter! Quarter!" The militia response on the part of many was "Tarleton's Quarter." For example, learning that his father, Colonel John Sevier, had been killed during the Battle of Kings Mountain, his son Joseph proclaimed "I'll keep loading and shooting till I kill every son of a bitch of them!" Eventually cooler heads prevailed, and the carnage ended. The offending militiamen were later tried in military courts and several hanged for their misconduct. In addition, several of the captured British who had participated in the killing of the Continentals at the hands of Tarleton were later tried and hanged.

The tide in the south was now turning. The "Over the Mountain" or Over Mountain militia organizations had been brought directly into the fight with the British. It

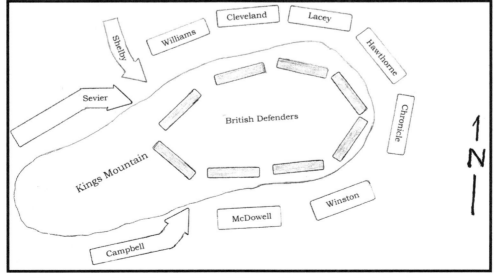

Illustration 5-3: The Battle of Kings Mountain, October 7, 1780

was now more than just the Indians threatening their homes; it was Cornwallis and his British regulars. The militia brought a new level of energy to the American cause in the south. Threatening their homes and families was not a good tactic as Cornwallis would learn throughout the winter of 1780. A tentative General Horatio Gates had been replaced by Washington's choice, General Nathanael Greene, as Commander in the South. Kings Mountain had bolstered the cause of the Revolution, and the number of soldiers in the Southern Army was beginning to grow. As the British withdrew to reorganize, the militia returned "over the mountain," its presence having been felt in the war for independence.

In Virginia, December of 1780 found former American, now British General Benedict Arnold, the famous traitor, with a force arriving in Portsmouth to attack Virginia from the east. Virginia's Governor Thomas Jefferson immediately called out the Virginia Militia. In his manuscript on the "Line of Senior Ancestor Regiments of the 116th Infantry," Reese T. Grubert points out that "With the invasion of Virginia by Benedict Arnold in January 1781 the entire regiment was called out. This was the first time since the Battle of Point Pleasant in 1774 that the regiment marched as a whole." Commanding all forces in Virginia was a Lutheran minister, now General, Peter Muhlenberg from Woodstock, in the Valley of Virginia. In the fall of 1775, General Washington and Virginia's first elected Governor, Patrick Henry, had urged him to accept an appointment as a Colonel in the Continental Army. He resisted initially, but on January 12, 1776, he gave a farewell sermon to his congregation saying, "There is a time of war and a time of peace, and now the time to fight has come." With that, he opened his robe to reveal his uniform as a member of the 8th Virginia Regiment, a German Regiment. Within a year he would be promoted to the rank of Brigadier General, and put in charge of the defense of his beloved Virginia. The British made it as far as Richmond before they were repulsed after destroying a few public buildings, but were successful in capturing a large number of military supplies. Arnold went into winter quarters, and the militia, for the most part, returned home.

In South Carolina, one of General Greene's first moves as the new commander in the South was to split his force and select Brigadier General Daniel Morgan to command his light infantry and militia units. Greene would move east, where he would be pursued by Cornwallis, while Morgan moved west followed by Tarleton. Morgan was immediately accepted by the soldiers, particularly the militia, since he had come from their ranks. He was well versed in militia tactics and experienced in how the British fought. He chose the ground at Cowpens, South Carolina, to present his force for Colonel Tarleton to attack. Cowpens was just that, a field where farmers in this part of South Carolina wintered their livestock. General Morgan chose a defensive position where he could see the entire field and maneuver his forces accordingly. The high ground was practically surrounded by streams, making escape by any defeated force very difficult. It was to be an "all or nothing" fight.

On the afternoon of January 17, 1781, Morgan was arrayed with his Militia up front and just behind his skirmishers. His primary defense position in the rear was

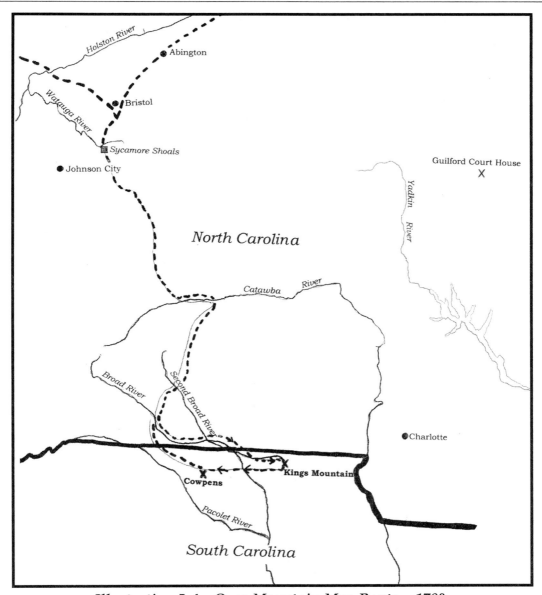

Illustration 5-4: Over Mountain Men Route - 1780

comprised of Continentals. Upon assessing the American position, Tarleton was delighted and thought this an opportunity to route the militia and overrun Morgan's position. Around 7 a.m. he sent a detachment of his Dragoons to force the American skirmishers to retreat, and then moved his Fusiliers forward to attack. The Militia fired a deadly volley as the British closed to within 150 yards, reloaded and fired another volley that staggered the oncoming line. Now following orders, the Militia filed off to the rear. Morgan's next line was 450 Continentals who further slowed the British advance. Tarleton saw the Militia withdrawal as a full retreat and ordered his Dragoons to charge after them. Morgan countered with his cavalry force under Colonel William Washington.

As the British continued forward, the Militia and Continentals continued to withdraw. Morgan was at the front with them, and as they reached higher ground and with the Fusiliers in hot pursuit, Morgan ordered his force to "turn about and fire!" The volley from a range of only about thirty to forty yards stunned the oncoming British infantry. Before they could recover, the Americans had fixed bayonets and were attacking. Almost simultaneously, Colonel Washington's cavalry swept to the attack, resulting in a double envelopment. The shocked British began to throw down their arms and fall to the ground. A momentary cry for "Tarleton's Quarter" was overcome by Morgan's leadership, and the prisoners were spared. Two British three pound cannon were captured as Tarleton tried to rally his Dragoons, but it was too late. Confusion became chaos as the British broke and ran in all directions. Tarleton, having lost his horse, took that of his surgeon and headed to the rear with Colonel Washington in hot pursuit. With the help of two Dragoons, Tarleton wheeled and was close to killing Washington when more Americans arrived on the scene. Tarleton

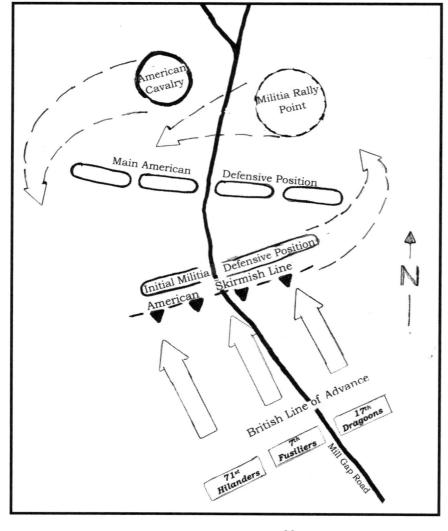

Illustration 5-5: Battle of Cowpens, January 17, 1781

continued his flight, stopping briefly at his supply trains and ordering them destroyed before racing on. Washington pursued him some twenty miles before returning to the scene of another great victory for the cause of the Revolution.

In less than an hour, Tarleton had lost 110 killed, 200 wounded, and 630 more captured. His force, comprising twenty-five percent of Cornwallis' army, had been destroyed. Additionally, two stands of colors, 800 muskets, 100 horses, and 35 wagons were lost. Against this, Morgan counted only twelve soldiers killed and sixty-one wounded. It was a smashing victory for the Patriot forces, again helped by the Militia, many of whom came from the Augusta Regiment.

Cornwallis was greatly distressed by the terrible losses at Cowpens and vowed to destroy the Americans once and for all. He was determined to find Morgan before his force could link up with Greene, but he was unsuccessful in doing so. In his effort to prevent the linkup, however, he made a critical decision to lighten his force by destroying his supplies. All tents, personal items, and anything that could not be carried in a knapsack were ordered destroyed despite the late January weather. The only wagons escaping destruction were those carrying ammunition, salt, the wounded, and necessary medical supplies. Cornwallis was going for broke.

After the victory at Kings Mountain, many of the militia returned to their homes. General Greene's situation was made worse by the deteriorating health of General Morgan whom he released to return to his home to receive needed medical care. Before departing, Morgan recommended the tactics he used at Kings Mountain to Greene. The proper use of the Militia was the key to success. Realizing the supply challenges now facing Cornwallis, Greene set about to play a game of cat and mouse, forcing the British to pursue him as long as possible before giving battle. Stretching Cornwallis' supply lines further and further, he moved his force north to a position he was familiar with, Guilford Court House in North Carolina. The terrain here was different from Cowpens, as would be the result of this last battle in the southern theater.

On March 15, 1781, Greene deployed his troops as Morgan had recommended, but the wooded area around Guilford Court House made his ability to react to the British attack difficult at best. The early part of the battle saw great holes torn in the attacking British formations from Greene's infantry and artillery three-pounders, but the tide turned as Cornwallis directed grape shot from his artillery be fired into the melee. The firing caused casualties in the British ranks as well as the American defenders, but it turned the tide, and the North Carolina Militia broke. When Greene learned that the British were maneuvering to attack him from the rear, he ordered his regiments to disengage and withdraw. The members of the Augusta Militia in the second line of the American defense had fought well and escaped with minor losses. The retreat was orderly and the arrival of a driving rain ended any British pursuit. Cornwallis was left in command of the field, but at a high price: ninety-three killed, over four hundred wounded, and twenty-six missing. The losses represented almost twenty-seven percent of the British force. It was a hollow victory and left Cornwallis with little choice but to abandon the Southern strategy, attempt to combine his force with General Clinton's, and seek an overwhelming victory in Virginia. The time had come to move north on a route closer to the coast and bypassing the resurgent militia.

The Americans awaited the British pursuit that never came. Their losses included seventy-nine killed and 184 wounded, a mere six percent of Greene's force. There were 885 missing, but they were the North Carolina Militia that had chosen to go home. Cornwallis now withdrew to resupply at the port of Wilmington, North Carolina before moving his force northeast to Virginia's Tidewater region. Greene went south in an attempt to recover the losses at Charleston and Savannah. He had not achieved the victory he had sought at Guilford Court House, but the end result, the departure of the British from the Carolinas, was satisfying.

As Cornwallis moved his forces into Virginia, he dispatched Colonel Tarleton to make a surprise attack through the Piedmont region. Learning of the movement, on June 3, Virginia Governor Thomas Jefferson ordered the removal of the General Assembly from Richmond to the safety of Charlottesville, some sixty miles to the west. Tarleton, also known as "The Hunting Leopard," pursued the withdrawing government, determined to surprise and capture as many as possible. (See Illustration 5-7) He stopped

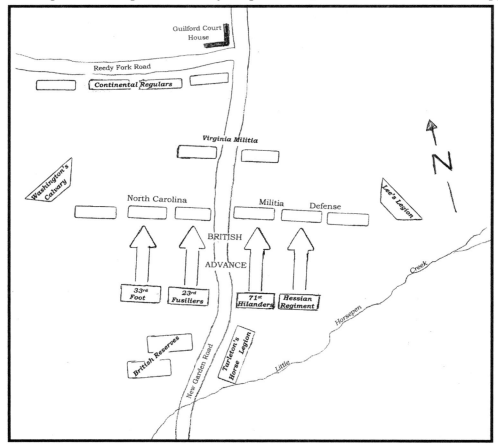

Illustration 5-6: Battle of Guilford Court House, March 15, 1781

briefly at a tavern in Louisa County where a young Captain in the Virginia Militia, John "Jack" Jouett, Jr., overheard the British plans. Leaping on his horse, Captain Jouett rode the forty miles to Charlottesville to warn the sleeping Virginia government. He roused the assemblymen, who withdrew another forty miles over the Blue Ridge Mountains to Staunton, the home of the Augusta Militia. Governor Jefferson, slow in leaving his home at Monticello, was nearly captured. Captain Daniel Boone, representing Kentucky County in the Virginia General Assembly, was captured when his identity was revealed in error by a departing comrade. Boone was eventually released, and made the trek to the safety of Augusta County and the militia in which he had once served.

The alarm was spread throughout the Valley. When Colonel Samuel Lewis, Andrew's son, learned of the impending danger, he rode to the home place at Bellefonte outside Staunton. Here he gave the news to his aunt Anne and requested the assistance of her sons. According to historian Virgil Lewis, she quickly readied the young boys and dispatched them saying, "Go my children. I spare not my youngest, my faired-hair boy, and the comfort of my declining years. I devote you all to my country. Keep back the foot of the invader from the soil of Augusta or see my face no more." Thus was the passion for the defense of the Valley, and hundreds of the Augusta Militia rushed to Rockfish Gap to protect their beloved county and homes. Tarleton wisely withdrew without moving further west. The crisis was diverted. Learning of the response throughout the county, General Washington was heard to say, "Leave me but a banner to plant upon the mountains of Augusta, and I will rally around me the men who will lift our bleeding country from the dust and set her free." Their former regimental commander clearly knew the Augusta Militia would not stand for any British intrusion into their Valley.

Virginia's government convened at Trinity Episcopal Church in Staunton, electing Thomas Nelson as their new governor. The die was cast now. The Augusta Militia was aroused along with militia from across Virginia. It was time to end this war for independence and drive the British from Virginia. French General Marquis de Lafayette took command of the forces in Virginia, and General Washington dispatched additional troops from General Von Steuben to join him. As Cornwallis withdrew further east, Washington, now also convinced that victory could be had in Virginia, moved the bulk of his entire army and that of French General Jean-Baptiste Rochambeau south to seal the British fate. As they were arriving, French Admiral Francois De Grasse was driving the British fleet under Admiral Thomas Graves from the Chesapeake, Bay. This blocked Cornwallis from any chance of combining his force with that of General Clinton. Cornwallis and his army were trapped! (See Illustration 5-8)

The Americans and French began tightening the noose around the British with the arrival of sixteen thousand troops under Washington and Rochambeau in early September. Trenches were dug and steadily moved closer to Cornwallis' encircled army. Artillery pieces were brought forward to pound the British positions that could provide little response as a result of the terrain sloping off to the waters of the York River. The impossibility

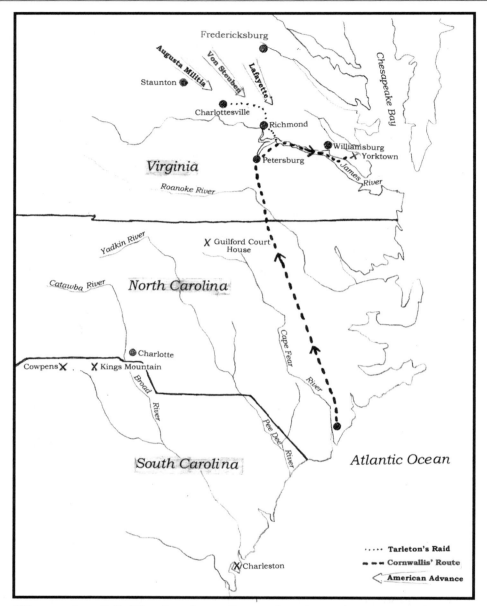

Illustration 5-7: The Southern Campaign & Tarleton's Raid Route

of his situation was evident to the British Commander at Yorktown. He had requested help from General Clinton in New York, but only promises came in return. On October 17, Cornwallis sent forth a white flag to the American lines with a note stating "I request a cessation of hostilities for twenty-four hours to settle terms of surrender." The parties met at the Moore house and, just two days later, the surrender was finalized. Cornwallis, according to author Virginius Dabney, "pleaded indisposition and named Brigadier Charles O'Hara to perform the unpleasant and humiliating office." On October 19, 1781, the British marched out from their defensive positions, passing between lines of American and French troops to lay down their arms. The surrender was complete.

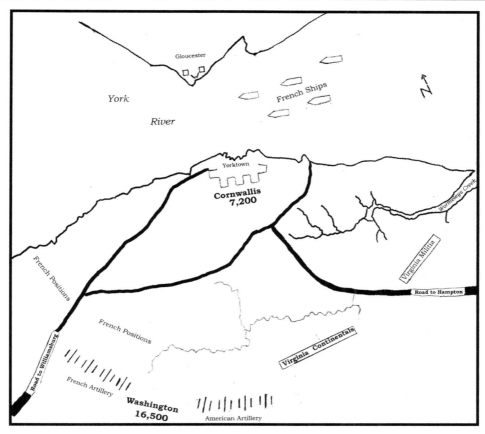

Illustration 5-8: Siege of Yorktown

The following Augusta County Companies were present at Yorktown under Colonel Thomas Hugart to witness Cornwallis's surrender on October 19, 1781:

Captain James Bell's Company
Captain Patrick Buchanan's Company
Captain William Finlay's Company
Captain Peter Hull's Company
Captain Zachariah Johnston's Company
Captain Francis Long's Company
Captain William McCutchen's Company
Captain Thomas Smith's Company
Captain William Tate's Company

Yorktown was not the end of the Revolutionary War, however; it would take almost sixteen months more before the Treaty of Paris brought the final end of the war on February 3, 1783. Most of the Augusta Militia returned home following Yorktown, but those serving in the Continental line remained on duty with Washington. Though difficult to prove, it can be surmised that Augusta County provided more troops to the cause of independence than any other county in the soon to be United States of America.

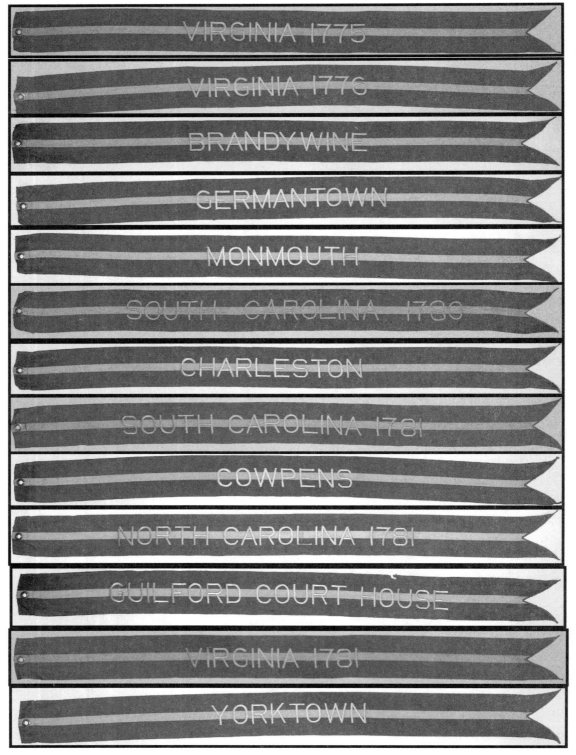

Battle streamers earned: Virginia 1775, Virginia 1776, Brandywine, Germantown, Monmouth, South Carolina 1780, Charleston, South Carolina 1781, Guilford Court House, Virginia 1781, Yorktown

Six

The Building
of a Nation

With the war behind them, the men of Augusta County returned to the peace and prosperity of their rich farm land in the Shenandoah Valley. Their involve-ment in the Indian Wars in the west diminished greatly with the organization of the new nation. In December of 1783, Thomas Jefferson and the Virginia General Assembly ceded all their previous claims northwest of the Ohio River to the authority of the new United States. This territory would one day be further divided into the present-day states of Ohio, Indiana, Illinois, Michigan, Minnesota, and Wisconsin. The area was beyond the Proclamation Line of 1763, and the British continued to claim this land and maintain forts there. Many members of the new American Congress agreed and wanted to take no responsibility for the settlements in the land north of the Ohio River.

In addition, once the Indians realized the British had been defeated, they banded together to prevent any further western expansion by the Americans. Representatives from the Delawares, Miamis, Mingos, Shawnees, Wyandots, and other western tribes met and determined they would continue to resist the American settlements, with or without the British. The Indian resistance and the uncertainty of the British claims in this western area would result in continued turbulence there until the end of the second war for American independence, the War of 1812.

Even before the Revolutionary War had ended, many of the inhabitants of what is now present-day Kentucky began rumblings for their own independence from Virginia. It would take until June 1, 1791, for the nine western Virginia counties to become the Commonwealth of Kentucky, but with former members of the Augusta Militia like Daniel Boone, they assumed more and more responsibility for their own security. It is estimated that between the British surrender at Yorktown in 1781 and the year 1790, more than one thousand settlers were killed or taken captive by Indian raiding parties moving through Kentucky. Most notable was the Battle of Blue Licks on August 19, 1782, where over two hundred Indians ambushed a militia force under Colonel John Todd on the Licking River in present-day Nicholas County, Kentucky. This attack was followed by sieges at Fort Henry and other frontier outposts.

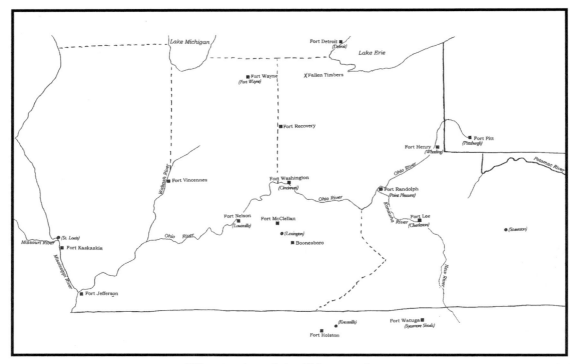

Illustration 6-1: Western forts

The settlers in the western territories were pretty much on their own for security until the new national government dispatched General Anthony Wayne to Fort Pitt in June of 1792 to address the Indian issue. Negotiations with the Indians had been going on unsuccessfully for years when General Wayne gathered his forces and moved further west to Fort Washington, the site of present-day Cincinnati, Ohio, in 1793. In April, when negotiations finally failed, Wayne's "Legion of the United States" had been built to 3,500 with the addition of Kentuckians under General Charles Scott. An Indian force of roughly 3,000 Chippewas, Delawares, Miamis, Pottawatomies, Shawnees, Tawas, and Wyandots were arrayed against them in what would become known as the Fight at Fallen Timbers, south of present-day Detroit, Michigan. On August 28, 1794, General Wayne's force defeated the Indians and soon began construction of Fort Wayne where the Indiana city with the same name now stands.

On January 1, 1795, the Indians requested further peace talks that resulted in the Treaty of Greenville, ceding more of their lands to the United States in return for $20,000 and a promise of $9,000 annually. Additionally, this forced the British to sign Jay's Treaty relinquishing all forts in America's Northwest Territory to the United States government. The struggle with the British was now over, yet the new American government had designs on much of the land that would later become Canada. The challenges opening up and defending the western lands of the United States now rested with the settlers moving into these areas. Many of these pioneers, however, would continue to come from the ranks of the Augusta militia. The Lewis family members, for example, remained active in the western movement and used their experience to organize and lead the militia units that would continue to win the west.

Most notable in the western expansion were the efforts of George Rogers Clark. Already recognized for his leadership in the Virginia Militia as early as 1777, when he was only twenty-four, he would continue to lead expeditions against the Indians, achieving the rank of General before being relieved by Virginia Governor Benjamin Harrison effective June 2, 1783. He was recalled in 1786, and commissioned to lead a force to defeat the Indians in the area of the Wabash River in what is now Indiana. Always offensive minded, Clark refused to build forts to protect the western settlements, insisting on attacking and destroying the Indians in the west as a better strategy. Clark had a difficult time raising an effective militia force, and later failures by militia organizations fueled the fires burning for the permanent establishment of a standing United States Army.

George Washington, who had become President in 1788, had over thirty-five years of serving with the militia. He had commanded the Augusta Militia on three occasions during the Indian wars and counted on the citizen soldiers to defend the Shenandoah Valley throughout the Revolutionary War. As John K. Mahon reveals in his *History of the Militia and the National Guard*, Washington "knew, and often voiced concern, about their faults, but he also appreciated the new nation's commitment to reliance on them."

During this post war period and leading up to the War of 1812, much controversy raged over the future of the militia in the new United States. Many of the citizens of the new nation strongly opposed a standing military, as a result of their European heritage. They feared their newly found independence would be suppressed and felt that citizen soldiers had provided the foundation of the emerging country. The militia would be sufficient enough to insure the young nation's future security. Others, however, favored a standing army instead of what they considered to be the undependable militia forces. The Articles of Confederation declared that "Every state shall always keep up a well regulated and disciplined militia, ..." Each state was pledged to help defend the others. The articles were vague concerning a peacetime army, so the debate raged throughout the 1780s.

The issue was finally resolved when Congress approved the Uniform Militia Act on May 8, 1792. The act required military service for all free and able-bodied white men from the age of eighteen to forty-five. The soldiers were required to provide their own musket and essentials for firing. Their service commitment was to both their state and the nation. Their federal service was limited to three months. It further provided a structure of brigades in each state, with each brigade consisting of four regiments. It established the position of an adjutant general in each state, responsible for maintaining uniformity among the militia organizations. Each of the fifteen states moved to enact supporting laws in response to the Uniform Militia Act. Similar to the recent day controversy over the overseas deployment of the National Guard, the founding fathers wrestled with using the citizen soldiers outside of the new country. The governors of the New England states were outraged at the federal government using its militia in any overseas conflict and passed state laws prohibiting such an action.

On December 31, 1792, the Virginia General Assembly adapted the Virginia Militia to the federal Uniform Militia Act. The Augusta Regiment became part of the 7th Brigade and was split between the new 32nd Regiment in the northern part of the county and the 93rd Regiment to the south. Regiments were generally organized with ten companies. This new militia system was soon tested in 1794 with the outbreak of the Whiskey Rebellion. On August 7, 1794, President Washington issued a proclamation ordering the end of the uprising in Pennsylvania. When the order failed to obtain positive results, he ordered out militia units on September 1 to end the rebellion. The Augusta County Militia, members from both of the new regiments, was ordered to assist in quelling the insurgency. They joined forces with militia units from Maryland, New Jersey and Pennsylvania, a force of some 12,900 soldiers to suppress the uprising. The Augusta Militia was on duty until early December, when the leaders of the rebellion had been arrested and the rest of the participants returned to their homes peacefully.

In 1793, President Washington called upon Congress to make numerous changes to the Uniform Militia Act. Each state had a little different idea on how the militia should be organized, trained, and utilized. The differences were never resolved despite the efforts of subsequent administrations to bring uniformity to the militia. The result left the United States with a small standing army and a large, but inconsistent militia force as the clouds of another war with England grew darker.

A number of incidents led to renewed conflict between the United States and Great Britain which resulted in the War of 1812. First, there was the continuing conflict in what would become known as the Northern Theater of War, the area around the Great Lakes. Then there was concern over issues in the Eastern Theater around Maine and New Brunswick. Finally, naval conflicts such as the engagement between the *USS Chesapeake* and the *HMS Leopard* in June of 1807, had stirred the growing conflict. The fervor for a fight, however, in the citizens of Augusta County, was not there when hostilities with the British exploded in 1812. The events leading up to war were of little impact to the residents of Augusta County. That wasn't to say that the Augusta Militia did not participate. When Virginia was called upon to furnish a regiment to the United States Army, both regiments of the Augusta Militia were ordered to send a company as part of this organization.

The two companies moved north across the Potomac River in support of neighboring Maryland and the new capital of the United States in the District of Columbia where it had relocated in 1800. The War of 1812 involved action in the north, west, and south, but generally outside the Commonwealth of Virginia, and there was never a serious threat to the Shenandoah Valley. The British did attempt to take Craney Island off the Virginia coast in June of 1813, in order to seize Norfolk and Portsmouth. This attack was unsuccessful, as a force of Virginia Militia and sailors defeated the much larger British force. Later, however, the British were successful in taking Hampton and burning the city to the ground, but proceeded no further inland.

In the summer of 1814, the British returned to the Chesapeake Bay, proceeding up the Patuxent River to attack the American capital in Washington from the east. (See Illustration 6-2) The militia responded, moving to Bladensburg, Maryland, to halt the British force of 4,500 regulars who had been put ashore at Benedict. The American defenses crumbled after heavy British bombardment and the advance of the impressive enemy force. The withdrawal became a rout and turned into what would become known as the "Bladensburg Races" which left the American capital in the hands of the British on August 24, 1814. They destroyed the new and partially completed government buildings in Washington, including the Capitol and President's Mansion. President Madison escaped along with his cabinet and Congress, but the new Capitol was in ruins. Governor James Barbour called out the militia and the Augusta Regiments responded vigorously as they realized their beloved state was under attack. Governor Barbour was delighted with the militia's response, calling it "the proudest day which Virginia has seen since the foundation of the commonwealth."

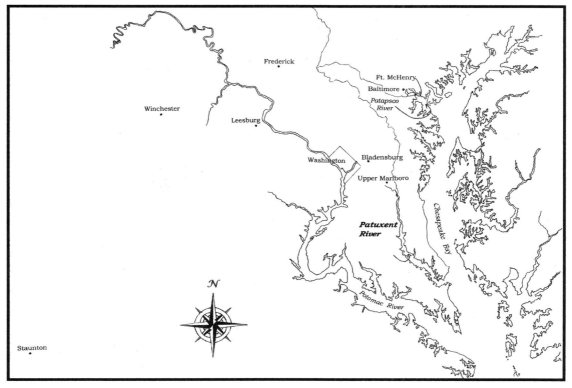

Illustration 6-2: War of 1812

The British withdrew under the threat of the overwhelming militia force being arrayed against it. Whenever there was a threat, riders would move about Virginia seeking militia support. When the British moved further up the Chesapeake Bay to attack Fort McHenry outside Baltimore, two companies, one from Winchester and one from Leesburg, responded to the threat. They helped defeat the British infantry attacks and defended the fort against the strong British naval bombardment. This famous American victory in Baltimore inspired Francis Scott Key to pen the national anthem.

The war had become a stalemate, and fighting was to end with the signing of the Treaty of Ghent, which is today located in Belgium, on Christmas Eve, 1814. Members of the Augusta Militia were also with General Andrew Jackson at New Orleans when his American Army handed the British a staggering defeat almost two weeks after the peace treaty had been signed. News traveled slowly and neither side was aware of the new peace. When the United States Senate ratified the treaty, the War of 1812 was officially over. The bottom line was that the Augusta Militia participated, but did not play a significant role in this second war with Great Britain.

Following the War of 1812, interest and support for militia organizations generally began to wane across the United States. The Augusta Militia, however, continued to be an integral part of its communities. Militia companies continued to be created as part of the 7th Brigade and the 32nd and 93rd Regiments. The population growth resulted in a third regiment, the 160th, being formed in 1839. Strong organizations sprang up throughout the central Shenandoah Valley. Local units, like the Middlebrook Rifles, West Augusta Guards, the Rockingham Grays, and the Rockbridge Rifles, drilled regularly and stood ready to respond to any call to state or federal service. The militia was an important part of life in the Shenandoah Valley.

The militia organization of the period consisted of a company of sixty privates, with four corporals, four sergeants, an ensign, a first and second lieutenant, and a captain. The officers were elected by the company, while the captain chose those to serve as corporals and sergeants. The next level in the structure was a battalion with four to eight companies and two battalions comprised a regiment. The next highest level was a brigade which consisted of from two to four regiments. Officers above the rank of captain were normally elected by the other officers in the organization, with generals being chosen by the governor of the state. This basic structure remained in place until the Civil War. The influence of the Augusta Militia remained strong during the western expansion of this period. William Irvine Lewis, for example, a descendent of John Lewis, was killed at the Alamo in 1836, along with Davy Crockett and others who had moved into Tennessee and then into other regions beyond the Mississippi River.

When Texas achieved statehood on December 29, 1845, Mexico broke off diplomatic relations, fearing the continuing expansion of the United States. General Zachary Taylor, "Old Rough-and-Ready," was spoiling for a fight, and when an American patrol was ambushed, the United States declared war on Mexico. In April of 1846,

President James Polk dispatched a force under General Taylor to Texas in a show of force to pressure Mexico into accepting an offer of thirty million dollars for its northern territories. What followed were a number of American attacks driving the Mexican Army south to Mexico City where they were defeated at Chapultepec on September 12, 1847. The resulting peace treaty ceded Mexico's entire northern territory, a vast area stretching from the new state of Texas to the Pacific Ocean and north to the Oregon Territory, to the United States at the reduced price of fifteen million dollars. Present-day states of Arizona, California, New Mexico, Nevada, Utah, and parts of Colorado and Wyoming were carved out of this vast region.

Existing militia units in Virginia were not called to serve in the Mexican War, but one regiment, the 1st Virginia Volunteer Infantry, was formed for service in northern Mexico, and the Augusta Regiments provided one company, the Augusta Volunteers. The unit was initially commanded by Captain Kenton Harper and later Captain George Washington Shuey. They were mustered into federal service in December of 1847 and moved to Fort Monroe where then embarked for the port of Corpus Christi, Texas. The regiment saw little or no action, as it was assigned mainly to provide security on the American supply lines in the area of Monterrey. It returned to Virginia in July of 1848 and mustered out of service at Fort Monroe on August 3. The unit then took stage coaches through Richmond and Charlottesville to Staunton where they received a heroes' welcome from the local residents.

The war with Mexico had created more American casualties than any previous conflict. Thirty percent of the army was lost, 1,721 from combat and another 11,155 from disease. Many young officers, among them Ulysses Grant, Robert E. Lee, James Longstreet, George McClellan, Thomas Jackson, and William Sherman, were recognized for valor and prepared for a greater conflict to come. The west was now open, and the discovery of gold at Sutter's Mill in 1848, near present-day Sacramento, California, would speed the migration.

The next eleven years saw a period of peace and prosperity in Augusta County and the growing United States. That would change quickly on October 16, 1859, when John Brown and a small force of abolitionists conducted a raid on Harpers Ferry, Virginia, taking possession of the small town located in the extreme northern end of the Shenandoah Valley. Brown believed the time was right to draw attention to the issue of slavery, particularly in the southern states, and planned an armed insurrection to end the practice. He had hoped that when word spread of his occupation of Harpers Ferry, he would be joined there by other abolitionists. The gathering force could use the weapons located in town's Federal Arsenal to overcome any attempt to stop them from expanding their cause to other areas. The militia units in the area of Harpers Ferry provided the initial response to the raid and forced Brown's small party to retreat to the protection of the building housing the arsenal.

That night, Colonel Robert E. Lee arrived with a company of ninety United States Marines to take control of the situation. Colonel Lee dispatched his aide,

Lieutenant J. E. B. Stuart to talk with Brown and try to find a peaceful end to the standoff. This effort failed, however, so the Marines stormed into the arsenal and in a matter of minutes it was all over, with Brown and four others taken prisoner. The survivors were taken to nearby Charles Town, the seat of government in Jefferson County, Virginia, to be tried. News of the attack spread quickly up the Valley and some members of the Augusta Militia went to Harpers Ferry when news of the raid reached Staunton. This was an invasion of their beloved Shenandoah Valley, and they wanted to be there for the trial. Many remained throughout the proceedings and were present when John Brown and his conspirators were hanged on December 2.

There were many threats from abolitionists against Virginia if Brown was executed, so Governor John Letcher ordered a few militia units to provide a strong military presence in Charles Town to insure justice was served without incident. Members of the militia came from Augusta County and other units throughout the Shenandoah Valley. Prominent among the units providing security was the Corps of Cadets from the Virginia Military Institute (VMI) in Lexington, Virginia, under the command of Major Thomas J. Jackson. This was the first time any members of the Augusta Militia saw their future commander. They were not impressed. His appearance and command presence were unremarkable. The Cadets even called him "Tom Fool" Jackson behind his back.

Now events began to spiral out of control, and the country seemed headed to a civil war with the election of Abraham Lincoln to the presidency in 1860. The Shenandoah Valley was not deeply involved in the slavery debate; there was strong Union sentiment throughout the region, and feelings were clearly mixed when several southern states began to secede to form the Confederacy early in 1861. Virginians in general wanted to avert a war, and this was reflected in the first vote of the Virginia Convention on April 4 against secession. However, three days after the fall of Fort Sumter, when President Lincoln called for volunteers from Virginia to squash the rebellion, the mood changed. A secret session of the Virginia convention was convened on April 17, and even then the votes of the Valley delegates were mixed with the delegates representing counties beyond the Appalachians, the original Augusta County, strongly against Virginia's secession and initially voting against it. Late that night, however, the final vote, eighty-eight to fifty-five, confirmed secession. Virginia's fate was sealed, and soon her most western counties would withdraw to form the new state of West Virginia, choosing to remain in the Union.

Virginia Governor Letcher immediately called upon the militia units in the Valley to move to Harpers Ferry to secure the valuable Federal Arsenal and machine shops there. Captain William S. H. Baylor and the West Augusta Guards joined militia units converging on Harpers Ferry as early as the evening of April 18. The Valley militia found the arsenal ablaze and the Union troops withdrawing across the Potomac River. They were able to seize a few small arms, but most importantly, they saved the machinery to produce such weapons. On April 22, Colonel Robert E. Lee, who had declined the opportunity to command the entire United States Army, arrived in Richmond to assume command of all of Virginia's military forces now a part of the Confederate Army. One of his first moves was to give Major Thomas J. Jackson the stars of a Colonel and place him in command of all of the forces at Harpers Ferry. The foundation of the Lee-Jackson command relationship was laid.

Illustration 6-3: West Augusta Militia officers (L-R): Lieutenant James Bumgardner, Jr., Lieutenant Henry King Cochran, Captain W.S.H. Baylor (center back), Lieutenant Thomas J. Burke, and Lieutenant J.H. Waters

Battle streamer earned: Maryland 1814

-Seven-

The Foundation
of the Stone Wall

ivil war was now inevitable, and the militia from the Shenandoah Valley continued to pour into Harpers Ferry. Lincoln's call to arms was considered an intrusion of Virginia's right to exist as an independent state, and daily, as rumors of a Union invasion spread, the Valley residents became more and more aroused. As militiaman George Baylor put it, "I felt it my duty to lay down the plow and pruning-hood and take up the sword and the battle-ax." Spirits were high and as one soldier wrote to the *Staunton Vindicator*, "our people are united as one man, and are determined to maintain their rights at every sacrifice." Volunteers and recruits rolled into Harpers Ferry to join the Valley Army to defend Virginia from any invading northern army.

Colonel Thomas Jackson had initially gone to Richmond with the VMI Cadets to train recruits, but on April 27 moved to Harpers Ferry to take command of the more than 4,500 volunteers assembling there to answer Governor Letcher's call to defend the gateway to the Shenandoah Valley. What Jackson found, according to Dr. James I. Robertson, Jr., was "undisciplined Virginians who were armed with everything from hunting knives to shotguns and who were attired in motley clothing ranging from gaudy militia uniforms to homespun shirts and coonskin caps." They were in dire need of leadership and discipline, and Jackson was just the commander to provide both.

As was usually the case when the militia was called to active duty, its officers, who had mostly been elected, were sent packing and replaced with younger, military schooled commanders. The age of the group assembled at Harpers Ferry ranged from fifteen to sixty. What they may have lacked in experience they made up for with a "can do" attitude that still permeates the organization of today. Jackson established reveille at five a.m. each morning, and the order of the day was drilling and marching, drilling and marching. Though resentful at first, the men became accustomed to the intense training and would soon see its value when confronting an equally determined enemy.

The organization at Harpers Ferry became known as "The Army of the Shenandoah." The Valley had initially provided four infantry regiments plus one artillery battery and they were organized as the First Brigade of Virginia Volunteers. As the Militia Reform Act of 1792 had outlined, each regiment was to have ten companies and in this newly organized brigade, each company was identified by the location they were drawn from. The result was some interesting names from which many of the Valley's National Guard units can still be identified. The following units comprised the First Brigade of Virginia Volunteers organized in Harpers Ferry:

The **Fifth Virginia Regiment** was formed from the primary descendents of the Augusta Militia and the 93rd Brigade:

Company A	Marion Rifles	Winchester
Company B	Rockbridge Rifles	Rockbridge Co.
Company C	Mountain Guards	Spring Hill
Company D	Southern Guard	Middlebrook
Company E	Greenville Greys	Greenville
Company F	West View Infantry	West View

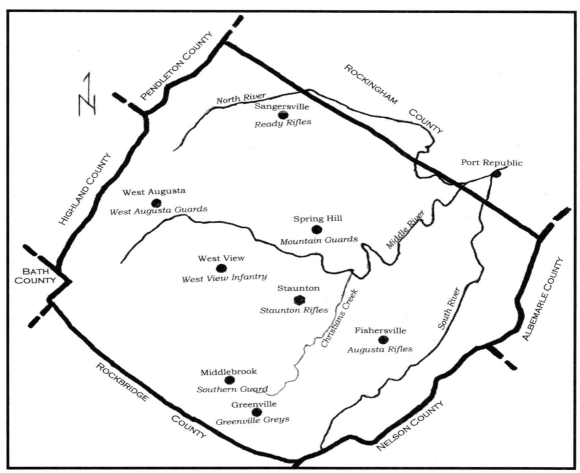

Illustration 7-1: Augusta County's 5th Regiment Communities - 1861

Company G	Staunton Rifles	Staunton
Company H	Augusta Rifles	Fishersville
Company I	Ready Rifles	Sangerville
Company K	Continental Morgan Guards	Frederick Co.
Company L	West Augusta Guards	West Augusta

The **Second Virginia Regiment** came from units drawn from many northern and western Virginia communities including men from areas that would split with Virginia and form the new state, West Virginia:

Company A	Jefferson Guards	Charles Town
Company B	Hamtranck Guards	Shepherdstown
Company C	Nelson Guards	Millwood
Company D	Berkeley Border Guards	Berkeley
Company E	Hedgesville Blues	Martinsburg
Company F	Winchester Riflemen	Winchester
Company G	Botts Greys	Charles Town
Company H	Letcher Riflemen	Duffields area
Company I	Clarke Riflemen	Berryville
Company K	Floyd Guard	Harpers Ferry

The **Fourth Virginia Regiment** was formed from communities that were generally south of Staunton and part of the former 32nd Brigade:

Company A	Wythe Grays	Wytheville
Company B	Fort Lewis Volunteers	Big Spring area
Company C	Pulaski Guards	Pulaski Co.
Company D	Smyth Blues	Marion
Company E	Montgomery Highlanders	Blacksburg
Company F	Grayson Dare Devils	Elk Creek
Company G	Montgomery Fencibles	Montgomery Co.
Company H	Rockbridge Grays	Buffalo Forge
Company I	Liberty Hall Volunteers	Lexington
Company K	Montgomery Mountain Boys	Montgomery Co.

The **Twenty-Seventh Regiment** was comprised of communities south and west of Augusta County, several of which would also become a part of West Virginia:

| Company A | Allegheny Light Infantry | Covington |
| Company B | Virginia Riflemen | Allegheny Co. |

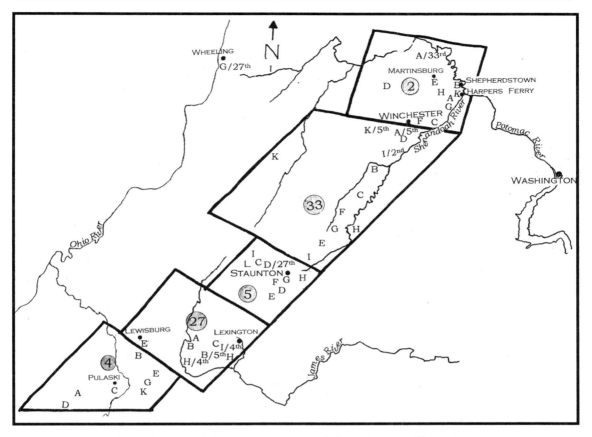

7-2: Regimental communities of the Stonewall Brigade

Company C	Allegheny Rifles	Clifton Forge
Company D	Monroe Guards	Staunton
Company E	Greenbrier Rifles	Lewisburg
Company G	Shriver Grays	Wheeling
Company H	Rockbridge Rifles	Lexington

The **Rockbridge Artillery** from Lexington and Rockbridge County primarily served as the brigade's artillery battery. The unit was commanded by the Episcopal rector in Lexington, Reverend Doctor, now Captain, William Nelson Pendleton. The four light guns, consisting of one twelve-pound howitzer and three six-pounders, were named Matthew, Mark, Luke, and John, and would become known for belching "Hell fire" upon the enemy. Pendleton was a West Point graduate and would later become General Robert E. Lee's Chief of Artillery. In the early part of the war, however, he would work effectively for Jackson and the Army of the Shenandoah. Today the guns reside on the parade field at VMI.

On May 10, Lieutenant Colonel J.E.B. Stuart arrived in Harpers Ferry and, due to his previous active duty experience in the cavalry, was tasked to organize the mounted units. This did not sit well with Captain Turner Ashby, who had arrived on April 16 with a company he had organized called the Mountain Rangers and seized the town and its arsenal. He had already gathered several companies of mounted soldiers, knew the men and the Valley, and thought himself best to be in charge. Jackson wisely tasked Ashby with scouting responsibilities and requested his immediate promotion, while giving Stuart command of the organized cavalry units. This defused the conflict, and both officers contributed significantly to the early success of the brigade.

Thus was formed the First Brigade, Virginia Volunteers: thirty-eight companies, one artillery battery, and cavalry, soldiers eager and ready to defend Virginia from the northern invaders. Many of the brigade members were only second or third generation Americans, but they loved their independence and were more than ready to defend their beloved Virginia. They were a cross section of the Valley residents, Germans, Scotch-Irish with a spattering of English.

The main occupation of the soldiers in the brigade was farming, with a mix of professional men, doctors, lawyers, teachers, and one minister. Almost a hundred and fifty were students, primarily from Washington College, now Washington and Lee University, and the University of Virginia. These young men left school for what they felt was a greater calling. Many would not live to return to their books. Jackson wrote to his wife to say, "I am very thankful to our Heavenly Father for having given me such a fine brigade." In describing the soldiers of the First Brigade, it was stated that "a finer body of men were never mustered. Among them were to be found men of culture, men of gentle training, men of intellect, men of social position, men of character at home, men endeared to domestic circles of refinement and elegance, men of wealth . . ."

General Joseph E. Johnston arrived at Harpers Ferry on May 23 to organize and assume command of an Army of the Shenandoah. In addition to the First Brigade already assembled there, this new army would have three additional brigade size units. The Second Brigade was the command of South Carolinian Bernard E. Bee and comprised of four regiments from Alabama, Mississippi, and Tennessee. The Third Brigade, primarily of soldiers from Maryland, Virginia, and Tennessee, was led by Marylander, Kirby Smith. The Fourth Brigade was comprised of troops from Georgia and Kentucky and was led by Georgia planter Francis S. Bartow. Brigade command brought with it a promotion to the rank of Brigadier General.

In mid June, General Johnston determined Winchester to be of more strategic significance than Harpers Ferry. (See Illustration 7-4) A superior Union force under General Robert Patterson was approaching the Valley from the north, and

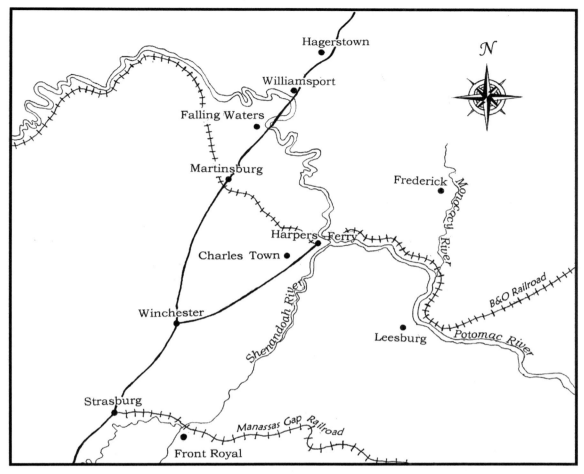

Illustration 7-3: Jackson's Brigade in the Lower Valley

Harpers Ferry was simply indefensible. The town was surrounded by high ground and located at the confluence of the Shenandoah River coming from the south and the Potomac River flowing in from the west. Jackson was ordered north to provide security for the Army as it withdrew to Winchester. Charges were set to destroy the bridge over the Potomac River, and on June 14 at five a.m. it was blown up for the first of the nine times that it would be destroyed during the war. Armory buildings, the machine shop, train depot, and telegraph office were burned and the bridge over the Shenandoah River was also destroyed.

Arriving in Martinsburg on June 19, Jackson was under orders to destroy the B&O railroad shops and equipment there. He was displeased with the mission, hoping to at least salvage some of the locomotives for the Confederacy. In the end, he did manage to dismantle and send thirteen engines on the thirty-eight mile trek to Strasburg and the Manassas Gap Railroad. The brigade then assumed a blocking position on the Valley Pike north of Martinsburg, with now Colonel J.E.B. Stuart and the cavalry screening the Potomac River to their front. Here they would camp for the next two weeks, drilling and awaiting their first action.

On July 2, Stuart's cavalry discovered a Union force crossing the Potomac River at Williamsport. The 5th Regiment was moved forward, followed by the 2nd, but after a brief encounter at Falling Waters, the Union force withdrew, choosing not to press the encounter. Jackson was under strict orders not to become decisively engaged and slowly withdrew south to Winchester. The First Brigade had seen its first action of the Civil War and was left wanting for more. Jackson and the Brigade had shown well in this first engagement, and a positive report of the action went from General Johnston to Richmond. On July 3, the brigade commander received word from General Lee: "My dear general, I have the pleasure of sending you a commission of brigadier-general in the Provisional Army, and to feel that you merit it. May your advancement increase your usefulness to the State." The orders did not reach Jackson until July 8, but were retroactive to June 17.

A significant event occurred on July 15 when the 33rd Virginia Regiment was ordered to become part of Jackson's First Brigade. It was a small regiment consisting of roughly 450 soldiers distributed between eight companies. The addition of this regiment would bring the brigade strength to 2,600.

The **Thirty-Third Regiment** was formed late from units in the lower part of the Shenandoah Valley north of Staunton:

Company A	Potomac Guards	Hampshire County
Company B	Toms Brook Guards	Toms Brook
Company C	Shenandoah Riflemen	Woodstock
Company D	Mountain Rangers	Winchester
Company E	Emerald Guards	New Market
Company F	The Independent Greys	Shenandoah County
Company G	Mount Jackson Rifles	Mount Jackson
Company H	Page Greys	Page County
Company I	Rockingham Confederates	Rockingham County
Company K	Moorefield Grays	Hardy County

The small engagement at Falling Waters, as the encounter on July 2 would become known, had a large impact on Union planners. It was assumed that the Army of the Shenandoah consisted of a large force determined to defend the Shenandoah Valley. It was mid-summer, and the crops and livestock of the region were critical to the Confederacy, so the Union determined it best to hold its positions north of the Potomac River and begin an assault into the south from Washington. Accordingly, General Irvin McDowell, commanding the army there, was ordered to move south.

McDowell was to advance on Richmond, now the capital of the Confederacy, with his force of 33,000, by way of Manassas Junction where he was ordered to

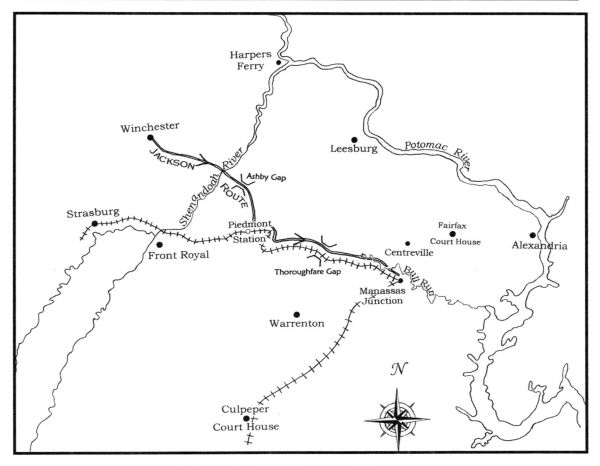

Illustration 7-4: Route to Manassas

destroy the railroad junction located there. The southern commander in the area, General P.G.T. Beauregard, was known to have a force of only 22,000. The Union plan fell apart quickly, however, as the Union Commander north of Johnston's force around Winchester, General Robert Patterson, chose to withdraw his army to Charles Town. Leaving the militia to guard the Valley, the Army of the Shenandoah seized the opportunity to slip over the mountain to the aid of General Beauregard. It was a dangerous maneuver, leaving the Shenandoah Valley basically undefended, but it was typical of the risk taking strategy southern commanders utilized throughout the Civil War.

The orders came on July 18, and the First Brigade took the lead moving east. They crossed the Shenandoah River and climbed the Blue Ridge, passing through Ashby's Gap and descending into the Piedmont region of Virginia. When they collapsed around 2 a.m. and began to rest from their exhausting up and downhill trek of over twenty miles, Jackson was heard to say, "Let the poor fellows sleep, I'll guard the camp myself." The aura of Jackson's "foot cavalry" and their hard driving commander had begun. In the morning the troops marched further east where they were picked up by the Manassas Gap Railroad, at Piedmont Station, and carried to Manassas Junction. It took almost eight hours for the trains to move the thirty-four miles to Manassas, a small community on the creek known as Bull Run. Here the units formed up and moved forward about three miles to a position in the center of the Confederate line.The next morning, the weary troops of the First Brigade fixed breakfast and began looking around at their surroundings. It quickly became another hot mid-summer day. General Johnston arrived around noon with the brigades of Bee and Bartow. When Smith's regiment arrived later, the Confederate force would be up to 32,000, almost identical to the Union strength. A skirmish had already occurred several days earlier, and members of the First Brigade had their first look at freshly dug graves and the damage of battle. Their date with destiny was approaching.

The troops were awakened the morning of July 21, 1861, by the sound of cannons. Excitement grew as the brigade assembled and prepared to support General James Longstreet's Brigade to the right, but suddenly their orders were changed, and at 9:30 a.m. they moved at double-quick time to the rear and around to the Confederate left. Reaching the area of the stone bridge over the Bull Run creek around 11 a.m., Jackson carefully placed the regiment on the reverse slope of the now famous Henry House Hill. The lines were formed inside a row of pine trees with the 5th Virginia Regiment on the right, then the 4th Virginia, 27th Virginia, 2nd Virginia, with the 33rd Virginia on the extreme left. Forward of the infantry were nine guns in line, attempting to counter the fire of twenty-four Union guns.

Jackson's brigade remained in position while the artillery exchanged fire. Many of the Union rounds hit in the trees above the soldiers and a number were killed or wounded by falling shot and timber. Lieutenant Benjamin Franklin Shuey of the Middlebrook's C Company of the 5th Regiment was struck by falling tree limbs from the bombardment and would die in a field hospital within a week. The soldiers were restless, thirsty, and suffering from the heat of the summer afternoon as the artillery duel continued. Crouching along the wood line, they could not see the enemy, but clearly knew from the sounds of the battle that they were approaching.

General Jackson was dressed in his old blue VMI professor's uniform with Colonel shoulder boards; some insist that he did wear the stars of a Brigadier General, as he calmly sat mounted, watching the fight develop. A round broke the middle finger of his left hand, but he refused aid and used a handkerchief to stop the bleeding. He did not move from his position on the top of the hill, as a strong Union force assaulted the Confederates under General Bernard Bee of South Carolina. As Bee's lines began to crumble, he rode to Jackson and announced, "They are beating us back," to which Jackson replied, "Then, sir, we will give them the bayonet!" Jackson had always favored the shock effect of a bayonet attack, and it was not unusual for him to call for this tactic to blunt the Union advance.

Illustration 7-5: Jackson – "...standing like a stone wall!"

Observing the demeanor of Jackson and his brigade, General Bee rode about his retreating men shouting, "Look! There is Jackson standing like a stone wall! Rally behind the Virginians!" As the Confederate position began to stiffen, two Union batteries were called forward to the Henry House Hill. As they were setting up, Stuart and his cavalry attacked the Union left, and the excitement became more than Colonel Arthur Cummings and his 33rd Virginia Regiment could take. Amidst the confusion on the Confederate left, the 33rd jumped up from their position and attacked the Union guns. Their initial success has been attributed by some to their still wearing, for the most part, blue uniforms left from their service prior to the outbreak of the Civil War. The Regiment now found itself facing a superior force, and within minutes about a third of their strength was lost and the survivors retreated to their original position on the Brigade's left. Their ill-timed attack was probably a result of their lack of disciplined training. They had just joined the First Brigade less than a week before the action and did not have the benefits of Old Jack's emphasis on drill and discipline.

One of the regiments attacking the Henry House Hill in the afternoon was the 2nd Wisconsin Brigade, later to become known as the Black Hat or Iron Brigade. Wearing grey uniforms as many of the Union regiments did on this day, they were fired upon, not only by the First Brigade, but also by Union Regiments to their rear. Their attack failed, like those of other Union regiments, and they were forced to withdraw under

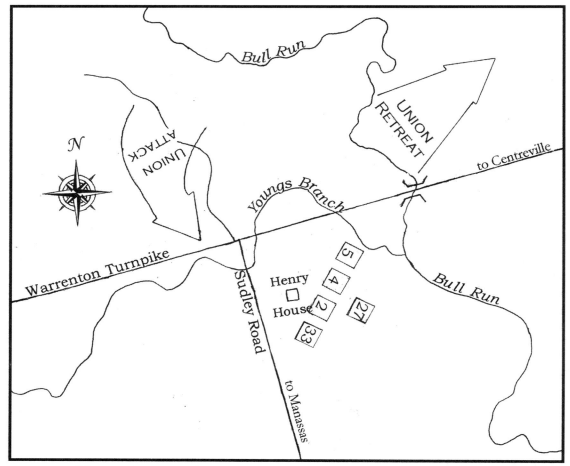

Illustration 7-6: The First Brigade at First Manassas, July 21, 1861

withering Confederate fire, but the 2nd Wisconsin and the First Brigade were destined to meet again. Through it all, General Jackson remained calm, and when the moment was right, at 3:30, he ordered the First Brigade to counterattack. The rest is history as the Union assault lost its momentum and dissolved under the onslaught of some two thousand fresh troops. The First Brigade, having earned its future name as "The Stonewall Brigade," now surged forward to the counterattack. The "rebel yell" was born as Jackson directed his men to *"yell like furies."* The Valley soldiers seized the Henry House Hill and raced down the slope in pursuit of the stunned Union attackers. The retreat suddenly became a rout, chaos turned to panic, and the Washington races were on with the entire Union Army high-tailing it back to Centreville.

Jackson, wanting to seize this opportunity to continue the attack, begged for the opportunity to pursue the Union forces and take the capital in Washington. When Jefferson Davis, the President of the Confederacy and an experienced military commander in his own right, arrived on the scene, the decision, however, was made not to pursue the enemy. Rain began to dampen the spirits of the First Brigade as they withdraw to their camp at Manassas. It was a glorious, but costly day with 111 brigade members killed and 373 wounded. The heaviest losses were, of course, in the 33rd Regiment. The joyful news that would sweep the Shenandoah Valley in the days ahead would be tempered with sorrow for those lost as fame was earned for their regiment.

The next few weeks found the brigade encamped just south of the battlefield and back in the routine of marching and drilling. The soldiers called the site "Camp Maggot" for obvious reasons, but even that name did not express entirely their distaste for the location. On August 2, Jackson moved the brigade further north to much better ground just east of Centreville. The site was named Camp Harman, since the soldiers approved of its selection by their Quartermaster, Major John Harman. They would remain there for six weeks, marching and drilling under the watchful eye of their commander. On several occasions, they hurriedly mustered in response to what would be false alarms of the Union Army advancing south.

On September 17, the brigade moved further northeast and set up camp on the farm of the Burke family, only three miles from Fairfax Courthouse. In his *Four Years in the Stonewall Brigade*, John O. Casler wrote:

> While in this camp near Centreville we had a grand review before Governor John Letcher, then Governor of Virginia, who presented each Virginia regiment with a beautiful state flag, and made a short speech, in which he told us we had a long and bloody war before us.

These were prophetic words for the Valley soldiers. On October 7, Jackson was promoted to Major General in the newly organized Provisional Forces of Virginia. He was given command of a Division, but would be leaving his beloved Stonewall Brigade. Virginia was now divided into the Aquia, Potomac, and Valley Military Districts. Jackson was given command of the Valley District. On November 4, Jackson spoke to his old brigade, as recalled by his aide, Captain Kyd Douglas in his book, *I Rode with Stonewall*:

> Officers and men of the First Brigade, I am not here to make a speech, but simply to say farewell. I first met you at Harpers Ferry at the commencement of the war, and I cannot take leave of you without giving my admiration of your conduct from that day to this, whether on the march, in the bivouac, the tented field, or on the bloody plains of Manassas, where you gained the well-deserved reputation of having decided the fate of the battle.

Throughout the broad extent of the country through which you have marched, by your respect of the rights and property of citizens, you have shown that you were soldiers not only to defend, but able and willing both to defend and protect. You have already gained a brilliant and deservedly high reputation, throughout the army and the whole Confederacy, and I trust in the future by your own deeds on the field, and by the assistance of the same kind of Providence who heretofore favored our cause, you will win more victories and add additional luster to the reputation you now enjoy. You have already gained a proud position in the history of this, our second War of Independence. I shall look with great anxiety to your future movements, and I trust whenever I shall hear of the First Brigade on the field of battle, it will be of still nobler deeds achieved and higher reputation won.

In the 120 years prior to this speech and over 146 years since, clearly the men of the original Augusta Militia, through today's National Guard units from the Shenandoah Valley and beyond the Blue Ridge Mountains, have lived up to General Jackson's charge on this fall day in 1861. To his wife Anna, Jackson wrote "If my brigade can always play an important & useful apart as in the last battle, I shall always be very grateful, I trust." Prophetic words which were fulfilled by this brigade, time and time again through America's wars, up to and including, today. Few military units have ever come close to serving a more critical role in the history of the United States than the men from the Shenandoah Valley. Again and again, this unit has found itself at the defining moment, at the right time, and in exactly the critical place, to influence the history of this great country.

Arriving in Winchester, Major General Jackson did his commander's assessment and quickly requested the services of his old brigade on November 5. Request granted, the First Brigade arrived in high spirits, looking forward to the comforts of Winchester as they waited out the winter. They were disgusted to learn, instead, that Jackson had assigned them a camp to the south near Kernstown, and then to Camp Stephenson some four miles north of Winchester. Jackson was delighted with his new command and the opportunity to again serve with his old brigade back in the Valley. In a letter some time later he wrote: "It is but natural that I should feel a deep and abiding interest in the people of the Valley, where are the homes of so many of my brave soldiers."

Battle streamers earned: Virginia 1861, 1st Manassas

Eight

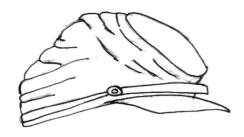

The Valley Campaign

In addition to the First Brigade, General Jackson was given the Army of the North-west, under General William W. Loring, for his Valley Army. It consisted of the brigades of Colonel William B. Taliaferro, Colonel William Gilham, and Brigadier General R.S. Anderson. His cavalry was to be commanded by now Colonel Turner Ashby, and the little army had twenty-six guns. It would take until Christmas day for all of the new units to arrive in Winchester. The last units of General Loring's army reported to Jackson's Headquarters on Christmas Eve.

Jackson had been unable to recommend someone to succeed himself in command of the First Brigade and finally on December 2, he wrote to Richmond requesting that the Military Department select a new commander for his old brigade. Two days later the response arrived in the person of Brigadier General Richard B. Garnett. Later Jackson would surely wish he had been more influential in the selection of his replacement. Assuming command of Jackson's First Brigade, already being talked about as the "Stonewall Brigade," would have been a daunting task for any officer. The shoes to be filled were probably too big for anyone; the expectation too great. There was also an immediate dislike of an "outsider" taking command of the Brigade. In time however, the veterans of the Brigade began to appreciate and respect their new commander. They recognized him as a leader who cared for his soldiers. Jackson, the harsh disciplinarian, was almost immediately at odds with Garnett. The new commander was somewhat deliberate and clearly spoke up in defense of the common soldier, while to Jackson, the mission always came first, and the men could endure any hardship if they believed in their cause.

In one of his first decisions for the defense of the region, Jackson focused on disrupting the Union supply lines along the Potomac River to the north. He was determined to destroy Dam No.5, located on that river, providing the water for the C&O Canal. Additionally, he wanted to again cut the B&O rail lines. When the first attempt failed, Jackson personally took command of the second effort, using 380 members of the 5th Regiment of the First Brigade and a group of Scotch-Irish soldiers from the 27th Regiment experienced in construction. John O. Casler of the Stonewall Brigade best describes the scene:

On the 17th day of December we struck tents and marched about fifteen miles towards Martinsburg, and camped within three miles of that place. The next morning we were on the march, and went through Martinsburg down to Dam No. 5, on the Potomac River—another fifteen miles. We had about twenty flatboats with us, in covered wagons. They were not so much concealed but they could be easily seen by any spies there might be about, and there were plenty of them. This was a ruse to make the Federals think we were going to cross the Potomac, while our object was to destroy the dam, so the Chesapeake and Ohio canal could not be used by the enemy.

The deception worked and after some brief resistance, the dam was destroyed. The damage was limited, however, and repairs completed by Union engineers in a matter of days.

This ended the activities of the First Brigade in their first year of war, 1861. Their combat experience to this point was limited, but their ranks had been hit hard from the sickness and disease that was present in every camp. The living conditions of the soldiers were never very good, and they often wanted for food

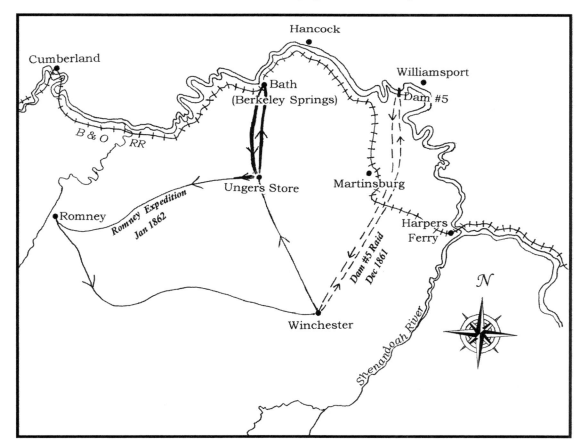

Illustration 8-1: Jackson Threatens Western Maryland

and uniforms, especially now with winter in the northern Valley approaching. "French furloughs," leaving camp without permission, infested the brigade as morale decreased. Jackson was not only a "Stonewall" on the battlefield, but also in camp. Drilling the soldiers hard and denying requests for leave, even when the wife of a regimental commander, Colonel Kenton Harper of the 5th Regiment, lay dying a month after First Manassas. The mission always came first. The proximity to Winchester, however, was too much for many soldiers to take and frequently they would slip, without permission, from their camp to enjoy the comforts and companionship found in the nearby town.

With the New Year came a new campaign. Jackson remained determined to break the Union lines of communication (supply lines) crossing just north of his position. On the first of January, 1862, he formed his army and began moving toward the small town of Bath, now Berkley Springs, to the northwest of Winchester. (See Illustration 8-1) The town was a part of the new state of West Virginia. Jackson's superior force would take the town easily, capturing supplies and weapons left by the Union soldiers as they hurried north across the Potomac River. Breaking camp at five a.m. in the morning, the First Brigade moved out on what began as a beautiful winter day. That changed quickly, however, and snow began to fall and the temperature plummeted. The soldiers were traveling light, having packed their tents in the supply trains which followed in the rear of the column. Their movement was slowed terribly by what had all the makings of a blizzard. Troops were suffering greatly at the outset of this march that would become known as the Romney Expedition. In two days, they had only moved the distance of fifteen miles to bivouac on the Washington Unger farm, or Unger's Store area.

Awaking the next morning, Jackson's army rose from their snow covered blankets to find that the supply wagons and food had finally caught up to them. General Garnett gave orders for the First Brigade to "fall out" and prepare for a hot breakfast. Cooking fires were just beginning to roar when General Jackson appeared, demanding an explanation. Garnett told his superior that the men needed the hot rations and "it is impossible for the men to march farther without them." Jackson snapped back, "I have never found anything impossible for this brigade!" Thus began the tumultuous relationship between the former and current First Brigade commanders. Word of the confrontation spread quickly throughout the unit, immediately improving the average soldier's opinion of Garnett. Here was a general who appeared willing to look out for their personal needs.

After capturing Bath, Jackson moved his army the short distance north to the Potomac River, intending to cross and capture Hancock, Maryland. The Union forces there were being reinforced, however, so Jackson left a force to monitor the area and withdrew south back to Unger's Store. The worsening weather kept the army there under miserable conditions until the storm broke on January 13. As the ice and snow began to thaw, the First Brigade took the lead, moving west to Jackson's ultimate objective, Romney. On the fourteenth, he marched into the town with his old brigade, capturing large amounts of equipment and supplies. In the worst way, General Jackson wanted to continue the push west and capture Cumberland, Maryland, but his force was simply too small and the weather much too bad to proceed. On January 23, he chose instead to leave Loring's Brigade to hold Romney and moved the First Brigade back to Winchester. Here his experienced brigade could be positioned as a "quick reaction force" should the Union Army cross the Potomac at any point in his area of responsibility and attempt to attack south, up the Shenandoah Valley.

Now began a long dispute between Jackson and the Confederate War Department that ultimately led to his resignation, which, fortunately, was not accepted. Loring bypassed Jackson and appealed to the Confederate government to be withdrawn from Romney, citing the terrible winter conditions there and the favoritism his division commander had shown to his old brigade. On January 31, J.P. Benjamin, Confederate Secretary of War, sent orders to Jackson to withdraw Loring's forces to Winchester. Jackson was livid and tendered his resignation. After much effort by his Virginia friends, and reassurance that this type of intervention by the Confederate government would not occur again, Jackson withdrew his resignation. In the old Army adage of "mess up and move up," Loring was promoted to Major General and transferred to southwest Virginia. His brigade was disbanded and integrated into other units. Jackson had won a tactical political victory, but strategically failed to fulfill his vision of cutting the Union supply lines to the west and preventing them from building up forces at multiple sites across the Potomac River. Any gains were short lived as the spring of 1862 approached.

Despite the difficult winter, tough campaigns, and lack of supplies, the morale of the First Brigade was improving as spring came to the Shenandoah Valley. On March 7, when General Johnston and the main Confederate Army in Virginia began moving south from Manassas, Jackson's position at Winchester became untenable. His division was reduced to less than 3,600 fit for duty, but it was an "all Virginia" force centered on his old brigade, and one to be reckoned with as history would soon show. With his right now exposed, Jackson had no choice but to consider withdrawing. He remained optimistic and devised a plan to conduct a feint, moving briefly south from Winchester, then turning his army north and conducting a night attack against the encamped Union forces moving into the Valley. He called a "Council of War" to consider his plan and was shocked when his subordinates voted the plan down, not once, but twice. Their input was negative and depressing. The withdrawal would begin in earnest, but a disgusted Jackson told his good friend and physician, Dr. Hunter Holmes McGuire, "That is the last Council of War I will ever hold!" Old Jack would keep his word.

Throughout the day of March 11, Jackson's army withdrew south. It was a sad departure for both the soldiers of the First Brigade and the citizens who had grown to love them. Ten days later, assuming Jackson's force to be departing in search of better positions further south and too weak for a fight, Union General Nathaniel Banks, whose army had been following Jackson's withdrawal, began moving his forward elements under General James Shields back to Winchester, ending the pursuit. When Turner Ashby reported the movement to Jackson's Headquarters, Old Jack sprang into action. Ashby's intelligence gathering ability was excellent and his information was rarely wrong, but in this case, he had unknowingly misled his commander; a major Union force still lay south of Winchester.

As the sun rose on March 22, Jackson's Army had reversed its course and was moving north. Around 2:00 p.m. the next day, Sunday, March 23, Jackson's little army was back just south of Winchester in the community known as Kernstown. Jackson's "foot cavalry" had covered some thirty-eight miles since leaving Mount Jackson and were within four miles of Winchester. Morale was high at the thought of the Yankees retreating and Jackson's Valley District Army returning to Winchester. Their optimism changed quickly, however, as Shield's force was spotted to the north, and Jackson made disposition for battle. His plan was to turn the Union right, believing the total force before him to be just several regiments. In reality, Shields had a force of about 10,000, including a division that Jackson was completely unaware of. The unknowing Stonewall ordered Colonel Samuel Fulkerson's brigade, and his 23rd and 37th Virginia Regiments, forward. Their assault began around four p.m. followed by the First Brigade. Garnett led the 33rd Virginia into position, followed by the 2nd and 4th Virginia, with the 27th on the right, initially supporting an artillery position, with the 5th Virginia in reserve.

The best thing Jackson had going for him was surprise. Shields had given little thought to a Confederate attack, but quickly positioned his division and the supporting regiments to meet the oncoming enemy. In short order, three Union brigades were responding, and the advance of the Confederates, already running low on ammunition, was stopped at a stone wall. (See Illustration 8-2) The First Brigade was in a position in the middle of the Confederate line, with the 5th Virginia still in a reserve position to the rear. Around 6:30 p.m., Garnett, acting without Jackson's approval, ordered the First Brigade, which was out of ammunition, to withdraw. This left Fulkerson's position to the left exposed, and the entire Confederate line began to collapse. The 5th Virginia was just arriving, and Garnett ordered them to cover the retreat. Jackson was furious; he would have attacked with the bayonet and carried the day with the reinforcements coming up. Garnett had lost the Battle of Kernstown and with it any possibility for Jackson to remain in the lower Valley. As night set in, the Confederate forces retraced their steps south.

Jackson's Army had suffered some seven hundred casualties, eighty of whom

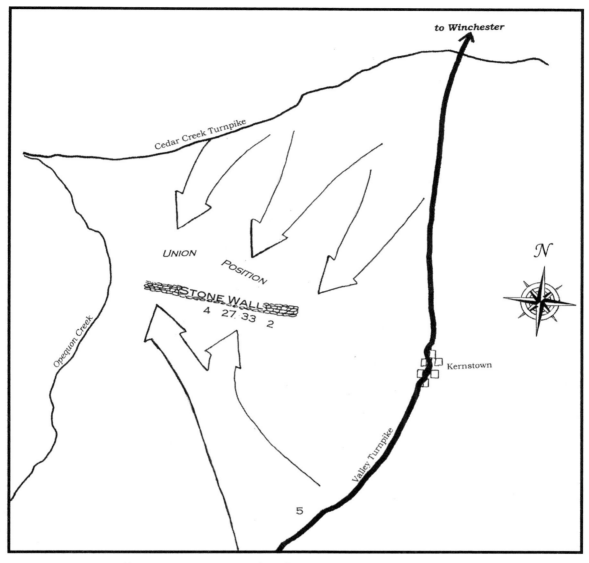

Illustration 8-2: Battle of Kernstown, March 23, 1862

were killed. The First Brigade had lost 343, or about half of the Confederate losses. The 2nd Virginia incurred more loses at Kernstown than they would at any subsequent battle until the fiasco of the "Bloody Angle" at Spotsylvania, almost two years later. Forty members of the First Brigade were killed in all, with 150 wounded and a like number captured primarily by Union cavalry during the retreat. The total Union losses were similar to those of the Confederates, but they had held their ground, and it was Jackson's Army that was forced to withdraw. It was a tactical Union victory, but strategically, Jackson had won the day. Initially, Shields reported that he had been attacked by 15,000 Confederates. The entire

Union plan for the capture of the Confederate capital in Richmond now came un-hinged. General McDowell, who was to attack from the north in support of McClellan, beginning his move up the Peninsula, was ordered to hold his army to protect Washington in the event Jackson continued to attack north. In addition, Lincoln personally reassigned Brigadier General Louis Blenker's 10,000 man division from McClellan's Penninsula Army to duty in western Virginia.

In his well researched book on the Battle of Kernstown, *We Are In For It!*, Gary L. Ecelbarger concludes:

> Despite his tactical lapse on the Kernstown battlefield, General Thomas
> J. Jackson profited from the misinterpretation of and overreaction to his
> audacious attack, and his subsequent Shenandoah Valley Campaign
> graces the list of all-time military endeavors and earns him respect as
> one of America's most perceptive and respected generals.

Jackson's bold strike on a superior Union force clearly had a dramatic impact on the Union plans in the spring of 1862, particularly the effort to capture the Confederate capital at Richmond.

Kernstown was a tough fight for both sides. Henry Kyd Douglas, soon to be aide to General Jackson, recalled: "In that fight I commanded as a lieutenant the color company of the Second Virginia Regiment, General Richard B. Garnett's brigade and saw seven color bearers fall." When their color-sergeant fell, a lieutenant from K Company, John B. Davis, grabbed the colors only to fall, passing them to Richard Henry Lee of G Company. Four additional soldiers attempted to carry the colors before succumbing to wounds. In the end, Regimental Commander Colonel James W. Allen grabbed the blood-stained standard. In his book, *2nd Virginia Infantry*, Dennis E. Frye writes that at the end of the battle, "Fourteen bullet holes had shredded the colors and the flagstaff had been shot in two." Lieutenant Colonel G.F.R Henderson in *Stonewall Jackson and the American Civil War* states that the Union pressed the 5th Regiment, covering the Brigade's withdrawal furiously. "In front of the 5th Virginia" he writes, "the colours of the 5th Ohio changed hands no less than six times, and one of them was pierced by no less than eight-and-forty holes." Firing stopped briefly when, late in the day, the color bearer of the 5th Virginia Regiment jumped atop a wall with its colors. A member of the 62nd Ohio had shouted, "Don't shoot that man; he is too brave to die."

The First Brigade had performed well in its second major battle. Unfortunately, it had not shown well in the eyes of Old Jack. He blamed its conduct on General Garnett, though, relieving him of command on April 1, placing him under arrest, and ordering him court martialed. Jackson placed the blame for Kernstown squarely on Garnett. The charges according to Douglas Southall Freeman in his *Lee's Lieutenants*, indicated:

Garnett was charged with neglect of duty under seven specifications— that he had not put his brigade into position properly, that he had separated himself from his command, that he had not been with his leading unit, that he had no troops with supporting distance of his front regiment, that regiments had become intermingled, that he had absented himself from his command, that he had given the order to fall back 'when he should have encouraged his command to hold its position,' and that he had sent an order to reserve forces to withdraw.

These were quite serious charges, and Jackson meant to pursue them. Members of the Brigade supported Garnett, however, feeling he had done the right thing and taken care of them. They saw little more that could have been done with their ammunition practically depleted and fresh Union forces moving against them.

Jackson, in an unrelated matter, reorganized the cavalry units in his army, leaving Turner Ashby, who had succeeded Colonel J.E.B. Stuart as Valley District Calvary Commander, with little or no responsibility. There were issues regarding drinking, general misconduct, and a lack of discipline within Ashby's cavalry units. They performed extremely well on the battlefield, but were unruly in camp. Ashby immediately responded to the reorganization by resigning, as Jackson had earlier in the year. This resulted in Jackson rescinding the order, and asking Ashby to stay. This decision would be an important one, for the Valley Campaign was just beginning, and Colonel Turner Ashby and his cavalry would have a critical role to play.

Old Jack now paused briefly to complete selection of his personal headquarters staff and to organize the remnants of his little army. On March 26, he resumed the march further south, reaching Rude's Hill, three miles south of Mount Jackson, on April 2. Here he camped until April 17, when the Union force pursuing him up the Valley closed in on his position. A new commander of the First Brigade was selected, Brigadier General Charles S. Winder. He would never be appreciated by the Valley soldiers, who felt Garnett had been wronged. They also disliked Winder since he was from Maryland, not a Virginian. He was a strong disciplinarian, though, a capable commander, and liked by Old Jack. In another move, Jackson obtained the division of Major General Richard S. Ewell, approximately 8,000 strong, to support his Valley Army. Ewell had been encamped at Brandy Station, just north of Culpeper, and was now ordered by Jackson to withdraw south for a future link-up with his Valley Army. Since Kernstown, new enlistees had joined Jackson's army and soon it swelled to some 6,000 troops, plus those of Ewell.

On April 16, The Confederate Congress passed the Conscription Act, requiring all white males between the ages of eighteen and thirty-five to join the military or be subject to the draft. General Robert E. Lee, responsible for Virginia's forces and needing soldiers to fill Virginia's one hundred regiments, had wanted the upper limit to be age forty-five, but the Virginia General Assembly supported the act approved by the Confederate Congress. Nevertheless, it immediately prompted volunteers from the Shenandoah Valley to pour into the resting First Brigade. The legislation also resulted in the reorganization of the regiments of the Brigade, and elections were held for officer positions. Colonel Allen remained in command of the 2nd Virginia, Charles Ronald assumed command of the 4th Virginia, Will Baylor replaced the retiring Colonel Harman in the 5th Virginia, Andrew Jackson Grigsby would lead the 27th Virginia, and John Francis Neff, only twenty-seven years of age, became the youngest regimental commander, replacing Colonel Cummings in the 33rd Virginia, who had resigned. As April became May, the Brigade grew in strength to over 3,600, the largest it would ever be during the war.

As part of the reorganization, a new unit was added to the First Brigade, the 5th Regiment Band. Former members of Staunton's Mountain Sax Horn Band, organized in 1855, had been with the Brigade since Harpers Ferry. They were well known for their music, and provided care to the wounded on the battlefield as they served in an additional duty as medical corpsmen. The band was also known as Turner's Silver Coronet Band, in honor of their organizer, Professor Augustus J. Turner, who taught music at the Wesleyan Female Collegiate Institute in Staunton prior to secession. Originally comprised of five volunteers in the 5th Regiment, the Band temporarily, but officially, become the 5th Regiment Band, and later the Stonewall Brigade Band. Old Jack loved their music and asked the Band to play for him at every opportunity. The Stonewall Brigade Band is still in existence today in Staunton and continues to play a significant role in the community. During the summer, it performs regularly in Gypsy Hill Park, just down the hill from Staunton's National Guard Armory, and the current home of the Headquarters of the 116th Infantry Brigade Combat Team.

It took the Union Army thirty days to cover the sixty-seven miles from Winchester and find Jackson. Not ready for an engagement, Jackson ordered his army to Conrad's Store, the site of present-day Elkton, and then further south before ascending the Blue Ridge Mountains and passing east through Brown's Gap, to depart the Valley. On April 22, Union General Banks surmised Jackson was headed for Richmond and sent word to Washington that "Jackson has abandoned the Valley of Virginia permanently, ..." The soldiers of the First Brigade were disheartened to leave their beloved Valley and confused when they reached the trains waiting for them at the Mechum's River Station. The locomotives, pulling the awaiting cars of the Virginia Central Rail Road, were on the wrong end of the train, they were pointing west. Soon the soldiers were elated to find themselves boarding these trains and heading west to Staunton, not east to Richmond. The residents of Staunton, the home of the Augusta Militia and the heart of the First Brigade, were joyful to see the trains arriving. They were expecting the Union Army under Banks or John C. Frémont to come and destroy their city, but instead found members of their brigade home to save it. It was Sunday morning, May 5, and church bells throughout the town were ringing. Secrecy would soon become the order of the day, as Old Jack wanted no one to know the whereabouts of his command.

On May 6, Jackson reviewed the newly arrived cadets from his old Virginia Military Institute, while his Army rested and re-supplied. The next day, the First Brigade, third in the order of march and followed by the VMI cadets that Jackson had selected from the Corps upon their arrival in Staunton, moved west along the Parkersburg road, now Virginia Route 254. Jackson had joined forces in Staunton with General Edward Johnson's Brigade that had been stationed there to defend Confederate supplies and rail lines. Johnson had the lead as Jackson's Valley Army moved to attack a much smaller Union force under General Robert H. Milroy approaching from West Virginia. Climbing the Bull Pasture Mountain roughly ten miles west of Staunton, they reached the town of McDowell and attacked Milroy's force on the afternoon of May 8. After a brief fight, Milroy was forced to withdraw in the face of Jackson's superior numbers. The next day the First Brigade was relegated to burying the dead and cleaning up the battlefield. Finally, it was called forward to pursue the retreating Union enemy headed north to Franklin. The Brigade's route took them west from McDowell, and using Strait Creek Road to bypass present-day Monterey, it turned north toward Franklin.

During the withdrawal, Union Brigadier General Robert Schenck ordered piles of hay to be set afire to slow the Confederate advance. The thick billowing smoke was an effective delaying tactic as the retreating army moved north along Strait Creek and the rich farmland between the steep ridges of the valley. After a pursuit of two days, the 4th Virginia Regiment in the lead found Union skirmishers just south of Franklin. General Milroy had already been reinforced by Schenck and would soon have support from Major General Frémont. After scouting the Union position, Jackson determined it to be too strong and risky to consider attack. His goal of blunting the Union movements from the west had been accomplished though, and now he wanted to focus his army on General Banks and his force of 17,000 remaining in the Valley. The Brigade withdrew the thirty-four miles back to McDowell, leaving cavalry to continue threatening the Union position and engineers felling trees to further delay any attempted Union pursuit.

On May 14, Jackson's Army left McDowell, heading back toward Staunton, but upon reaching Lebanon Springs, they turned northeast to Mount Solon, arriving on the eighteenth. Now for the first time, Jackson appeared dressed in a gray uniform bearing the Confederate rank of Major General. He ordered the forces of Ewell's Division to move immediately to a position near the Massanutten

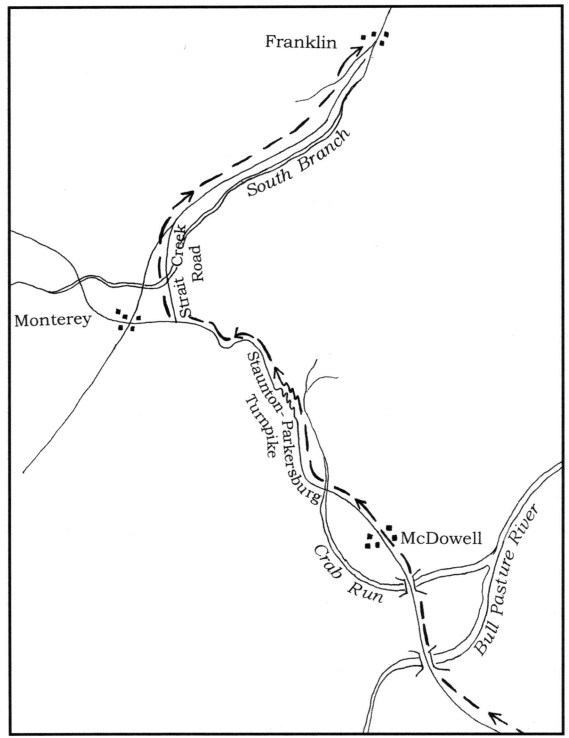

Illustration 8-3: McDowell and Franklin

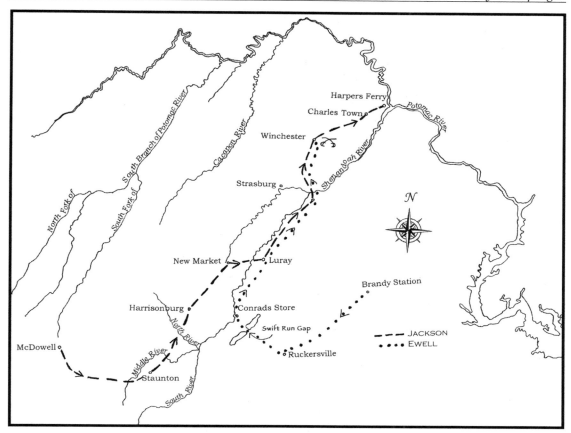

Illustration 8-4: McDowell to Winchester, Spring 1862

Gap, to the east of Mount Jackson, to link up with the rest of his army. General Banks and his force were camped along the Valley Pike around Strasburg with advanced troops as far south as Woodstock. Learning of Banks' position, Jackson, using the detailed mapping of one of his newest staff officers, Jed Hotchkiss, intended to move the united force north toward the town of Front Royal. He hoped to remain undetected by advancing along the eastern side of the Massanutten Mountain Range. Its movement would be protected by the high mountains to its left, and his army could fall upon the Union rear positioned near Front Royal without being detected. He would use Ashby's cavalry to demonstrate in front of Banks and keep him fixed, as the Valley Army swung east. The Brigade was put in motion in the early morning hours of May 21, initially moving north down the Valley Pike to New Market before turning east to descend into the Luray Valley.

May 22 dawned as a beautifully warm day. Ewell's fresh division took the lead down the Luray Valley, as Jackson's old division with the First Brigade fell in behind them. On the afternoon of the following day, the Louisiana Brigade of Brigadier General Richard Taylor was in the lead as Jackson's force struck the rear of the unsuspecting Union force garrisoned at Front Royal. The close fight here brought the Confederate First Maryland Regiment face to face with the Union First Maryland Regiment. It was a classic fight with neighbors fighting neighbors and occasionally even brothers facing off against brothers, but Jackson's superior forces were no match for the unsuspecting Union defenders around Front Royal. Wagon loads of supplies were captured along with two trains and some artillery. Jackson incurred only fifty casualties to achieve a stunning success. When the bad news reached Banks, he immediately ordered his entire Union force to withdraw back to Winchester. The race was on.

The First Brigade was counter-marched by General Winder and now placed in the lead and moved west to the Valley Pike. Ewell's Division was to race north to Winchester on the Front Royal-Winchester Road, while Jackson led his old brigade in pursuit of Banks. The 33rd Virginia was forward in the advance down the pike and tasked to clear Union ambushes set to delay the oncoming Confederates. It was a cloudless night as General Winder and the Brigade pushed north. After midnight Colonel Fulkerson approached Jackson, asking that the troops have the opportunity to rest. Jackson's reply was firm, "Colonel, I yield to no man in sympathy for the gallant men under my command; but am obliged to sweat them tonight, that I may save their blood tomorrow." Relenting, however, his old Brigade was given a short rest, but at four a.m. on the morning of May 25, they were back in motion.

The continuous forty-four days of marching and fighting, with only two days of rest, had taken its toll on the ranks of the First Brigade, and only around 1,500 men were able to fall in that morning to continue the push to Winchester. After a short march, Union skirmishers were spotted on the high ground southwest of Winchester. This was the terrain critical to the defense of the town, and the Union had to hold it to have any chance of continuing to retain Winchester and the huge stores of supplies there. Jackson ordered Winder to attack immediately. Winder sent the 5th Virginia Regiment forward as skirmishers, positioning the 2nd Virginia Regiment to the right, with the 27th Virginia to their left and the 33rd Virginia protecting Cutshaw's artillery battery, while the 4th Virginia was in reserve. (See Illustration 8-5) When the Union force put forth a galling fire which stopped the advance of his old Brigade, Jackson sent Taylor's Brigade to the left in support. As the Union defenders were about to be turned on their right, Ewell's Division emerged on the Union left, and the entire defense collapsed as the soldiers in blue began to withdraw quickly under the overwhelming attack from two sides. Their retreat quickly became a route, and soon Winchester once again belonged to Jackson.

Old Jack wanted more than Winchester; he wanted the destruction of Banks' Army. He personally led his old First Brigade in the pursuit north for about five miles, but the tired infantry could not keep up, and a halt was called near Stephenson's Depot. Darkness and exhaustion made further pursuit to the Potomac River impossible. To the victors went the spoils, and the weary soldiers of Old Jack's Army literally tasted their sweet victory as they plunged into the commissary wagons and quartermaster's stores left from the Union retreat. Barefoot men found shoes; ragged clothes were replaced with the new un-issued Union supplies. Jackson had captured some 9,300 small arms, two

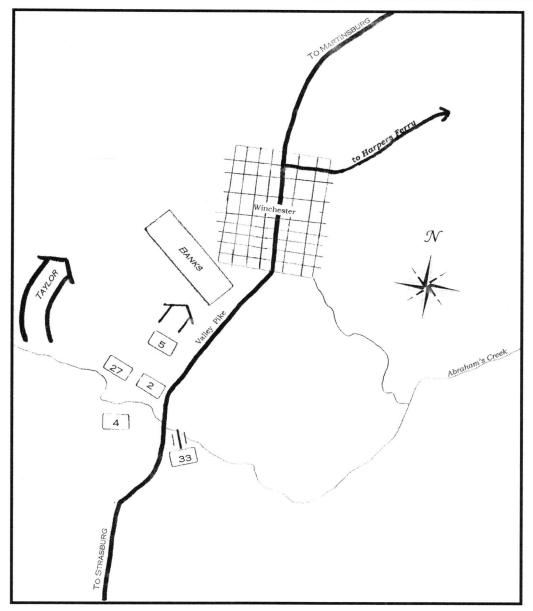

Illustration 8-5: Battle of Winchester, May 25, 1862

field guns, and over three thousand prisoners. Banks had lost over thirty percent of his army. It was another stunning victory for Jackson. Kernstown had been revenged. Winchester again lay in Confederate hands. Since the battle for Winchester was on a Sunday, Jackson declared Monday, May 26, as a day for rest and prayer.

Winchester was a great victory for the Confederacy and a tremendous strategic loss for the Union. General McDowell's Army, that had resumed moving on Richmond from Fredericksburg, was again halted and returned north. Two divisions and at least one regiment were ordered to the Shenandoah Valley. Jackson had stopped

McDowell's Army from linking with General McClellan, thus preventing their assault on Richmond from two sides. The Army of the Valley was now in a position to threaten Washington. Jackson allowed his force to rest one more day and then on May 28, he moved on Charles Town and Harpers Ferry. Alarm spread throughout the Union capital. Jackson had to be stopped! General Shields was dispatched west to Front Royal, while General Frémont was directed to move east to Strasburg. The two converging armies would trap Jackson and destroy his Army of the Valley once and for all.

Winder left the 2nd Virginia on duty in Winchester and took the other four regiments, the 5th Virginia in the lead, on a successful attack into Charles Town, capturing even more Union supplies. The Brigade then moved to Harpers Ferry, where they identified a strong force positioned on the commanding Bolivar Heights above the town. The next day, May 29, Jackson personally led the 2nd Virginia forward to link up with the rest of the Brigade, and ordered them to prepare to attack the defenders on Bolivar Heights. The following morning, the Regiment successfully scaled the high ground overlooking Harpers Ferry and was enjoying an excellent view of the activities in the town when a messenger arrived indicating that Jackson was being forced to abandon Winchester. The 2nd Virginia was the unit farthest north and would suffer terribly as they struggled through rainstorms and over muddy roads to catch up with the rest of the Brigade hurrying south, avoiding the Union trap. When they finally reached Jackson's main body in Strasburg, they collapsed from exhaustion and from not having any rations for almost two days. Dennis E. Frye, *2nd Virginia Infantry* indicates "This march rated as a major highlight in the history recorded by the Second Virginia Infantry. Through a drenching rainfall and over slippery mud-caked roads, the Second had trampled thirty-six miles in fourteen hours!"

The entire Brigade had suffered greatly in achieving their linkup with Jackson, but again validated their "foot cavalry" reputation. It was now June 1, and the Confederate retreat had avoided being cut off by the armies of Shields and Frémont converging on Strasburg. The Army of the Valley, however, vastly outnumbered, began another withdrawal up the Valley. The victories at Front Royal and Winchester were sweet and a tremendous boast to the Confederacy. The Union stores they had captured, especially much needed medical supplies, would prove invaluable. Jackson had moved the Union prisoners and some 275 wagon loads of supplies south, well ahead of the advancing enemy. The Brigade brought up the rear of the army and served as its protection from advancing Union cavalry. It took four days for them to shuffle up the Valley Pike, finally arriving in Harrisonburg on June 5.

The evening of June 7 brought sad news to General Jackson. His thirty-three year old cavalry commander, General Turner Ashby, had been killed leading a charge against Union forces moving south outside of Harrisonburg. Jackson's opinion of Ashby had been rising as the Valley Campaign progressed. Ashby's inaccurate intelligence had been very costly at Kernstown, but since that fight, he had done a masterful job gathering information on Union forces and delaying their advance. The loss was stinging to the entire Army of the Valley. Ashby was loved by his troopers and genuinely admired by all members of the First Brigade. He was aggressive, daring, and was determined to drive the Union from his beloved Shenandoah Valley.

On June 8, Jackson moved his entire army east toward Port Republic, destroying any bridges that could assist his pursuers. The First Brigade moved to the high ground north of the little village, while Ewell's force was positioned at Cross Keys a few miles to the northwest. From this position Jackson could again slip through Brown's Gap to the Virginia Central Railroad, but his plan was to deal first with his pursuers. He wanted to prevent Frémont and Shields from linking up and forming an overwhelming force which would be difficult to deal with. On June 8, Ewell's Army repulsed Frémont's force of 15,000, sending them reeling west. Winder and the First Brigade, deployed to protect a bridge over the South Fork of the Shenandoah River,

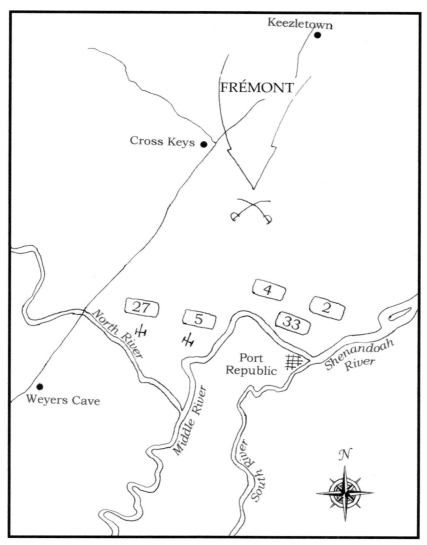

Illustration 8-6: Battle of Cross Keys, June 8, 1962

were not involved in the battle. The 2nd and 4th Virginia Regiments were forward, and the 33rd Virginia was held in reserve. The 5th and 27th Regiments were assigned the protection of Poague and Carpenter's artillery batteries, respectively.

Early the next morning, June 9, Jackson initiated an attack on the flank of Shields' recently arrived Army. The First Brigade was moved across a temporary bridge over the Shenandoah River. As the sun was breaking through the morning mist, Winder sent the 2nd Virginia Regiment forward to the right and the 4th Virginia to its left in support. The 5th Virginia and 27th Virginia led the main attack, but faltered against the superior Union force. The 33rd Virginia Regiment had been placed in reserve and awaited orders to move forward. Ammunition was running low, but Winder, remembering the mistake of the previous Brigade commander General Garnett, held his ground awaiting support. At the critical moment in the battle, General Ewell's Army arrived from its victory of the day before at Cross Keys to support the First

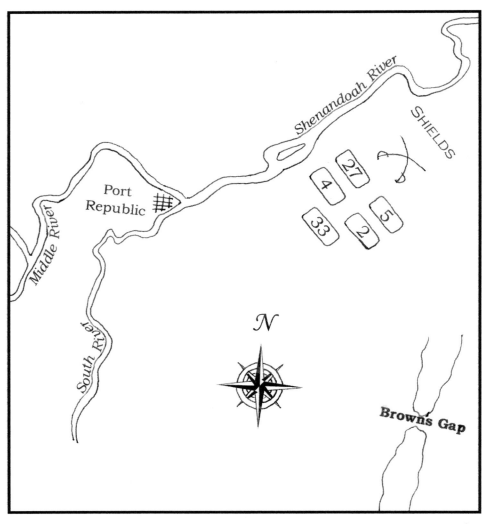

Illustration 8-7: Battle of Port Republic, June 9, 1862

Brigade. Still the Federals pressed their attack. Suddenly Jackson arrived on the scene shouting, "The Stonewall Brigade never retreats! Follow me!" At that moment, the 33rd led by Colonel Neff reached the field and turned the tide of battle. Soon Shields' Army was in retreat, fleeing north with the First Brigade hot on its heels. The chase lasted for five miles before the pursuers fell to the ground exhausted. Shields' force of 10,000, like Frémont's force the day before, had been routed.

The First Brigade withdrew to Brown's Gap that evening and made camp. The

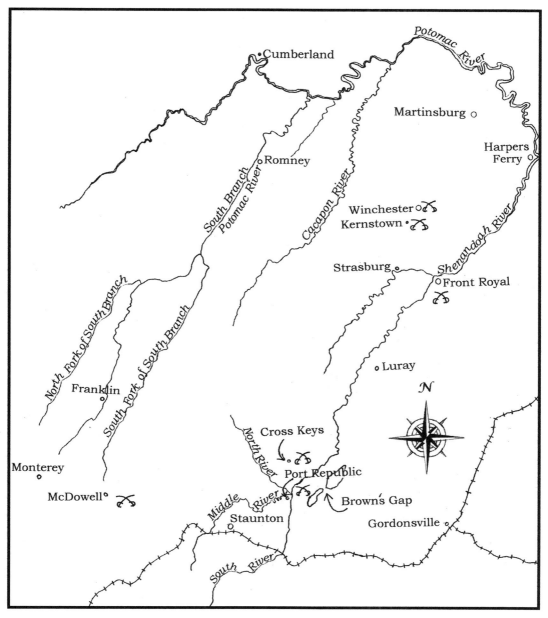

Illustration 8-8: The Valley Campaign

next two days were spent wondering what they would be called upon to do next. On June 12, Jackson moved his entire Valley Army to lush ground between Weyers Cave and Mount Meridian. Here the soldiers enjoyed the fresh water of the Shenandoah River and the shade of the surrounding woods as the June sun began to warm the Valley. There were also excellent pastures where their horses could graze while the Valley Army rested. Worship services, including Communion, were well attended, and Jackson proclaimed Saturday, June 14 as a day for prayers and thanksgiving. The rest and worship continued on Sunday. On June 18, the Valley Army packed up and began moving south to Brown's Gap. The First Brigade was about to depart its beloved Shenandoah Valley once more. Tragically this time, few would return.

During the Valley Campaign, the First Brigade had marched over 650 miles in only forty-eight days. They had been at the forefront at Kernstown, Winchester, and Port Republic. They led the pursuit to Franklin, Charles Town, and Harpers Ferry, and the chase after their victory at Port Republic. They had been a part of the defeat of a Union force made up of three armies totaling over sixty thousand. Once again they were the centerpiece of another Stonewall Jackson strategic masterpiece. Jackson's actions in the Valley had probably saved Richmond; now he was off with his Valley Army to end the siege on the Confederate capital and drive Union General McClellan from the Virginia peninsula between the James and York Rivers.

Battle streamers earned: Virginia 1862, Valley, Shenandoah

Nine

The Peninsula
to Appomattox

here were certainly some long gazes back to the west as the First Brigade again passed through Brown's Gap headed east. The soldiers were looking at the trains of the Virginia Central Railroad as they arrived at the Mechum's River Station, and this time they were pointed east toward Richmond. Unfortunately, there were not enough cars to move the entire Valley Army, resulting in the Valley Army being forced to march most of the distance to Gordonsville. The troops were basically "leap frogged" forward from there. The ten available trains, with a mix of less than twenty cars each, would move forward for several hours; the soldiers would then detrain and resume marching while the engines reversed their course and moved back to bring the next unit forward. Marching for a while on the edge of the railroad ties or roads nearby, the soldiers would anxiously await their next ride.

The walk-ride process got the Brigade to Gordonsville on Saturday, June 21. General Jackson rode off to confer with General Lee, who was now in command of the defenses at Richmond after the wounding of the previous commander, General Sidney Johnson. Old Jack ordered his Army to rest and observe the Sabbath, which they did gladly. The march east resumed the next day, and the Brigade covered twenty-one miles on June 25, going into camp near Ashland, directly north of Richmond. They pushed on the next day, pressed by Jackson, who had returned with knowledge of an offensive scheduled to begin at 3 p.m. that afternoon, June 26. The Army of the Valley arrived late however, with Ewell in the lead, appearing at the front around 4:30 p.m., but the First Brigade not arriving until 6 p.m., too late to participate in this, the first day of the Seven Days Campaign to defeat McClellan's Union force threatening Richmond.

The following morning at 5 a.m., the Brigade went forward to the attack, moving further east and then south to Cold Harbor. The 2nd and 5th Virginia Regiments were initially ordered to protect artillery positions while General Winder moved the 4th Virginia, 27th Virginia, and 33rd Virginia forward to join the Confederate attack, which erupted around 2 p.m. in the afternoon. It was almost 6 p.m. when General Winder ordered his Brigade to attack. The 2nd and 5th Virginia had returned to the

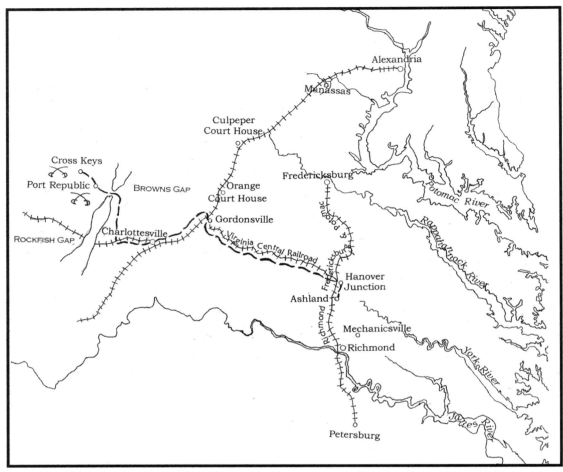

Illustration 9-1: First Brigade Route to the Peninsula – June 1862

Brigade, and they took the lead in the advance. Almost immediately, Colonel Allen, the commander of the 2nd Virginia, was killed. Shortly thereafter the second in command, Lieutenant Colonel Raleigh Colston, was severely wounded, and the third in command, Major Frank Jones, received a fatal wound. Still, the First Brigade moved forward, and within an hour, the strong Union position on the high ground had been wrenched from the defenders who were withdrawing. Winder's soldiers continued the pursuit briefly, but darkness soon brought an end to the advance. The Brigade withdrew to the high ground for the night.

The next day was spent cleaning up the battlefield, caring for the wounded, and burying the dead. The Brigade losses seemed light considering the terrible Union infantry and artillery fire from the day before. There were thirty killed and 150 wounded. One of the interesting events of June 28 was the capture of Union General John Reynolds and his aides by members of the 4th Virginia on picket duty. The next day the Brigade made its deliberate movement further south toward Malvern Hill. On the evening of Monday, June 29, the First Brigade conducted a night move, crossing the Chickahominy

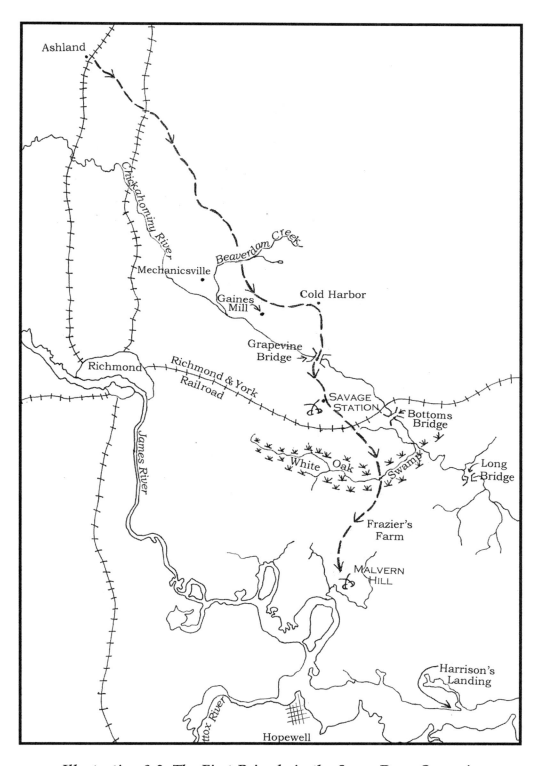

Illustration 9-2: The First Brigade in the Seven Days Campaign

River and passing through Savage Station to White Oak Swamp. Here they bivouacked and the next day, finding the far side of the river undefended, they continued their movement south to Malvern Hill and the heavily defended Union position there.

Malvern Hill was a Union strongpoint consisting of heavy concentrations of artillery, possibility as many as 250 guns. The firepower included ten, twenty, and thirty pound Parrott field pieces, plus one hundred pound Parrott guns and nine-inch Dahlgrens firing from the *USS Galena* and the gunboat *USS Aroostook,* floating on the James River over two miles away. There was even fire coming from the heavy guns of a siege train. Ammunition was plentiful, and the supply base at Harrison's Landing was only a short distance from the guns. McClellan was withdrawing, but it was not a rout. The defenses covering his movement were positioned on the high ground of Malvern Hill, prepared to repulse any Confederate advance.

Throughout the heat of July 1, the First Brigade moved forward to Frazier's Farm and continued toward Malvern Hill, finally assuming a reserve position in support of General D.H. Hill's Division attacking the Union center. The combination of rugged wooded terrain, underbrush, and swamp had broken the regimental formations during their movement. Command and control were difficult in this terrain, and some of the units, particularly elements of the 4th and 5th Virginia, became separated from the Brigade. General Hill's units attacked into the strength of the Union position and took heavy losses. It was almost 7 p.m. before the Brigade was ordered forward to continue the attack. The 4th and 33rd Virginia were in the middle of the line and directly controlled by General Winder, with the 27th Virginia to the right, and the 2nd and 5th Virginia on the left. The Brigade struggled forward under the galling fire from the Union positions on Malvern Hill. Almost three hundred yards separated the Brigade from its initial assault position to the Union defenses to their front. The concentrated fires from the Union artillery made any movement slow and difficult.

Unable to advance successfully, and clearly not capable of penetrating the strong Union position, at 10 p.m. General Winder ordered the advance halted and withdrew the units to the protection of a wooded area to regroup. This withdrawal ended the Union shelling and any further attempt by the Confederates to take Malvern Hill that day. The next morning the Brigade again pushed forward, but McClellan had withdrawn his force to Harrison's Landing during the night. The Seven Days Campaign had ended. Richmond was saved for now.

Although the total Confederate casualties at Malvern Hill was heavy, over 5,000, the First Brigade, protected by the darkness of their night attack, suffered only eighteen killed and five times that number wounded. Winder described the Union artillery as producing "the most terrific fire I have ever seen. There was a continuous stream of shot, shell, and balls for some two hours…!" The Brigade would spend the next several days with battlefield cleanup chores. They remained in the vicinity of Malvern Hill, occasionally sending patrols as far forward as ten miles to scout Union activity. On July 8, they were moved to within three miles of Richmond. Here the soldiers of the Brigade were able to briefly enjoy the hospitality of the grateful citizens of the Confederate capital. The rest ended on July 10, when the Brigade moved five miles north to Mechanicsville, to defend against any attack by Union General McDowell, still positioned around Fredericksburg.

Soon the concern would not be McDowell's force, but a new Union Army being formed to threaten Virginia. On June 27, Major General John Pope had been ordered to take command and combine the three Union armies defeated by Jackson in the Valley. He was to take the force south to the vicinity of Gordonsville, Virginia, to relieve the pressure on McClellan. General Pope was very cautious and moved so slowly that the Seven Days Campaign was lost before his force could become a threat. Now his mission completely changed, and the focus was once again on the protection of Washington. It would soon make little sense to have two Union Armies in Virginia, so on August 4, McClellan was ordered to complete his withdrawal and provide Pope the additional forces necessary to move on Richmond from the north. The Peninsula Campaign was officially over.

General Lee was quick to learn of the new Union plan of attack, and ordered Jackson's Army to move northwest to meet any threat from that direction. On July 17, the Brigade retraced its route to Gordonsville. The tracks of the Virginia Central Railroad had been cut in several places, so Jackson's force was able to ride part of the way, but had to march the balance in the summer heat. During The Seven Days fight, the First Brigade had suffered significant losses, and its ranks were seriously depleted from the strength they had enjoyed during the Valley Campaign. Still, they were a formidable veteran organization and a mainstay in Jackson's Valley Army. Jackson was pleased to learn in late July that the six brigades of General A.P. Hill's Division would be leaving Richmond to join his veteran force. This addition would bring Jackson's Army to over 24,000, despite his heavy losses over the previous three months.

As the First Brigade reached Gordonsville, Jackson realized there was no immediate Union threat. He used the lull to hold court martial proceedings against Brigadier General Garnett. Old Jack had not forgotten Kernstown. The proceedings were held at General Ewell's Headquarters, but were disrupted as a Union Army under an old adversary, General Banks, approached. On August 7, the Brigade was ordered to prepare two days' rations and begin its move toward Orange Court House. The troops crossed the Rapidan River, moving through Orange and camping that night at Madison Mills. The next day, August 9, the Brigade moved north toward Culpeper, unaware that Bank's Union force was moving south to Cedar Mountain, just to the north. General Winder, who had also been serving as the commander of Jackson's Division, had been ill for several days and in bed when awakened by the sound of gunfire as the two forces collided. He was extremely weak, but left immediately, conveyed by ambulance to the front. Always the artilleryman, Winder moved forward to the position of the Rockbridge Artillery, and was adjusting their fire when he was struck by a shell and mortally wounded.

Colonel Charles Ronald, commanding the 4th Virginia Regiment, assumed command of the Brigade as it moved forward to the fight, third in the order of march. After moving some seven miles to the north, Colonel Ronald formed the Brigade for the upcoming fight, with the 27th Virginia on the right, and the 33rd, 5th, 2nd, and 4th Virginia Regiments, in that order, to their left. Jackson ordered the Brigade forward around four p.m., shouting, according to Jed Hotchkiss, "Remember that you are the Stonewall Brigade!" Soon the soldiers collided with an attacking Union force supported by artillery. The Union attack found a gap to the right of the 27th Virginia and were about to penetrate the Confederate line when fresh reinforcements from Major General A.P. Hill's "Light" Division arrived. Colonel Ronald now ordered the Bri-

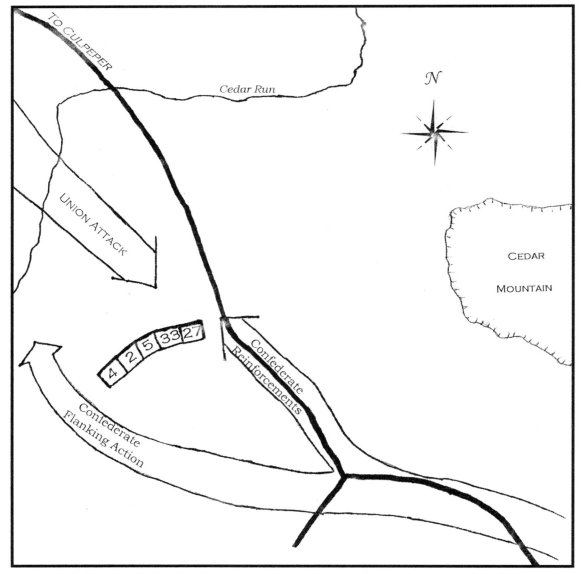

Illustration 9-3: The First Brigade at Cedar Mountain, August 9, 1862

gade to charge the Union lines. Banks' Army broke under the pressure of the renewed attack, and darkness fell as the Brigade pursued them from the field. Colonel Allen would later relate, "The conduct of the troops in this brigade was, indeed, splendid. Men never behaved better in battle."

The First Brigade collapsed that night in a wheat field near Cedar Mountain, completely exhausted from the battle. Despite the desperate fight, they had lost only ten killed and fifty-two wounded. The loss of Winder was significant, however. Although not liked, he was clearly respected by the soldiers of the Brigade and recognized for his courage and demeanor under fire. The next day they moved back to Gordonsville and enjoyed five days of rest. In mid-August, they were pleased to learn that Colonel William S.H. Baylor of the 5th Virginia Regiment had been selected to replace General Winder. Baylor had overcome being demoted by Jackson at Harpers Ferry and stayed with his Regiment, clearly earning Old Jack's respect. He was well liked throughout the Brigade, and morale was high as they moved out toward Orange Court House on August 15, camping for the night at Pisgah Church. Here they would enjoy another five days of rest, for many their last.

On August 19, the Brigade, now numbering just over six hundred, again crossed the Rapidan River, heading north through pouring rain. They moved northwest, protected by Bull Run Mountain, passing through Thoroughfare Gap and moved to Gainesville, with the 2nd Virginia in the lead. On the morning of August 27, Jackson's Army struck General Pope's rear in the vicinity of the Union supply depot at Manassas Junction. The Brigade joined in ravaging the huge stores of rations and other much

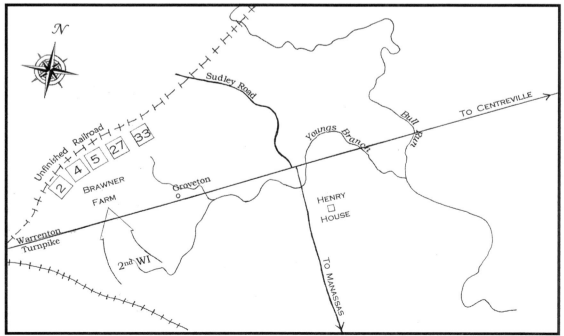

Illustration 9-4: Groveton – August 28, 1862

needed supplies. They had moved fifty miles in only forty-eight hours, and it was time to again enjoy the spoils of war. They filled their stomachs, then their packs, and finally anything that could hold food as they moved off to the northwest. Late in the evening, they halted at Groveton for the night.

The morning of August 28 revealed features familiar to many of the remaining members of the Brigade. A short distance away was the Henry House Hill and even closer was the Warrenton to Washington Road running from right to left. Late in the day a Union force was detected to the front, moving north in search of Jackson's Army. It was the unsuspecting Major General Rufus King's Division with Brigadier John Gibbon's 2nd Wisconsin Brigade. The Confederates, undetected, jumped to the attack, with the First Brigade colliding directly with the tough black-hatted Midwesterners forming the soon to be famous "Iron Brigade." For the next several hours the lines of these two brigades faced each other, each refusing to give ground. Neither side was willing to back down despite accurate, withering fire that one observer called "one of the most intensely concentrated fires of musketry probably ever experienced by any troops in this or any other war." For almost half an hour, alone on the Brawner Farm, the two great regiments fired at each other over a distance of only about fifty yards in places. Soon reinforcements arrived, filling gaps and extending the lines of both sides. Finally, after nine p.m., the Union force began a slow, orderly withdrawal.

The First Brigade had held its ground at the Brawner Farm, but at a terrific price. Lieutenant Colonel Lawson Botts, commanding the 2nd Virginia, was shot from his horse, Colonel Andrew Grigsby commanding the 27th Virginia was severely wounded, and Colonel John Neff fell, riddled with bullets. General William Taliaferro, in command of Jackson's Division, was wounded, and General Richard Ewell would lose a leg to amputation from a severe wound. Company commanders fared little better during the struggle. The leadership of the First Brigade suffered irreplaceable casualties, and total losses numbered over two hundred. The Brigade looked more like a regiment, having lost almost forty percent of it strength. The 27th Virginia Regiment had been depleted to only twenty-five effectives.

There was no time to rest, however, as Jackson redeployed his army of 18,000 that night for the impending attack by General Pope's superior force of over 50,000. The First Brigade was last in the order of march, and on the morning of August 29, its remnants held the Valley Army's right, awaiting the Union attack. The soldiers were located on high ground, five hundred yards above an unfinished cut for the Manassas Gap Railroad. As another hot August day developed, a strong Union force appeared and prepared to attack. Supplies and ammunition were brought forward as the Brigade prepared to defend its position. As expected, the Union attack opened with artillery pounding Jackson's position, and then wave after wave of infantry assaulted his defense. Cheers went up when a cloud of dust to the south signaled the approach of General Longstreet's Army to halt the Union attack. Soon General Pope's

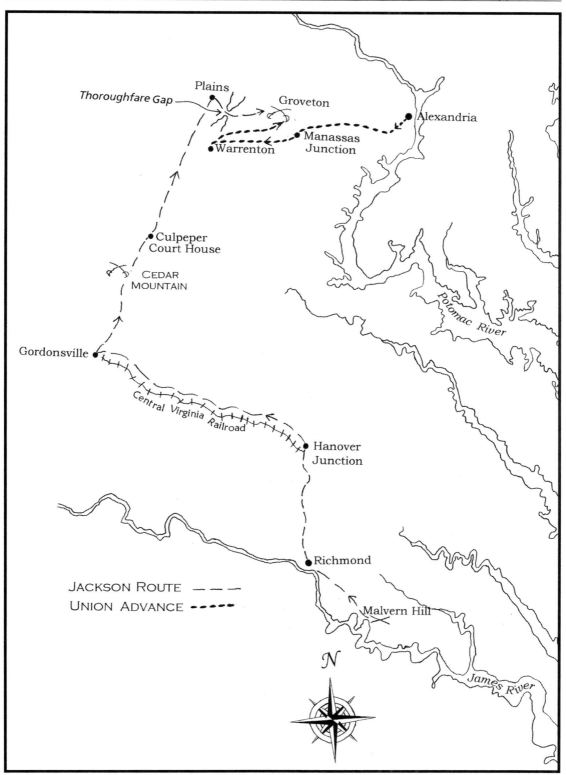

Illustration 9-5: The Route to 2ⁿᵈ Manassas

entire force was withdrawing. As the sun set, the railroad cut in front of Jackson's position was filled with hundreds of brave dead and wounded Union soldiers.

That night, Colonel Baylor organized a prayer service around his tent, and probably every remaining member of the Brigade paused to reflect on the terrific losses of the previous days. The fight was not over, however, as dawn on August 30 brought a renewed artillery barrage and a strong attack on the Confederate right, which the First Brigade was defending. At three in the afternoon, as many as thirty-seven Union regiments were sent forward to the attack. The Confederate line of infantry lay in the railroad cut, with the First Brigade part of the second line of defense still on the high ground. As the Union forces began to break through the first defensive line, Colonel Baylor grabbed a set of fallen colors and ran forward shouting, "Boys! Follow Me!" He was quickly cut down, as was young Captain Hugh White, who tried to rally the Brigade waving regimental colors. Now Colonel Grigsby, the senior Brigade leader remaining, moved the five regiments forward to the railroad cut to close the holes that the advancing Union attack had opened.

When a courier informed Jackson as to what was happening to the right, Old Jack shouted out, "Go back, give my compliments to them and tell the First Brigade to maintain their reputation!" Jackson dispatched Brigadier General Dorsey Pender's Brigade to reinforce the right, and now Longstreet on the Union left flank unleashed his artillery and sent 25,000 infantry to the attack. The Union offensive disintegrated, and Pope ordered a withdrawal. On this day the Confederate Army came as close as

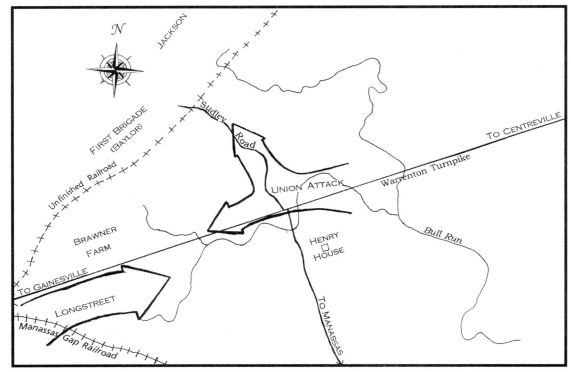

Illustration 9-6: Second Manassas, August 29-30, 1862

it ever would to the complete destruction of its northern enemy in the east. In a period of less than two months, two Union Armies had been defeated and driven from Virginia and, in each case, the First Brigade played a pivotal role, but the price was high. Colonels Baylor and Neff were both killed. Captains and Lieutenants now led the regiments of the Brigade, and there were just over 200 soldiers remaining in the Brigade at the end of Second Manassas.

During the next few days some members of the First Brigade buried hundreds of Union soldiers who had died in the railroad cut. Their new commander, Colonel Grigsby, moved the majority of the Brigade north on September 1, where they served as a reserve during the Battle of Chantilly. A steady rain had soaked the battlefield for two days for those remaining around Manassas and mourning the losses incurred during the three days of heavy fighting. Morale began to soar, however, when the entire Confederate Army began moving north to Leesburg. Finally they were carrying the Civil War into the north to the homes of their Union enemies.

At dawn on September 3, Old Jack led his divisions, including what remained of the First Brigade, northwest for ten miles in the direction of Leesburg. The next day they pushed on, moving through that little town, camping two miles to the north. Then they crossed the Potomac River and moved thirteen miles further north to Frederick, Maryland. While encamped there, Generals Lee, Longstreet, and Jackson finalized their invasion plans. Jackson was to move southwest to capture Harpers Ferry, while Longstreet moved northwest to threaten Hagerstown. The First Brigade was ordered to prepare rations for three days, and on September 10, they moved south and re-crossed the Potomac River, moving to Boonsboro. Marching some twenty miles the next day, they were on familiar ground and only a short distance from the Baltimore and Ohio Railroad depot in Williamsport. In the early morning hours of September 13, they slipped into Martinsburg, but the enemy there had already withdrawn to Harpers Ferry. The Brigade followed and on September 14, they were once again in control of Bolivar Heights, overlooking the Union supply depot there.

The depleted 2nd Virginia Regiment was assigned provost guard duty and remained in Martinsburg. The fight at Harpers Ferry never developed, and the entire garrison surrendered with little resistance. Old Jack had taken over 12,000 prisoners and a like number of small arms, along with seventy-three artillery pieces and two hundred wagons. Around midnight, the First Brigade moved out on a seventeen-mile night march, first moving west, crossing the Potomac River at Boteler's Ford, and following a canal towpath along the river to a position just south of Sharpsburg, Maryland. After resting on their arms for only two hours, the Brigade continued the move north to a position on the Confederate left, west of the town. They numbered only around 250 as the sun rose on the morning of September 17 on the soon-to-be battlefield of Antietam. Again, they found themselves on the front line, positioned near the Dunker Church, which would become one of the pivotal positions in the upcoming battle. Their location, to the west side of the church and just beyond the

Hagerstown Road, was on a piece of wooded high ground known as the West Woods. Jackson knew this area had to be held, and positioned his old First Brigade here.

The Union forces began moving into assault positions at three a.m. Artillery began to range the West Woods and, as the sun rose, the blue wave began its attack on the Confederate left. General Abner Doubleday's Division was in the lead as three divisions, totaling over 10,000 soldiers, headed straight for the First Brigade. The soldiers lay prone in a low area just south of the Hagerstown Road. Concealed by a fence until the Union advance was within point blank range, they then sprang up to deliver a deadly volley into the attackers. The wave of blue staggered momentarily,

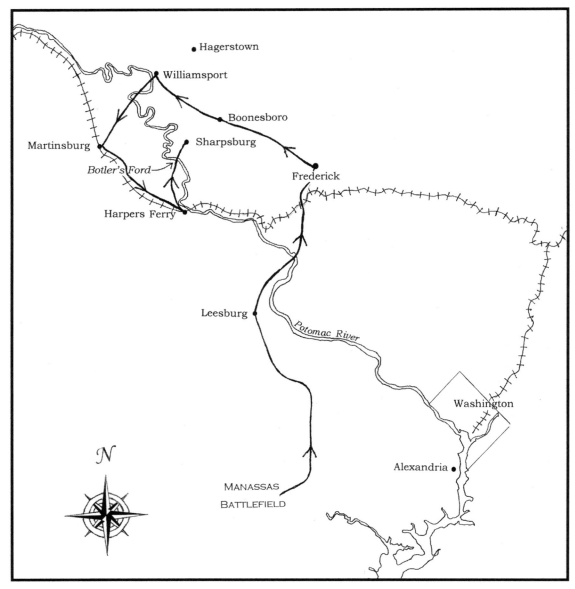

Illustration 9-7: Route to Antietam, September 1862

but its superior numbers recovered quickly and continued forward. In short order, the outnumbered Confederates were in turmoil, with many of their key leaders killed. Colonel Grigsby took over Jackson's Division, as its chain of command fell in succession. The Confederate left withdrew back, then, reinforced, attacked forward to its original positions. The tide of battle ebbed and flowed, but in the end the First Bri-

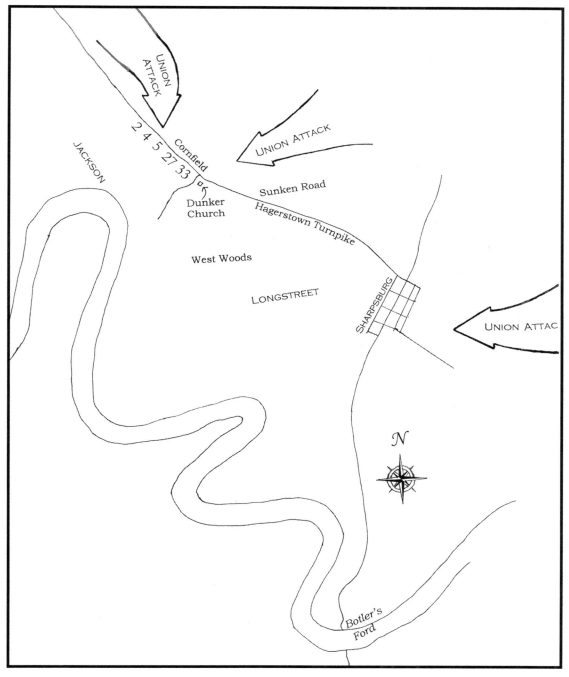

Illustration 9-8: Antietam, September 17, 1862

gade remained in the West Woods as the Union attack swung around to the Confederate right. The Confederate left had held, and by day's end, the entire southern army, its back to the Potomac River, had held its ground.

The Brigade was given the opportunity to withdraw to the rear, to re-supply, and consume the few rations available, mostly salt bacon. They left behind eleven dead and approximately seventy-five wounded. It was no longer a brigade, but an organization with only enough soldiers to fill two companies. The next day the two armies faced each other with little activity, and that evening, General Lee's Army of Northern Virginia began its withdrawal across the Potomac River. The Battle of Antietam had ended without a decisive victory by either side, but the losses were staggering. The combined Confederate and Union casualties on September 17 were greater than on any other single day during the Civil War.

The Confederate Army was reorganized on September 18. Jackson was now to command the Second Corps of the Army of Northern Virginia, which would include his old Division and its First Brigade, which some were now calling the First Brigade. With their numbers reduced so dramatically, the Brigade would lose the Rockbridge Artillery to become a unit of the Corps Reserve. Jackson had to officially appoint a new commander for the First Brigade, and much to the displeasure of the soldiers, he bypassed Colonel Grigsby, who had taken over after Colonel Baylor was killed at Manassas and had led the unit well during the past few weeks. Jackson chose, instead, a friend from Lexington and a member of his staff, thirty-four-year-old Frank Paxton, to succeed Baylor. The outraged Grigsby, who was described as "mad as thunder," resigned and left for Richmond to appeal the decision. He had successfully led the "Bloody" 27th Virginia Regiment and deserved to command the Brigade. His appeal was to no avail, however, and Paxton was appointed to the rank of Brigadier General in early November and took command of the First Brigade. He was a strong man with a deep voice, which had earned him the name of "Bull." The soldiers of the Brigade would have other names for him before he earned their respect and support.

Leaving Maryland, the First Brigade crossed the Potomac River, returning to its beloved Shenandoah Valley where it was rejoined by the 2nd Virginia Regiment. For the next two months they would remain camped in the area north of Winchester, seeing very little action. Units would conduct patrols and destroy the tracks of the Baltimore and Ohio Railroad whenever possible, in an attempt to disrupt Union troops and supplies moving west. There was one exchange near Kearneysville in mid-October which cost the 4th Virginia Regiment three killed and eleven wounded. During the lull, recruits and recovering wounded began to swell the ranks, and the organization began to look more like a Brigade again.

Snow covered the ground on November 22 when Jackson's Corps made its first move. It numbered some 38,500 soldiers in four divisions. Jackson's old Division was the smallest, with barely 6,800 members, and the First Brigade provided 1,200 of

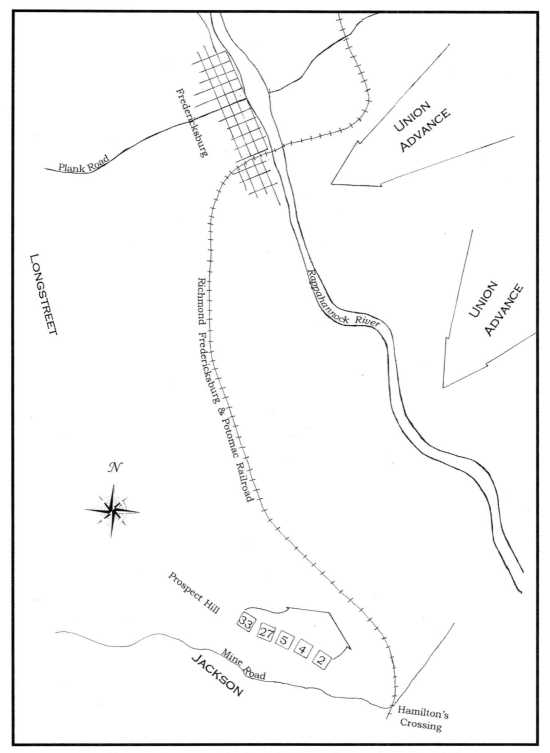

Illustration 9-9: Fredericksburg, December 13, 1862

these soldiers. The Second Corps headed south, up the Valley, to New Market, where it turned east. The Brigade crossed the Massanutten Mountain Range on November 24 and the Blue Ridge Mountains the next day. Then it was on to Madison Court House and Gordonsville, finally reaching Guiney's Station, ten miles south of Fredericksburg, on December 2. At this stop on the Richmond, Fredericksburg, and Potomac Railroad, the major north-south line, the troops camped for ten days, fighting the December cold. On December 12th, they were ordered north to Fredericksburg and placed in a position on the right of the strong Confederate line, directly south of the town. Union forces under new Commander General Ambrose Burnside were preparing to cross the Rappahannock River, determined to conduct a winter attack on the Confederate positions on the high ground south of the town.

The Brigade was in a reserve position as the sun attempted to break through the morning fog of December 13. By ten a.m., the lifting haze revealed a strong Union force to the front and preparing to attack. Two Union charges were repulsed without the First Brigade's participation, but when a breach in the Confederate lines occurred around 11 a.m., the Brigade rushed to the rescue. The 2nd and 4th Virginia Regiments were on the right, the 5th Virginia in the middle, with the 27th and 33rd Virginia to the left. The charge plugged the gap and halted the third Union advance, their last of the day, on the Confederate right. The First Brigade was again successful and had sustained losses of only three killed and sixty-eight wounded. The main battle that day at Fredericksburg was along the sunken road below the high ground directly south of the town. By day's end, the Union Army of the Potomac was soundly defeated and another "on to Richmond" offensive stopped. It was a lopsided southern victory fought under difficult winter conditions.

During the next four days the First Brigade endured extreme cold, but remained prepared to repulse any further attempt by Burnside to renew the attack. Finally orders arrived, sending the Brigade south along the Rappahannock River to long awaited winter quarters. The camp would be established close to Jackson's Headquarters at Moss Neck, the home of the Corbin family. It was also close to the Richmond, Fredericksburg & Potomac Railroad's Guiney's Station, providing the opportunity for the troops to visit Richmond. The site, named Camp Winder, would see difficult winter conditions. As best they could, the soldiers built log cabins and used tents as insulation to protect themselves from the cold. Jackson, viewing the soldiers' primitive living conditions, told an associate to "Call them suffering angels." It was certainly not going to be as comfortable as their first winter quarters at Winchester.

With the arrival of the warmer spring weather, the Brigade again prepared for action. Breaking camp on April 28, 1863, the soldiers moved to a new temporary camp at Hamilton's Crossing. The spring rain soaked the soldiers for several days before they were marched thirty miles north to the western flank of General Lee's Army of Northern Virginia, stopping south of the small community of Chancellorsville. The new Union Commander of the Army of the Potomac, General Joseph Hooker, who had replaced Burnside, had his Army crossing the Rappahannock River west of

Fredericksburg at United States Ford and preparing to march south to capture Richmond. Significantly outnumbered, Lee was forced to assume great risk as he ordered Jackson's Second Corps to attempt to move undetected further west and conduct a flank attack on the Union forces that had already crossed the Rappahannock and were confronting him. The morning of May 2 found the Brigade holding a critical position protecting Jackson's right flank south of the Plank Road, as the Second Corps began a twelve-mile movement. The force marched quietly, just beyond the sight of the enemy lines, to assume an attack position on the Union's unsuspecting right flank. When the attack was initiated at five p.m. the First Brigade was still on the Corps' right and attacked along the Orange Plank Road. The charging Confederates quickly overran the Union defenders, who began to withdraw in great disorder. Jackson's Second Corps' attack was now joined by his old Brigade on the right, and the rout was on.

It was late in the evening when the Brigade finally halted and rested on their arms. Through the night they could hear the Union forces constructing defenses in an attempt to stop any further Confederate attack. Tragically, in the darkness of that night General Jackson was wounded by his own men, troops from the 18th North Carolina Regiment, who mistook his scouting party for Union Cavalry. The General had been reconnoitering forward in the darkness, attempting to locate the enemy positions and making plans to continue the attack. The rumor of Jackson's wound-

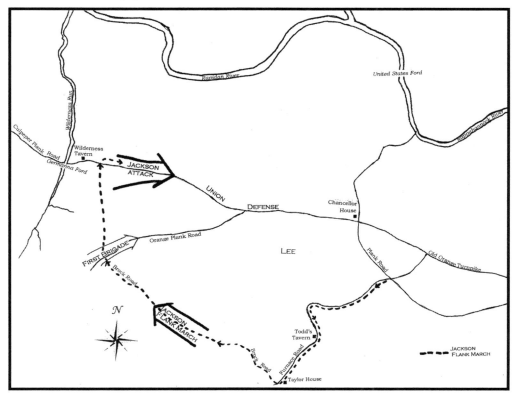

Illustration 9-10: Chancellorsville, May 2, 1863

ing added to the cold night chill as it spread through the ranks of his old Brigade, Division, and the Second Corps. The General was moved to the rear by wagon, further southeast to Guiney's Station located on the Richmond, Potomac, and Fredericksburg railroad. As the morning of May 3 broke, there was great concern over Old Jack's condition, but his men had to focus on routing the Union forces to their front. The day opened with resumption of heavy Union artillery fire.

The First Brigade moved to the attack, with the 2nd and 4th Virginia Regiments on the right, the 5th Virginia in the center, and the 27th Virginia and 33rd Virginia on the left. They advanced under galling fire, taking the Union position, to be known as Slocum's log works, which had been hastily prepared during the night, using timbers and dirt. During the attack General Paxton, the Brigade commander, fell mortally wounded. Colonel John H.S. Funk commanding the 5th Virginia Regiment, was ordered, by acting Second Corps Commander Jeb Stuart, to take command of the Brigade. A coordinated attack at this point seemed impossible since the Brigade's right flank had fallen behind in the dense wooded terrain and swampy areas along the Plank Road, and the raking fire from the Union gunners continued to take a toll. The Brigade's men fell back to the protection of the breastworks they had just taken, reformed, and with additional forces coming up in support, prepared to resume the attack. They were spurred on by General Stuart, who arrived on the scene, urging them to "Charge, and remember Jackson!"

The Rebel yell signaled the charge of the First Brigade as it raced forward, eventually passing through the grounds of the Chancellor House, which had earlier been the headquarters of General Hooker. Now his headquarters was in the saddle, as he led his army back to the United States Ford crossing from where it had come. The Brigade was exhausted and out of ammunition. Fortunately, the Army of the Potomac had little will to continue the fight, and its withdrawal continued. The Brigade set up camp near the captured earthworks and would remain there for the next several days. They had played a major roll in another great victory, but it had been costly. Their Brigade commander was dead, General Jackson lay seriously wounded, and 493 comrades had become casualties. It would be the highest one day casualty rate the First Brigade would encounter during the entire Civil War. Reviewing the Confederate losses at Chancellorsville in his *Lee's Lieutenants*, Volume II, Douglas Southall Freeman wrote, "Jackson's old First Brigade never was itself in full might after that battle."

A week later, May 10, word would come that General Jackson had died of pneumonia at Guiney's Station, while recovering from his wounds. The news was devastating to his old Brigade. Old Jack gone? It simply couldn't be. The next day the five Regiments of the Brigade were united in requesting to serve as the honor guard in the upcoming events leading up to General Jackson's burial. With the Army of the Potomac still threatening to cross the Rappahannock River and drive south, however, General Lee denied the request. He could not afford to lose the entire First Brigade, but would allow a few members to escort the body. The Brigade was very displeased with this decision, but accepted it grudgingly from their new camp back at Hamilton's Crossing, named Camp Paxton. On May 16, they petitioned the President of the Confederacy, Jefferson Davis, to designate them officially as "The Stonewall Brigade." The War Department honored this request on May 30, 1863, and by Special Orders 129, the Brigade became the only unit of its size in the Confederate Army authorized to carry a distinctive nickname. From this point on, soldiers of the Stonewall Brigade have been affectionately called "Stonewallers."

Replacing General Paxton was a real challenge for the Confederate leadership. There were certainly several very qualified leaders within the Stonewall Brigade, including their acting commander, Colonel Funk, who had performed well at Chancellorsville. The decision, however, gave the command to Colonel James Walker, an original member of the Brigade, who organized and commanded Company C, the "Pulaski Guards" of the 2nd Virginia Regiment. The Brigade was very displeased with the decision, especially the leaders, and all of the regimental commanders resigned. In short order, though, the soldiers would take a liking to Walker and nickname him Stonewall Jim. A native of Augusta County, Walker came from strong Scotch-Irish stock. He had attended Virginia Military Institute, but was expelled in his senior year when he challenged Professor Thomas J. Jackson to a duel as a result of a classroom incident. He had displayed his leadership and courage as a Regimental commander at Gaines Mill and Cedar Run, and while serving as an acting Brigade commander at Antietam. He was a fighter!

In early June, the Stonewall Brigade, now in General Edward Johnson's Division of Second Corps, commanded by General Richard Ewell, left Camp Paxton, fourth in the order of march. The column moved west to Culpeper Court House, then through the Chester Gap to Front Royal. June 11 was an especially happy day as the Brigade crossed the Blue Ridge Mountains, filing through Chester Gap and looking down into their beloved Valley. Crossing the Shenandoah River, they were back in Front Royal, which stirred memories of the previous victories in the Valley Campaign just over a year before. In the early morning hours of June 13, the Brigade moved north toward Winchester, with the 2nd Virginia Regiment on the left of the road and the remaining regiments to the right. They halted in the evening, less than a mile from the Union defenses, but shortly after midnight resumed their movement, proceeding to the east and around the town.

Masked by early morning fog, the soldiers moved back toward the Valley Turnpike where they fell upon the retreating Union forces. The 5th Virginia Regiment led the Brigade's attack, assisted by the 2nd Virginia. Nearly 900 prisoners and six stands of Union colors were captured, practically without any losses. It was a joyous day, as the Valley soldiers were allowed to return to Winchester where the streets were full of grateful citizens. The celebration was short lived, however, and on June 16, the Brigade moved to Shepardstown, then crossed the Potomac, headed to Sharpsburg, Maryland. There they camped on the old battlefield of Antietam for six days, then continued their move north on June 24. They foraged into Pennsylvania via Greencastle and Chambersburg, finally stopping for several days just south of Carlisle. Here they awaited orders to continue the attack to the Pennsylvania state capital at Harrisburg. The orders that came, however, on June 29, directed the Second Corps to countermarch southeast to join General Lee and the rest of the Army of Northern Virginia positioned to the east of Chambersburg.

The Brigade retraced its steps and camped at Fayetteville, just east of Chambersburg.

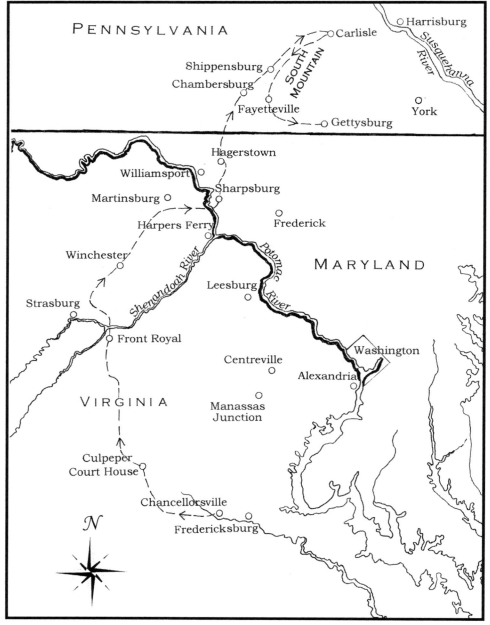

Illustration 9-11: Route to Gettysburg

There, on July 1, the Second Corps received additional orders to move to the Pennsylvania crossroads town of Gettysburg. Crossing South Mountain, excitement grew as they marched toward the sound of the guns and the ensuing battle to the east. Reaching Gettysburg as the sun was setting, the Second Corps helped push the Union forces from Gettysburg to the high ground just east of the town. It was dark as the Brigade moved northeast following the tracks of the Gettysburg & Hanover Railroad to set up camp on the Confederate left near Culp's Hill. This high ground would be the focus of their activities for the next two days. The farm there was the home of twenty-four-year-old John Wesley Culp of the 2nd Virginia Regiment and, tragically, he would become the only soldier from this unit killed during the battle.

July 2 was practically an uneventful day on the Confederate left, while General Longstreet attempted to turn the Union left. The 2nd Virginia was involved in some minor skirmishing as General Walker moved the Brigade to the north side of the Hanover Road. Activities on July 3, however, got started early as the Brigade formed up around two a.m. and began moving to capture Union trench works at the base of Culp's Hill. Soldiers of the Federal Twelfth Corps counter-attacked at dawn but were repulsed, primarily by companies of the 2nd Virginia, which turned back the assault and remained in a defensive position for most of the day. The remainder of the Brigade, however, surged to the attack, attempting to take Culp's Hill boulder by boulder. The terrific combination of artillery and musket fire from the Union positions atop the hill took their toll, particularly on the 4th Virginia Regiment, which lost almost seventy-five percent of its strength on this day. For five hours the Brigade struggled without success to reach the crest of Culp's Hill. After a brief rest, orders came to resume the attack a second and then a third time until, finally, General Walker ordered a withdrawal, later stating "I suffered the brigade to fall back to a more secure position, as it was a useless sacrifice of life to keep them longer under so galling a fire."

The next day the two armies lay resting, and later that evening, General Lee ordered his Army to withdraw. The Brigade joined the retreat as torrential rains turned the roads into mud and misery. High water delayed the crossing of the Potomac River at Williamsport until July 13. The battle of Gettysburg was behind them but not to be forgotten. It had cost thirty-five killed, over two hundred wounded, many of whom would die later on the difficult return to Virginia, and eighty-seven captured. Even worse was the despair the defeat brought to the ranks, and many soldiers deserted as the Brigade moved back to the Valley. Several days were spent destroying railroad tracks around Martinsburg, then back to Front Royal and across the mountains to a new camp, Camp Stonewall, near Orange Court House, just a short distance from Montpelier, the home of former President James Madison. They arrived at their new home on August 1, almost two months and 247 miles of marches since being ordered north. The joyous victory at Chancellorsville had been followed by a tragic defeat at Gettysburg, but what was to come now? With regiments down to company size, some even smaller, what would become of the famed brigade?

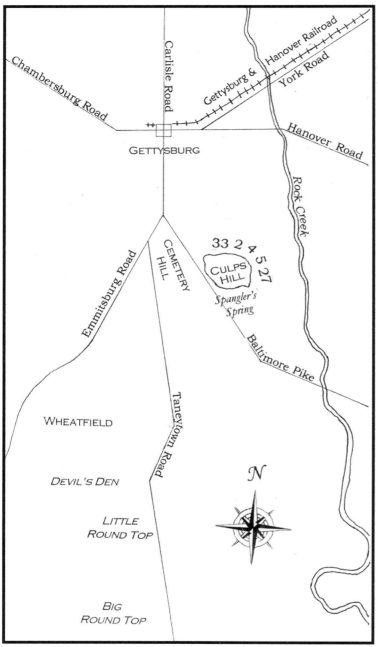

Illustration 9-12: Brigade position at Gettysburg, July 3, 1863

Word spread through the Valley, calling for additional volunteers to fill the depleted ranks. Newspapers were filled with the news from Gettysburg and the needs of the Stonewall Brigade. The *Lexington Gazette* called for volunteers for the Brigade in order to "help continue its reputation." The unit was clearly the Valley's own, and the citizens were proud of what it had accomplished and more than willing to support its future endeavors. The conscripts and volunteers who stepped forward to fill the Brigade were unfortunately not of the caliber of the original members, now seasoned veterans. Down, but not out, the Brigade valued the recovery time they enjoyed for the next few months. Morale was being restored as indicated in a letter home from Daniel Sheetz of the 2nd Virginia Regiment when he said, "You must not get discouraged yet we can fight them a long time yet."

As summer turned into fall, the Regiments of the Brigade took turns performing picket duty and providing watch on river crossing sites to the north. The peaceful camp life ended on November 26, when orders came to move north to the Rapidan River. The next day they marched to a position on a tributary known as Mine Run, which flowed north to the river. The Brigade was third in the order of march when they were attacked by a superior Union force attempting to turn the Confederate right flank. The Brigade took a position to the right, with the 2nd Virginia Regiment deployed forward, protecting the rest of the Stonewallers as they prepared defensive positions for the anticipated assault. The entire Union Third Corps had fallen upon the Confederates, supported by heavy artillery fire, but the momentum of the attack stopped when it neared the front of General Johnson's Division and the Stonewall Brigade. The pause was broken around four p.m. when General Johnson ordered his division forward. Darkness was approaching as the Union force began to withdraw. General Walker pressed the Brigade's attack into the fields of Payne's Farm, where the lack of ammunition and mixing of formations caused General Johnson to order a withdrawal to the west bank of Mine Run. The little known battle had cost the Brigade dearly. Colonel Colston of the 2nd Virginia Regiment was wounded and would later die of pneumonia and Colonel William Terry, leading the 4th Virginia, was also severely wounded. Twenty Stonewallers were dead with five times that number wounded. At the end of the day, the Stonewall Brigade had again found itself in the critical place and time of another costly close fight. For several days both sides held their position, but General Meade, never the aggressor, withdrew his forces on the night of December 1, 1863. Another battle had ended.

The Battle of Mine Run ended fighting for the year of 1863. The Union had failed for almost five months to follow up its victory at Gettysburg, and when it did, General Meade had his nose bloodied by the Stonewall Brigade. President Lincoln needed to find a "fighter" who could press the attack and bring an end to the war. In the meantime, the Brigade would move back to the south and settle into winter quarters at Camp Randolph, and also at Camp Stonewall Jackson in Orange County close to Pisgah Church. Crude small cabins were constructed for protection against the winter cold. The 2nd Virginia's Tom Gold noted,

> Our houses were small log huts, capable of holding three or four men, and were quite comfortable. Chimneys built of sticks of wood plastered on the inside answered well. The roof of clapboards or pieces of tents, a bed of straw or pine shats on pieces of split wood...made us quite luxurious.

In his *33rd Virginia Infantry*, historian Lowell Reidenbaugh indicates

> Daily rations were reduced to four ounces of bacon and 12 ounces of meat. Moreover, the bacon frequently was little more than lard and the beef was tainted. Flour rations were cut from 18 to 10 ounces daily and the men expected further reduction momentarily.

The Christmas season brought thoughts of better days but also special rations. In *A History of the Laurel Brigade*, William N. McDonald writes,

> It was Christmas time too, and in spite of the ruin wrought by war, thanks to careful housewives, many good things remained. The half-starved troopers made the best of their opportunity, and gladly banishing thoughts of 'grim-visaged war,' yielded themselves to the cheerful festivities of Christmas time. If turkeys were hard to get, the savory sausage of the forehanded farmers was accepted as a fair substitute, and the apple, peach, and pumpkin pies, rye coffee, and sorghum molasses galore, made one think that plenty, if not peace, had again returned to the land.

The second year of the war closed with no end in sight. Winter quarters meant drilling, picket duty, and reacting to Union incursions across the Rapidan River. One of the most challenging confrontations, though, occurred in the Confederate camp

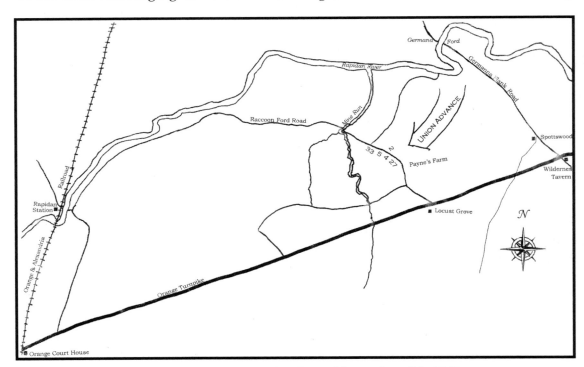

Illustration 9-13: Mine Run, November 27, 1863

as spring approached, and it became known as "The Great Snowball Battle." In the afternoon of March 23, 1864, following a surprising wet, heavy snow, the Stonewall Brigade joined Stafford's Louisiana Brigade in a struggle against Dole's Georgia Brigade and Ramseur's North Carolina Brigade. The opposing formations moved back and forth until finally the Rebel yell of the Stonewall Brigade indicated a successful offensive was underway. General Walker mounted his horse and led the charge into the opposing lines. It was a five-hour struggle and many a gray uniform was covered in white snow as darkness set in. Flags, hats, and prisoners were returned, and foes became friends again after an experience none of them would ever forget.

Clothing and supplies came to the Stonewall Brigade from the Valley, but with so many homes and communities now under Union control, some units were unable to receive any support from their family and friends. Hundreds were without socks and many did not even have shoes. General Lee personally assisted by forwarding what he could from the Army's stores and appealing to the citizens of Richmond, including his own family, to send whatever they could to the suffering soldiers of the Stonewall Brigade. In a letter to his wife, General Lee asked her to "Tell the young women to work hard for the brave Stonewallers." It was a difficult winter for these heroes who had sacrificed so much. The strength of the regiments began to grow with the beginning of spring, as wounded soldiers returned along with more conscripts to help fill the depleted ranks. It was still a sad organization to look upon, as many visitors to the Brigade would attest.

In April of 1864, President Lincoln announced that General Ulysses S. Grant was taking command of the Union Army. The offensive minded Grant appeared to be exactly what the army needed to complete the drive to Richmond and end the war. As May approached, the Union Army of the Potomac was crossing the Rapidan in great numbers. On May 2, the Stonewall Brigade broke camp and moved north to confront the new threat. In his *Battle of the Wilderness May 5-6, 1864*, Gordon C. Rhea indicates "All told, Grant was preparing to move against Lee's 65,000 veterans with a combined force of nearly 200,000 combatants." In addition, the Union force consisted of some four hundred cannon and 12,000 cavalry. On May 4, the Brigade was positioned on the Confederate left on the edge of a dense forest of pine and oak trees, with thick briars, brush, and blooming honeysuckle at their bases. The area, known as the Wilderness, was almost impenetrable. As the beautiful morning of May 5 dawned, Walker moved his Brigade into the thick Wilderness, colliding almost immediately with a huge force of Federals assembled in the deep woods. The fight started immediately, catching the Brigade in disarray. The superior Union numbers staggered the advancing Stonewallers, and they began to fall back.

At the critical moment, Colonel Terry reformed the 4th Virginia Regiment at right angles, blunting the attack. The 5th and 27th Virginia, which had suffered most during the initial confrontation, now joined the 2nd and 33rd Regiments in support of the Brigade's defensive position. In the midst of the fight, "Stonewall" Jim Walker was heard rallying his men with shouts of "Remember your name." As the day's fighting wore on, the Union attackers began to sustain heavy losses, and around 5 p.m., after a costly five-hour fight, the Brigade was replaced at the front by Hayes' Louisiana Brigade. In rallying his Regiment, Colonel William Randolph of the 2nd Virginia was killed, and although accurate numbers are not available, the Wilderness had been another costly fight for the Stonewall Brigade. The surviving soldiers withdrew to the rear for ammunition, re-supply, and a much-needed rest. The next day they remained in defensive positions, but there was no resumption of the Union attack.

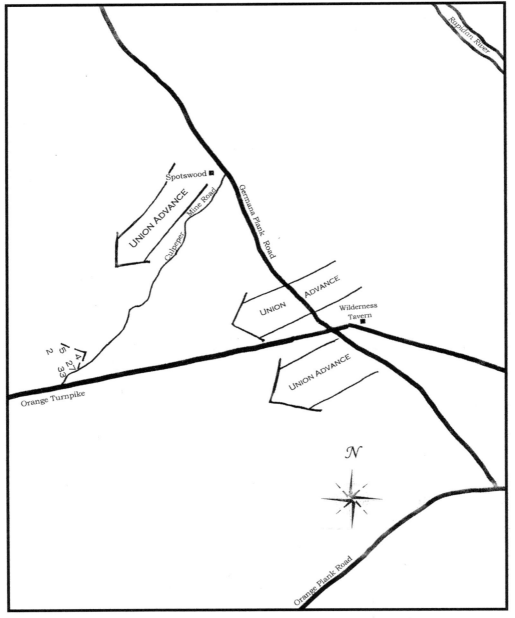

Illustration 9-14: The Wilderness, May 5, 1864

May 7 found the Union positions empty, as General Grant moved to outflank the Confederates. Now General Lee had to shift his forces, and the Stonewall Brigade would march all night and into the next afternoon to a new position at Spotsylvania Court House. It was a sixteen-hour march for the "foot cavalry," with little rest and no sleep. Initially, the 2nd, 27th, and 33rd Virginia Regiments were ordered to establish defensive positions on a small hill, with the 4th and 5th Virginia in a swampy area below. Walker found the terrain unacceptable and withdrew the Brigade to more defensible positions slightly to the rear. Reaching this better ground, the Stonewallers began digging in. The remnants of the 4th Virginia Regiment held the right, with the 5th and 27th Virginia, in that order, to the left. The 33rd Virginia was positioned next, with the 2nd Virginia to its left. The combined Confederate positions held by Johnson's Division took the shape of a horseshoe, and the salient that was created would become known as the "Mule Shoe."

"Soldiers in the Stonewall Brigade awoke on May 9 to find themselves occupying the most important point along the Confederate line," writes Dr. Robertson in *The Stonewall Brigade*. Using bayonets, a few picks and shovels, whatever they could find, the Stonewallers began digging and working feverishly to prepare their part of the Mule Shoe. The open field to their front was only 150 yards from the Union Second Corps, forming in the woods before them. On May 10, the first Union attack struck the Brigade. The 2nd and 33rd Virginia Regiments staggered, but the Confederate line remained intact as night fell. A steady rain began the next day as the Brigade's men continued to improve their positions by piling logs atop their breastworks.

The morning of May 12 brought continuing rain and thick fog which greatly reduced the Brigade's visibility. They could hear the Union forces forming as they watched from the muddy trenches, but could not see them. When the attack finally was in sight, the Stonewallers opened fire only to find that their powder was too damp to ignite, and their weapons would not fire. Suddenly the overwhelming Union force fell upon the Brigade's defenses. Desperate hand-to-hand fighting ensued as the Brigade struggled to hold its position. Some Stonewallers used their rifle butts to club their attackers, while others used their fists, bayonets, knives; some even threw rocks, but to no avail. The tide of Union blue just kept coming. The 4th, 5th, 27th, and 33rd Virginia Regiments were trapped as the Mule Shoe was pinched off from the rest of the Confederate Army. The members of the Brigade who escaped, raced to the second line of defense and fell in on other regiments. "Stonewall" Jim Walker was wounded, and only two regimental commanders and some two hundred soldiers survived the attack. For the rest, killed, wounded, and captured, the war was over. Most, taken prisoner, were transported to Fort Delaware until June following the end of the war. The unit's last famous stand at the Bloody Angle closed the book on the Stonewall Brigade in the Civil War. Its wounded commander would declare that on this day his famous Stonewall Brigade "was annihilated & ceased to exist," according to National Park historian Robert K. Krick in *The Spotsylvania Campaign*.

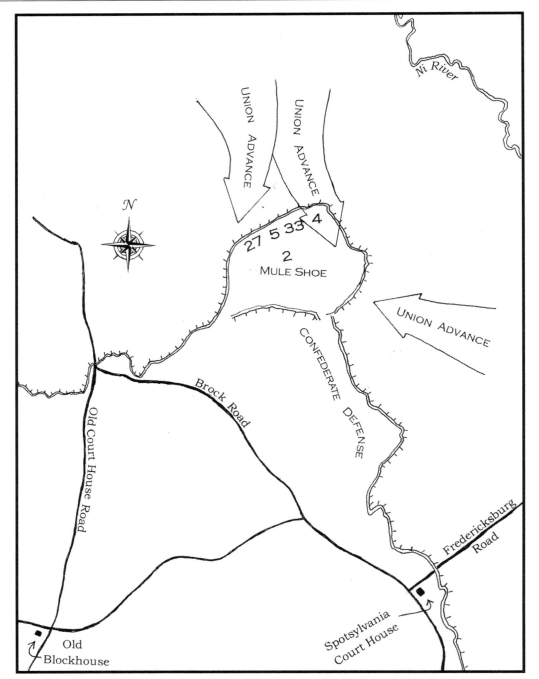

Illustration 9-15: Bloody Angle, May 12, 1864

The war continued on, however, and there were some Stonewallers, many of whom were seasoned veterans, still ready to continue the fight. These roughly two hundred survivors of the Bloody Angle and their five regiments were consolidated into one brigade to serve along with the remnants of Jones', Steuart's, and Walker's brigades. The new brigade would contain a total of fourteen regiments, but the strength of many consisted of just a handful of soldiers. The end strength of the new organization was not even equal to that of any one of its regiments when they were formed. The reorganization took place on May 14, and the now General Terry of the Stonewall Brigade's 4th Virginia Regiment, still recovering from a wound, became their new Brigade commander. The five famed regiments from the Shenandoah Valley of Virginia were now a part of Terry's Brigade in General John B. Gordon's Division.

Henry Kyd Douglas in his book, *I Rode With Stonewall*, points out that after Stonewall Jackson, "no general of that brigade ever lived long enough to secure further promotion: none either escaped wounds or death long enough to be made a Major General." Garnett was killed leading his new brigade of General Pickett's Division during the famous charge at Gettysburg; Winder, Baylor, and Paxton were all killed on the battlefield. Now "Stonewall" Jim Walker lay severely wounded. He alone would survive the war, returning to practice law in Pulaski and later become the lieutenant governor of Virginia. Brave men all, who led from the front and moved to the sound of the guns.

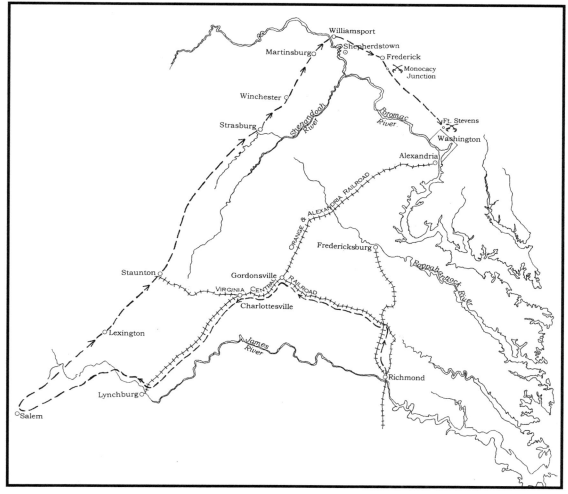

Illustration 9-16: Headed to Washington – Summer 1864

Over the next month, Terry's Brigade saw little action as it was pushed south with the rest of General Lee's Army into positions defending Richmond. Then on June 13, 1864, the soldiers were ordered to join Jackson's old Second Corps, now commanded by General Jubal Early, to drive the forces of Union General David Hunter from their beloved Shenandoah Valley. Hunter had taken command of the Union forces in the Valley following their defeat at the Battle of New Market, and he was intent on revenge. After crushing a makeshift Confederate force at Piedmont, northeast of Staunton, he entered the city and destroyed everything that could provide support to the Confederate cause. He then proceeded south and burned the Virginia Military Institute, before heading east over the Blue Ridge Mountains to cut the major rail lines in Lynchburg.

Terry's Stonewall Brigade departed Petersburg by train, but soon the train broke down, forcing the soldiers to continue west in their traditional "foot cavalry" mode. They marched to Charlottesville, then south to Lynchburg. Learning of the arrival of the Confederate Second Corps, Hunter withdrew west to Salem and then further into West Virginia. The Valley was once again under Confederate control, and "old Jube" was determined to take advantage of the opportunity. He turned the Second Corps north, down the Valley, to threaten Washington. The morale of the remaining Stonewallers had to soar as they moved down the Valley Pike through Lexington, Staunton, and Winchester. Along the way, they were cheered and welcomed with water and what food the citizens could spare. On July 5, the force crossed the Potomac River at Williamsport, and many veterans were pleased to be back in Union Maryland. On July 9, the 5th Virginia Regiment and most of the remaining Stonewallers helped break the defenses around Frederick and open the way to Washington.

As General Early approached the outskirts of Washington and the Union position at Fort Stevens, he became tentative, fearing Union reinforcements had arrived to defend the city. Instead of attacking, to the dismay of the Stonewallers, Early began to withdraw his forces on July 12. Back in the Valley, his force rested until General Grant dispatched General Philip Sheridan to crush the Confederates there once and for all. During the pause, Terry's Brigade was divided into three brigades with the 2nd, 4th, 5th, 27th, and 33rd Virginia Regiments comprising the First Brigade again. Terry's entire organization was now just over 850 strong.

During the Third Battle of Winchester on September 19, Early's small force was soundly defeated by Sheridan. The Stonewallers fought well under General Terry, but were no match for the superior Union forces. Terry was seriously wounded at Winchester. General Early retreated south to Fisher's Hill, where his attempt to halt Sheridan's advance failed on September 22. He continued his retreat all the way up the Valley to the area of Port Republic, where he could escape through Brown's Gap if needed. Sheridan pursued the Confederates going as far as Staunto,n before withdrawing back down the Valley to positions south of Winchester. Instead of leaving the Valley, Early followed his enemy cautiously, and on October 19, ordered a surprise attack on Sheridan's forces encamped along Cedar Creek just north of Strasburg. The early morning attack shocked the sleeping Union forces, driving them back north. Sheridan, who had just returned from Washington, was sleeping in Winchester when he was awakened by the gunfire. Mounting his horse, he made his famous ride that turned the tide of the battle as he shouted, "Turn boys we're going back!" The counterattack routed Early's forces, many of whom had stopped to partake of the Union stores left in their captured campsites. The Second Valley Campaign was now ended. The Valley was lost for good.

The Second Corps and its few Stonewallers, who had once again fought well in the Shenandoah Valley, crossed the Blue Ridge Mountains on December 6 to join Lee's Army now at Petersburg. It had to be a difficult journey for the remaining members of the Stonewall Brigade, who had to know their final opportunity to hold the Valley was lost and their little army would probably never be able to return. From June to December, through marches and battles with Early, many a veteran was heard to say, "Oh, if we only had Jackson." General Terry would recover from his wounds and again return to command his brigade as they defended the position known as Hatcher's Run in the trenches around Petersburg. It was another very difficult winter. The Stonewallers spent more time fighting famine, disease, and cold, than they would General Grant's forces, until March 25, when they joined in the

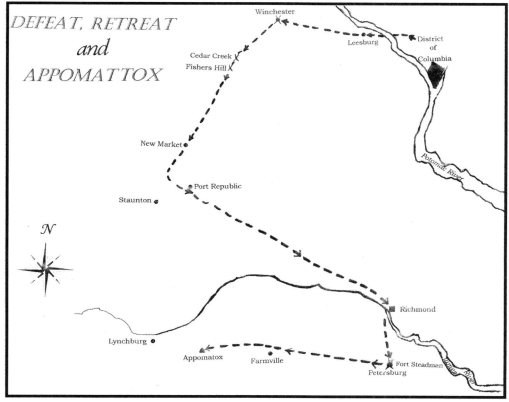

Illustration 9-17: Defeat, Retreat, and Appomattox

attack on Fort Stedman, a key position in the Union line. This, the last attack by the remnants of the Stonewall Brigade, was initially successful, but ended as fresh Union troops counterattacked, driving the Confederates back to their original positions. A week later, Grant's cavalry broke through the Confederate lines at Five Forks, forcing Lee to withdraw west, in an effort to link up with the Confederate Army still holding out in North Carolina under General Joe Johnston.

A miserable week of retreat ended near the small town of Appomattox, Virginia, where, on April 8, 1865, General Lee's remaining little army was surrounded and forced to surrender. On April 12, General John B. Gordon's Division led the Army of Northern Virginia on its last march. At its front was Colonel Terry's Brigade with his First Brigade, the units of the old Stonewall Brigade, leading the way. The weary, ragged veterans moved across the Appomattox River, carrying every emotion from anger to fear. They marched before the victorious Union Army's First Division of the V Corps. These troops stood smartly behind their Division Commander, General Joshua Chamberlain of Gettysburg's Little Round Top fame. The lines of blue snapped to attention and presented arms as the remnants of the famed Stonewall Brigade passed by. The Stonewallers halted to the left of the Union formation, faced south, and fixed bayonets before stacking their weapons. Cartridge boxes were removed and hung over the stacked arms. Colors were also stacked, but most had already been cut up and distributed to the remaining Valley soldiers, so that only the staffs were present.

On that chilly April morning, the 2nd Virginia Regiment consisted of sixty-nine soldiers; there were forty-six from the 4th Virginia, forty-seven from the 5th Virginia, thirty-three from the 27th Virginia, and only fifteen remained from the 33rd Virginia. Of the over seven thousand soldiers who had served in the five regiments during the Civil War, only 210 were present at Appomattox. Many of these were noncombatants such as doctors, litter bearers, and, of course, seven members of the Stonewall Brigade Band. The sorrow of the day began to lift as the men left Appomattox and headed for their homes and families. The war was over. The Brigade had fought the great fight, they had kept the faith, and they had earned a name that would last into infinity. Never again would they have to fight to defend their Valley, although throughout history they have continued to serve their communities and the Commonwealth of Virginia during floods, snow storms, forest fires, and other emergencies where public safety was threatened. Going forward however, their combat service would be on foreign soil as they continued to add more glory to the name "Stonewall Brigade."

The efforts of the soldiers of the Stonewall Brigade during the Civil War may best be described by one of their own, previously quoted Private John O. Casler of the 33rd Virginia Regiment, who wrote, "The laws of the human body seemed to have been reversed for these men. They fought and marched and triumphed like war machines which felt no need for rest, or food, or sleep." Some eighty years later, Lieutenant Charles R. Cawthon, who joined the Brigade just prior to World War II, may have best described its Civil War achievements in writing,

When chance threw my lot with the 116th (Infantry Regiment), I had not known that it was the direct descendant of the 2d Virginia regiment of the legendary Stonewall Brigade of the Civil War, which, until it was fought and marched into extinction, may well have been the most deadly single formation of infantry that this country—North or South—has produced.

Civil War Engagements of the Stonewall Brigade

July 2, 1861	Falling Waters	November 27, 1863	Mine Run
July 21, 1861	First Manassas		(Payne's Farm)
January, 1862	Romney Expedition	February 10, 1864	Morton's Ford
March 23, 1862	Kernstown		(skirmish)
May 9, 1862	McDowell	May 5, 1864	The Wilderness
May 25, 1862	First Winchester	May 12, 1864	Spotsylvania
June 9, 1862	Port Republic		(Bloody Angle)
June 27, 1862	Cold Harbor	May 18, 1864	Harrison
July 1, 1862	Malvern Hill		House
August 9, 1862	Cedar Mountain	May 19, 1864	Ni River
August 28, 1862	Grovetown	July 19, 1864	Monocacy
	(Brawner Farm)	August 11, 1864	Newtown
August 29-30, 1862	Second Manassas		(skirmish)
September 14, 1862	Harper's Ferry	September 19, 1864	3rd Winchester
September 17, 1862	Sharpsburg (Antietam)	September 24, 1864	Fisher's Hill
December 13-14, 1862	Fredericksburg	October 19, 1864	Cedar Creek
May 2-3, 1863	Chancellorsville	February 6, 1865	Hatcher's Run
June 14-15, 1863	Second Winchester		(Burgess Mill)
July 1-3, 1863	Gettysburg	March 25, 1865	Ft. Stedman
November 5, 1863	Bealton (skirmish)	April 9, 1865	Appomattox

Battle streamers earned: Virginia 1862, Peninsula, Cold Harbor, 2nd Manassas

Battle streamers earned: Sharpsburg, Fredericksburg, Virginia 1863, Chancellorsville, Gettysburg, Wilderness, Spotsylvania, Virginia 1864, Maryland 1864, Petersburg, Appomattox

-Ten-

Reconstruction, Reorganization, & Over There

Following the Civil War, Union troops occupied the South, and military units, even the militia, were prevented from reforming in the former Confederate states. The Army Appropriations Act, passed by the United States Congress on March 2, 1867, included a provision specifying this position. Time seems to heal all things, however, and just two years later on March 2, 1869, Congress agreed to allow militia units to be organized in the southern states except for Georgia, Mississippi, Texas, and Virginia, since their strength in these states could lead to political conflict. The military occupation of Virginia finally ended on January 31, 1870, and on July 15, Virginia was again authorized to form militia organizations. Blacks were now allowed to serve as citizen-soldiers, and the new militia would be built around volunteers. Initially, only company-sized units were organized, and on February 19, 1874, a company of volunteers was formed once again in Staunton.

Similar company-sized volunteer units began to spring up in the towns and communities throughout the Shenandoah Valley. Finally, on May 2, 1881, the Second Virginia Regiment was again formed in the Valley of Virginia, and among its ranks were found many veterans from the Civil War. Some wonderful stories were told around campfires, as the mix of veterans and young volunteers came forward to reestablish the militia tradition of service in Virginia's Valley. There were no uniforms or weapons, so the command set about to raise funds to equip their growing numbers. Initially, there was no federal funding and limited support from the state, but over time the Second Virginia began to take shape.

The citizens of the reunited nation had seen all of the war and sacrifice they wanted. There was little support for military funding, so the Second Virginia struggled to obtain modern equipment. In 1878, militia leaders from across the country gathered in Richmond, Virginia, to form a national organization. In October of 1879, the leadership of the militia held its first conference in St. Louis, Missouri, forming the National Guard Association of the United States (NGAUS) and electing Brigadier

General George W. Wingate of New York as its first president. The organization immediately focused on obtaining additional funding for militia units, and finally in 1887, the annual federal funding was increased from the $200,000 it had been receiving since 1808 to $400,000. NGAUS successfully argued that it cost only twenty-four dollars annually to fund a member of the militia, while a regular soldier cost one thousand dollars.

All militia units, including the Second Virginia Regiment, the re-emerging Stonewall Brigade, benefited from the increased funding. In 1887, the first National Encampment brought citizen soldiers from across the nation to Washington, D.C., to compete in drill competition and show their readiness. The concept of conducting summer camps grew, and in 1893 the Adjutant General of Virginia determined a permanent site for this training should be purchased. In 1904, an experiment was conducted, and Ocean View, a beach area at the entrance to Hampton Roads, was used to conduct a week of unit training. The experiment was considered so successful that in the following year every unit of the Second Virginia Regiment conducted its first week of summer training there. In 1908, $15,000 of state funding was appropriated to purchase a permanent site for a future summer training camp and rifle range. In 1910, a decision was made to purchase 350 acres of oceanfront land beyond Rudee Inlet, just south of the growing resort area of Virginia Beach. Virginia's new training site was initially known as the State Rifle Range, and building construction was completed in November, 1912.

During the military preparation for World War I, Virginia's State Rifle Range would become a federal installation, and in 1917 the name changed to the U. S. Navy Rifle Range at Virginia Beach. After the war it was returned to Virginia's control and renamed the State Military Reservation (SMR) through General Orders Number 7, issued by the Adjutant General of Virginia. In 1940, the U. S. War Department again took possession of the property, naming it Camp Pendleton, for Confederate Brigadier General William Nelson Pendleton, who commanded the Rockbridge Artillery of the Stonewall Brigade at the outbreak of the Civil War. He later rose to become Chief of Artillery for General Lee and his Army of Northern Virginia. In 1948, it again became the property of Virginia and its National Guard. Though much of the land has been turned over to the City of Virginia Beach for development, SMR still remains a training site for the Virginia National Guard. Units of the Stonewall Brigade utilize the training facilities at SMR whenever possible, but the distance to the post often makes it difficult to utilize its facilities during normal weekend training assemblies.

In 1891, the Civil War veterans of the Stonewall Brigade mustered for the last time. The site was Lexington, Virginia, and it was the thirtieth anniversary of the First Battle of Manassas, July 21, 1891. Thousands of spectators gathered to view the veterans assembling in their old faded Confederate gray uniforms. The night before the anniversary activities, the local citizens and planners of the event were in a panic when they could not locate the veterans. They seemed to have left the little town of Lexington to find accommodations elsewhere. Finally, around midnight, they were spotted, sleeping on the ground around old Jack's grave and the memorial to be dedicated the next day. Protected by only blankets, the citizens begged them to return to the homes and hospitality that had been planned for them. The answer was a firm "no." They were going to spend one last night bivouacking with the commander who had led them to so many victories and an eternal legacy. When the ceremonies concluded the next day, the veterans fell into formation for the last time and marched away. From a Rebel song:

> They will tell their children
> Though all the other memories fade,
> That they fought with Stonewall Jackson
> In the old Stonewall Brigade

When the *USS Maine* exploded in Cuba's Havana harbor on the morning of February 15, 1898, the Valley soldiers were more than ready to serve in the imminent war with Spain. Volunteers from the 2nd Virginia were mustered into federal service at Camp Lee, which had been established on the site of the Richmond fairgrounds. The Regiment left Richmond on June 2, moving to Jacksonville, Florida, where it became part of the Army's VII Corps, commanded by Major General Fitzhugh Lee. They would train at Camp Pablo Beach, Florida, located sixteen miles northeast of Jacksonville. The peace with Spain was concluded on August 12, 1898, long before the Regiment was able to be shipped overseas. They departed their campsite on September 19, returning to Richmond by train. From there they moved back to their home station armories, where they were allowed a one month furlough before finally being mustered out of service in December. The next generation of Stonewallers had been quick to volunteer, but many regretted that they never got into the shortest war in America's history.

With the approach of the twentieth century, America's military clearly needed reshaping. On August 1, 1899, Elihu Root was appointed by President William McKinley to serve as his new Secretary of War and to reform the military. His first impact was on officer education, and a school system was established beginning with basic officer training and going all the way up to an Army War College. Additionally, he worked with the National Guard Association to successfully increase the appropriations for the citizen soldiers from $400,000 to $1 million. In 1903, Congress passed the Dick Act, sponsored by Congressman Charles Dick, who was also a Major General commanding an Ohio militia division. It became law on January 21, 1903, replacing the Militia Act of 1792 and creating the modern National Guard.

The Dick Act was critical to the emergence of the National Guard in the past century. Citizen soldiers would now receive pay for their five days of summer camp. Additionally, they would be required to perform twenty-four drill periods at their home station for which they would not be paid. Federal call-ups for duty within the United States borders would be limited to nine months, and soldiers failing to respond to their nation's call would be subject to court martial. There would be organized training to include maneuvers, modern equipment, and a more formal command structure. Another provision created a Division of Military Affairs within the War Department, but the Chief of the Division and its entire staff would be chosen from the active Army. In 1916, the National Defense Act once and for all mandated that the militias would be known as the National Guard and serve as the primary reserve force for the regular Army. The number of drills was increased to forty-eight, and pay authorized for each of these periods. Additionally, the annual training period extended to fifteen days, and the National Guard was provided the opportunity to train with regular Army units. The Chief of the National Guard still had to be selected from the Army, but he could now have two citizen soldiers on his staff. These were momentous changes and helped shape the National Guard of today. From 1916 to the present, federal funding for the Guard has been greater than that provided by the states.

In 1903, units of the Stonewall Brigade were placed on state active duty and sent to Richmond in response to a debilitating street car strike there. The year 1904 found the Brigade participating in the Manassas Maneuvers, a joint exercise integrating Virginia National Guard units and regular Army units. In 1905, the Second Regiment was consolidated with the Third Regiment, which was comprised of units from central Virginia. The new organization was to become known as the 72nd Virginia Infantry. After several years, it was re-designated to its origins as the Second Virginia Regiment, but the units from areas beyond the Blue Ridge Mountains remained a part of the historic Stonewall Brigade. This brigade structure would be modified again to a regimental system, then back to brigade, and finally restructured again in 2006, when the Army's Transformation reorganized the Stonewall Brigade into its present status as an Infantry Brigade Combat Team, or IBCT. Units of the Brigade participated in the three hundredth anniversary of the landings at Jamestown in 1907 and the fiftieth anniversary of numerous civil war battles.

In 1916, the Second Virginia was part of the new Virginia National Guard and was mobilized for duty in Texas, in response to Mexican bandit Pancho Villa's raid into the New Mexico town of Columbus on March 9. Seventeen citizens were killed during this incursion across the Rio Grande River and America's southern border. Citizens were outraged, and President Woodrow Wilson, who had been born in Staunton, ordered a strong military response. The soldiers of the Second Virginia were called to duty and mustered into federal service on the fairgrounds outside Richmond on June 30, 1916. The camp was named Henry Carter Stuart in honor of Virginia's seated governor. From there the Regiment was transported to Brownsville, Texas, where they established a camp and training site. Serving in the southwestern heat was unpleasant, but the men from Virginia's Shenandoah Valley made the best of it. During the seven months of duty on the border, the Regiment saw very little action. Soon the crisis had ended, and the unit returned to Richmond where it was housed in local armories there until being mustered from active service on January 16, 1917. The soldiers were delighted to have the opportunity to return to their home, families, and jobs.

The return home lasted only a brief time, however, as the Regiment was called to active duty in April, 1917. President Wilson had won re-election for keeping America out of the war raging in Europe, but German U-boats continued to attack American shipping, and relations with Germany worsened. As events spiraled out of control he was forced to ask Congress to declare war on Germany. On April 6, both chambers overwhelmingly voted for war, and America began mobilizing an army to go "over there." The Valley citizen soldiers were about to be deployed overseas and fight on another continent for the first time. With the threat of a draft, the ranks of the National Guard filled up quickly with volunteers. Initially, the units trained at their home armories and provided local security, protecting railroads and other infrastructure within the Commonwealth from any possible sabotage. In August, the Regiment boarded trains and moved south to Anniston, Alabama, and a new installation there, Camp McClellan, being constructed to accommodate the large numbers of soldiers needing to be trained for combat. Learning individual skills was their first task: weapons qualification, bayonet drills, wearing a gas mask, marching and field craft. Those first weeks at Camp McClellan could be compared with what would later become known as "basic training." Additionally, discipline had to be instilled and leaders trained.

October 4, 1917, was a momentous day as the Stonewallers were given a new unit designation. They were now part of the new 116th Infantry Regiment, of the 58th Brigade, of the newly formed 29th Division, a force comprised of all three of Virginia's existing Infantry Regiments, the 1st, 2nd, and 4th Virginia. The new organization came primarily from the following communities:

Regimental HQS	Staunton, Richmond, Charlottesville, Alexandria
Company A	Alexandria, Richmond, Staunton
Company B	Richmond
Company C	Richmond, Charlottesville, Danville
Company D	Warrenton, Staunton, Front Royal
Company E	Richmond, Alexandria
Company F	Chase City, Richmond, Suffolk
Company G	Richmond, Staunton, Farmville
Company H	Charlottesville, Covington
Company I	Culpeper, Winchester
Company K	Lynchburg, Covington, Fredericksburg, Norfolk
Company L	Lynchburg, Alexandria, Staunton, Norfolk
Company M	Lynchburg, Radford
Supply Company	Staunton, Cape Charles, Norfolk, Roanoke
MG Company	Staunton, Cape Charles
Sanitation Det.	Richmond, Staunton

In preparing the Army for the challenging combat ahead, General John J. "Black-jack" Pershing determined he needed larger, more lethal divisions than those previously organized. They were to be known as "square" divisions, since each would consist of two large infantry brigades consisting of two regiments each. In addition, each division would have two artillery regiments and an engineer regiment. The end strength would be a whopping 28,061 soldiers. Divisions would be numbered with numbers 1 through 25 being assigned to regular Army units, 26-75 to be for National Guard units, and those above 75 organized for volunteers and draftees. The entire United States Army was undergoing change as it prepared to become the American Expeditionary Forces, or AEF, and the National Guard was included.

The new 29th Division would have two infantry brigades, the 57th from New Jersey with the 113th and 114th regiments, and the 58th from Maryland with the 115th from Maryland, and 116th from Virginia. The 54th Artillery Brigade was from Virginia and consisted of the 110th Artillery Regiment from Maryland and the 111th Artillery Regiment from Virginia. Combining the former Civil War foes from the north and south drew considerable speculation concerning how well the two groups could perform together. The resulting name for the new formation was the Blue and Gray Division, and its patch, the first divisional insignia officially registered with the Ad-

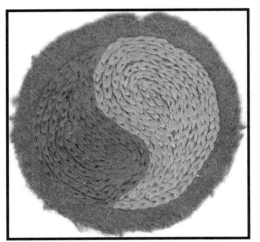

10-1: Original stitched 29th patch

jutant General of the Army, took the shape of the Korean "symbol of life," the yin and the yang. The patch design suggested by Division Adjutant Major James Ulio was to be worn on the left shoulder and would be half blue and half gray, blending the two Civil War adversaries into one cohesive fighting unit.

Reorganization complete, the new 116th Infantry Regiment focused on its training and preparation for deployment to France. In mid-October, 1917, British and French officers arrived at Camp McClellan to begin the specialty training the 29th Division would need for its upcoming deployment. The concept of "trench warfare" must have reminded the descendents of the Stonewall Brigade of the days they had heard about from their predecessors, who had survived the hardships of Petersburg in 1864-65.

The most frightening and newest weapon, poisonous gas, was unsettling to all of the soldiers being trained. Life or death could be determined in only a matter of moments, and life depended on how fast the men could put on their gas masks. During a gas attack, there would be two types of soldiers, the quick and the dead. Tanks, trucks, biplanes, a new and more destructive war lay ahead, but soldiers still had to know how to put gas masks on their horses. Several canteens and post exchanges were constructed at Camp McClellan to provide the soldiers with some diversion from the day-to-day training routine. Occasionally passes were distributed, and the men had the opportunity to go into the nearby small town of Anniston. Many used the opportunity to attend church or just relax away from the confines of camp life.

The Regular Army, in taking control of the 29th Division and thus the 116th, shuffled its senior leadership, sending many of the commanders home. This was not the first, nor would it be the last time, that the Army would place its officers in the ranking positions of National Guard units. In *A Brief History of the Militia and the National Guard*, Robert K. Wright, Jr. indicates "Much of the Regular Army hierarchy had nothing but contempt for militia officers, and many higher-ranking Guardsmen at regimental, brigade, and division level were relieved." This had occurred to the leadership of the Augusta Militia under the British during the Indian Wars, to the Regimental leadership arriving to serve with General Jackson at Harpers Ferry at the outbreak of the

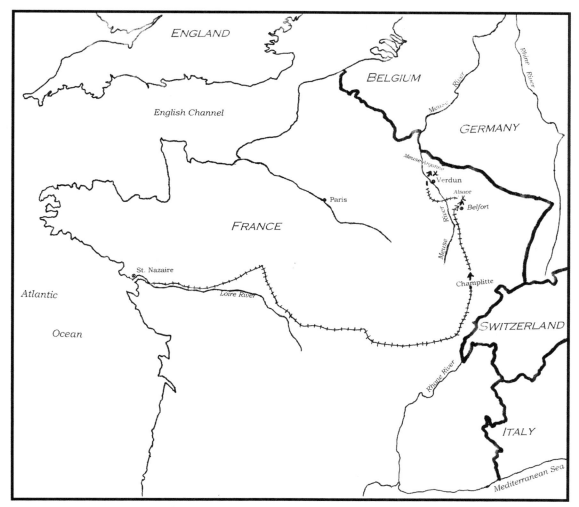

Illustration 10-2: Route to the Front

Civil War, and now during the preparation of the 116th Infantry Regiment for overseas deployment in the Great War. "They want the Joes (soldiers), but not the Os (officers)" was heard as senior leaders were found unfit for duty and sent home. This would occur again during the mobilizations for World War II. As has always been the case, the citizen soldiers would respond professionally and accept their new leaders.

Orders for overseas duty were issued on May 25, 1918. On June 11, the soldiers of the 116th Regiment boarded trains and moved north through Cleveland, Tennessee, and into Bristol, then to Lynchburg, Washington, D.C., and Philadelphia. It was a long ride to their port of embarkation at Hoboken, New Jersey, in the port of New York. The Stonewallers boarded the *USS Finland* on June 15, landing at St. Nazaire, France, in the Bay of Biscay and at the mouth of the Loire River on the 27th, after the thirteen-day Atlantic crossing. The *Finland* was part of the thirteen ship convoy which brought the entire 29th Division through U-boat infested waters to its first entrance into Europe. The Stonewallers' next landings on the coast of France, less than twenty-seven years later, would not go as easily. Disembarking, the units formed up and moved to their temporary camp and three days later on to Argillieres. They headed to other sites further east near the Swiss border and continued preparing to go into the trenches. On August 28, they were moved to the front lines going into the defenses of Haute Marne Sector in Alsace, as part of General "Blackjack" Pershing's First United States Army. They found themselves in the southern-most point of the allied lines. Action was quick in coming as the 116th was attacked on August 26, in an obvious test of the new American troops. The attack was repelled, and the Stonewallers became the first unit of the 29th Division to face combat in the Great War. They stopped an enemy advance, inflicting heavy casualties on the German army. During the next month they became acclimated to trench warfare, splitting their time between the trenches and billets to the rear. For their service there, the 116th would earn the Alsace Campaign streamer.

In early October, the 29th Division became part of the French Army preparing to take to the offensive along the Meuse River. The 116th Regiment joined the French 18th Division and on October 8, at five a.m. went "over the top" to attack the strong German positions on the Marne heights. During the attack, SGT Earle Gregory of Headquarters Company earned the Medal of Honor, the first ever given to a Stonewaller. His medal citation would read

For conspicuous gallantry and intrepidity above and beyond the call of duty in action with the enemy at Bois de Consenvoye, north of Verdun, France October 8, 1918. With the remark, "I will get them," Sergeant Gregory seized a rifle and a trench mortar shell, which he used as a hand grenade, left his detachment of the trench mortar platoon, and advancing ahead of the infantry, captured a machine gun and three of the enemy. Advancing still farther from the machine-gun nest, he captured a 7.5 centimeter mountain howitzer, and, entering a dugout in the immediate vicinity, single-handed captured nineteen of the enemy.

Illustration 10-3: Alsace Map

Later wounded, he would survive the war and return to his home in Chase City, Virginia.

The 116th's attack had been a success, and during the night the soldiers consolidated their positions and awaited the German counter attack. Their position was bombarded throughout the night, and in the morning fog of the next day, they encountered a vicious German attack. In close fighting, the "Huns" were defeated and forced to withdraw. The 116th again took to the offensive. Despite heavy casualties, during the next three weeks, the Stonewallers would continue pushing the Germans back some five miles in places.

In *The Long Line of Splendor*, John W. Schildt summarizes that "During those October days of 1918" the 116th "exhibited the courage of their ancestors on the frontier, against the British, and on the plains of Manassas." Clearly their efforts contributed to the German surrender and earned them their regimental motto, "Ever Forward!" Throughout World War I, the 116th steadily advanced against the German defenses, despite galling direct and indirect fire, gas attacks, and restrictive terrain. They never gave any ground, but steadily advanced, driving the German invaders to the northeast from whence they had come four years earlier. Their movement under fire caused some observers to say "they moved as if they were on maneuvers." In addition to earning their motto during this offensive action, the regiment would receive the Meuse-Argonne Campaign streamer for their colors.

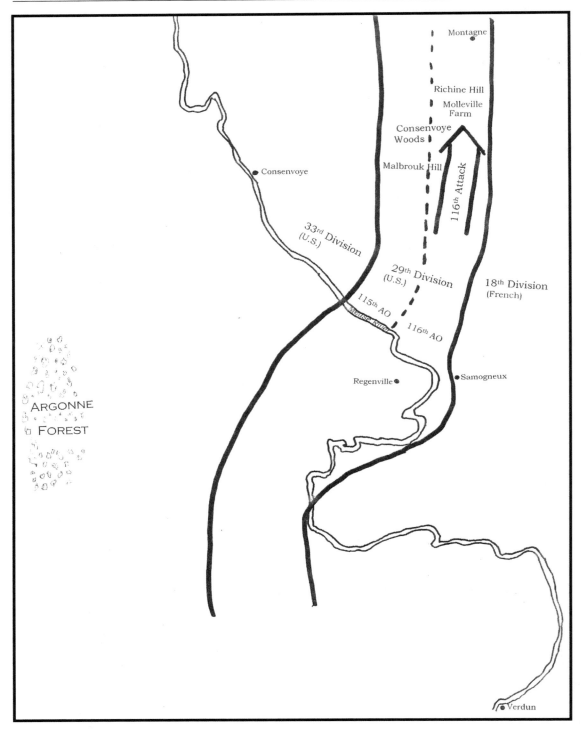

Illustration 10-4: Meuse-Argonne Map

The Great War, the war to end all wars, was finally over. On the eleventh day, of the eleventh month, and at the eleventh hour, an armistice took effect. It would be a costly victory for the Americans who suffered some 100,000 casualties. The 116th would suffer almost 1,300 losses, with 188 killed, and eight hundred wounded, and over three hundred suffering from the consequences of gas attacks. The Regiment would remain in France for almost six more months before beginning its journey home. On Christmas Day, 1918, M Company was reviewed by President Woodrow Wilson as part of the American Expeditionary Force. It was the first time a United States President would review American troops on foreign soil. On March 24, 1919, the 29th Division was reviewed by General Pershing who, following the ceremony, presented individual and unit awards earned during the war. The 116th Regiment had the lone honor of representing all the forces of the AEF and was reviewed by Field Marshall Sir Douglas Haig, the Commander-in-Chief of the British Army on April 4. Clearly the Stonewallers were recognized as one of the most outstanding units of the American Expeditionary Force.

On April 2, 1919, the 116th moved by truck to Jussey, then by train to Beaumont, marching the distance to Braults in the Le Mans area before embarking on their journey home from St. Nazaire on May 10, 1919. They sailed on the *USS Matsonia*, reaching Newport News, Virginia, on May 20, in just ten days. It had to be great to be back in the Commonwealth. Gone "over there" for just less than a year, they had helped turn the tide in the war to end all wars. Leaving the ship, they moved to Camp Lee, Virginia, outside Petersburg, demobilized on May 30, 1919, and returned to their home armories and families.

10-5: Regimental Crest

The Regimental Crest of the 116th grew out of the reorganization for World War I. It is comprised of the shield and motto of the coat of arms. The *Shield* consists of Gules, a saltire argent voided throughout per saltire gray and azure per cross counterchanged; in chief a fleur-de-lis or. It is red with the familiar saltire cross, with blue and gray edged in white reflecting the Civil War service. The chief is a single gold fleur-de-lis, to recall the World War I service in France. The *Motto* of the 116th, "Ever Forward," is displayed on the bottom of the crest. This crest has been proudly worn by Stonewallers since it was introduced and officially approved by the Department of the Army.

The Seal of Virginia, similar to the regimental crests of the Virginia National Guard

10-6: Seal of Virginia

of the period, reveals a wreath of colors (argent and gules) Virtus, the genius of the Commonwealth, dressed in Amazon, resting on a spear with one hand and holding a sword in the other, and treading on Tyranny, represented by a man prostrate, a crown falling from his head, a broken chain in his left hand and a scourge in his right, all proper. The Latin words *Sic Semper Tyrannis* mean "Thus always to tyrants."

On the April 20, General Orders No. 13 dissolved the 29th Division of the American Expeditionary Force. The 116th Regiment briefly ceased to exist and was again known as Virginia's 2nd Regiment. This change was a result of the National Defense Act of 1916, which provided that the National Guard units would be disbanded when called into Federal service and then reverted back to Guard status after demobilization. The 116th was a designation of the regular Army, while the 2nd Regiment provided a Virginia identity. This problem was remedied by the National Defense Act of 1920. In *I am the Guard*, published in 2001, Michael D. Doubler reveals,

> The National Defense Act authorized the postwar organization of the National Guard, designated the Guard as the primary Federal reserve force and set its strength at a maximum of 435,000 soldiers. The organized Reserves would provide a pool of officers in wartime and man nine Reserve Divisions to absorb and train conscripts during national emergencies.

In addition, the Act provided that the Chief of the National Guard Bureau would come from the ranks of the citizen soldiers, be appointed by the President of the United States, and serve a four-year term. In addition, it increased the number of positions in the Bureau which would be filled by the Guard.

On March 9, 1922, as a result of the National Defense Act of 1920, the Stonewall Brigade was again designated under the regular Army system as the 116th Infantry. The site of the headquarters would be in Staunton. In 1933, Congress would again amend the National Defense Act to clarify the role of the National Guard. First, the

Act created a new component of the Army, the National Guard of the United States. This would allow the Guard to be called to active duty without having to be drafted, which had been the case in 1917. The citizen soldiers would still retain their ability to respond to emergencies within their state as their governor might deem necessary. Dr. Samuel J. Newland, a professor at the United State Army War College in Carlisle, Pennsylvania, summarized the end result of the National Defense Act and its amendments,

> Thus, today every Guardsman is both a member of the Army's reserve and of his/her state militia. The Guard can be called to service as militia, through the Militia clause, or ordered to active duty as part of the Army's reserve.

The status of the citizen soldier had come a long way.

Battle streamers earned: Alsace - 1918, Meuse-Argonne

Eleven

Great Depression
& War Again

D uring the twenty-three years following the Great War, America would go
through some of the "best of times" and then "the worst of times" as the
Great Depression set in from 1929 until World War II. Throughout this difficult period, however, the 116th Infantry continued to play an important role in its
communities. The local armory became the place for social gatherings, dances, and
other events which were provided free of charge. It assisted with the growing number of homeless and worked with the Salvation Army to help as many of the suffering Americans as possible. The National Guard has always brought stability to
America's communities during difficult and challenging times. It responded quickly
to natural disasters and emergencies, and firmly to areas where labor strikes threatened public safety. As had been the case since 1742, whether called the Augusta
Militia, the Stonewall Brigade, the 2nd Regiment, the 116th Infantry, or simply citizen
soldiers, the National Guard in western Virginia was always ready, always there.

The Great Depression was also very difficult for the citizen-soldiers. Many lost
their jobs and even their homes. Still, they loved their military duty, and volunteers
continued to fill the ranks. Military pay helped recruiting, as soldiers would receive
about a dollar for their drills, normally held one evening a week, and summer camp
meant almost another twenty dollars for a private. It may not sound like much, but
in many cases those dollars meant the difference between eating or going without
food for days at a time. The men complained only slightly as federal funds were
reduced in 1933, and they would only be paid for thirty-six of the forty-eight drills
they were required to attend. There were appropriations for new agencies to provide
jobs, such as the Civilian Conservation Corps or CCC. Their creation resulted in the
construction of several new armories, to include Lynchburg where the Headquarters
of the 116th was moved in 1933. The Virginia Adjutant General's newsletter, *The Virginia Guardsman* which was started in 1920, changed its format during the depression to be more of a newspaper with photographs and stories to boost morale.

In the fall of 1930, as a direct result of the Great Depression, a crisis began to
emerge at the Dan River Cotton Mills located in Danville, Virginia. Half of the 4,500

workers at the plant had been laid off by early November, resulting in unrest in the town and surrounding communities. A union was formed and many of the remaining workers left the job in protest of the layoffs and lower wages being forced upon them. It was the union's hope that this action would force Dan River Cotton Mills to reconsider its employee and wage reductions. Instead, the mill responded by hiring replacement workers, further inflaming the situation. National Guard Historian John Listman noted in his article entitled, "Guardsmen keep peace during strike," found in the Spring 1996 edition of the *Virginia GuardPost*, "The city of Danville and the sheriff's office of Pittsylvania County combined employed only about 25 men, far too few to control any riotous behavior." He went on to note, "The Virginia State Police as we know it today did not exist."

For the first 350 years of its existence, the Commonwealth of Virginia had only its militia/National Guard to protect lives and property during a major crisis. The role of the Virginia State Police would emerge to its current status as the popularity of the automobile grew and roads improved. As conditions in Danville worsened, Virginia's Governor John Pollard alerted the 116th Infantry Regiment for possible mobilization to provide "Aid To Civil Authorities." Colonel Hierome Opie of Staunton, commanding the 116th, quietly notified his subordinate commanders to prepare to be called up. On November 26, threats against nonunion workers escalated to the bombing of several homes of these employees. Although fortunately no one was hurt, the situation was clearly getting worse, and the community officials requested Governor Pollard to call out the Guard. Using the authority of Article V, Section 4 of the Military Code of Virginia, the governor ordered Colonel Opie to mobilize the 116th Regiment and move to Danville immediately. Transportation was a major problem since the 116th only had seven trucks in the command. Additional trucks were sent from Richmond, and some of the officers and NCOs utilized their personal vehicles for the move. Despite the challenges, almost the entire regiment, 887 Stonewallers, arrived that evening. Housing and rations would also soon become quite a challenge.

Checkpoints were set up, and motor and foot patrolling begun. In addition, key parts of the local infrastructure, particularly bridges and intersections, were guarded. The normal duty day was four hours on, followed by eight off, then another four on. The winter conditions made the soldier's life unpleasant since he had only two uniforms and limited winter clothing. Discipline, for the most part, was good, despite some excessive drinking, gambling, and fighting - the usual soldier issues. There were very few confrontations with the strikers since the soldierly presence of the Stonewallers created the overpowering impact Governor Pollard had hoped it would. The daily routine and duty were boring, but the 116th was successful in restoring peace and calm to Danville and the surrounding Pittsylvania County. As Christmas approached, Colonel Opie reduced his force to just over four hundred, allowing many soldiers to return home to their families. The remaining men enjoyed the traditional Christmas dinner and the opportunity to call home.

As January and the snowy winter dragged on, the union strikers became more desperate as their money began running out. Acts of violence increased, but negotiations began in earnest as the 116th's tour of duty began winding down. The Military Code of Virginia restricted state duty to a maximum of sixty days, so on January 23, the regiment turned the mission over to the 246th Coast Artillery and headed home. Fortunately, before the Stonewallers had settled back into civilian life, Dan River Cotton Mills and the strikers reached a settlement on February 7, ending the largest and longest state duty call up of the 116th Regiment during the twentieth century. Back in their homes and communities, the men resumed their own fight for survival during the difficult Thirties. Few realized that they were enjoying a time of peace but preparing for a future federal activation and a date with destiny.

As the outbreak of war in Europe approached, and the end of the Great Depression was in sight, positive changes began to occur for the soldiers of the 116th Infantry. Full drill pay was back by 1937, plus soon President Franklin D. Roosevelt would see that each citizen soldier got an additional twelve drills and another week of summer camp. America was beginning to ready itself for the reality of another war. The 1903 Springfield rifles that the soldiers had been training with since their return from France were gradually replaced by the new M-1 rifle. Training intensified and in August, 1939, the 116th Infantry participated in First Army maneuvers conducted near Manassas, Virginia. Training on the historic Civil War battleground made for interesting stories around the campfires of this new generation of Stonewallers. It had been almost eighty years since the 116th had earned its designation as the Stonewall Brigade on Henry House Hill nearby. There was lots of lore to be recalled as the unit again camped and maneuvered on this historic ground.

Only a few weeks had passed since the maneuvers at Manassas when Adolf Hitler triggered the German invasion on Poland on September 1, 1939. Two days later, Britain and France responded by declaring war on Germany. The Great War would hereafter be known as World War I, as a second world war began taking shape. Following seven months of inactivity in what was called the "phoney war," a German offensive, known as the Blitzkrieg, starting on May 10, drove the forces of Britain, France, Belgium, the Netherlands, and Poland west to the French coast. Here they consolidated in an area known as the Dunkirk Pocket, where their evacuation across the Channel to England began on May 27. By June, 338,226 soldiers had been evacuated, leaving behind their wounded comrades and thousands of weapons and pieces of equipment. On June 24, 1940, Hitler announced that "the war in the West was won." The defeat of the British and French would embolden the Japanese to continue their expansion across China and into Indochina. Hitler moved now to support his ally, Italy, in its occupation of North Africa, spreading the horrors of war to a third continent.

President Roosevelt had pledged to keep American out of the growing war, but began to prepare for the reality that diplomacy might fail. Additional training for National Guard units was authorized and in August, 1940, Major General

Milton Reckord, commanding the 29th Division, led the members of the 116th Infantry and Maryland's 115th to a summer encampment at Camp Drum, New York. Special trains were sent to transport the majority of the soldiers. Many, however, had to move by truck, and convoys clogged the roads as vehicles transporting men and equipment moved north down the Shenandoah Valley, along the similar route followed today by Interstate 81. It took them across Pennsylvania and into western New York for their final summer camp before being called to active duty. The cooler climate of this area, just south of the Canadian border, provided some relief from the summer heat during the three-week training period.

The success of recruiting in the National Guard has always been the unit members talking their friends into joining. Ralph Coffman remembered clearly how his

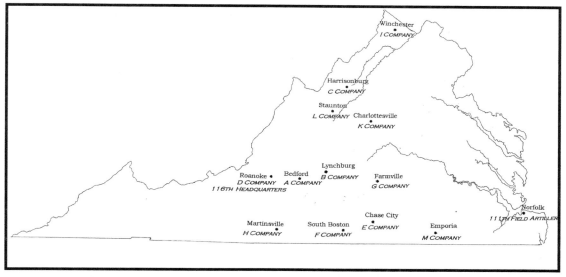

Illustration 11-1: 116th Infantry Regiment Company locations

co-worker at the DuPont Factory in Waynesboro, Virginia, encouraged him to join the local unit in Staunton. He recalled how Woodrow Ashby had approached him one day saying, "you better come on up to the armory tonight and sign up in Company L, 116th Infantry, 29th Division as we are taking in some new ones tonight." With a military draft looming in preparation for war, Ashby closed the deal with "You will also be with the home town boys that you know." The appeal of serving with neighbors and friends had been the hallmark of the Valley units for almost two hundred years, and it certainly made sense to the soon-to-be Private Coffman. In this way the National Guardsmen have always been successful in its recruiting, first to defend their communities, then their state, and their emerging nation. There has always existed a bond in National Guard units, a cohesiveness that can be matched by very few other military organizations in history.

On September 16, 1940, Congress adopted the Selective Service Act, and all men age twenty-one to twenty-six were now required to register for military training. This action instantly improved recruiting for the National Guard and by year's end; the 116th Infantry was near one hundred percent strength. One of the provisions of the new Selective Service Act directed that National Guard units be called up for one year to receive additional training. By October, it was clear the 116th would be called to active duty in early 1941. The first notice set the call-up date as January 15, but labor strikes delayed the construction of the proposed mobilization site at Fort Meade, just south of Baltimore, Maryland. Although the date slipped by several weeks, finally the Stonewallers, along with the rest of the units of the 29th Division, got the word to report to their local armories on February 3, 1941. The communities of the Shenandoah Valley buzzed with excitement as the soldiers mustered at their facilities in a tradition going back almost two hundred years. The order to "fall in" was followed by roll call and inspections. Some things never change.

In Staunton, the local unit assembled at its armory. Many had cars and were able to slip home at night; for most, however, a cot on the armory drill floor would be their bed. The soldiers trained in the nearby Gypsy Hill Park and occasionally marched up the hill to the Staunton Military Academy to take advantage of the facilities there. It was there that a teacher, Thomas D. Howie, also a member of the 116th, provided the best instruction the soldiers remembered receiving. They recognized immediately that Lieutenant Howie was a great leader who took care of his men. Meals were taken at local restaurants, and the town provided numerous evening activities for the Guardsmen, including parties and dances. On one of their last nights before leaving home, a dance was held at the Stonewall Jackson Hotel, and the men enjoyed the company of the local young ladies before departing. This hotel has been recently renovated and now hosts the annual Muster of the 116th each year on Veteran's Day Weekend. Since its origin, this dinner has honored the veterans of the Stonewall Brigade and their spouses.

Over the Blue Ridge Mountains to the east in Charlottesville, Virginia, K Company of the 116th assembled for its year on active duty. Following the Revolutionary War, Thomas Jefferson invited the Marquis de Lafayette to visit him at his home at Monticello just outside the town. Jefferson asked the local militia unit, now K Company of the 116th, to assemble on the grounds of Monticello to honor the young French general. Upon seeing the unit in formation, Lafayette called them the "Monticello Guard," a name that they still carry today. Among those assembling at the downtown armory on February 3, 1941, was Sergeant Frank Peregoy. Only fifteen years old when he joined K Company in 1931 (he had lied about his age), Frank had grown up in difficult times and had responded with a toughness that quickly gained him respect among the members of the Charlottesville National Guard unit. His sister Daisy remembered "Those were hard years, but we lived on our garden crops, and we raised bees so we had honey. We'd sell the honey for 15 cents a pint and berries we'd pick for 10 cents a gallon." Frank was destined to be a leader and add to the legacy of the Monticello Guard.

In Bedford, Virginia, just a short distance east of Roanoke, A Company formed up with six officers and ninety-two enlisted soldiers reporting. It was Monday, February 3, and the "Bedford Boys" were being inducted into federal service. The town and surrounding area were excited and assembled along with veterans of the Great War to show support for their home unit. Meals were a problem, so the men were dismissed each night to go home for supper. Occasionally some local moonshine was made available to lift morale. When A Company's departure for Fort Meade was set for February 18, the town arranged for a dance at the Bedford High School to honor the unit. Led by the Fireman's Band, the Bedford Boys marched to the local high school for an evening of dancing and socializing on February 17. The next day, the company assembled at the local station and boarded the train, as the Fireman's Band played and the community cheered. The Bedford Boys were on their way to join the rest of the 116th at Fort Meade.

While at their home station armories, all of the units of the 116th were issued new woolen uniforms which arrived just in time to help offset the cold winter weather. Physicals were conducted, along with classes on military courtesy, weapons cleaning, and basic maneuvering. Physical training, known as calisthenics then, marching, and close order drill filled the daily armory routine. Families and local politicians came to visit, and the communities reached out to do what they could for the soldiers. Charles R. Cawthon recounted in his book, *Other Clay*, how one night ladies of a local church provided his H Company in Martinsville, Virginia, with a splendid dinner in return for the soldiers singing "God Bless America," which he said "we did in a heavy rumble." The long days at the armory were soon over, however, and the soldiers bid goodbye to their families. The pain of departure was lessened somewhat by the slogan, "so long dear, I'll be back in a year!"

The commander of the 116th was Colonel E. Walton Opie who was from Staunton where he published the local newspaper along with his brother, the former 116th Commander, now Brigadier General (Retired) Hierome Opie of World War I fame. The departure of the Brigade began on February 13, with the trucks and equipment moving north. Many soldiers would move by train, and some with rank would be permitted to drive their own cars to Fort Meade. Their vehicles and large equipment already gone, Company L in Staunton moved to the C&O train station on February 20, carrying only their packs and individual weapons. The town turned out in great numbers to see their sons, friends, and co-workers off for a year of training. The train station area remains pretty much the same today, housing several excellent restaurants and providing a boarding area for the Amtrak passenger train that still stops there.

Arriving at Fort Meade, the soldiers of the 116th found conditions there to be similar to what their predecessors had found at Camp McClellan, Alabama, in 1917.

Some of the current soldiers were veterans of the Great War and remembered only too well the new facilities they occupied there. The installation was still being constructed as the troops arrived. One of the first tasks was to remove the scrap pieces of lumber from the new barracks and sweep the sawdust from the floors. Again, the Army was creating itself as it was mobilizing. The days there were spent drawing equipment and conducting basic maneuver training. The last blast of winter left knee deep snow which turned to mud as the weather warmed. Nights were spent in the barracks, singing songs and sharing thoughts of home. Each unit now had its own cooks, and there was stiff competition between the companies for who had the best mess (food service facility). One of the many additional duties involved fire watch detail and responsibility for keeping the furnaces burning throughout the night. Some of the unit members had cars, so occasional trips to Baltimore and Washington, D.C., helped to ease the boredom after long days of training. Weekend passes allowed six or seven men to pack into a car and head for home for a short visit. In March, young men being inducted into the Army began pouring into Fort Meade to begin their thirteen-weeks of mobilization training, before joining the ranks of the 29th Division units now on active duty.

Coming from the Shenandoah Valley and the Piedmont region of Virginia, most of the members of the 116th grew up in a rural environment, and hunting was often a part of daily life, especially during the Great Depression. For this reason, marksmanship was one of the strong suits of a Stonewaller. They loved their new M-1 Rifles and had no problem emptying the eight-shot clip in a minute. Rapid firing was new and a lot of fun. Bayonet training was also a new adventure, and it took some work to get the men to understand how to thrust and recover. They were great on moving quietly in the woods and navigating at night. A lot of the training at Fort Meade was second nature to the original Stonewallers going on active duty in February, 1941, but it was often challenging to the new recruits joining the 116th Stonewall Brigade. It would seem that little had changed from the early days of mobilizations going back to the days of the Indian Wars.

With warmer weather came the 116th's first opportunity to leave Fort Meade. In late June they were moved south to Camp A. P. Hill to conduct field training. They were able to cross the Potomac River utilizing a newly completed bridge connecting southern Maryland to Virginia. Tents were erected, with the men sleeping six to a shelter. The Stonewallers were very much at home operating in the large training areas of Camp Hill and the familiar pine forests there. Mosquitoes and chiggers were everywhere, and the summer heat kept the soldiers looking for shade during every ten-minute break they were afforded. The field training in their beloved Commonwealth of Virginia lasted only ten days before the Stonewallers returned to their barracks at Fort Meade.

July brought the unsettling news that President Roosevelt was proposing a six-month extension for the National Guard units and draftees. He considered the country to be facing a national emergency, and much to the dismay of the Stonewallers, the House of Representatives passed the Service Extension Act by one vote. The biggest issue they had faced during the last five months was boredom, and now they found they might have to face another year of the inactivity of camp life. There were just so many times you could clean your weapon or go out on Reconnaissance, Observation, Operation, and Position exercises (ROOPs), without wondering why. Rarely did anyone explain to the soldiers why they were doing something; they were simply told to do it even if it made no sense to them. Opportunities for leave were rare, and the short weekend passes failed to satisfy the need to see home and family. Active duty training seemed to be a terrible waste of a soldier's time, and morale reached an all-time low in the summer heat.

In September, the 116th again moved to Camp A. P. Hill, this time for two weeks of training before heading further south to neighboring North Carolina. The 29th Division would be participating in First Army exercises along with the 26th National Guard Division from Massachusetts and the 28th National Guard Division from Pennsylvania. The roads south were choked with rolling military stock as the thousands of soldiers descended to their camp sites at what is now Fort Bragg, North Carolina, on September 27. From here they would conduct force-on-force maneuvers in the recently picked cotton fields along the border between North and South Carolina. They would live in tents and be constantly moving in what was to become known as the First Carolina Maneuvers. This was the first extensive field exercise, and for the next two months, the Blue Army Corps, wearing their Olive Drab (OD) uniforms, would be pitted against the Red Army Corps, wearing the lighter weight blue denim uniform. The 29th Division was part of the Fredendall Second Blue Corps, named for Major General Lloyd R. Fredendall, its commander. The maneuvers were war games, and nights were filled in the various camps with tales of who had been shot and who had been captured.

There was a severe shortage of equipment throughout the 116th's first nine months of active duty training. Mortars were very scarce and antitank weapons were unavailable. The soldiers cut up stove pipes to simulate the crew served weapons which they were missing, such as bazookas and mortars. They used their initiative to create other pieces of dummy equipment to substitute for the real thing they had not been issued. Trucks with signs on their side with the word "tank" on them denoted the vast shortage of armor in these units training for war. The soldiers would mount vehicles and move down the dirt roads, dismount and take positions briefly before they were recalled to mount up and do it all again. The First Carolina Maneuvers left a great deal to be desired.

A number of issues arose which distracted from the tactical effectiveness of the Carolina Maneuvers. As the units moved across the Carolinas, they were followed closely by local vendors, offering everything from ice cream and cold drinks to tobacco. The prices were ridiculous, but in most cases the men were more than willing to pay, in order to have some of the pleasures of civilian life. Additionally, the closeness to home often brought family and friends to visit. America was on wheels now, and the trip from Virginia was very do-able, but often served to distract the attention of the soldiers. Prostitutes were also known to frequent the camps at night. As the exercises moved across the dusty open ground of the Carolinas, it was impossible for commanders to control the civilian presence and keep the soldiers focused totally on the war games.

Finally, the cold of the oncoming winter ended the maneuvers and the 116th headed back to better conditions at Meade in late November. Rumors spread that the 29th Division was considered trained and ready, and would now be demobilized. Morale soared as the thought of being home for Christmas replaced the boredom and frustration. The 116th halted at South Hill, Virginia, just south of Richmond to rest before completing the final leg of its return trip to Fort Meade. There were only fifteen shopping days left before Christmas as the soldiers turned on their radios on the evening of December 7, 1941, and learned the news of the Japanese attack on Pearl Harbor. The initial shock and disappointment turned to anger as the news of the destruction of the Navy's Pacific fleet began to sink in on the Stonewallers. A "sneak attack, a lousy, rotten sneak attack." The 116th was fighting mad; "they were fighting mad!" They continued on to their quarters at Fort Meade and, despite the war, most were still allowed to enjoy a Christmas furlough back at their homes.

In a very short time, orders came extending active duty service and assigning the 116th to patrolling the shores of the east coast from Atlantic City, New Jersey, to the Outer Banks of North Carolina. During this duty, Corporal Frank Peregoy of K Company became an early wartime hero.

The incident is described best by an article in the December, 1999 issue of the magazine *Albemarle*.

> On Sunday, January 11, 1942—thirty-five days after Pearl Harbor—Frank Peregoy became the 29th Division's first wartime hero. Early that frost-bitten morning, elements of the 116th Infantry were patrolling the North Carolina coast, close to New Bern, when a Company K weapons carrier slid on an icy road and nose-dived into the deep waters of an adjacent canal. Most of the men swam out but a quick roll-call revealed that Private Stanley P. Major was missing. (Evidently, a strap from his backpack was caught on the truck.)
>
> Without a thought, Peregoy dove back into the frigid water, an army knife clutched between his teeth Tarzan-style. Slicing his way through the vehicle's tarpaulin cover Frank swam down into the back of the truck and cut the unfortunate private loose. When he pushed the lifeless body back up through the hole other men from Company K grabbed it and pulled it ashore. Thankfully, although Major had lost consciousness, he was revived several hours later, back in camp.

For his courage Corporal Peregoy would be awarded America's highest non-combat award, the Soldier's Medal.

The winter cold and tent living made it difficult for the soldiers of the 116th as they performed coastal defense duty. A normal day consisted of sentry duty along a six mile stretch of beach. As part of their training, some of the units of the 116th were pitted against units of the 1st Division that were learning to conduct amphibious landings on the beaches at Cape Henry near Virginia Beach. The anti-invasion exercises of January 12-14 saw the 116th repel the landings attempted by the 1st Division. The cold winter weather was difficult for the soldiers on both sides, but especially hard for the men of the Big Red One, who were soaked by icy ocean water as they attempted to come ashore. This was the most exciting part of the coastal duty that lasted for about another month, before the units were again assembled at Fort Meade. The soldiers were glad to get out of the temporary pup tents they had been using for protection against the cold coastal winter and back to the warmth of their barracks and regular showers again.

Now a change could be seen in the men of the 116th and the entire 29th Division. It was no longer business as usual; the country was at war. The men began to take pride in the wearing of their uniforms, even after duty hours and while on pass. They were becoming tougher and beginning to prepare for what lay ahead. Air raid drills became a part of the daily routine, and at night, Fort Meade began blackout exercises. Learning from the tragedy at Pearl Harbor, vehicles were dispersed rather than parked in straight lines, and drivers were prepared to move the vehicles away from the installation at the first sign of an air raid. Again, America was at war.

The stay at Fort Meade was brief, however, and soon there was more coastal defense duty beginning in February, this time on the Eastern Shore of Maryland and Virginia. Assignments were being made by the Headquarters Chesapeake Bay Frontier Defense Command located at Fort Monroe. The men patrolled around the clock, armed with their loaded M-1s and prepared to repel any landing attempts. Whenever possible, the patrols were motorized. The soldiers were warned to be on the lookout for German spies attempting to infiltrate the east coast. Following duty on the Eastern Shore, the 116th was assigned along with the rest of the 29th Division, to serve as a mobile reserve for the coastal area between Philadelphia and New York City, including Atlantic City.

March brought numerous changes within the 29th Division. On March 2, Major General Leonard T. Gerow took command of the Division, replacing the beloved Milton A. Reckord, who was deemed too old to continue serving in command. Major General Gerow was a regular officer, a Virginian, and a graduate of the Virginia Military Institute, so he was an acceptable replacement in the eyes of the 116th. Very shortly thereafter, on March 11, General Orders Number 13 restructured the 29th Division from the old square configuration of four regiments used in the Great War to provide mass during frontal attacks on prepared defenses. The new triangular structure, which had already been introduced into the active Army divisions, depended less on mass and more on mobility. The bottom line was that there would be three maneuver regiments in the 29th Division instead of four, which sent Virginia's 176th Regiment away for a new assignment.

The new triangularized 29th Division would consist of the 116th Regiment from Virginia, and the 115th and 175th Regiments from Maryland. It was intended to be more lethal and mobile. The Army had looked closely at the German Blitzkrieg tactics and determined that the future of maneuver lay in speed and armament. The artillery support would come from three excellent artillery units, the 110th from Maryland, Virginia's 111th, and the 176th from Pennsylvania. The authorized strength of the Division was much leaner, down to 15,500 men. Shortly after reorganization, the 29th Division received orders to leave Fort Meade again, but this time it was destined not to return. Before leaving, the 116th was honored on April 6, by a trip to Baltimore and a parade before some half a million Marylanders assembled to wish them well. They stepped off from the Fifth Regiment Armory, marching downtown past the reviewing stand at Baltimore City Hall.

On April 15, 1942, the 116th said a final good-bye to Maryland and Fort Meade. They moved for days by foot and truck back into Virginia and the familiar training grounds at Camp A. P. Hill, just south of Fredericksburg. The song "Carry me back to old Virginny" could be heard as the troops set up their tent cities for another hot summer at "the Hill." At night, soldiers slipped into nearby Bowling Green, and Fredericksburg was close enough if your ride could get you back before taps at eleven p.m. Their home communities were also much closer, so weekend passes allowed for visits to the family and home cooking. The training was tougher than that of their previous summer, with long road marches and more physical training. They were trained to respond to artillery fire and attacks by aircraft. A new vehicle, the Jeep, became part of their inventory.

In early June, the 116th was selected to go to Washington, D.C., to be part of a parade to encourage the government workers there to a new level of efficiency. The trip out of the dust and misery of Camp Hill was greatly appreciated, and the soldiers made a special effort to present themselves well. They marched proudly down Constitution Avenue to the cheers of the crowd assembled to watch. It was truly a proud day for the 116th and one most would remember for a long time.

On July 6, the 116th joined the rest of the 29th Division moving south to participate in the Second Carolina Maneuvers. Once there, the training was very different from the previous year. There was a real effort to conduct the exercise as close to what real combat would look like as possible. Dismounted maneuvering replaced the motor moves, and there was a great deal of marching. Weekend passes and leave were severely limited. There were umpires to evaluate and score the maneuvers. There were exercises conducted on the handling of prisoners of war (POWs), preparing defensive positions, and river crossings. This was serious business. The Division was clearly being prepared for a mission. Since there was some training in swampy terrain, rumors spread that the Blue and Gray were going to the Pacific to fight the Japanese.

Just as quickly as they had started, the Second Carolina Maneuvers ended, and the men of the 116th found themselves on August 17 boarding trains south. The troops were delighted to detrain in Florida, where, unlike the Carolinas, there was water to go along with the sand. The site was Camp Blanding, located between Jacksonville and Gainesville, and once again they were in buildings. The truck convoy bringing the Division's equipment south was followed by a procession of wives and girlfriends driving their civilian cars. Soon the rationing of oil and gas and limited availability of rubber would end this distraction. For now, however, life was good as there were weekend trips to the Atlantic and Gulf Coast beaches. The soldiers hoped they would be able to winter in the Sunshine State. Their hopes were dashed quickly when in early September orders came that the 29th Division was to deploy overseas.

In a few days, the 116th was moved to the railroad siding at Camp Blanding where they were loaded onto passenger cars for the move north. Although secrecy and security were now surrounding every move, the wives had little trouble determining where the trains were going; it was Camp Kilmer, New Jersey. Immediately they headed north to beat the trains there. The soldiers were quiet and thoughtful as their train moved north, crossing the familiar training grounds in the Carolinas, then on through Richmond, passing near Camp A. P. Hill, on through Washington, D.C., and past their first home at Fort Meade, Maryland. In just twenty-four hours, the 116th reached Camp Kilmer; it was Friday, September 18. They were stunned to learn that their commander, Colonel Opie, was getting promoted and would be replaced by forty-six-year-old Colonel Charles D. Canham. The Stonewallers were concerned about this regular Army officer taking command, even if he was a friend of their Division Commander, Major General Gerow. In time, however, they would appreciate his leadership.

The week at Camp Kilmer was filled with preparations for going overseas. More new equipment arrived, to include a new "coal-scuttle" helmet much different from their old "dish pan," new green herringbone uniforms, and new M-1 rifles. There were immunizations, new photographs taken, and identification cards produced. Each man got at least one day's pass to say good-bye to loved ones or have one last blowout before departing. In a May 30, 2001, article in the *Bedford Bulletin*, Bettie (Krantz) Wilkes Hooper, the widow of Master Sergeant John Wilkes, remembered her last trip to see her husband and prior trips to other installations.

> When we learned our men would sail for England out of New York harbor on the *Queen Mary*, I decided to go there to see John before his leaving. Prior to this, other wives and girlfriends of these men had accompanied me and we made many trips back and forth to Fort Meade or Camp Blanding when we were lucky enough to find someone who had a car who would drive us there. Gas was rationed and cars were becoming a rarity because of the war.

Then, on September 26, the 116th marched to New Brunswick, where they boarded trains to take them to Hoboken. Here they dismounted, carrying all of their equipment, including their A bag, with their personnel gear to stay with them, and their B bag, which was to be stored aboard ship. The men had to march almost

Illustration 11-2: Fort Meade to Camp Blanding

a mile to the ferry landing at Jersey City. After the short ferry ride across the choppy Hudson River to the Port of New York, they again grabbed their gear and moved to the dock where two large ships were berthed. The Stonewallers stood quietly in formation in full combat gear with all their military wares, as their names were called to board. Moving past the checkers, they climbed the gangplank and boarded their transport, the *Queen Mary*, berthed at Pier 92. Once on board, they were given their berth assignments and moved below to settle in for the trip ahead. The entire process took most of the night, and with the morning light of September 27, 1942, the *Queen Mary* slipped away from her berth, assisted by tug boats, passed the Statute of Liberty at eight a.m., and moved down the Hudson River through the Narrows and out to sea.

The *Queen Mary* had been a luxury liner before the war, but was converted to a troop ship to ferry soldiers across the Atlantic Ocean to England. The twelve decks provided a mix of bunks and hammocks for the roughly 15,000 men to sleep in during their seven days at sea. Today the ship has a permanent home in Long Beach, California, where visitors are welcome to visit and learn first hand how this ship supported the Allied efforts of World War II. There are displays that reveal how the bunks and hammocks were configured to sleep all of the soldiers aboard. The ship is a treasure of history and worth a visit.

The week on the *Queen Mary* was basically uneventful for the members of the 116th. The zigzagging at twenty-five plus knots made movement difficult at times and created some seasickness. The soldiers didn't like having to wear their life jackets everywhere they went but understood that if they fell overboard, the ship would not be stopping to pick them up. At night, the ship was completely blacked out. Meals had to be taken in three shifts starting at six a.m. each morning, but the English food was not to the liking of the Stonewallers. Poor ventilation also contributed to the soldier's discomfort. The *Queen Mary* was built as a luxury liner, not a troop ship. It was simply not equipped to handle the large number of soldiers it carried to war.

The German U-Boat threat was very real, but the *Queen Mary's* speed made it a difficult target to acquire. Still, every precaution was taken to assure a safe passage. On October 2, six English destroyers met the *Queen Mary* along with the cruiser *HMS Curacao*. This told the soldiers they were indeed headed to England. The destroyers would provide a screen against any German submarine attack, while the cruiser would add additional anti-aircraft firepower in the event of a Luftwaffe air strike. The *HMS Curacao's* mission required it to stay close to the *Queen Mary*. At 2:10 p.m. of the first afternoon the *Curacao* was in support, its crew misjudged the speed of the *Queen Mary* and crossed too close to the bow of the much larger troop vessel. The huge transport cut the small cruiser in half, and the two parts sank quickly after the collision. Many Stonewallers were on the decks and witnessed the tragedy which cost the lives of some 300 British sailors and left the bow of the *Queen Mary* damaged. The ship's Captain Gordon Illingworth impressed upon the Stonewallers the need to keep the accident a secret after they arrived in the British Isles, for fear German spies would reveal his ship's damage to submarines lurking in the area.

The next day, the *Queen Mary* arrived in Scotland, slipping down the River Forth of Clyde and into Greenock Harbor and the protection of the barrage balloons overhead. Again, loaded down by their equipment and bags, the men of the 116th boarded "lighters," or ferry boats, for the trip to shore. The units formed up on the docks and then marched to the nearby train station. George Homan of C Company recalled "After landing we went to a railroad station where there was some Scotsmen playing *Carry me Back to Old Virginia*." Here they boarded strange looking passenger cars pulled by train engines half the size of those at home. The Stonewallers settled in for what was to be a long ride south on the London, Midland and Scottish Railroad. Lieutenant Charles Cawthorn in his *Other Clay*, writes that

> Occasionally, the train ground to a halt at station platforms, dimly lit by blackout lamps, where ladies in dark uniform poked trays of vaguely sweet buns and mugs of hot tea at us. By sight, sound, and taste, it was as though we had landed on a strange planet…

The men of the 116th were getting their first taste of tea and crumpets from the English equivalent of the American Red Cross, but they were not enjoying it at all.

The trains chugged along though the English countryside. The men could see cottages and fields of sheep, rolling hills and stone walls. The weather was cool and damp, as expected. Some of the soldiers tried to sleep while others spent the trip gambling or exchanging stories about home. There was a lot of nervous energy and uneasiness as the train continued traveling through the night. Occasionally the screams of air raid sirens could be heard. Clearly, the Stonewallers were a long way from their homes in Virginia.

The next afternoon, the train moved onto a siding and stopped near a large brick complex of buildings known as Tidworth Barracks. They were on the Salisbury Plain near Andover, roughly ten miles from the ancient prehistoric marvel known as Stonehenge. The quarters were the remnants of an old British army cavalry unit and had been there for a long time. Constructed of concrete, brick, and slate, their gloomy appearance did not help the morale of the Stonewallers. Each building was two stories in height and inside was found a long room with double bunks on each side and a fireplace or pot bellied stove to provide heat. There were two old bath tubs on iron legs to be used by fifty men. Mattresses were made from straw, and there were no pillows. The soldiers did have their two issue blankets to help ward off the cold, raw air.

Most of the 116th's equipment was to arrive later by much slower ships, but training began immediately. The schedule called for activities seven days a week for four weeks, followed by a two-day pass. The training was intense, as Division Commander Gerow was determined to show that his National Guard soldiers could be-

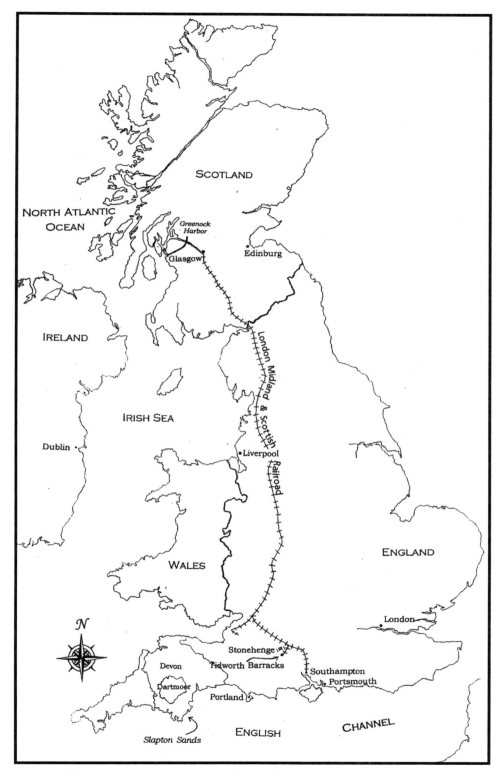

Illustration 11-3: Greenock Harbor to Tidworth Barracks

Illustration 11-4: Tidworth Barracks today

come every bit as effective as the soldiers in the active Army. Part of this determination came from the constant criticism by the commander of Army Ground Forces, Lieutenant General Lesley McNair. Thirty-mile marches became routine, and during their time at Tidworth Barracks the Stonewallers would march over three thousand miles. There was extensive individual training, focused on earning each man the Expert Infantryman's Badge as described by Alex Kershaw in *The Bedford Boys*.

> To qualify, first the men had to run a hundred yards in twelve seconds in army combat boots and uniform, do thirty-five push-ups and ten chin-ups, get across an obstacle course at a sprint, then show themselves to be deadly accurate with a Colt .45, the Garand M-1 rifle, and a BAR (Browning Automatic Rifle), the standard issue submachine gun.

Achieving the badge would get you five dollars more each month, while failing it could result in transfer to a support unit. There were live fire exercises, testing how each man would react under fire. Collective or unit training involved maneuvers during the day and at night, building up to live fire exercises.

The two-day pass would earn you a two-hour train ride to Waterloo Station in London where you could get a room for fifty cents per night. There was lot to see— Buckingham Palace, Big Ben, and the Piccadilly Circus. A visit to London was pretty exciting for all of the Stonewallers, but especially so for the many that had never been outside of their home communities prior to mobilization. There was drinking and dancing, coupled with propositions from young ladies willing

Illustration 11-5: Another view of Tidworth Barracks

to take you to their apartment for a special party. The devastation from the Luftwaffe bombings during the battle of Britain was everywhere, but the Brits were resilient and life went on. Back at Tidworth Barracks, recreation was limited to shooting snooker pool or playing rugby American style (football). The American Red Cross moved into the adjoining Tidworth House, which had been the home of the Duke of Wellington. Entertainment there included dances, which brought in many of the young local girls

Christmas of 1942 was a memorable occasion for the men of the 116th and the entire 29th Division. The 1st Division, the first American division to arrive in England, had moved out to begin its invasion of North Africa. This left the second arriving division, the Blue and Gray, alone to celebrate the holiday season with their English hosts. The American celebration of Christmas was looked upon by the Brits with great curiosity. The English press descended on Tidworth, making the Stonewallers feel like celebrities. To a man, they would have traded this opportunity for one day at home with their families. The holiday season gave the Stonewallers some relief from the rigorous training, and they had some time to write home and read over and over again the mail they received from their friends and family there.

The winter of 1942-43 was one of the coldest on record in England. The soldiers remembered nine days of rain, fog, and cold, with one day of limited sunshine, and then the cycle started all over again. The constant dampness was penetrating, and staying warm was very difficult. English tea was no replacement for American coffee. In place of beer, they had to drink something called "bitter." It was served warm and had very little taste, but it was all they had in the English Pubs. Daylight hours were limited, with the sun coming up around nine a.m. each morning and setting just eight hours later at around five p.m. The dismal conditions made the Stonewallers miss home and family even more.

With the approach of spring and warmer weather, morale in the 116th began to improve. On May 23, 1943, the unit led the operation known as Exercise Hanover, which saw the entire 29th Division move some 160 miles southeast. The six-day trip resulted in four days of marching and two days riding in trucks. The men finally reached their new home near Ivybridge in Devon. Here they took over the quarters at Crown Hill, left behind by the British 55th Division, that had previously been stationed there as part of the coastal defenses. The camp was adjacent to the little town of Bridestowe on the edge of Dartmoor, a soggy, spongy piece of terrain the men would learn to hate. The 116th was now just twelve miles from the English Channel and the port of Plymouth. On June 5, the Stonewallers marched in a parade in the nearby port town to help in raising money for a war bond drive being held throughout England. In less than a year, they would be marching to a port for a different reason.

In July, General Gerow was selected to command V Corps, and he was replaced by Major General Charles H. Gerhardt on July 22. The new commander was a graduate of West Point and only forty-eight years old. He came with the knowledge of a plan later to be known as Overlord and knew the 29th Division was to play an important role in this effort to liberate France. It was doubtful that he knew just how critical a role the 116th would play, but he knew there was a lot of work to be done to get ready for the task ahead. Gerhardt was a spit and polish cavalryman, who took command determined to improve the discipline and appearance of the Division. His driver, Sergeant Robert Cuff, often bore the brunt of the General's attention to cleanliness, sometimes washing the commander's jeep called *Vixen Tor*, as often as five times a day. The men would nickname Gerhardt "Uncle Charlie." *Vixen Tor* can still be seen today in the National Guard museum located within the historic Fifth Regiment Armory in Baltimore, Maryland.

Major General Gerhardt would be joined in the fall of 1943 by Brigadier General Norman Cota, who became the Assistant Division Commander. A born trainer, Cota had come from the 1st Division, where he had most recently served as their Chief of Staff during the invasion of North Africa. He was a solid infantryman and considered an expert in amphibious operations. He was fearless and set an example that inspired the soldiers. They nicknamed him "Dutch," and always held him in high regard. He was perfectly suited to train the 29th Division, especially its infantrymen, for what lay ahead. His experience and leadership would be critical to the success of the Division.

The 116th was designated as a "Combat Team" which gave them an Artillery Battalion, Medical Company and Engineer Company. The men were assigned a defensive sector with responsibility along the southern coast of England in the event of any German invasion. Their main focus, however, remained training. Soon their operations included specialty training with a particular focus on amphibious assaults, and the Stonewallers began to realize they were preparing for more than the defense of England. Non-swimmers received swimming lessons, and units practiced wading ashore through surf. Now Sergeant Ralph Coffman of L Company remembered,

> We trained in boat teams of 30 men each. I was the squad leader of the 1st Squad of the first boat team of Company L. We trained with the British Navy for a while until the American Navy came to Plymouth in late summer of 1943. The U. S. Navy Assault boats would go full speed ahead to the Beach and drive their boat on the beach and drop the ramp and many a time we would step out on dry land and not even get our feet wet. This was a good feeling riding in a boat that would really go, after poking around with the British Navy.

The 116th began enhanced amphibious training at the beach assault center developed at Woolacombe, located on the southwest coast of England, on the north shore of Devon. Here the men got their first glimpse of the new amphibious truck dubbed the DUKW. Lieutenant Charles Cawthon recalled,

> The tactics were based on thirty man boat teams—the capacity of the personnel landing craft—organized to fight independently against the complexes of bunkers and field fortifications in the landing areas. A typical boat team was made up of rifle and machine gun sections, and flame thrower, wire-cutting, and demolitions sections.

The training evolved to live fire exercises, and the soldiers began to get a good understanding of what they were in for.

One of General Gerhardt's first initiatives after taking command was to implement the battle cry of "Twenty-Nine Let's Go!" It was to become a part of all paperwork produced by the Division and a motto to be used in every training exercise. He hoped it would increase the Division's esprit de corps and pride. The Stonewallers, whose predecessors had created the famous "Rebel Yell," became particularly adept at the new Division shout. Gerhardt was very conscious of the mistrust and contempt many senior Army officers had for the National Guard unit, and although the 29th Division had been on active duty for over two years, they were still talked about as being "a National Guard Division." Gerhardt's goal was to have the 29th Division become something special and recognized throughout the Army for its readiness.

As a second Christmas in England approached, the 116th's training level continued to increase, and the men began to conduct complete amphibious exercises on the beaches known as Slapton Sands. Lieutenant Charles Cawthorne remembered that

> Again and again, we loaded onto landing craft that pitched and rolled out into the Channel and then roared landward to drop ramps over which we lumbered to flounder through the surf to the beach and go through the assault drills.

In January, Operation Duck tested the entire Division's ability to load, move to an embarkation site, land, and successfully establish a beachhead. Almost two hundred replacement soldiers had arrived to bring the 116th up to strength. By now, only about one out of every five Stonewallers was an original Guardsman mobilized in February, 1941. Volunteers and draftees had joined the unit to fill in for the losses resulting from the difficult training and serving on active duty for over three years. In April, the final exercise was a full dress rehearsal in conjunction with the 1st Division. It was deemed a success ,and final plans were made for the invasion.

Colonel Canham, commanding the 116th, had been a tough taskmaster through all of the train up. Never one to mince words, Private Harold Baumgarten of B Company remembered Colonel Canham addressing his soldiers to announce that,

> ...we were going to be the first forces in to the Second Front in Europe, and that two out of three of us aren't expected to come back, and if anybody's got butterflies in the belly, to ask for a transfer now, because it's going to be that kind of operation.

The 116th was finally about to see action.

By May, the training was winding down, and the units began moving to a new cantonment area designated as D-1. May 19 found the 116th at Blandford, near their future embarkation points at Portland and Poole, living in tents in what was known as marshaling area "O" for Omaha. The camps were so crowded the men became known as "sausages." Security was unbelievably tight, with barbed wire surrounding the complex and no way in or out without a pass. The objectives of the Allied invasion of Europe, Operation Overlord, were now laid out in

Illustration 11-6: General Dwight D. Eisenhower, Supreme Allied Commander, Allied Forces visits with the officers of the 116th Regiment as they prepare for D-Day. Far left is the 116th Commander Colonel Charles Canham. Major General Charles Gerhardt, 29th Division Commander is to General Eisenhower's right and 5th Corps Commander Major General Leornard T. Gerow is to his left. First Army Commander Lieutenant General Omar Bradley can be partially seen behind General Gerhardt.

detail. The marshalling areas were completely sealed to prevent any of the information about the upcoming landings from falling into enemy hands. At all levels, the description of the events planned for the upcoming "D-Day" was revealed. May 30 brought a visit by General Omar Bradley, commander of all the American forces who were arrayed for the invasion. Speaking to the 3,500 Stonewallers before him, he told the men they would have "ringside seats for the greatest show on earth."

On June 3, the units began leaving their camps for their ports of embarkation. Once there, the units of the 116th boarded their assigned ships for the crossing. The First Battalion, A, B, C, and D Companies, commanded by Lieutenant Colonel John Metcalfe, would cross the English Channel on the Royal Navy's *HMS Empire Javelin*. The Second Battalion, under the command of Major Sidney Bingham, Jr., with company's E, F, G, and H, would cross on the *USS Thomas Jefferson*. Lieutenant Colonel Lawrence Meeks commanded the Third Battalion and its I, K, L, and M companies, and they would be transported on the *USS Charles Carroll*. Departure from England was set for the next evening, with "D-Day" to be launched on the morning of June 5. The 116th would land on the beach, code named "Omaha," with units of the First and Second Battalion leading as part of the first wave, followed by the Third Battalion.

Initially the Stonewallers would be attached to Major General Clarence Huebner and his 1st Division, which was responsible for the initial landings on Omaha Beach. The 16th Infantry Regiment of the 1st Division would be on their left, and off to their right, the 2nd Ranger Battalion would be responsible for seizing the cliffs known as Pointe du Hoc. In addition to their commander, Colonel Canham, the 116th's Executive Officer was Lieutenant Colonel Harold Cassell, and Major Thomas D. Howie, the teacher from the Staunton Military Academy, served as the S-3 Operations Officer. As the Stonewallers moved to their ships, Colonel Canham was with them, constantly reminding the soldiers of their motto, "Ever Forward." Standing on the dock as they boarded, he would warn them, "There will be no other way to go!" "Ever Forward" would be the key to survival.

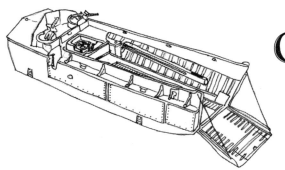

-Twelve-

Omaha Beach
to St. Lô

The men of the 116th Infantry Regiment were awed by the miles upon miles of soldiers, vehicles, and equipment lined up to be transported by the largest naval armada ever assembled. Barrage balloons floated over the ports to protect the invasion fleet from Luftwaffe air attack as they prepared to cross the English Channel, bound for the Norman coastal region of France. The soldiers boarded their assigned ships and then scurried below to find their berths. They quickly dropped their gear and then returned above deck to witness the spectacle. It was truly a sight to behold for the Stonewallers, most of whom had never been outside their rural communities before mobilization. Tragically, many were on a course that would prevent them from ever returning to their homes and families. When the ships were finally loaded, they slipped out to an assembly area to await the crossing order. During the next twenty-four hours, gale force winds, heavy rain, and fog would threaten to delay Operation Overlord until later in the summer. General Eisenhower chose to keep the force in readiness during this period in order to give the weather a chance to improve. D-Day and "H" hour would be postponed for one day. It was now set for the morning of June 6, 1944.

On the morning of June 5, the weather forecast for the Channel provided a positive outlook for the next morning. D-Day was back on, with H-Hour at 6:30 a.m. after low tide, which was scheduled to occur at 5:25 a.m., just before sunrise at 5:58 a.m. Throughout June 5, the preparations continued for the execution of Operation Overlord. The 116th was ready, but many soldiers found it hard to believe they were finally going into action. As described in *29 Let's Go!*, by Joseph H. Ewing,

> As the invasion fleet headed across the Channel some of the men still didn't believe it, and felt that somehow they would wind up again back on the beach at Slapton Sands, as they had done before. Most of them however appeared to be convinced that this was the real invasion, and the day of the dry run was over.

It most certainly was real, and, after twenty months in England, the 116th was leaving to play an integral role in what the Allied Supreme Commander, General Dwight D. Eisenhower, was calling the "great crusade to liberate Europe." The Stonewallers weren't really thinking about that now; they remembered the homes and families they had left behind and pondered what the next day would bring.

As darkness approached, the ships took their positions in the crossing formation and set their course for the French coast. The long hours of waiting and now the rough waters of the English Channel were no friend of the Stonewallers. Seasickness began to affect some of the soldiers, but not to the extent they would suffer hours later in the small landing craft. The winds and waves seemed to increase with the evening darkness, but the fleet pushed on. After dinner there were religious services for those wanting to attend, and many prayers were conducted in solitude. Some of the soldiers played cards and told stories, while others tried to rest. The ships were, of course, completely blacked out, and no smoking was allowed on deck. All too soon, it was midnight and then the beginning of "The Longest Day." In the sky above the fleet could be heard the drone of the aircraft engines of the B-24 bombers carrying their loads of destruction, and the C-47 cargo planes with the three Allied airborne divisions headed to their drop zones behind the German positions on the coast of Normandy.

Reveille sounded at two a.m. There was breakfast for those who felt up to it—steak, gravy, coffee, and then gearing up. A soldier's pack weighed roughly sixty pounds, plus the weight of individual equipment. The load was described in detail by Lieutenant Charles Cawthorn in *Other Clay*.

> It consisted of a special canvas assault jacket with large pockets front and back in which were grenades, rations, mess gear, raincoat, a Syrette of morphine, toilet articles, motion sickness pills, water purification tablets, DDT dusting powder, a paste to put on boots in case he encountered chemically contaminated areas, a small block of TNT for the quick blasting of a foxhole, and two hundred francs in a special currency issued by the Allied Military government in order that trade could start with the Normans as soon as he was ashore. Around his waist was strapped an entrenching tool, another first aid packet, and a canteen. From his neck hung a special assault gas mask and extra bandoliers of ammunition. In addition, each carried his individual weapon, and, if a member of a machine gun, mortar, flame-thrower, or demolitions team, his part of that load.

Their basic load consisted of 286 rounds of rifle ammunition and ten grenades. The last item that the soldiers put on was their rubberized life belt, to be inflated by using carbon dioxide capsules, if needed.

At three a.m., the boat teams of the first wave assembled at their stations to board their assigned vessel for the landing, either the Landing Craft, Assault (LCA) or Landing Craft Vehicle-Personnel (LCVP). Just as they had rehearsed so many times, there were thirty men to a boat, six boats per company in the assault, and one to follow with communications equipment and supplies. Even numbered boats were to the right, odd numbered to the left. The soldiers counted off, then slipped over the side to take their position in their assigned boat. First wave landing boats were located just off the decks of the *USS Thomas Jefferson* and *HMS Empire Javelin*, but soldiers in the follow-on waves would have to climb down cargo nets to their landing craft floating on the Channel surface below. Cables and chains began clanking as the landing craft were very carefully lowered into the rolling waters of the Atlantic. Once loaded, the landing boats formed up and began to circle in the high seas. The flat bottomed landing craft were unable to roll with the waves and pitched violently in the stormy Channel waters. They rose and then fell, tossing the soldiers about inside and splashing them with seawater. The waiting was horrible, and the Stonewallers, many seriously seasick, grew more and more impatient as the morning skies began to lighten. At five a.m., naval bombardment on Omaha Beach began, followed at 6 a.m. by the air bombardment. The guns of the battleship, the *USS Texas*, began to boom in front of the landing craft, still circling some twelve miles from the beach.

The first wave of Stonewallers had been afloat for three hours when finally H-Hour was approaching. The landing craft of the 116th's first wave turned for Omaha Beach. The landing sites began with D-1, or Dog Green, on the right as the Stonewallers approached the beach. This was the Vierville draw assigned to A Company from Bedford, Virginia. Next, on the left, was Dog White, assigned to G Company from Farmville, Virginia. Then came Dog Red, the objective of F Company from South Boston, Virginia, and last was Easy Green, where E Company, the unit from Chase City, Virginia, was to land. The next objective, Easy Red, was the right flank landing area of the 16th Infantry Regiment of the 1st Division. Between Dog Red and Easy Green lay the objective known as D-3, the Les Moulins draw. The draws on Omaha Beach had been opened by constant draining and erosion from the cliffs above the beach. They afforded the fastest route off the beach and therefore were the best defended positions. The coxswains commanding the first wave boats were told to locate the Vierville Church steeple and navigate using its location, since it would be the only identifiable landmark. In the confusion of the assault and morning fog, however, only A Company and F Company would land in the right location, while E and G Companies would drift to the left of their assigned landing zones.

Ramps began dropping right on time around 6:30 a.m. Landing correctly and alone on the 116th Regiment's right, A Company was destined for destruction. Two boats were lost on the way in, and the four that landed did so within 500 yards of well fortified German positions. As the ramps of the LCAs fell, and "the Bedford Boys" exited their landing craft, German MG42 machine guns began to cut the Stonewallers down. Their commander, Captain Taylor Fellers, was first from his boat, following the division order to lead by example. The 116th commanders at all levels were trained to be first off, thus, unfortunately, becoming the first casualties. The well intended directive left the survivors, not only of A Company, but all the 116[th's] landing craft, leaderless as they came under galling direct and indirect German fire. The result was predictable chaos, as soldiers in the first waves had to do whatever they could to survive until additional units landed. George Roach of A Company remembered looking around and finding only one other soldier alive, "...all of the officers, and all of the noncoms were dead, and he and I, as PFCs, were the senior men on the beach for as far as we could see."

When the first wave landed, the Channel tide was out, leaving some three hundred yards of open beach between the soldiers and the protection of a seawall. Subsequent waves were dropped off closer to the beach as the tide rose, but they were placed in additional peril if they floated too close to the mined obstacles the Germans had placed on the beach, assuming any eventual attack would come during high tide. Before the second wave landed around seven a.m., the tide had risen almost eight feet. The second wave came in on Landing Craft, Vehicle, Personnel (LCVP), a boat with less armor, thus capable of moving faster during an assault. The result was unfortunately the same. The soldiers came under terrific German fire. There was only supposed to be an ad hoc force in the defense, but unknown to Allied intelligence, on March 15, the 352nd German Division had been moved from St. Lô to Omaha Beach.

The Stonewallers were facing troops from a veteran division, with extensive combat experience at the Russian front. Additionally, they would be confronted by the 726th Regiment of the 716th Division, which had occupied a static defensive position prior to the arrival of the 352nd. This unit, of mixed composition and questionable readiness, was the only one with which the D-Day planners had concerned themselves. General Bradley learned of the presence of the 352nd shortly before the invasion fleet left the coast of England, but it was too late to make any adjustment to the landings on Omaha and Utah Beach. This was no small oversight, and the 116th was in for a serious fight.

In *Voices of Valor*, Douglas Brinkley and Ronald J. Drez wrote, "Still the boats of the 116th Regiment came on like moths drawn to a flame. Their reward for their perfect navigation to the correct landing beach was to enter into the jaws of hell."

Following A Company, Robert Scales of B Company described what happened as his boat arrived on the beach.

> Everybody who went off, they just cut them down. We got caught in crossfire. The only thing that saved me, I stumbled and went off the side of the ramp. I looked back and as fast as everybody was coming off that boat, they were just dropping. A, B, and D Companies, the ones that landed right there by those pillboxes by the Vierville draw were caught in a crossfire. Most of those men are in that cemetery there.

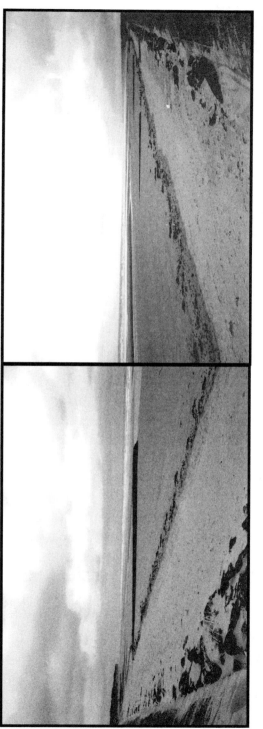

Illustration 12-1-1 & 12-1-2, and 12-2: Omaha Beach at low tide looking west (left) and east (right), and at high tide (below)

The deadly fire zeroing in on the First Battalion units was coming from 100 milli-meter guns of WN 73 on the cliffs above and the MG42s and 88s located in WNs 70, 71, and 72. WN is the abbreviation for the German word *Widerstandsnest,* used to identify the strong points constructed to stop any invasion. WNs 60 to 73 protected Omaha Beach. They were difficult to locate since they were positioned to provide interlocking fires into the flanks of any landing force. General William E. DePuy, the first com-mander of United States Army Training and Doctrine Command (TRADOC), would use this technique in developing a new defensive strategy for the Army in the 1970s. In *The Longest Day*, Cornelius Ryan described the Omaha Beach defenses in detail.

> There were 8 concrete bunkers with guns of 75 millimeters or larger caliber; 35 pillboxes with artillery pieces of various sizes and/or automatic weapons; 4 batteries of artillery; 18 antitank guns; 6 mortar pits; 35 rocket-launching sites, each with four 38-millimeter rocket tubes; and no less than 85 gun nests.

The situation on the left was not much better. E Company, having landed about one thousand yards from its assigned beach, was intermingled with soldiers of G Company of the 16th Infantry, struggling forward under heavy fire. F Company had landed close to its objective at the Les Moulins Draw and found the grass ablaze from the naval gunfire. Using the resulting smoke for protection, half of the com-pany was able to move quickly to the protection of a shingle bank. The rest of the unit, which was exposed, took heavy casualties in the forty-five minute slow move-ment to the same position. G Company also missed its landing zone, but fortunately came ashore protected by the smoke from the grass fires still burning and moved across the beach with the least resistance. Of their twenty-one remaining original unit members, only one would die this day, but all of the surviving members of G Company except for two, would be wounded or killed before the war ended. H Company, landing last, had drifted far to the east and found itself struggling with the soldiers of the 16th Infantry. The casualties in the Second Battalion continued to mount throughout the morning, and by 9:30 only half of the battalion remained.

Into the midst of the melee, around 7:30, the command groups with Colonel Canham and Brigadier General Cota arrived on Dog White, between the First and Second Battal-ions. Disliked by the Stonewallers in training, Canham became a hero to his men on Omaha Beach. Wounded in the right wrist shortly after landing, he began to urge his men forward, *Ever Forward!* Sergeant Bob Slaughter of D Company recalled,

> When I got to the bottom of the seawall and looked back, I saw a couple of the officers from the regimental and battalion level. I saw Colonel Canham with his right arm in a sling, and he had a .45 in his left hand and he was encouraging the people to get off the beach and get set up and to get up over the cliffs.

Illustration 12-3: Part of WN 71 showing a concrete pillbox at the top of the hill above Vierville Draw on Omaha Beach

Cota had been leery of a daylight assault from the start and was not surprised by the chaos he saw before him. Waving his pistol, he too began to shout to the leaders he could see, "We've got to get them off the beach. We've got to get them moving."

Now LCIs (Landing Craft, Infantry) landed, each carrying 150 men, but just as importantly, with more Bangalore torpedoes and satchel charges that would be critical to breaking through the initial German beach positions. Only one of the twelve DUKWs, carrying the guns of the 111th Field Artillery, made it to shore around nine a.m. All of the others were lost at sea. The Commander of the 111th, Lieutenant Colonel Thomas C. Mullins, would announce, "We're infantrymen now." Oh, the indignity of it all, the King of Battle having to fight as the "Queen of Battle." Also landing were LCTs (Landing Craft, Tank), carrying jeeps and more importantly, bulldozers and tanks to begin opening lanes through the obstacles ahead. A few floating tanks finally reached the beach. The first three waves of the 116th had been ineffective, but now their fortunes began to turn.

Brigadier General Cota linked up with C Company that had just landed and reached the seawall pretty much intact. He instructed a BAR (Browning Automatic Rifle) gunner to position his gun on the top of a sand dune and provide covering fire. Sergeant John Polyniak of C Company remembered what happened next.

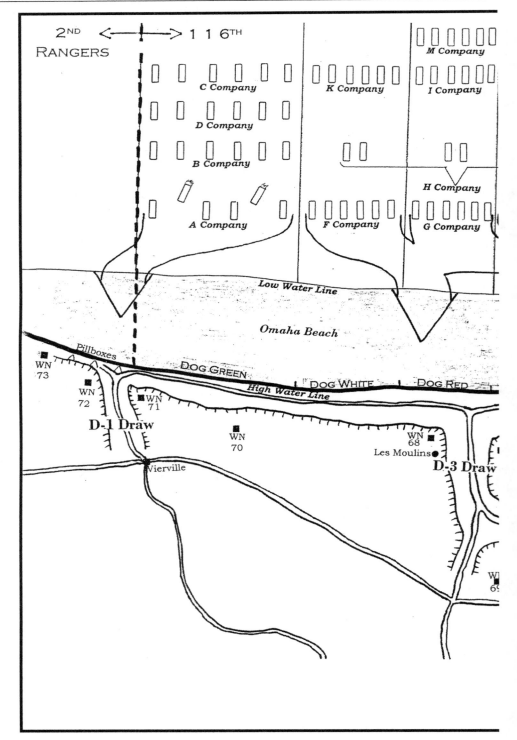

Illustration 12-4: 116th landings on Omaha Beach

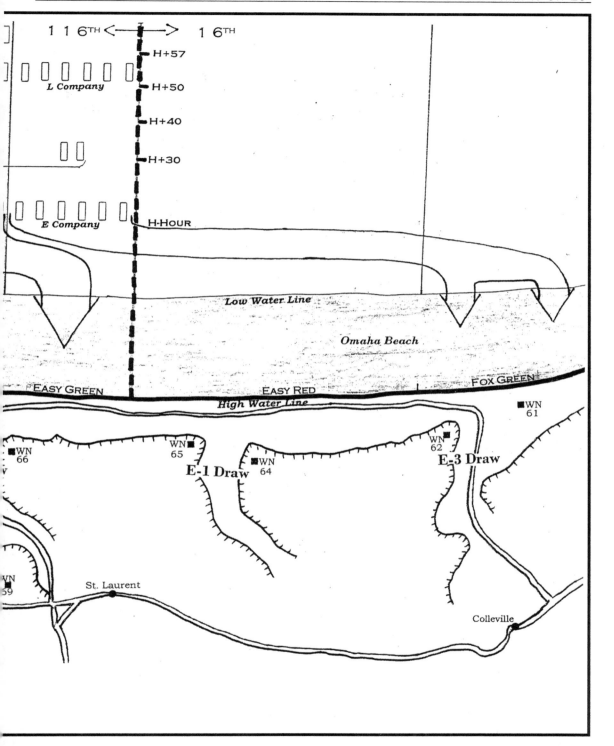

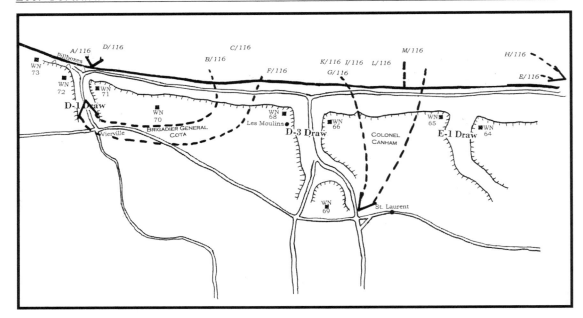

Illustration 12-5: The 116th breaks out from Omaha Beach

> I was carrying a Bangalore torpedo, and I reached over the wall, placed it under the enemy wire, and blew it with my igniter. The team made it through the gap safely, moved ahead until we reached the bluff, and climbed to the top.

Cota joined the soldiers who had angled to their right in reaching the top and began to move to the Vierville Draw. Along with a handful of Stonewallers, he would take the draw from the rear. Here he found the German gun emplacement that would later become the National Guard Memorial on Omaha Beach. It was disguised as a beach house, but it had brought deadly fire on the landings before being knocked out, probably by naval gunfire. The Vierville Draw also now houses the 29th Division Monument.

Colonel Canham had gone to the left, and collecting a mixed force of Stonewallers, worked up the cliffs to the left of the Les Moulins draw and was headed for St. Laurent. The decision was made to exploit success, so the Third Battalion, with I, K, L, and M Companies, would land to the right of the St. Laurent Draw, E-1, and move right up the cliffs, to link up with the rest of the 116th units. Succeeding waves would also land here and climb to the fields behind the objective D-3, the Les Moulins draw. The second objective, like the first, the Vierville Draw, would be breached from the rear. Around 10 a.m. Major General Gerow gave the command from V Corps for the 115th to begin its landing, following an opening created by the 1st Division's 16th Infantry Regiment which was located to the left of D-3. By afternoon, the Les Moulins draw had been opened for vehicle traffic, and men and equipment began streaming inland. There were many Germans now surrendering, as they were overwhelmed by the superior numbers of Stonewallers on the attack. Colonel Canham

Illustration 12-6: D-Day Veteran Sergeant John Polyniak, the author, and SFC Terry Howard during the 1999 visit to Omaha Beach

had a "take no prisoners" policy, which meant that some of those attempting to surrender were shot. Most of the enemy, however, would fall back into the fields and towns behind Omaha Beach and begin a delaying action. By day's end, the 116th Regiment had established a beachhead, but was far short of achieving its D-Day objectives. Scattered amongst the fields and barns behind the beach, the soldiers would get what rest they could before continuing the attack inland.

After the air Battle for Britain ended in the summer of 1941, British Prime Minister, Sir Winston Churchill, was quoted as saying, "Never in the field of human conflict was so much owed by so many to so few." This description would also have been appropriate to recognize the efforts of the soldiers of the 116th Regiment and other units on D-Day some three years later. By securing the beachhead at Normandy, they had opened the door to Europe and the eventual destruction of Adolph Hitler and Nazi Germany. The sacrifice of the 116th had been particularly heavy. At the end of this Longest Day, they had suffered 1,007 casualties, 247 of which were killed. The 116th would later receive a Distinguished Unit Citation for its role on D-Day. The accompanying narrative recognized its "extraordinary heroism and outstanding performance of duty in action in the initial assault on the northern coast of France." Old Jack and the two hundred years of veterans, from the Augusta Militia to the now 116th Regiment, would most certainly have been proud of these World War II Stonewallers.

Within the 116th, A Company had clearly suffered the worst on D-Day, as nineteen of the boys from the small town of Bedford lay dead. Five other members of the community's unit survived their boat capsizing, while only nine landed and survived the events of the Longest Day; three of these would not live through the Normandy Campaign to follow. It would be <u>thirty days</u> before the casualty letters began to reach the families of the "Bedford Boys." Then, almost daily, more bad news arrived until a complete picture of the community's loss was known.

On D-Day plus one, June 7, the 29th Division and Major General Gerhardt took control of the 116th Regiment after its release from being attached to the 1st Division on D-Day. His orders were to proceed west with the 29th Division toward Carentan, linking up along the way with the 2nd Rangers at Pointe du Hoc, and then moving on to linkup with the elements of the 101st Airborne and the 4th Division that had successfully landed on Utah Beach on D-Day. The first objective would be Isigny, a fishing village on the Vire River some nine miles away. Originally the plan was to use the 116th to lead this attack, but assessing the situation on D plus 1, Gerhardt was quick to realize the Stonewallers needed time to reorganize. The 175th, which would be landing soon, would have to take the lead west, allowing the 116th and 115th to conduct cleanup operations around Omaha Beach. There were still dangerous German positions which had to be eliminated before the beachhead was secure. The 2nd and 3rd Battalions of the 116th conducted the majority of the cleanup, despite being reduced to about fifty percent of their landing strength. The 1st Battalion was in even worse shape and in no position to continue the fight, but the threat of a German counterattack on the Rangers at Pointe du Hoc forced them into action.

The 1st Battalion got to within half a mile of the isolated Rangers before being stopped by the strong German defensive positions. They dug in for the night and on June 8, the 2nd and 3rd Battalions joined them, along with M-4 Sherman tanks from the 747th Tank Battalion. The 116th Regiment was reunited and moved to the attack. As other units of the 29th Division moved west, the Germans surrounding the Rangers were forced to withdraw or be cut off from the rest of the 352nd. Now the 116th, with Ranger comrades and tanks in support, pressed on toward the fishing port of Grandcamp. The route followed the coast road, the main route west. As the road narrowed at a bridge just east of Grandcamp, the Stonewallers began to take heavy fire from a strong German position on the high ground outside of the town. The first of the five tanks in support was knocked out in a minefield protecting the bridge, and the rest, with Colonel Canham directing their aim, fired on the German positions. Their 75mm rounds, however, just bounced off the hardened enemy positions. K and L Company were able to slip cross the bridge, but were stopped from going any further by terrific enemy fire coming from the hill to their front.

At this point, Sergeant Frank Peregoy of K Company dropped his gear and slipped out of the position where his unit had been pinned down for two hours. He crawled undetected to the flank of the first German position, which consisted of an MG-42. Using his expertise with his M-1 Rifle and grenades, Sergeant Peregoy rushed the position, destroying it and taking three prisoners. He then moved to the major enemy strong position and, using the same tactics, destroyed it, taking thirty-two more prisoners. In short order, Sergeant Peregoy eliminated the defenses outside Grandcamp, taking a total of thirty-five prisoners, and allowing the 116th to secure the town. For these actions, Sergeant Peregoy earned the Medal of Honor. Today, on the corner of University Avenue and Emmet Streets in Charlottesville, Virginia, Historical Marker G 27 provides a permanent reminder of his valor. Interestingly, his last name on this tribute is spelled Peregory, which was an error resulting from the Army's misspelling of his name. The family name has always been Peregoy, no second "r"!

By the middle of the afternoon of June 8, the 2nd and 3rd Battalions had completed the liberation of Grandcamp, and the 116th moved out to Isigny. German resistance was breaking down, and that town fell by the next morning, June 9. In less than three days, the Stonewallers had opened the coast road between Omaha Beach and Isigny. They now became the reserve regiment of the 29th Division and were finally given the opportunity to rest. George Homan of C Company, who had not seen his unit since his jeep sank during the D-Day landings, finally caught up with it and recalled that "By that time our kitchen had come in, so we had our first hot meal."

During their brief respite, the soldiers were re-supplied with K rations and ammunition for the tough days ahead. Squads and platoons were reorganized to provide a balanced force in each company. Many soldiers resisted this effort since they had trained together for so long and did not want to be broken up to serve with strangers. There was always comradery in the units of the 116th, but after several days of tough fighting together, an even stronger bond existed. Still, some reorganization did take place. There was finally time to write letters home to let loved ones know they were still alive. Most of the soldiers had their first opportunity to shave since arriving in France. It was great to finally be able to just hear the fighting and not be directly under fire, although German bombers would occasionally make night runs, dropping their bombs behind the 29th Division lines.

After the brief respite, the 116th moved out again, this time facing another difficult piece of terrain known as the *Bocage* in French, which translated means a grove. To the Stonewallers, however, it would become something that cannot be expressed in nice language. The bocage consisted of hedgerows, which had been used as early as the Roman times to mark off fields. They had an earthen or rock base from which thick vegetation grew, making them a nearly impassible barrier. In *BREAKOUT: Drive to the Seine*, David Mason may have written the best description of the maze the 29th Division found itself in.

> The hedgerow was a tangled mass of brambles and trees up to fifteen feet high, and was firmly based on a solid dirt parapet three or four feet thick and itself up to twelve feet high. These formidable natural obstacles divided the countryside into a patchwork of tiny rectangular fields. Built centuries previ-

ously to mark the limits of fields, and developed as shields to crops, animals and inhabitants against the howling ocean winds, in this month of June 1944 they proved an effective barrier to both man and vehicle.

The hedgerows were perfect for keeping cattle in, but also perfect for German ambushes to support their delaying action, in hopes that reinforcements would arrive to help them drive the Americans back into the sea. The Germans could hold off the advancing infantry easily with their MG-42s, and even a lone sniper could delay an advancing squad for days. Archibald Sproul, then a captain commanding Headquarters Company of the Third Battalion, remembered,

> The hedgerows were like having to take one field after another, because they were six or seven feet high and there were stone walls with growth and with trees growing out of them. Trying to take them was exactly like going back to World War I tactics, going from one trench to another trench.

Sproul would continue his service in the 29th Division and less than twenty years later rose to command it. The hedgerows were even more dangerous to the tanks supporting the 29th Division. Attempting to go over the top of the earthen wall exposed the bottom of the tank to German anti-armor weapons, particularly their effective Panzerfaust, a weapon similar to the American bazooka. Advancing across Omaha Beach had been difficult, but now roughly twenty miles of this new obstacle lay between the beach and the 116th Regiment's inland objective of St. Lô, targeted for D-Day +9 days.

On June 11, the Stonewallers were again on the move. They crossed the Aure River to support the 115th Regiment, which was positioned outside the French village of St. Marguerite. Still designated as Division reserve, the Stonewallers finally received clean uniforms and enjoyed partaking of a local beverage known as *calvados*. This was a very potent apple brandy that was rumored to be strong enough to use as fuel for everything from cigarette lighters to tanks. There was an abundance of *calvados* in the Norman region, and the soldiers were happy to exchange their K rations for a bottle. Often they simply found barns and storehouses filled with the beverage. When the 116th Regiment musters in Staunton each year, the remaining World War II veterans enjoy a toast of *calvados* and share memories of their time in France with today's Stonewallers.

The 116th Regiment's rest ended on June 12, with orders to prepare to attack across the Elle River. Colonel Canham called his battalion commanders together and prepared to launch an attack that evening at 7:30 p.m. There was little time, as often was the case, to develop detailed operation orders. The attack by the Stonewallers surprised the Germans as it penetrated a mile into their lines before getting bogged down. The 116th was now halfway to St. Lô. The next objective was the village of St. Clair-sur-l'Elle. As the dawn of June 13 broke through the thick fog, some of the Stonewallers could see the church steeple located in their objective just ahead. The

Illustration 12-7: The hedgerows of France

weather for those first days in France was tolerable, but drizzling rain often created a heavy morning mist, particularly in the low areas. Again, the superior numbers of the 116th Regiment forced the Germans to withdraw, and the attack pursued them two miles through the town of Couvains. St. Lô, was now only five miles away.

June 14 was a tragic day for the 116th and particularly K Company. In the hedgerows outside Couvains, Technical Sergeant Frank Peregoy's unit came upon a German strongpoint. Peregoy found a gap in the hedgerow and was leading his squad into the open field when he was shot and killed instantly. The soldier described as "the best enemy fighter" by his unit, recipient of the Soldiers Medal in 1942, and just six days earlier having earned the Medal of Honor, America's highest award, was gone, but he would never be forgotten by the Stonewallers. During the presentation of the medal to his wife Bessie Kirby Peregoy on June 4, 1945, Brigadier General E.R. Warner McCabe would say that

> You have the comfort and consolation and satisfaction of knowing that your heroic husband's memory will live forever in the hearts of his country and his valiant deeds will live in the hearts of his fellow citizens.

Today at Fort Pickett, Virginia, the brigade cantonment area on post is named for the 116th's World War II hero, Frank Peregoy. He rests in the American Cemetery at Colleville-Sur-Mer overlooking Omaha Beach. His grave is easily located by the gold embossed lettering of his name which is reserved for Medal of Honor recipients.

Illustrations 12-8: Peregoy memorial marker in Couvains, France, and his final resting place at Colleville-sur-Mer at the American Cemetery

On June 14, the 29th Division was transferred to the newly organized XIX Corps under the command of Major General Charles Corlett. This change was a result of the linkup of VII Corps coming off of Utah Beach, and V Corps, coming from Omaha Beach. Additional units would be moving to join the 29th Division in XIX Corps. The relationship with V Corps and its former commander, Major General Gerow, was now over. The new corps commander came with orders to temporarily delay further advances to allow other Allied units to achieve their objectives. The port of Cherbourg, for example, was critical to provide the basic logistics base needed to continue the offensive across Normandy. During the pause, replacements were brought in to bring the units of the 116th back up to roughly fifty percent strength. Real rations arrived to be cooked and, for only the second time since D-Day, the soldiers had the opportunity to enjoy hot food. Finally, something other than C or K rations.

The 29th Division finally resumed its attack on June 16, with the 116th on the left along with one battalion from the 115th. The 175th was on the right, with the balance of the 115th now in reserve. The 1st Battalion of the 116th took the lead, moving to the south, followed by the 2nd and 3rd Battalions to their right. As the 1st Battalion moved south supported by the 3rd Battalion of the 115th, the 2nd and 3rd Battalions would follow and turn southwest toward St. Lô. This four battalion attack had advanced roughly a mile, but just as it seemed nothing would stop it, a vicious German counterattack struck. The supporting 115th Battalion was hit particularly hard and fell back to its line of departure that morning. The battalions of the 116th held their ground, but found themselves in a precarious position as darkness approached. The difficult terrain had left large gaps between the battalions, and they were in no position to support each other. The 116th successfully held its position during the night, and the

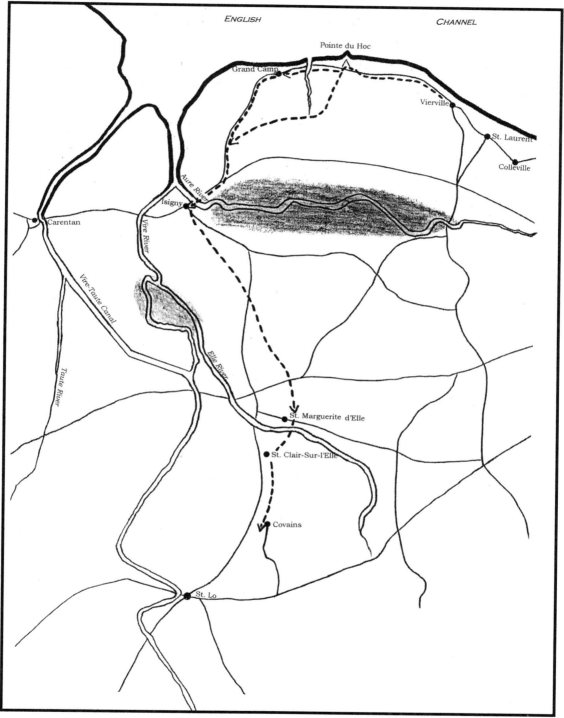

Illustration 12-9: Omaha Beach to St. Lô

next morning, it was ordered to continue the attack. Little, if any, progress was made that day. Throughout June 17, the Stonewallers would surge forward, only to be driven back.

On June 18, General Bradley ordered the 29th Division to cease offensive action, due to the high casualty rate and the need for fresh units to arrive to support the offensive. Colonel Canham was frustrated by the 116th's failure to advance, but Major Thomas D. Howie, the Regimental S-3, attributed the difficulty to the terrific losses the rifle companies had suffered. The replacement soldiers did not have the training and experience of the Stonewallers that had landed on D-Day. The units, he submitted, needed time to organize and develop into a cohesive fighting force. Major Howie always defended the soldiers of his beloved 116th Infantry Regiment and looked out for their welfare, even during the challenging conditions of Normandy. June 19 saw the miserable drizzling conditions turn to heavy rain and strong winds. The wet ground quickly turned to mud, and meteorologists were calling it the worst June conditions in the English Channel during the twentieth century. The rough seas destroyed the temporary harbors (Mulberries) on Omaha Beach, disrupting the flow of men and supplies to the front.

The lull in fighting lasted from that rainy day until July 11. During that period soldiers were given the opportunity to go to the rear, sometimes only a mile back, for a brief rest. The calm was broken occasionally by incoming German artillery and mortar fire, and the required combat patrol to probe the forward enemy lines. Training included more close order drill and instruction on how to breach the difficult Bocage defenses. Sherman tanks were fitted with metal prongs on their fronts to break through the dense growth and create an opening to allow infantry squads to quickly attack the German defenses across the open field. General Gerhardt developed a new strategy for the Blue and Gray Division, "one squad, one tank, one field" was the technique he wanted utilized to break the enemy defenses. The only problem was that there were only fifty-three tanks from the supporting 747th Tank Battalion available when the offensive resumed. During this period, the remnants of the 352nd, which the Stonewallers had been fighting since landing on D-Day, were replaced by the 3rd *Fallschirmjager* Division. These well-armed and highly motivated German paratroopers were determined to provide a formidable defense of St. Lô.

During the lull, planners developed the order for the attack to finally seize St. Lô. The new strategy made the 116th Regiment the XIX Corps' main effort, and they in turn chose the 2nd Battalion to lead the attack to breach the German lines and open a route to the French city. The 1st and 3rd Battalions would follow, and pass through the 2nd Battalion to complete the drive to St. Lô. The XIX Corps was building its combat power, with more units arriving daily. The 116th was on the 29th Division's left, bordering V Corps and the 38th Infantry Regiment of the 2nd Division. The 115th Regiment was on the right, and completing the XIX Corps' front lines was the 35th Division, a National Guard unit from the midwest. The morale of the units in the

116th improved when they learned that they had been picked again to lead the attack. The soldiers, even the replacements, took great pride in serving as part of the historic Stonewall Brigade, and they were determined to continue the legacy as they advanced to St. Lô. On July 4, the Stonewallers, along with the rest of the American forces, celebrated America's Independence Day by firing what seemed to be unlimited rounds of ammunition. Their British Allies did not share in the joy of the day.

The 2nd Battalion's attack was finally set for the morning of July 11. A one hour artillery barrage beginning at 0500 announced the start of a bad day for the German defenders. Promptly at 0600, with E and F Companies in the lead, the 2nd Battalion moved forward supported by A Company of the 747th Tank Battalion. The plan was to attack south and then make a right turn to attack St. Lô from the east. In the V Corps area, the 38th Division was tasked to capture Hill 192 on the 116th's left. The 115th was to initiate a supporting attack on the right, but it had suffered serious losses from a German counterattack in its area just a few hours before the 29th's offensive was set to kick off. Their ability to support was in question, as the Stonewallers moved out. Still, the attack seemed to go well as the battalion broke through the German front line. Major Bingham, commanding the 2nd Battalion, turned his companies to the right after achieving the successful move of some five hundred yards after Hill

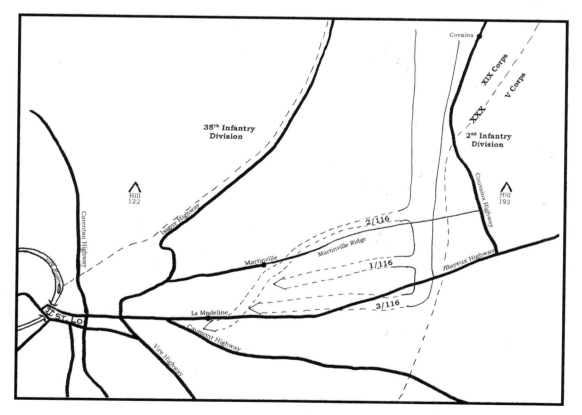

Illustration 12-10: Attack on St. Lô

192 had been captured. This action reduced the *Fallschirmjager* Division's ability to observe the 116th's movements and bring effective indirect fire on them. The German paratroopers were forced to withdraw almost a mile and half to better defensive positions closer to St. Lô.

Throughout the attack, the 116th Regiment's 2nd Battalion incurred heavy casualties, and finally its progress ground to a halt, and the soldiers began to dig defensive positions for the night. They had followed the line of the Martinville Ridge, and were close to taking the small town it was named for, when they halted. The 1st and 3rd Battalions had followed the 2nd during the afternoon and continued south to protect their left flank as Bingham's forces made their turn west. The entire 116th was committed to a curving front line, oriented from the west to the southwest. Major General Gerhart now brought forward the 175th Regiment to support the move to St. Lô. The 116th was ready to continue the attack on July 12 and had high hopes of reaching its objective within twenty-four hours.

Unfortunately, not enough attention was given to Hill 122, which lay north of St. Lô and in clear view of the Martinville Ridge and the 116th's approach to the city from the east. On the morning of July 12, the Germans had regrouped, and their artillery observers were positioned to direct effective fire on the Stonewallers and any 29th Division units attempting to support them. Throughout the day, the 116th was able to advance only some 650 yards against the galling indirect fire from the enemy artillery and mortars. The unit was within two miles of St. Lô, but still clearly visible to German observation posts on Hill 122 and the Martinville Ridge. The 116th Regiment's 3rd Battalion was oriented south, protecting the left flank. The 116th's front stretched only about three-quarters of a mile. The supporting attack of the 115th Regiment on the right was also coming under observation from Hill 122 and had been stopped by the effective German indirect fire. The closer the units got to St. Lô, the better the German forward observers could see them and direct destructive fire, stopping their advance.

The plan for July 13 was to pass the 175th Regiment through the 116th, hopefully with enough combat power to move into St. Lô. Unfortunately, the planned air strikes were called off due to bad weather, the tank support from the 747th did not materialize due to a lack of fuel and ammunition, and the 175th's capability to communicate was seriously damaged by German fire. Nothing went well throughout the day, and casualties in all of the 29th Division units continued to mount despite little progress. During the day, Major Thomas Howie assumed command of the 3rd Battalion, replacing LTC Meeks. Howie had been relieved of command by Major General Gerhardt in England for what was considered his lack of attention to the details that the commanding general felt important, and too much concern for soldier care. Now he would again turn to Howie to lead a battalion, this time concerned more about the big picture, breaking through to St. Lô.

Frustrated by the lack of progress, Gerhardt ordered the day of July 14 to be utilized to rest the command, while the plan for the final attack on St. Lô was formulated. He also used the opportunity to visit his unit at the front and impress upon them how critical the capture of St. Lô was to the entire American offensive. Seizing the crossroads of the city was critical, and necessary before kicking off the attack across France and into Germany which would be known as operation COBRA. His remarks were inspirational, but many of the soldiers were unhappy with his tactics that had cost so many casualties. The fight for St. Lô had already been more costly to the 116th than the D-Day landing on Omaha Beach.

The renewed attacks of July 15 brought more heavy losses and little gain on the ground until late in the afternoon, when the 1st and 2nd Battalions of the 116th created a break in the German lines. Gerhardt, unaware of the success, ordered the 29th to halt and dig in for the night. The 1st Battalion got the word, but Major Bingham and the 2nd Battalion were in close pursuit of the withdrawing enemy and surged forward through Martinville and to the village of La Madeleine before stopping. The problem now was that the bulk of the 2nd Battalion was almost a mile ahead of the rest of the 116th, digging in to their new positions on the Martinville Ridge. Fortunately, the 35th Division had finally taken Hill 122, reducing the German's ability to observe the positions of the 116th, but it was not hard for them to see that the 2nd Battalion was isolated in advance of the rest of the Regiment. During this day, Colonel Philip R. Dwyer took command of the 116th, replacing Colonel Canham, who had been selected for promotion and had departed to accept a new position as Assistant Division Commander of the 8th Division.

Despite the salient created by the 2nd Battalion's position, Sunday, July 16, was to be a day for the 29th Division forces to rest and re-supply, but as morning broke, the Germans initiated a strong counterattack against the 115th and 116th positions, strangely ignoring the 2nd Battalion, which was basically cut off and unsupported. The attackers used organized tank formations for the first time in the campaign, and the Stonewallers struggled to stop them with their anti-armor bazookas. The rounds seemed to just bounce off the advancing German armor, but at least got their attention, enough to result in their withdrawal back toward St. Lô. By day's end, the counterattacks had been defeated, but with significant loss to both sides. There was no rest, little re-supply, and the 2nd Battalion was still well forward and without rations. The country boys of the battalion slipped out to nearby farmhouses to obtain whatever food they could find and secure much needed water. Ammunition was becoming a real problem, though.

July 17 found the entire 29th Division, all nine battalions, ordered to attack. The assignment to relieve the 2nd Battalion was given to Major Tom Howie and his 3rd Battalion. The relief column fixed bayonets in the early morning hours and moved quickly toward La Madeleine, reaching the town just as the sun was rising. The defenders were delighted to see their fellow Stonewallers, but especially grateful for the rations they brought. Major Howie was quick to assess the condition of the 2nd

Battalion as essentially being combat ineffective at that point, and he called his commanders together to lay out the plan for his 3rd battalion to continue the attack into St. Lô. The meeting had just concluded when German mortar rounds began falling in the field around the command group. Major Howie paused to insure his subordinate leaders had found cover, and in doing so, fell victim to a shell fragment which struck him in the back, puncturing his lung. His Executive Officer, Captain William Puntenney, rushed to assist his fallen commander, but nothing could be done. After only four days in command, Major Tom Howie was dead. Word of his loss spread quickly, and coupled with German counterattacks, the 116th Regiment's momentum for the day was lost. The enemy counterattack was finally broken by the Stonewallers' effective use of air power. The 506th Fighter-Bomber Squadron arrived around 8:45 that evening, bombing and then strafing the German armor and infantry.

On July 18, Major General Gerhardt activated a secret weapon he had been developing - "Task Force C"- under the command of Brigadier General Cota. Task Force C had been organized back in Couvains and was comprised of Armor, Artillery, Engineer, Reconnaissance and Tank Destroyer units. The 29th Division launched the final attack to St. Lô on a broad front, but Task Force C would provide the concentrated combat power to finally allow the Blue and Gray Division to enter the city. The attack was successful, despite desperate German counterattacks and artillery bombardment. The long fight through the hedgerows to St. Lô was finally over. Though over a month late, the capture was significant, and soon would allow the launching of Operation Cobra. General George S. Patton would take command of the operation and race across France to take the war into Germany. The Stonewallers had suffered heavy losses and combined with the D-Day casualties, very few of the original National Guardsmen remained in the ranks.

On the morning of July 19, the flag draped body of Major Tom Howie was brought forward on the hood of a jeep and placed on a pile of rubble from an outside wall of the Saint Croix Church in the main square of St. Lô. Tom Howie, hereafter known as the "Major of St. Lô," had told his subordinates before his death "See you in St. Lô." This was a promise Gerhardt made sure was kept. Joseph Auslander recalled Major Howie's momentous entry into St. Lô with a eulogy published in *Life Magazine*, the close of which read:

> Ride soldier in your dusty, dingy jeep,
> Grander than Caesar's chariot, O ride
> Into the town they took for you to keep,
> Dead captain of their glory and their pride!
> Ride through our hearts forever, through our tears,
> More splendid than the hero hedged with spears!

Major Tom Howie was one of the most beloved leaders in the 116th Regiment during WWII. He had commanded the 2nd Battalion in England, served as Regimental Operations Officer, or S-3, and then commanded the 3nd Battalion. He had been a trainer and friend of the 116th's soldiers since their mobilization in February, 1941. He would be sorely missed, but not forgotten. The National Guard Armory housing the Headquarters of today's 116th IBCT in Staunton, Virginia, bears his name, as does the athletic field at the former Staunton Military Academy (SMA), where he instructed. Entering St. Lô on the Bayeux Highway from La Madeleine, it is easy to locate the memorial there to the "Major of St. Lô," Thomas D. Howie, dedicated in 1969. Major Howie rests with Technical Sergeant Frank Peregoy and 785 other Stonewallers at Colleville-sur-Mer Cemetery.

On July 19, the 116th Regiment was finally given the opportunity to withdraw from the line. They would be replaced initially by the 115th, but soon the responsibility for St. Lô would be turned over to the 35th Division. The entire 29th Division was given a well deserved rest. They had been continuously in action for six weeks, suffering some seven thousand total casualties. The Division and its 116th Regiment had endeared themselves to the people of the Norman Region of France, despite the destruction that was a tragic part of their liberation. The city of St. Lô lay in ruin, but the resilient people of the region rebounded with their freedom restored, and today

Illustration 12-11: Resting Place of the "Major of St. Lô"

Illustration 12-12: Thomas D. Howie Memorial in St. Lô

continue to honor the memory of their liberators in community events and parades. There is little more cherished in France's Norman region than the patch of the Blue and Gray Division and the legacy of the "Major of St. Lô." The affection may have been captured best by the Mayor of St. Lô, L'Baird during the dedication of the Howie Memorial there, "On this 25th anniversary of our liberation, I sincerely hope St. Lô's citizens will never forget in the years and centuries to come Major Howie, who, in 1944, gave his life so that we might live free."

Battle streamers earned: Normandy Beachhead, Beaches of Normandy, Normandy, Northern France

-Thirteen-

Vire to
the Elbe

O n July 28, rested, reorganized, and ready to continue the fight, the 29th Division mounted vehicles and returned to the front, now just three miles south of St. Lô. There were lots of new faces in the companies as they passed through the city the Division had fought forty-three days to occupy. Reaching the forward lines, the Stonewallers dismounted and watched the trucks return back toward St. Lô. It was after three in the morning before they were placed in their new positions at the front. The next objective was the city of Vire to the southeast. The 116th Regiment took its usual position in the lead, along with the 175th Regiment on its right, and the boundary with V Corps on its left. By the morning of July 29, the 116th completed its relief of the 66th Armored Regiment of the 2nd American Armored Division. This Division was now released to join Operation Cobra. On July 30, the 116th resumed its offensive operations against the elements of the German 2nd Panzer Division. Reports of enemy tanks slipping through to the rear sent G Company with its bazookas to locate and destroy the group of infiltrators. Near the crossroads of La Denisiere, the enemy was spotted, and the ensuing battle destroyed four Mark IV German tanks and a halftrack accompanying them. The engagement cost the Brigade several Tank Destroyers and a number of G Company soldiers, to include the Commander of Company F, Lieutenant Eugene Raggett, who had been in support. Lieutenant Colonel Sidney Bingham was wounded on this day and replaced by his Executive Officer Major Charles Cawthon.

The next day, July 30, German armor, mainly panzers, probed the lines of the 116th unsuccessfully. The dawn of July 31 found the Germans gone. The effects of Operation Cobra were being felt as Patton's Third Army was flanking the German forward positions and forcing them into a hasty withdrawal. The Stonewallers moved out in pursuit, covering about two miles without incident, before digging in as darkness fell. The next day, the advance continued. The 115th moved up to replace the 175th on the 116th's right, and the steady move continued southeast. At best, the Germans were only fighting a delaying action, with many staying behind to surrender. Everywhere there were the remains of destroyed tanks from both armies and tons of ruined German equipment left behind. By August 5, the 116th Regiment had reached the high ground to the north and northwest of Vire. On this day Lieutenant Colonel Tom Dallas, commanding the 1st Battalion was wounded and was replaced by Lieutenant Colonel Harold Cassell. In less than three weeks, two battalion commanders of the 116th were killed and two wounded.

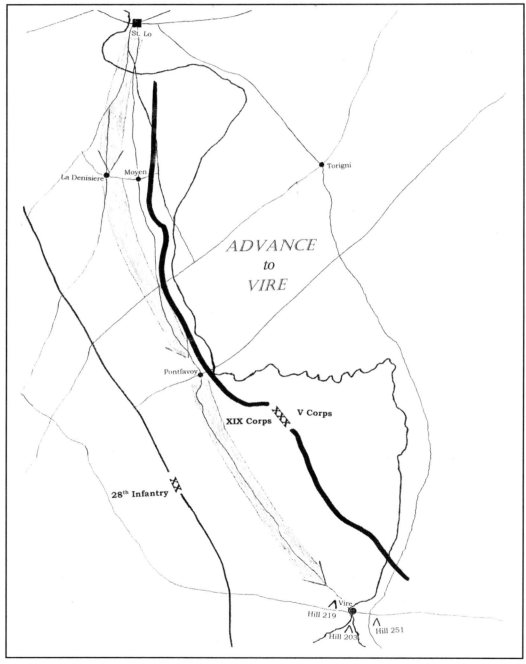

Illustration 13-1: Advance to Vire

On August 6, the 116th Regiment's 2nd Battalion attacked to capture Hill 219 overlooking the city of Vire. As their momentum was halted, the 3rd Battalion passed through and completed the capture of the strategic high ground to the west of city, setting the conditions for the Regiment to attack the urban area. That evening, around 7:15 p.m., with the 2nd battalion on the right and the 3rd Battalion on the left, the 116th moved down into a ravine, crossed the Vire River, and then climbed up the bank on the other side. Despite intense small arms fire, they succeeded in entering the city. During the night, the two battalions cleared the buildings, many of them still burning from bombing and shelling, and by the next day, the Stonewallers controlled the five major roads leading east and south from the city. German artillery now began to rain down on the 116th defenders. The fire was being directed by forward observers on Hill 203 overlooking the city, and the position had to be eliminated. The difficult mission of climbing this hill and capturing it fell to the 1st Battalion. Throughout the night, its companies made preparation for the attack on the morning of August 8. B and C Companies would make the assault, while A Company engaged the defenders with direct fire. The tactic worked, and the Germans were forced to withdraw or surrender under the pincer attack by B and C Companies.

The successful attack of the 1st Battalion can best be described in the narrative of the subsequent Distinguished Unit Citation they received for the action.

In the afternoon of 7 August 1944, the 1st Battalion, 116th Infantry was ordered to accomplish the seemingly impossible task of driving a strongly emplaced enemy force from the heights overlooking Vire. The battalion, weary from ten-days' continuous fighting during which it had lost two-thirds of its effective strength, started immediately to get in positions to attack its objective. During this advance the battalion was subjected to frequent and violent artillery concentrations but by its aggressive and skillful action it was able to get to the base of Hill 203 with light casualties. As the forward elements of the battalion advanced up the hill they were met by heavy fire of all weapons, stopping the attack for the night. Immediately thereafter the enemy artillery was directed on the rear elements of the battalion, which moved forward quickly to a defiladed position at the base of the hill where they held all night under an almost constant, but ineffective, artillery and mortar barrage. At 0530 hours on 8 August, the battalion executed a skillful maneuver under cover of its own supporting weapons to surprise and rout the enemy. The success of the action was made possible by innumerable acts of heroism on the part of the soldiers who advanced speedily and steadily in the face of enemy fire and uncertainty, not hesitating or swerving from their mission. On taking this hill they made possible the reopening of the Vire streets to our traffic and denied the enemy a very important point from which to direct artillery fire on our troops.

In the entire action the spirit, aggressiveness, and skill of the 1st Battalion, 116th Infantry, in the attack reflected great credit on the United States Army.

The capture of Hill 203 was complemented by the capture of Hill 251 by the 2nd Battalion, completing the elimination of the German presence on the high ground around the city. Vire had been identified early on by Supreme Allied Commander General Eisenhower as the "pivotal point" from which Patton's Third Army could begin its swing east. Soon the Falaise Pocket, a salient resulting from Patton's swift movement, was created, and this resulted in the German collapse in the area of the 29th Division. Another mission accomplished, the 116th Regiment was taken off the line to become the First United States Army Reserve and had an opportunity to rest and reorganize in Vire. The entire 29th Division would enjoy a brief period of rehabilitation from August 17-20. During the down time, General Gerhardt visited the 116th and presented Bronze Stars to several of the Stonewallers and praised their accomplishments. On August 12, Brigadier General Cota departed to take command of the 28th Infantry Division, a National Guard Division from Pennsylvania, which was located on the right of the 29th Division during its attack on Vire. He would be replaced later in the month by Colonel Leroy H. Watson of the 3rd Armored Division.

Sunday, August 20, was set aside as a day for rest and worship. Many a Stonewaller attended religious services, happy to be alive. Replacements filled the ranks again, youngsters, many only eighteen years of age. The new soldiers quickly learned the pride of serving in the historic Stonewall Brigade and soon understood what the veterans they were joining had accomplished. It was difficult for the newcomers to be accepted however. Green and minimally trained, the veterans knew that few would adapt fast enough to survive. On the morning of August 22, the 116th loaded onto trucks, the usual "deuce and a halfs" that carried twenty-five soldiers each, and headed off to the front. The Stonewallers were surprised, though, when the trucks did not turn east to follow the American advance toward Germany, but instead turned south. The Stonewallers were being assigned to serve as part of the VIII Corps, ordered to take the port city of Brest in the region of France known as Brittany. The convoy was greeted along the way by happy French citizens, cheering them on and calling them "liberators." It was a title well earned, but also greatly appreciated by the Stonewallers. Occasionally, the men of the 116th leading, the 29th Division column, stopped to enjoy fresh eggs and their old nemesis, *calvados*, provided by the grateful citizens of Brittany. The trip, which covered two hundred miles, ended that evening with the 116th Regiment units forming up in an assembly area roughly ten miles northwest of Brest. They would take positions on the right of the American VIII Corps, preparing to capture the port city and its U-boat pens.

The German Commander at Brest was Major General Hermann Ramcke, known for his tenacious defense at Monte Cassino in Italy. His orders were to hold Brest for at least three months, and he was committed to doing so with the experienced troops of his 2nd Parachute Division. His force also consisted of many sailors and naval personnel trapped by the Allied encirclement. There was no way to retreat. The defenders of Brest would either surrender or die.

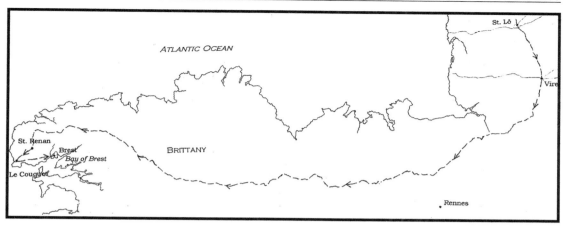

Illustration 13-2: 116th Movement to Brest

On August 25, the 116th Regiment was in position, and the attack kicked off at 0100 hours. Its 1st and 3rd Battalions would move forward together, with the 2nd Battalion initially in reserve. For the next twenty hours the Stonewallers moved forward against increasing resistance, finally stopping to dig defensive positions as night fell. Movement was slow over the next two days, and the 116th was moved to the extreme right of the 29th Division during the night of August 27. Here they were to continue the attack along le Conquet-Recouvrance Highway. The 2nd Battalion was now in the lead as the Regiment approached the outskirts of la Trinite, halfway to the objective. Casualties mounted as the 2nd Battalion tried to seize the small town, and a standoff developed. Joined by the 1st Battalion, the 2nd captured the small town with relative ease during the night attack of September 4. Now the 116th prepared for the German counterattack, which it withstood, partially through the heroics of Sergeant Wilson R. Carr of G Company, who single-handedly killed at least fifteen attackers. For this and for encouraging his platoon to successfully defend its position, he would be awarded the Distinguished Service Cross, one of the few earned in the 116th Regiment after D-Day. Awards for valor were hard to come by, and Major General Gerhardt was known for not recommending many, but the deeds of numerous Stonewallers certainly deserved recognition throughout the advance across France.

During the next few days, the noose around Brest continued to tighten, while the 116th was given a short break in a reserve role for the 29th Division. On September 11 the Stonewallers were back at the front, assisted by the 5th Ranger Battalion on their right. On the evening of September 13, they took up the attack of Fort Montbarey, one of the last bastions of the German defense. It was an old nineteenth century French castle with forty-foot thick exterior walls surrounded by a moat. The Germans had protected it with multiple defensive positions, and it was a formidable obstacle that had to be captured. At dawn of the next day, the 1st Battalion led the attack with the 2nd and 3rd Battalions in reserve. C Company took the lead to clear defenders outside the moat, west of the fortress. B Company followed up, using flame-throwing British Churchill tanks, to open lanes through the final defenses. The next day, the Stonewallers consolidated their positions and, on September 16, renewed their attack, forcing the final surrender of the fort. The 116th Regiment was in the center of the 29th Division's line of attack, and by the evening of the seventeenth had reached the outskirts of Recouvrance and then took the high ground overlooking the Bay of Brest and the submarine pens located there. The next day, the surviving German garrison surrendered to now Brigadier General Charles Canham and his Eighth Division. After three weeks, not three months, Brest had fallen under Allied control.

The delighted Stonewallers took full advantage of the peace brought about by the victory, partaking freely of the huge stores of wine they liberated and riding

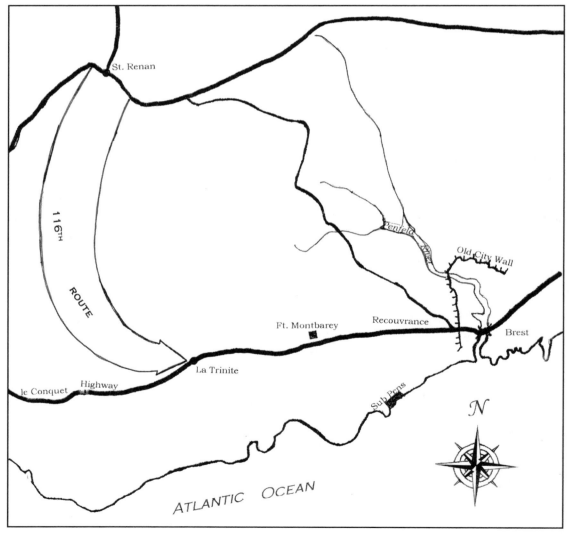

Illustration 13-3: Attack to Brest

about on captured horses, bicycles, motorcycles, cars, and trucks. On September 18, the units began moving back to rest on the Conquet Peninsula. The day before, September 17, the Allies had launched Operation Market Garden, the largest airborne offensive in history, jumping into Holland to capture crucial bridges and canals in the low country leading to Germany. The American 101st Airborne Division was tasked with securing the first objectives, which consisted of a series of canal bridges around Eindhoven. The American 82nd Division had the more difficult task of capturing the Grave Bridge over the Maas River and the bridges at Nijmegen. The British 1st Airborne Division had the challenge of seizing and holding the Rhine River bridge at Arnhem, the one to become known as "the bridge too far," in the words of British Lieutenant-General Browning, who had overall command of the operation. The attacks resulted in heavy losses in the airborne divisions and failed to capture the critical bridge over the Rhine at the town of Arnhem. There would be no quick entry into Germany.

At Brest, the 29th Division had suffered around 3,500 casualties. Major Jim Morris, formerly of the sister 115th and temporarily in command of the 1st Battalion during this period, had written to his mother, "I am still CO of the VA outfit, at least it used to be from VA, but now it is from all over." Most companies of the 116th were under fifty percent in strength and essentially combat ineffective until more new recruits joined their ranks. The remaining Stonewallers enjoyed the luxury of showers, movies, and the opportunity to write home. Plans were made for providing leave time, but all too soon, duty called and the down time was ended.

On September 23, the 116th Regiment was again in motion, with the Infantry first moving by trucks to the railhead at Landerneau, where the Stonewallers bivouacked before boarding trains to take them to rejoin XIX Corps, while the support elements began the long motor move to the link-up. The companies were only at about two-thirds strength, which meant roughly only forty men per train car, leaving enough room to make the trip somewhat comfortable. For three nights and four days, the Stonewallers rolled across France. During stops, the liberated French welcomed the soldiers, sharing wine on several occasions to celebrate their freedom. Along the way, the trains passed through Paris, but everything, including the cars carrying the 116th, was blacked out, leaving little to remember. Finally, on the evening of September 29, the trains reached Vise, Belgium, having covered roughly 650 miles. The 116th Regiment was now only about twenty miles from the German border. It was just fifty miles south of Eindhoven, which had been captured by the 101st Airborne in Operation Market Garden. Perhaps this terrible war would be over before Christmas, bringing an end to the horrible year of 1944. The soldiers again boarded trucks, this time for the two-hour ride to Valkenburg and the front. Here they were welcomed by their support elements that had already arrived by convoy.

The 29th Division and the 116th Regiment were back with XIX Corps, this time joining the 30th Division, a National Guard unit from neighboring North Carolina and Tennessee, and the 2nd Armored Division. The Stonewallers assumed the role of

Corps reserve, and the opportunity was utilized to issue wool uniforms and winter gear, to include overcoats, knit caps, gloves, and sweaters. Somebody was assuming the war would not be over soon. Makeshift rifle ranges were set up and daily battle drills conducted for the four days the 116th was in reserve, then it was time to move forward. The terrain here was very open, totally unlike the hedgerow hell that had taken the lives of so many Stonewallers. The soldiers could see vast open fields before them, with some trees lining the roads.

On October 1, the 116th was attached to the 30th Division, and each of the battalions tasked with varying missions. The 1st Battalion moved almost immediately to the German border and took up defensive positions roughly three miles northwest of Aachen. Here they would be responsible for protecting the Corps' right flank and remaining in contact with the 1st Division, which was the left flank unit for the VII Corps. A standard German tactic was to identify the boundaries between the American units and direct a counterattack into them. Maintaining contact with the adjacent unit was an important assignment as XIX Corps approached Germany, as it had been through all of the action since the D-Day landings. During this time, the 1st Battalion would be preparing for the upcoming offensive mission to widen the breach of the Siegfried Line and continue the attack east to the Roer River and Germany.

The first few days of October found the 116th Regiment's 2nd Battalion being bounced around the XIX Corps' area of operations and tasked to conduct a variety

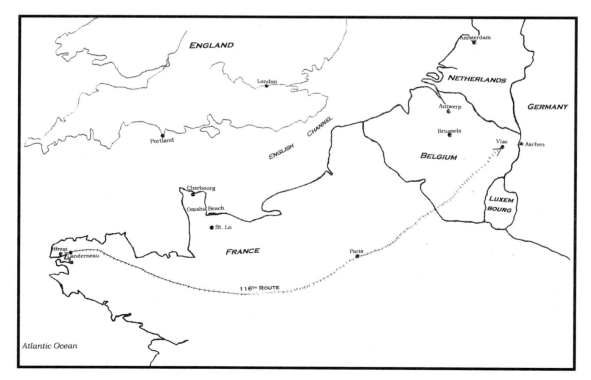

Illustration 13-4: 116th Movement to the Front - Vise

of missions. It was initially in a reserve role, located in the vicinity of Kerkrade, but constantly sent on reconnaissance missions trying to identify potential weaknesses in the Siegfried line. There were multiple probings in an effort to utilize the reserve to create an opening. It was obvious to the Stonewallers that an offensive operation was imminent to complete the breakthrough of the Siegfried Line and conduct a final attack to the Roer River and into Germany. On October 8, with very little notice, the 2nd Battalion was moved forward and attached to the 2nd Armored Division for several days as they prepared to attack east. Then on October 11, the 2nd Battalion joined the 30th Division preparing to attack south to Aachen and a linkup with the 1st Division.

On October 4, the 116th Regiment's 3rd Battalion, which had also spent several days in a Corps' reserve role, was sliced off from the 116th to become part of Combat Command A from the 2nd Armored Division. This heavy organization was to exploit the 30th Division's success after they penetrated the Siegfried Line. Initially the 3rd Battalion soldiers enjoyed riding on tanks, but they soon realized that the large armor formations attracted heavy German fire. Still, Combat Command A was able to successfully move east, and by October 7, the 3rd Battalion soldiers were cleaning up the town of Baesweiler. Throughout this period, casualties in the entire 116th mounted steadily from the continuous German mortar and artillery shelling. The historic Stonewall Brigade was inside Germany, and its presence was not appreciated. The relentless indirect fire was some of the worst the Stonewallers had experienced since D-Day. Assigned primarily to the Corps' reserve, however, their actual losses were insignificant compared to previous periods at the front.

Intelligence gathering completed and orders finalized, Friday, October 13, was established as the day XIX Corps would resume its offensive east. The 116th Regiment, minus the 3rd Battalion, was attached to the 30th Division and assembled in the area of North Bardenberg to prepare for the attack. The combat power of the 116th was plused up by the addition of the 3rd Battalion from the 66th Armor Regiment and the 3rd Battalion from the 120th Infantry Regiment. Final preparations on October 12 found tanks being brought forward and the infantry readied to kick off the action promptly at 9 a.m. the following morning. At H-Hour, the 116th moved forward, but the determined German defenders did not give ground easily. Their artillery, which had massed east of Wurselen, brought effective fire on the Stonewallers, staggering their advance. It took three difficult days for the 116th to succeed in linking up with the 1st Division on the Aachen-Julich highway. On October 20, the 116th continued its attacks to capture Wurselen, but with little success. Finally, the 1st Division was successful in capturing Aachen, allowing the 30th Division to take up defensive positions. The 116th was now returned to 29th Division control and pulled off the line on October 24, 1944.

The 116th withdrew to Eigelshoven and Merkstein to rearm, refit, re-supply, and train for its next mission. There was a focus on river crossing tactics, and many classes were conducted in a Dutch castle, which became known as "Uncle Charlie's University" for Major General Gerhardt. There was time for mail call and memories

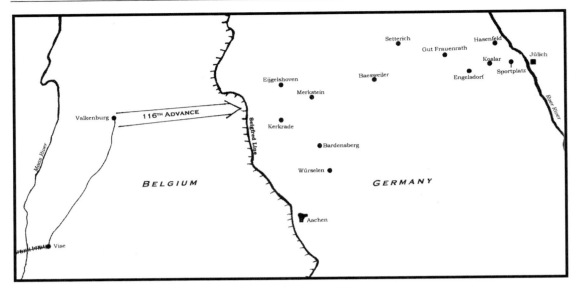

Illustration 13-5: Attack to the Roer River

of the upcoming holidays at home. The weather seemed to grow worse by the day, as one of the most difficult winters in European history approached. On November 7, the Stonewallers once again moved to the front, this time on the 29th Division left, with the 115th Regiment to their right and the 2nd Armored Division on their left. They were visited by General Eisenhower on November 10 to insure their readiness for continuing the attack deeper into Germany. Lieutenant Colonel Harold A. Cassel, the Executive Officer of the 116th, assumed command of the Regiment from Colonel Dwyer, who was transferred to another assignment. Uncle Charlie was still at the helm of the 29th Division, and Major General Raymond S. McLain was now in command of XIX Corps.

The Stonewallers renewed their attack on November 17. Their objective was the town of Setterich to the east, and they would have tank support from the 2nd Armored Division. The attack came from three sides, with B and C Company approaching from the south, while A Company came from the west, supported by the 2nd Armored elements to the north. The 1st Battalion's attack made good progress on the first day, and the capture of Setterich was completed on the second day, November 18. Stonewallers from the 2nd Battalion's E, F, and G Companies assisted in clearing the town, building by building, throughout that day and part of the next. The 116th then moved to an assembly area at Baesweiler to prepare to take Kolsar, five miles deeper into Germany. The 2nd Battalion approached the town from the west, with the 3rd Battalion conducting a supporting effort to the south. The attack kicked off on the afternoon of November 21, and the Stonewallers immediately ran into wire obstructions and minefields. Moving cautiously, but progressing steadily, they proceeded to the outskirts of the town by November 25, and concluded its capture with a night bayonet assault conducted by F and G Company. The two units, however, found themselves isolated and vulnerable to German Counterattack. The two companies held out until being relieved by the 1st Battalion, coming from their position as regimental reserve on the morning of November 27. It was a Thanksgiving week that few of these Stonewallers would ever forget.

The fall of Koslar left the 116th only two thousand yards from the Roer River. On December 1, the 1st Battalion moved east toward the river, with A and C Company attacking, and B Company positioned in reserve. The Germans had their backs to the river and fought tenaciously, using mortars and machine gun fire to stop the advancing Stonewallers. The next night they resumed the attack, but were forced to fall back with heavy losses. The defenders had laid extensive minefields to protect their positions west of the Roer and were effectively using artillery to lay down a curtain of steel to cover them. On December 3, Colonel Bingham assumed command of the 116th and made plans to renew the attack. The 3rd Battalion now moved forward on December 4, attempting to reach the river and came within three hundred yards of achieving its objective before being stopped. That night and into the next day I and L Companies struggled to advance but made it only as far as the *Sportplatz*, or athletic field, a short distance from the river. Ralph Coffman, now a Platoon Sergeant, who had recovered from the wound he had received outside of St. Lô and had just returned to the front, recalled reaching the dirt high ground in front of the *Sportplatz* before being stopped by a counterattack. "The German reinforcements were coming up in front of us and his artillery shells dropping right back of us," he recalled before being hit by shrapnel and having to withdraw, wounded again after only three days back at the front. Sergeant Coffman had been amazed at the few faces he recognized in the 116th during his brief return. The complexion of the regiment had changed dramatically since the D-Day landings.

A coordinated attack by the 116th was planned for the morning of December 6. The 1st Battalion, supported by the 3rd Battalion, was to attack and capture the *Sportplatz*, while the 2nd Battalion was to attack the Hasenfeld Gut, another heavily mined German strongpoint. The attack was initiated at 2:35 a.m., supported by bombing and strafing from the air corps and heavy artillery bombardment followed by a heavy smoke screen. Again the German defenders, using direct and indirect fire and thick minefields, prevented the 116th from achieving its objectives, and they paid a heavy price in losses for the attempt. Companies now looked more like platoons and battalions were down to only a company-sized unit in strength. The 116th Regiment was forced to conduct a battle handover to the 115th Regiment that finally completed the seizure of the west bank of the Roer River by the morning of December 9. The weary and depleted ranks of the Stonewallers withdrew to again rearm, refit, re-supply, and train for the next operation. "Ever Forward" was a difficult motto for the severely under strength units to live up to, especially when their ranks were filled mainly by new recruits brought in to replace the staggering losses the 116th had incurred.

For the next few days the Stonewallers resumed their training, with particular emphasis on river crossing. This was a much needed break that quickly restored the confidence of the 116th Regiment, shattered by the desperate German Roer River defense. The Stonewallers were shocked on December 16, to learn of an extensive counteroffensive to the south. It was centered in the Ardennes on a seventy-five mile front which was defended by only four divisions, one of which was the Pennsylvania National Guard's 28th Division. The right flank of the attack, which consisted of three German armies and twenty-four divisions, passed just thirty miles to the south of the 116th. The enemy plan, which caught the Allies completely unaware, was an effort to split the U. S. First and U. S. Ninth Armies and drive west to capture the critical port and supply base at Antwerp, Belgium. The resulting German offensive would become known as the Battle of the Bulge. Although the 116th would not participate directly, its training for a river crossing ceased immediately and attention turned to the defense. The Stonewallers would now be assigned a forward defensive position along the river, replacing the 2nd Armored Division. They would be on the 29th Division's left, as the Blue and Gray assumed responsibility for the entire XIX Corps defense on the west bank of the Roer. The 116th Regiment, with its 2nd and 3rd Battalions, took up defensive positions forward, with the 1st Battalion in reserve. The 175th Regiment was on their right in the center of the 29th Division's front, which covered twelve miles and overlooked the Roer River. The 115th Regiment was positioned on the Division's right.

The 29th Division assumed previous German and American defensive positions, and began to improve them in preparation for any German offensive that might come their way. Listening outposts were established forward, many as close as twenty yards to the Roer River. The winter cold made it hard on the soldiers who served in the outposts, but duty was rotated to give each of the men some time in better conditions. Duty back in the main defense and reserve was a luxury by comparison, with warm fires and beds of straw to sleep in. There were stoves, and that meant hot coffee and the ability to heat K-rations.

Replacements for the 116th Regiment were slow in coming, as the priority was to fill the units that had suffered the heavy losses during the Battle of the Bulge. There was a thick cloud cover during the first days of the German attack that headed west to Bastogne, but as the weather improved, Allied planes took to the air and brought a halt to Hitler's last great offensive scheme. In addition, General George Patton had turned his Third Army north toward Bastogne, cutting into the German left flank and relieving the besieged town. Christmas, 1944, found the Battle of the Bulge winding down, but there was now little hope that the war would end soon. For the 116th, there was not much action as the end of another year approached, except for routine patrolling and occasional indirect fire exchanges across the Roer. Christmas Day saw a scattering of trees decorated with German ornaments and a turkey dinner with all of the fixings. Some

Stonewallers had even received gifts from home, but unit chaplains made sure that everyone received something during the holiday.

The New Year, 1945, found the Allies cleaning up the remnants of the Germans left behind in the "bulge" south of the 116th Regiment. F Company, supported by a detachment of engineers, paddled across the Roer River on January 9, to conduct the first of the 29th Division's raids to help fix the German positions beyond the east bank. The town of Julich, for example, provided the enemy excellent observation of the movements within the Division's area of operations, and would clearly need to be taken when the Blue and Gray Division resumed its offensive into Germany. On January 27, the front of the 116th was expanded as the 175th Regiment was moved from the center of the line to the rear to become the Division's reserve. The 175th would prepare to lead the river crossing to capture Julich and create a hole in the German lines. When February 3 dawned, the Stonewallers paused to think of home and recall their day of activation four years earlier. Many of the original National Guardsmen were returning to the front, having recovered from being wounded in the fighting of the last nearly eight months. The combat readiness of the 116th was improving in time to resume the attack into Germany, but initially they would become the Division reserve as the 175th and 115th Regiments crossed the river. The attack was set for February 10.

The key to a successful Roer River crossing rested with the First United States Army's capture of a number of dams, to prevent the Germans from flooding the river as the 29th Division attempted to cross. The last dam was captured on schedule on February 9, but not before the enemy managed to damage one of the floodgates, allowing the river's water level to rise and prevent the 29th Division's crossing. As a result of the rushing torrents of water, the 175th and 115th withdrew to continue their training while the 116th held the Roer River line. The attack was delayed two weeks until February 23, allowing the water to recede. When the assault finally kicked off, the 29th Division had been held up at the Roer for three months, but now it was time to break the German defenses and end this miserable war. The 3rd Battalion of the 116th was attached to the 175th in a reserve role initially, and then assigned the mission of capturing the Citadel, a fortress within the city of Julich. The 175th would bypass this stronghold and leave it for the Stonewallers to take. Supported by tanks from the 739th Tank Battalion, the 116th Regiment's F Company poured into the fort, capturing the remaining Germans who had not escaped before the attack. The last defenses of Julich had fallen and on February 25, the 116th moved forward to continue the attack into Germany.

The next move of the 116th Regiment was focused on Dusseldorf to the northeast, and the Stonewallers captured Welldorf, Gusten, and Serrest in succession. They attacked with the help of the 330th Infantry and tanks from the 747th Tank Battalion attached to them. After achieving success, the 116th passed the lead to the 115th, as the 29th Division sped northeast against crumbling German resistance. The enemy

Cartoon and photograph 13-6: Delbert cartoon & Julich banner

had been prepared for the Allies to attack from the west, but were unable to halt the well conceived shift of Ninth Army to hit their southern flank. The Blue and Gray advanced steadily, utilizing coordinated infantry attacks supported by effective indirect and tank fires. Pausing only briefly on February 27 to consolidate and re-supply, the 116th moved out aggressively on the Division's right the next day, taking the towns of Holz, Hochneukirch, Mongshof, Sasserath, Durselen, and Waat. They proceeded roughly seven miles beyond Munchen-Gladbach, which was taken by the 175th on March 1. This was the largest German city captured to this point of the war, and the success spoke volumes about the effectiveness of the 29th Division and its regiments. They now paused to enjoy a well deserved break from combat and assumed a new role as Ninth Army Reserve.

Throughout March, the harsh winter turned to a milder spring as the Stonewallers joined the rest of the 29th Division in the occupation of Munchen-Gladbach. The city provided roofs, real beds, and running water. These were the best conditions the soldiers had seen since landing on D-Day. A light schedule was implemented, consisting of range firing, road marches, and physical training filling the days, while the nights were spent relaxing and enjoying the creature comforts of the city. There was mail from home, time to play cards, and stores of champagne to drink as the war moved further into Germany, leaving the Stonewallers behind. Rumors began to circulate that the 29th Division had done its part and was out of the war for good. This speculation, though erroneous, added to the excitement of the talk shared during organized athletic competition that the units enjoyed many afternoons. Softball and volleyball were especially entertaining. Replacements began to pour into the units of the 116th, along with more former members who had recovered from wounds. Life in March was good until orders came down on March 29, attaching the Division to the XVI Corps and sending it back to the front.

On March 31, trucks arrived to pick up the 116th and move the soldiers across the Rhine River. It was Easter Sunday, April 1 when the Stonewallers reached the river. They paused for church services before moving across the narrow bridges the engineers had constructed. Soon they arrived at Marl, to the northwest of Recklinghausen and northeast of Dusseldorf on the east bank of the Rhine, and were attached to the 75th Division. Initially they were placed in a reserve role for an upcoming attack into the German industrial center, located in the Ruhr Pocket. On April 4, at one in the morning, they moved to the front line, with orders to attack south toward the 75th Division objective at Dortmund. They moved out with the 1st and 2nd Battalions abreast, and the 3rd Battalion serving in regimental reserve. The 116th was protecting the 75th's left, as they crossed the Dortmund-Ems Canal and moved south, capturing the small town of Waltrop. During the night, engineers bridged the captured canal, allowing armor to move up to support the Stonewallers. The next morning the 116th continued its move south, crossing the famous German *Autobahn*, now route A2. Late in the afternoon of April 6, the Germans attempted a weak counterattack against the 116th, but it was easily defeated. This action was the last the Stonewallers would see as part of the 75th Division, as they reverted back to 29th Division control where they would serve as XVI Corps' reserve.

As the German army defenses dissolved, the Allies were faced with the challenge of masses of prisoners of war, POWs, and displaced civilian personnel or DPs. The 29th Division was now called upon to assist with this new challenge in the Ninth Army area, and the 116th Regiment, along with the other regiments and Division Artillery, was given a sector that it would be responsible for. The Stonewallers were tasked to clear the roads in their sector of all the POWs and DPs, by moving them to camps which had been established to provide them food and shelter. Western Europeans could return home, while the displaced civilians and soldiers from Eastern Europe, who were taken prisoner by the Germans, would have to await the conclusion of the war before repatriation could occur. There were thousands of captured military and civilian personnel who had been used as slaves to keep the German war machine going. Then there were the German soldiers, now prisoners of war, surrendering daily by the thousands as the Allies advanced into their homeland. Fearing reprisals from the Russians advancing from the east, the Germans, civilian and military alike, streamed west, hoping for humane treatment from the Americans and British. The mission given to the 29th Division in the Ninth Army rear was not an easy one, but at least it was a break from the day-to-day risk of serving at the front. The rear duty lasted from April 8 to April 18, when the Stonewallers boarded trucks and moved east again.

For the next several days, the 116th Regiment advanced against little resistance, mopping up small German elements left behind by the rapid Ninth Army advance. Finally, on April 24, they reached the high ground overlooking the Elbe River, just south of Neu Darchau, near the town of Dannenberg. Continuing on, they conducted a passage of lines through units of the 5th Armored Division and assumed the lead in the advance to the west bank of the Elbe. The final German resistance was light as the Stonewallers reached the river. Here they would stop, although there seemed to be little stopping them from proceeding to the east bank and beyond. The German capital of Berlin was less than seventy miles to the east. The Elbe River, however, had been determined by the Allied leadership to represent the new international boundary which would divide Germany. The Americans, British, Canadians, and French would remain on the west side of the Elbe, while the Russians took control of everything to the east, including Berlin. For the next few days there would be continued German shelling,

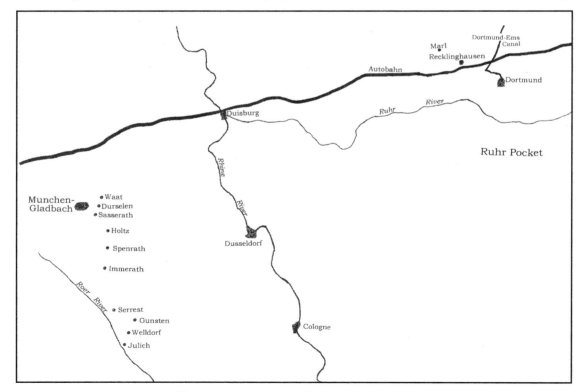

Illustration 13-7: Julich to Dortmund

occasional bombing raids, and several enemy patrols against the 116th, but its mission was to hold its position and await the arrival of the Russian Army. By April 30, when Adolph Hitler committed suicide, the Elbe River duty had become peaceful, and the soldiers moved about with little fear of hostile German activity.

On May 2, white flags appeared on the east bank of the Elbe, as scores of German soldiers sought to surrender to the Americans. The bulk of the Germans were from the V-2 Rocket Division, and they sought to avoid capture by the Russians to ensure their rocket technology was preserved for the west. The 29th Division engineers assisted in ferrying their previous enemy to the safety of the American lines. By the next day, 10,367 German soldiers and civilians had surrendered and crossed to the west bank of the Elbe. That same day, Russian soldiers appeared, and the linkup at the river was completed. Almost immediately, the 29th Division was ordered from XIII Corps to XVI Corps to begin occupation duty. The 116th was moved by open trucks northwest to the port at Bremerhaven on the North Sea. Division policy allowed supplies to travel in covered trucks, but not soldiers. At Bremerhaven, the Stonewallers would establish "watch posts" to control ships entering or leaving the Weser River at any point other than Bremerhaven where a Navy Task Force supervised all movement. It was here that they would learn of the German surrender on May 8, 1945. For the 116th Stonewall Brigade, another war was finally over. Victory Europe, or VE-Day, had finally arrived. The command had suffered 7,113 casualties,

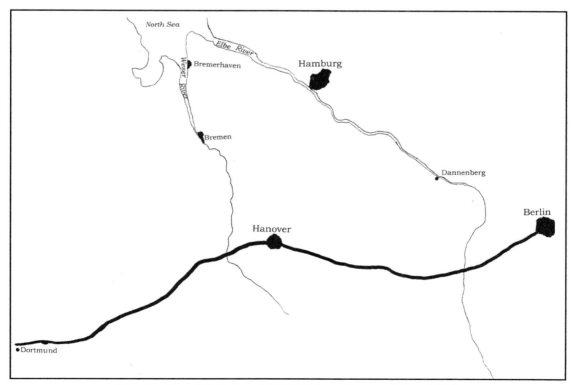

Illustration 13-8: Last WWII locations of the 116th

beginning with the landings on Omaha Beach eleven months earlier. The 116th Regiment had again paid a high price for the freedom and security of America.

A concern remained that the 29th Division might be redeployed to the Pacific, but a "point system" had been established that would send many Stonewallers home almost immediately. Soldiers received an Adjusted Service Rating by earning points for their length of service, months overseas, battle credits, wounds, marital status, and even the number of children they had. The first level needed to go home was eighty-five points. On May 9, Platoon Sergeant Ralph Coffman of L Company, who had just returned to the front as the company approached the Elbe River, found himself with one hundred and eighteen points and a trip home. He would be reunited with his good friend Woodrow Ashby, who had encouraged him to join the National Guard over five years earlier. The two, and many others, would be the first Stonewallers to board trucks on May 19, and head west back to France for the trip home. Six days later the veterans would arrive at the familiar port of Grandcamp, where they boarded ships to England. Here on June 2, from the port of Southampton, they would finally sail back to their homes. The men would land at Boston and make

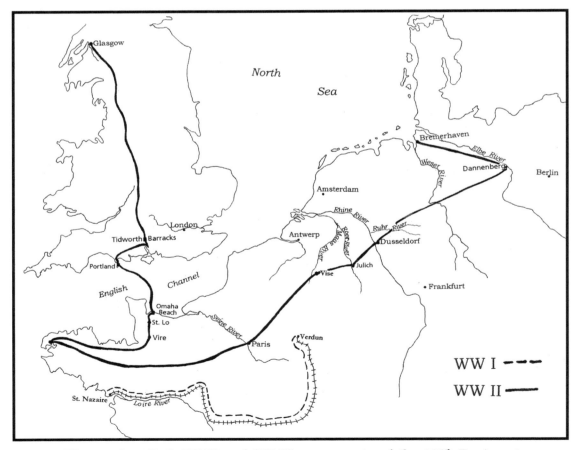

Illustration 13-9: WWI and WWII movements of the 116th Regiment

their way south via train, to family and friends back in Staunton and Augusta County.

Other Stonewallers would make their way home in a similar fashion when they achieved the required Adjusted Service Rating. The majority, however, would become part of the American occupation force in Germany. They would participate in victory parades and pass-in-reviews for visiting dignitaries, but for the most part, occupation duty was boring. The motto became "29 Let's Go Home" after the surrender of the Japanese in August and the conclusion of World War II, but still occupation duty dragged on. Finally, in December, the departure order arrived. The 116th would be the first to leave, and everyone hoped to be home by Christmas, 1945. Unfortunately the departure date gradually slipped, and Christmas Day found the 116th just leaving German waters. The winter crossing did little to dampen the morale of the Stonewallers, who arrived in New York City where they were sent by train to Camp Kilmer--the same place from which they had departed over three years earlier. There were no bands playing, no parades or great crowds; it was simply a time to stand-down and prepare to return home. The 116th Regimental Commander, LTC Harold Cassell, wrote that of the 4,410 Stonewallers he brought home aboard the U.S.S. Navy Transport *LeJune*, only fifty were unit members who had been mobilized in February of 1941. He added that the Brigade members had adopted eight-year-old Eddie Nichichuk whom they had found in an internment camp and smuggled aboard ship to bring to the United States. Before leaving Camp Kilmer, the boy was taken to Ellis Island to begin his new life in America. On January 6, 1946, equipment turned in and paperwork complete, the 116th Regiment headed home after almost five years on active duty and 242 days in combat; mission accomplished!

Battle streamers earned: Rhineland and Central Europe

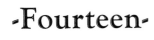

Fourteen

Reorganizations & the Cold War

The end of World War II closed one more chapter in the proud history of the 116th Infantry, Stonewall Brigade but opened another. After only a few months home, efforts began to reorganize the units of the Virginia National Guard. Federal authority was provided on July 2, 1946, and by fall, units of the 116th began reforming. Fittingly, on November 11, Veteran's Day, the Army returned unit guidons and World War II battle flags to the various Virginia communities to restore the local pride and encourage enlistments. During ceremonies conducted in the Nation's Capital, President Harry S. Truman, a former National Guardsman in World War I, commented, *"I return these colors to the National Guard. I hope they will use them to train young men in the interests of peace and the welfare of the country."* Similar ceremonies occurred in a number of states throughout the United States that Veteran's Day. As the colors were returned to the 116th Regiment armories, six new battle streamers had been added, bringing the total number to twenty-nine. In addition, the action on Omaha Beach on D-Day had added a Presidential Unit Citation and a French Croix de Guerre with Palm to the numerous other awards Stonewallers had earned during its more than two hundred year history.

Tragically, the price of World War II was too high for some communities, and in locations like Chase City, Virginia, where their E Company had been in the first wave on D-Day, suffering heavy casualties that day and throughout the war, were simply not ready to create another National Guard unit. Still, most of the 116th communities could see the value of reforming their local company. In Bedford, D-Day veteran Lieutenant Ray Nance led the effort to insure the tradition of National Guard service in that town was continued. After reorganization and recruiting, some of the 116th units received Federal recognition as early as January, 1947. Bedford had 124 men volunteer to serve when the unit mustered for duty again in 1948. The initial formations throughout the 116th included a mix of World War II veterans and young men of another generation, eager to join and serve. With the Second World War over, it was difficult for America to envision another international conflict, resulting in dramatic defense spending cuts and downsizing throughout the military. Funding for defense seemed unnecessary, but the National Guard and its service to the community and the state was recognized as "value added" at less cost. The initial result was the reinstitution of a National Guard structure larger than the units prior to the mobilizations of 1941. Another significant event which occurred during this period, as part of the National Security Act of 1947, was the creation of the United States Air Force from the Army Air Corps. Now there would be an Army and an Air National Guard.

One of the biggest obstacles facing the National Guard was the lack of proper facilities to house the re-emerging force. Many existing armories had been neglected during the war, and some communities still had not established a facility for their soldiers to use for drills. This was certainly the situation in the Commonwealth of Virginia and the units of the 116th. In addition, the new National Guard was authorized armor units, and this would require substantially more space to house tanks and the additional equipment which was part of the heavier unit's organization. The 116th was authorized a regimental tank unit which would be located in Lexington, Virginia. With Federal funds and appropriations from the Virginia General Assembly, facilities for the 116th began to improve. It was not until 1950 that Congress provided substantial financial assistance for new armory construction, as long as the states would participate with twenty-five per cent of the cost. The result was a number of new facilities constructed for units of the 116th, to include Staunton, Harrisonburg, and Roanoke. The legislation also provided much needed funding for armory repair. In 1952, Virginia re-established an Armory Commission to oversee the National Guard facilities throughout the Commonwealth.

The new armory in Staunton was completed and dedicated in 1956. It would be known as the Thomas D. Howie Memorial Armory, in memory of the Major of St. Lo. Tom Howie's wife Elizabeth and daughter Sally were present for the dedication. A bust of Major Howie is enchased in the wall to the right side of the main entrance; a similar bust was dedicated at the Staunton Military Academy, a short distance away. The walls surrounding the drill floor are adorned with replica streamers revealing the Stonewall Brigade's historic past. In addition, the driveway to the Staunton armory is today identified as the 116th Infantry Regiment Road.

The fight for funding within the military soon began to take its toll on the National Guard. The initial post war strength authorizations were cut in half. A board was appointed to review the future of the National Guard and Reserves. It reported that the dual status of the National Guard reduced its ability to focus on national security, and it should be merged into a reserve organization. The findings completely ignored the roots of the National Guard going all the way back to the founding fathers, and minimized the contribution of the Guard to national defense for the past two hundred and seventy years. The National Guard Association of the United States was outraged and responded that *"The Battle Is On!"* With defense spending being reduced, every branch of the military was fighting for survival, a struggle that has permeated the history of the American military and significantly affected the funding of the National Guard.

The Stonewallers of World War II were unaware that as they had gazed east across the Elbe River in May, 1944, awaiting the Russians, they were looking at a dividing line that would soon become known as the "Iron Curtain." The Russians, now known as the Soviet Union, were determined to spread their Communist doctrine to other parts of Europe and Asia. They made moves to threaten Greece and Turkey and invaded Czechoslovakia. In 1948, the Soviets cut the land routes to Berlin. The resulting Berlin Airlift revealed that America was equally determined to maintain its presence in the region and would not back down under Communist pressure. Another war was now looming, but it would be a Cold War, and one in which the 116th would, for the first time in its history, not be called upon to directly participate.

Throughout this period, the 116th fulfilled its commitment to respond effectively to emergency situations that developed within the Commonwealth of Virginia. In 1947, the units in Winchester were called upon to secure the site of a civilian plane crash at Hillsboro. In 1959, Charlottesville's A Company was called out three times in less than thirty days. First they responded when a damaging tornado struck the little town of Ivy just west of Charlottesville. Then they assisted with security and recovery at the sight of two plane crashes, first that of a Navy fighter and the second a civilian DC-3. Additionally, the Stonewallers assisted several communities after flood waters damaged homes and property. They even assisted after high winds and heavy rains resulted in losses following hurricanes. Hurricane Hazel in 1955 was especially destructive and the response of the Virginia National Guard was critical to preserving life and restoring property. The 116th played a large part in every natural disaster affecting the Commonwealth. Its units were always there, responding to the needs of their communities.

The first major conflict of the Cold War broke out on the Korean Peninsula on June 25, 1950, when Russian-backed North Korea crossed the 38th Parallel launching a surprise invasion into U. S.-backed South Korea. The 38th Parallel had been the line established after World War II to divide the peninsula between the evolving Communist North and the Democratic South. America's reduction of its military forces had left its active forces unprepared to respond quickly, and they were slow in coming to the aid of South Korea, in what was called initially a "police action." Even with the support of the United Nations, it would take years to defeat the Communist efforts to dominate the entire Korean Peninsula. Before the 38th Parallel boundary and peace were restored, eight National Guard Divisions would be called to active duty, but not the 29th Division and its subordinate 116th Regiment. The Blue and Gray and its Stonewall Brigade would sit this one out.

Following the Korean War, Congress passed legislation to consolidate and improve the organization of America's military. Title 10 was created as a status for all active duty personnel, and it became the authority for future National Guard per-

Illustrations 14-1 and 14-1b: Typical training activities conducted during Summer Camp in the 1950s.

sonnel called to federal duty. Additionally, they established Title 32 status for members of the Guard called to perform national defense at a state level. For the first time, members of the National Guard were required to attend initial training on an active duty installation, beginning with basic combat training. Advanced training for both officers and enlisted men would now be conducted as part the Army's School system.

The year of 1959 saw the first major reorganization of the 116th since the end of World War II. President Dwight D. Eisenhower had made it clear that he would use nuclear weapons to protect the United States, and it was understood that the Soviet Union was prepared to do the same. Army planners soon determined that the old triangular structure of their combat organizations would no longer fit the threat of a nuclear environment. The battlefield of the future was pictured as being very chaotic, requiring units to be self-sustaining and capable of operating independently. In "The Tradition Continues," National Guard Historians John W. Listman, Jr., Robert K. Wright, Jr., and Bruce D. Hardcastle summarized, "*Pentagon analysts had concluded that the introduction of tactical nuclear weapons to the battlefield left the familiar World War II-style structure too vulnerable to enemy action, and inefficiently ar-*

ranged to make use of the latest advances in technology." The Army had restructured to a new organization referred to as the "PENTOMIC" division, two years earlier, and now it was the National Guard's turn to transition. The pentomic structure consisted of divisions with "battle groups," the new name given to what had previously been units similar to regiments in organization. Battle Groups, however, were smaller than the old regiments, but larger than the triangular battalions. The word Pentomic came from the Greek word *penta*, meaning <u>five</u>. The Pentagon, for example, is known for its five sides. Divisions, for the atomic age, had five Battle Groups, and each was comprised of five companies with five platoons.

On June 1, 1959, the 116th became part of the new pentomic force and reorganized under the Combat Arms Regimental System, or CARS. This structure had resulted in the historical redesignation of some National Guard units, but the 116th was able to retain its identity in the new force. Instead of three battalions, with four companies each, the regiment would now have two battle groups consisting of a Headquarters Company, a Combat Support Company, and five infantry companies. These new regiments would now have artillery battalions with three different caliber howitzers and mortars, plus helicopters and light tanks. This new combined arms effort brought a lot more combat power under the control of a CARS Regiment and spread the organization among a larger number of units. The new structure of the 116th after the pentomic reorganization was complete reflected the following final unit designations and their locations:

First Battle Group

Headquarters Company	Roanoke
A Company	Bedford
B Company	Farmville
C Company	Radford
D Company	Roanoke
E Company	Christiansburg
Combat Support Company	Lynchburg

Second Battle Group

Headquarters Company	Winchester
A Company	Charlottesville
B Company	Staunton
C Company	Harrisonburg
D Company	Lexington
E Company	Lynchburg
Combat Support Company	Berryville

In June, 1961, the Soviet Union announced that it was time for the Allies to end their occupation of Berlin and turn the entire city over to Communist control. The resulting "Berlin Crisis" drew an immediate and unpredicted response by the United States. President John F. Kennedy placed American forces on high alert, and by the end of July Congress had authorized him to mobilize up to two hundred and fifty thousand members of the National Guard and Reserves to answer the Soviet threat. Although one hundred and seven units of the Army National Guard were alerted, the 116th Infantry Regiment was not one of them. Among those called up were three National Guard Divisions, but not the 29th Division. The substantial American response, however, was effective, and the Soviet Union backed away from its original threats, choosing only to build a wall around the western portion of Berlin to further isolate that part of the former capital of Nazi Germany. The National Guard units which had responded quickly and efficiently were returned home after less than a year on active duty. The year of 1961 also saw the one hundredth anniversary of the Battle of First Manassas, and the Stonewall Brigade returned to participate in that historic event.

By 1963, the Army had determined that the Pentomic divisional structure presented a number of challenges, particularly in providing effective command and con-

14-2: Major General Paul Booth, the Adjutant General of Virginia visits with Colonel Mifflin Clowe Commanding the 116th Infantry and Brigadier General Archibald Sproul, Assistant Division Commander, 29th Infantry Division

trol. Another restructuring was necessary. The new organization would be known as the "Reorganization Objectives Army Division" (ROAD), and it would look similar to the previous triangular configuration. The focus was on developing a combined arms task force with increased tactical capabilities. A Division would now have three brigades and each brigade would have three battalions. The designation of battle group had given way to the "battalion" structure once again. Each battalion would consist of four companies, but with a brigade headquarters to improve command and control. The Stonewall Brigade would become the Second Brigade of the 29th Division. It was to be headquartered in Staunton with two Infantry battalions: the 1st Battalion of the 116th in Roanoke and the 2nd Battalion of the 116th in Lynchburg, plus the 116th Armor Battalion in Winchester.

The ROAD Division structure did not please the National Guard leadership, since it meant a reduction of the number of units and less presence in communities throughout the United States. An even greater impact was felt when President Lyndon B. Johnson announced the reduction in the number of National Guard divisions from twenty-three to only eight. He further proposed merging the Army Reserve into the National Guard, an effort which Congress defeated in the 1966 Appropriations Act. In another critical decision by President Johnson and Defense Secretary Robert McNamara, the escalating war in Viet Nam would be fought with draftees and not involve the mobilization of the National Guard. The reasoning was based on the administration's decision to conceal the growing war from the American people and retain the National Guard to assist in responding to any new threat which might develop. In 1968, a limited number of Guard units were quietly mobilized into federal service, as a result of the North Korean seizure of the *USS Pueblo*; thirty-four units comprised of 12,234 Guardsmen were called to active duty. After the *Pueblo* crisis ended, 7,000 of these soldiers were detached from their National Guard units and found themselves serving as fillers in active Army units in Viet Nam.

Starting in 1967, the Virginia Army National Guard began conducting its drills on weekends instead of evenings during the week. Consolidating drill time improved training efficiency and attendance. The two weeks of summer camp still provided the soldiers and their units the most realistic training for their wartime mission. In 1969, when Hurricane Camille devastated portions of central Virginia, in particular Nelson County, the soldiers of the 116th responded immediately to assist the affected citizens. They searched for survivors and would later provide security for damaged homes and commercial buildings. In 1972, Hurricane Agnes caused widespread flooding throughout the Commonwealth of Virginia, and the 116th provided a substantial response, particularly in the Roanoke Valley. It joined the largest state activation of the National Guard in the Commonwealth of Virginia's long history.

In 1965, Secretary of Defense Robert McNamara began a sweeping reorganization of the National Guard. It was clear early on that the 29th Division was targeted as one of the fifteen Guard divisions to be eliminated from the Army's new force structure. A new battle cry arose within the Division, *"29 Don't Go!"*, but nothing could stop the Army's reorganization as America's role in the war in Viet Nam expanded. When the final decision was announced, Division Commander Major General Archibald Sproul, a company commander on D-Day and a former Commander of the Stonewall Brigade, would respond *"This is a sad day for the State of Maryland and the Common-wealth of Virginia. They are breaking up a unit with a fighting record and an esprit de corps second to none"*. The official deactivation of the 29th Division would be set for January, 1968. The Stonewall Brigade, the 2nd Brigade, headquartered in Staunton would then be re-designated as the 116th Brigade of the 28th Infantry Division. It joined Maryland's 3rd Brigade, which had already transitioned to the 28th Division in 1966.

The year of 1967 was significant in the history of America's Stonewall Brigade. Virginia Governor Mills Godwin officially designated Staunton, Virginia, as the official home of the 116th Infantry Regiment (CARS). On Memorial Day, May 30, a ceremony was held to dedicate a Monument and Memorial Garden at Staunton's Thomas D. Howie Armory to honor the eleven residents of Staunton and Augusta County "who made the supreme sacrifice while in service to their country in World War II." Major General (Ret.) E. Walton Opie, who made the dedication address, was introduced by another Staunton resident, Major General Archibald Sproul, the last commander of the 29th Division. Later that year, in an effort to keep the "spirit of Omaha Beach" alive and insure that the heritage of the Stonewall Brigade was continued, an Annual Muster of the 116th Infantry Regiment was created. The first event was held on November 18, 1967, and Major General (Ret.) Opie, a former commander of the 116th Infantry, was selected to serve as the first Honorary Colonel of the Regiment. From a slow initial start, the event grew into an annual reunion of the Omaha Beach and World War II Stonewallers. The muster was later scheduled in conjunction with the Veteran's Day weekend. As time progressed and fewer Veterans were able to attend, the event was continued by a new generation of citizen soldiers. The Annual Muster of the 116th Infantry has been held continuously since 1967, and it draws a new group of Stonewall Brigade veterans and their families committed to preserving the history of this great unit. The torch is being passed to a new generation, insuring the legacy of comradery and esprit de corps will be continued into the future.

The last summer camp of the 29th Division with its 116th Infantry Brigade was a challenging event which occurred in June, 1967. The units were split between Fort A. P. Hill and Fort Pickett, with the Division Headquarters and Major General Sproul at Fort Pickett. There were multiple training events, extensive live fire exercises and other activities focused on showing the readiness of the Division. On the national scene, the outbreak of war between the Israeli and Arab Armies brought conflict to an area of the world other than Viet Nam. Although the 29th Division was about to stand down, there was a brief glimmer of hope that the United States might still need the Blue and Gray Division. The conflict in the Middle East ended quickly, however, and the 29th Division would proceed on the path to roll its colors. The final activities of the Division included a final "pass in review" attended by the governors of Mary-

**14-3: Monticello Guard retiring the colors
at the 1st Muster, November 18, 1967**

land and Virginia and numerous other dignitaries from the state and federal level. The end was clearly near.

The 28th Division was another outstanding and historic National Guard division. It had served in the Spanish American War as the 7th Infantry Division and was re-designated the 28th Infantry Division in the fall of 1917 as part of the mobilization for World War I. It became known as the Keystone Division, and a red keystone-shaped patch was adopted on October 27, 1917, to identify the unit. The Division had served effectively during World War I and was mobilized along with the 29th Division on February 1, 1941. It had trained that year along with the Stonewallers during a number of maneuvers. With the outbreak of World War II, the 28th moved to Camp Livingston, Louisiana, where it was commanded by Major General J. G. Ord and later Major General Omar Bradley. Like the Stonewallers, they would also sail to England on the *Queen Mary*, arriving in September, 1943. After the capture of St. Lo, the 28th Division would replace the 35th Division and sweep east to Paris. There on August 29, 1944, it would become the first American Division to parade through the Arc de Triomphe, preceding down the Champs Elysees, led by Major General Norm Cota, the former Assistant Division Commander of the 29th Division.

The 28th Division would continue to attack east to Germany, but in December, it would bear the brunt of the German counterattack in the Ardennes, which would become known as the Battle of the Bulge. Here it would hold out for four days, December 16-20, and against overwhelming odds, blunt the German advance. Its defense allowed Allied reinforcements to reach Bastogne and other critical positions along the front and eventually defeat the German effort to reach the port city of Antwerp, Belgium. After World War II, the 28th Division returned home in December, 1945, but less than five years later, it was recalled to active duty by President Truman in September, 1950, at the outbreak of the Korean War. The Keystone Division clearly had a proud history and with the 29th Division gone, the 116th was pleased to be able to serve as part of another great National Guard Division.

The headquarters of the 28th Division was located in Harrisburg, Pennsylvania and the reorganized Stonewall Brigade would remain located in Staunton's Thomas D. Howie Armory. The 116th would be supervised by a one star Assistant Division Commander from Virginia, who would also have responsibility for a Military Police Platoon, a Cavalry Squadron, an Engineer Company, plus an Aviation Company. In addition, there was a Medical Company, Maintenance Company, and an Administration Section located in Virginia to support the 116th, plus a truck platoon and forward supply section. All of these units would be a part of the 28th Division and wear the distinctive Keystone, also known as the "Bloody Bucket," patch. The first Assistant Division Commander from Virginia was Brigadier General Samuel R. Gay of Lynchburg, a veteran of WWII and the Italian campaign, where he served as an officer with the famed 442nd Infantry comprised of Japanese Americans. The Stonewall Brigade Commander would be Colonel Julian R. Bradshaw, also a combat veteran of World War II.

As it became evident that National Guard units would not be called upon to serve in Viet Nam, its units began to attract enlistees wanting to avoid the unpopular war. The ranks of the 116th were quickly filled, and a waiting list developed for those wanting to join. The interest in joining the Guard reached a new level when a draft lottery took effect as part of the 1967 Selective Service Act. Although the obligation for recruits joining the National Guard was six years, as opposed to only two years on active duty, the opportunity to serve without having to go to Viet Nam kept waiting lists growing. Still, many members of the National Guard and the 116th chose to volunteer to serve on active duty and go to Viet Nam in support of the war there. Through the difficult years of the Viet Nam "conflict," the 116th stayed home. Its training was enhanced by new equipment, to include the M-16 rifle issued in 1970 for the first time, which replaced the M-1s the Stonewall Brigade had been using since World War II. Summer camp was conducted at Camp Pickett, located on Route 460 and thirty miles west of Petersburg and outside Blackstone, Virginia, and at Camp A. P. Hill, south of Fredericksburg. In 1971, Major General William J. McCaddin became the Adjutant General of Virginia. In July, 1972, the Stonewallers made the challenging twenty-seven hour convoy move to Camp Drum, New York, in July, where they trained with other units of the 28th Infantry Division. The tragic Johnstown Flood would result in many of the Pennsylvania National Guard soldiers serving on flood duty and missing the entire Camp Drum experience.

The year 1972 will be remembered as the year hostilities broke out between the Arab nations in the Middle East and Israel. In what would be become known as the Yom Kipper War, since the Arab attacks were started on this Jewish Holiday, the Egyptians re-crossed the Suez Canal and attacked into the Sinai, while Syrian tanks headed for the Golan Heights overlooking Israel. With the Soviet Union providing the Arab nations with their latest technology, and the United States supporting Israel, another world war loomed on the horizon. The United States was committed to the survival of Israel and began preparations to provide military support if the situation worsened. The 28th Division was alerted and mobilization plans reviewed in the event ground forces were needed to support Israel. Fortunately, the Israelis, though clearly set back by the initial Arab attacks, gained the initiative and drove the Arab armies to the original borders and beyond. World war was averted and the 28th Division and its Stonewall Brigade stood down.

When General Creighton W. Abrams, Jr. became the Army's Chief of Staff, he was committed to rebuilding the Army in the post Viet Nam era. One of his initiatives would become known as The Total Force Policy. General Abrams realized the value of the National Guard and was determined to enhance Guard readiness, modernize it, and improve its relationship with the active Army. His efforts would ultimately lead to the CAPSTONE Program, which required active units to develop a relationship with National Guard units. The 116th was now provided with active duty Army advisors to assist in their training and readiness.

Another notable change was the transition to the "all volunteer" Army, which impacted recruiting for all military units as well as the Stonewall Brigade. In 1972, the Selective Service System or "the draft" was abolished. Many of the soldiers who had enlisted during the Viet Nam era were reaching the end of their six year enlistment and leaving the Guard. The anti-war, anti-military sentiment that was sweeping America also had a very negative impact on recruiting. The "Try One in the Guard" program, which attempted to attract trained soldiers leaving active duty, had been somewhat successful, but new enlistments, the historical strength of the Guard, remained down. The Stonewall Brigade implemented "Operation Muster," Operation "Ever Forward" and other initiatives to build recruiting and improved retention.

The plans to get its strength back up focused on the Stonewall Brigade returning to its roots and appealed to its communities for support. The National Guard had proven itself a valuable asset to the Valley of Virginia for over two hundred years, and that service needed to be emphasized. For the first time, selected noncommissioned officers were hired fulltime and trained to recruit new members of the National Guard. Advertisements were provided to the local media, telling the story of the historic Stonewall Brigade. Recruiting was initiated in local high schools, emphasizing the history of the local units and their contribution to their communities, the Commonwealth of Virginia, and the Nation. The units of the Brigade again made their presence known during numerous community activities and special events. Then too, Stonewallers were there in the 1970s when disasters struck; through hurricanes, floods, fires, and blizzards, the communities of the Shenandoah Valley and central Virginia were reminded of how important their National Guard units were. Renewed support for the Stonewall Brigade was taking hold.

On April 1, 1975, the 116th, left the 28th Division to become the 116th Brigade (Separate), headquartered in Staunton. The Brigade would now be commanded by a Brigadier General, with a Colonel as Deputy Commander. Colonel Bradshaw was promoted and continued his command while Colonel Bruce Grover of Staunton became the Deputy Commander. The new organization would have three Infantry Battalions, but it was also given artillery, cavalry, engineer, signal, and support assets. This new 116th as indicated, was structured to be completely separate, organized to be self sustaining and capable of operating independently. A new patch, the image of Stonewall Jackson at First Manassas, nicknamed "Stony on the Pony," would identify the members of the 116th Brigade for the next ten years. The patch was formally approved by the Army's Institute of Heraldry in 1978. Their motto would be "Rally on the Virginians," as they organized to meet the challenges of the post Viet Nam era. African-Americans began joining the Stonewall Brigade in 1965, and their numbers grew steadily and contributed greatly to the successful reorganization to separate brigade status. The new organization, with its own support units, allowed females to join the 116th for the first time to serve in non-combat roles. There was a new, revitalized Stonewall Brigade.

14-4: 116ᵗʰ Separate patch

116ᵗʰ Separate Brigade Units and locations
    Headquarters   Staunton

First Battalion
        Headquarters Company   Roanoke
        Company A (-)   Bedford
        Det. 1, Company A   Roanoke
        Company B (-)   Christiansburg
        Det. 1, Company B   Radford
        Company C (-)   Covington
        Det. 1, Company C   Clifton Forge
        Combat Support Company   Pulaski

Second Battalion
        Headquarters Company   Lynchburg
        Company A (-)   Charlottesville
        Det. 1, Company A   Harrisonburg
        Company B (-)   Altavista
        Det. 1 Company B   Rocky Mount
        Company C   Lynchburg
        Combat Support Company (-)   Farmville
        Det. 1, Combat Support Company Chase City

Third Battalion
        Headquarters Company   Winchester
        Company A   Manassas
        Company B   Manassas
        Company C (-)   Warrenton
        Det. 1, Company C   Winchester
        Combat Support Company   Berryville

Support Battalion

Headquarters Company (-)	Petersburg
Det. 1, Headquarters	Blackstone
Company A	Richmond
Company B	Charlottesville
Company C	Petersburg
Company D	Blackstone

246th Field Artillery

Headquarters Battery	Danville
Battery A	Martinsburg
Battery B	Chatham
Battery C	South Boston
Service Battery	Danville

183rd Cavalry	Richmond
237th Engineer Company	Fredericksburg
212th Signal Detachment	Roanoke
616th Ordinance Detachment	Blackstone

There was a renewed emphasis on tactical training and federal funds to go with it. The Capstone initiative resulted in each National Guard Brigade being matched with an active duty unit with similar organizations. A relationship would then be developed, with the active duty unit tasked to assist in training and improving the readiness of the Guard unit. The 116th was extremely fortunate, and became a member of the XVIII Airborne Corps family and began a long and successful association with the 82nd Airborne Division and Fort Bragg, North Carolina. The Brigade's level of training was quickly intensified. In the summer of 1975, some of the units of the Stonewall Brigade participated in a training event known as Atlas Force One. This joint exercise, with the Navy and Marines, culminated with amphibious landings on the beaches of the State Military Reservation at Virginia Beach. Thirty-one years after D-Day, the 116th still had a few World War II veterans within its ranks for this assault, but the number was dropping quickly.

In 1977, Brigadier General John G. Castles took command of the 116th Infantry Brigade (Separate) upon the retirement of Brigadier General Bradshaw. The 116th Infantry Brigade (Separate) conducted most of its monthly training at home station, with some weekends at Fort A. P. Hill or Fort Pickett for individual and crew served weapons qualification and collective training. There was emphasis on basic soldier skills and physical fitness. Passing the Army's Physical Fitness Test, APFT, became a requirement to be able to remain in the Guard. There was also emphasis on weight control with regular weigh-ins and diet and fitness programs for those unable to meet the Army's weight table requirements or body fat level. Annual physicals became a requirement, later extended to every three years due to a shortage of doctors and medical facilities to administer them. Summer Camp was now called Annual Training. The 116th was to be kept trained and ready in the event the Soviet Union attempted to invade Western Europe. The National Guard was the follow-on-force in the event of war.

The year of 1979 saw the first overseas opportunity for a Stonewall Brigade unit since World War II, when Charlottesville's Company A was chosen to conduct its annual training at the Sennybridge Training Area in South Wales, June 9-23. It was quite an experience for the old K Company, also known as the Monticello Guard, to receive this honor, and the announcement was made by Brigade Commander, Brigadier General Castles, who had served in the unit while attending the University of Virginia. A Company, under the command of Captain Jim Harmon, a local teacher and coach whose family had a long tradition of service going back to the old Augusta Militia, was ready for the challenge. It was an unforgettable training experience with numerous challenges, not the least of which was the thousands of sheep grazing throughout the hilly terrain at Sennybridge. Staff Sergeant Clarence Vencil, Jr. recalled "when the sheep weren't around, there were reminders of them!"

A Company trained with the 3rd Battalion, 51st Highlanders; know as the Queens Own Highlanders, while D Company, 4th (Volunteer) Battalion Welsh Company came to Virginia to train with the 2/116th during their annual training at Fort Pickett. The old Augusta Militia had previous experience with the Fusiliers, going back to their presence on Virginia soil during the War of 1812, but now they were again on the same side. The Fusiliers were descendents of the company best known for its defense

14-5: Sennybridge Training Area, South Wales

of Roark's Drift in 1858 in South Africa where it defeated over six thousand Zulu Warriors. Two of the Welsh platoons trained with C Company of the 2/116th. The C Company Commander, CPT Buddy Faulconer remembered, "our NCOs and soldiers were shocked by the stringent enforcement of discipline within the Highlanders and the harsh punishment for what many of us considered being minor infractions." The Welsh Color Sergeant clearly used a "hands on" approach when disciplining subordinates.

In 1979, the 116th Regiment Memorial Museum Association was formed with a goal of building an addition to the Thomas D. Howie Memorial Armory in Staunton to house a facility which would capture complete history of the regiment. Funds trickled in slowly, but enthusiasm for the project diminished as the Regiment's World War II veteran population began to fade. Additionally, complications developed on the legality of a memorial museum on an armory site and perpetual funding for its upkeep. The project was finally put on hold.

There were two major call-ups of the 116th during 1979 to assist communities with natural disasters. In February, heavy snow and bitter cold struck northern Virginia and the National Guard responded to assist in emergency evacuation of residents who could not be reached by normal emergency vehicles. Spring flooding left Buchanan and Russell counties, near Roanoke, damaged and many of their residents without palatable drinking water until August 2. The Stonewallers provided relief and assistance, to include transporting water to those in need.

On a lighter note, the new commander of the 116th, Brigadier General James Baber, III, hosted the first "dining-in" of the Stonewall Brigade. The event can be traced back to early European history and the need to build esprit de corps and camaraderie within the unit. The dining-in was held in the Mess Hall of the Staunton Military Academy and was well attended by the officers and senior enlisted members of the Brigade. A chair draped in black recognized the members of the 116th Regiment who had made the supreme sacrifice for their country. The attendees partook of "Brigade Punch" which consisted of a variety of beverages, including wine from France and lemon juice in honor of Stonewall Jackson, who frequently sucked on lemons to relief a stomach disorder.

The summer of 1980 found the 116th training at Fort A. P. Hill, with assistance from its counterpart of the 82nd Airborne Division. New weapons systems were introduced, including the two anti-armor weapons, the "TOW" (Tactical Optical Weapon) and the smaller "Dragon" which replaced the LAW (light anti-tank weapon) which was now ineffective against the enhanced armor threat of the Soviet block nations. A new program was initiated to improve the fulltime support for the National Guard units. It was the AGR (Active, Guard, and Reserve) employment option that provided opportunities for Guard members to serve their units fulltime in an active duty status. Soon, about half of the fulltime support force converted to the AGR program.

On January 30, 1981, John O. Marsh, Jr., a Stonewaller for many years and

14-6: Deployment Pictures: CPT Harman and 1SG Hobart Addington are welcomed to Wales by their host for AT-80 (top photo); at left MG William J. McCaddin extends "best wishes" to CPT Harman and A Company as they depart the VaANG base at Sandston, Va.

former commander of M Company, Heavy Weapons in Harrisonburg, became the Secretary of Army. Secretary Marsh retired from the Virginia National Guard with the rank of Lieutenant Colonel in 1976, having served in, not only the 116th, but also on the staff of the 29th Division and Headquarters, Virginia Army National Guard. He served four terms as the Congressman from the Seventh District of Virginia, principally located in the Shenandoah Valley. He became the Assistant Secretary of Defense for legislative affairs in 1973 and later as Assistant for National Security Affairs to President Gerald Ford. Accepting his new position, Secretary Marsh announced the Army's theme for 1981 would be "Yorktown, the Spirit of Victory" to commemorate the two hundredth anniversary since the defeat of British General Cornwallis.

Annual training in 1981 saw the 116th returning to Fort Pickett. There was a variety of tactical training from soldier to battalion level. A new initiative was announced known as KPUP (Key Personnel Upgrade Program), which would allow Guard members to have the opportunity to request additional individual training with an active duty unit stationed overseas or in the United States. Tours were generally for two weeks, but there were short tours and opportunities for up to thirty days. The soldier would work in their MOS (Military Occupational Skill), and gain valuable additional experience which would benefit themselves and their unit. A new piece of equipment was introduced, the Multiple Integrated Laser Equipment System (MILES), to increase the realism of tactical operations. Each soldier would be provided a harness and a helmet headband with buttons to detect any hits from weapons equipped with the MILES laser system. A "hit" set off a buzzing noise in a control box on the back of the harness, identifying the soldier as being shot. The buzz could only be stopped by a control key carried by Observer Controllers (OCs) who were managing the tactical play. The MILES system took the realism of force-on-force tactics to a new level. It would be incorporated into all of the Army Training Centers and even placed on armor and aircraft.

In 1982, it was back to Fort A. P. Hill. Here the Stonewall Brigade would face an opposing force comprised of Second Battalion, 325th Infantry from the 82nd Airborne Division that had parachuted into the air strip there. The high speed 82nd soldiers provided quite a challenging test to the Stonewallers during the tactical war games conducted in the wooded terrain of "the Hill". As the exercises concluded, Major Jim Holt, the Executive Officer of the 325th's Second Battalion, noted the 116th was "well trained and motivated and would complement any unit in the active Army." During the annual training, the soldiers of the 116th were introduced to MREs (Meals Ready to Eat) which had replaced the canned C Ration. The MRE came in an Olive Drab pouch with a variety of meals, snack items, and fruit inside small, tear-open packages. The new meals were quite a topic for discussion among the Stonewallers, but they were here to stay.

Summer training in 1983 found the 116th moving to Fort Bragg, a major convoy exercise for the organization. The excellent training facilities there and the access to major post facilities, particularly the Post Exchange and Commissary, made the Stonewallers feel like they were really a part of America's Army. The 82nd Airborne Division was America's Rapid Deployment unit, so the training also included the opportunity to work with the most current military equipment the Army had to offer. The training focus was on MOUT (Military Operations in Urban Terrain): taking advantage of the forty-two newly constructed buildings of the village developed for Special Forces and XVIII Airborne Corps units at Fort Bragg. There was training on grappling hooks to gain entry to buildings and rappelling to exit. Soldiers were taught to clear buildings, room by room, and then defend them by booby trapping the doors and windows. Annual Training 1983 was a new experience for the soldiers of the Stonewall Brigade, young and old alike.

In October, command of the Brigade would pass to Brigadier General Gilbert J. Sullivan a veteran of many years in the 116th. A resident of Charlottesville, General Sullivan was the Alumni Director for the University of Virginia there. In the winter of 1983, a terrific snow storm hit Virginia, and the 116th called many soldiers to "state active duty," to assist local authorities by using military equipment to reach citizens experiencing emergencies and unreachable by normal emergency services equipment. Annual Training that year would send the Brigade back at Fort Pickett to conduct routine field training and weapons qualification, where Training and Doctrine Command (TRADOC) directed that all operations were to be conducted in the field. This presented a real challenge, particularly for the support elements of the 116th trying to feed and supply at multiple field locations. Battalions had very limited mobility with a small support platoon and vehicles for mortars and the new TOW anti-armor weapons system. Companies had only one organic vehicle, the company commander's jeep, for support. The 116th Support Battalion was sorely tested.

Annual Training in 1984 was also the year of OPFOR and MOPP 4. The units would deploy directly to the field and test their soldier skills for two difficult weeks in a continuous field environment. Soldiers had been training with protective masks since the days of the Pentomic Division, but now protective clothing was added to enhance a soldier's ability to survive in a nuclear environment. The gear was difficult to work in, however, and the summer conditions limited its use at level 4, the most extreme conditions, to just six continuous hours. The opposing force throughout the annual training period was again provided by the 82nd Airborne Division. The second week of training saw the 3/116 convoying to Fort Bragg, North Carolina, to continue its urban training to include a live fire facility.

Throughout the CAPSTONE era with the 82nd Airborne Division, the 116th Infantry Brigade enjoyed an excellent relationship with that great Division. The 82nd's support provided critical assistance throughout the annual training periods, including introduction to new equipment, mentoring at all levels, and playing the role of aggressor during many exercises. On numerous occasions it provided teams to assist unit training at local armories and local training areas. As the premier Infantry Division, the 82nd Airborne was an exceptional partner for the Stonewall Brigade during the cold war period of America's history, but the world and the future of the 116th was about to change.

Fifteen

29 Let's Go Again

I t was an exciting day on June 6, 1984, the Fortieth Anniversary of D-Day, when Defense Secretary Casper Weinberger announced plans for the re-activation of the 29th Division. The decision was in no small part a result of the vision of Secretary of the Army, John O. Marsh, Jr., who had grown up in the Stonewall Brigade, and the Adjutant General of Virginia, Major General John Castles, a former commander of the 116th Brigade (Separate). The structure would be "Light" and followed a new concept which was intended to provide a very mobile, but lethal division with expertise in warfare in restricted terrain and urban areas. In addition to the ongoing Soviet threat in Europe, the Army needed a force which could respond to low intensity conflicts. There would be emphasis on both anti-tank and airmobile operations. The new headquarters of the 29th Division would be located at Ft. Belvoir, Virginia, with two Infantry Brigades and the Divarty (Artillery Brigade) also in Virginia, with one Infantry Brigade, an Aviation Brigade, and the DISCOM (Division Support Command) located in Maryland.

Illustration 15-1: Captains Castles and Marsh test the .30 Caliber machine gun during Summer Camp

Immediately, the members of the 116th began preparations to rejoin the 29th Division. In early 1985, several company level officers and NCOs (Non Commissioned Officers) volunteered for and successfully completed the Army's 28 day "Light Leader" Course (LLC) at Fort Benning, Georgia. The training conducted by the Ranger department consisted of rappelling, helo-casting, hand-to-hand combat, and survival techniques. There was emphasis on leadership development and weapons familiarization. The concept was for this basic cadre to return to their units and train additional Light Leaders.

Annual Training in 1985 found the 116th at Fort Pickett, spending two weeks conducting "field craft" or basic soldier tasks now known as the "rites of passage," necessary to be a member of the new Light Division. There would be emphasis on combatatives, rappelling, land navigation, movements during limited hours of visibility, and weapons qualification. All operations would be conducted in a continuous field environment. There was the usual crew-served weapons training, 4.2 and 81 mm mortar live fires, but this year also live fires for the Dragon and TOW anti-armor weapons. The Brigade Commander, Brigadier General Wendell Seldon, was selected to become the Assistant Division Commander for Maneuver for the new 29th Division, passing command of the Stonewall Brigade to COL Rodney McNeil of Roanoke. COL McNeil had spent most of his career in the Brigade and commanded the 1st Battalion.

After months of planning, on October 5, 1985, the 29th Infantry Division (Light) was officially re-activated on the parade field at Fort Belvoir, Virginia, the new home of the Blue and Gray Division. The units of the Stonewall Brigade were reorganized effective 1 May, 1986, and the Division became operational on September 30, 1986. The 116th Infantry Brigade (Separate), America's "Stonewall Brigade," was redesignated as the First Brigade of the 29th ID (L). As Training Year 1987 began on November 1, 1986 (TY-07), the Blue and Gray Division was back in America's arsenal. The Stonewall Brigade would, of course, continue to be headquartered in Staunton. The formation of a Second Infantry Brigade, headquartered at Fort A. P. Hill in Virginia, meant a number of former Stonewall Brigade units would be reassigned to this new organization. Those losses would return the old Brigade, which retained its 116th designation, to its roots in the Shenandoah Valley and Central Virginia regions. Several new units would be created in the reorganization to round out the new First Brigade.

First Brigade, 29th Infantry Division (Light) 1985 Structure and Locations

Headquarters	Staunton
First Battalion	
Headquarters Company (-)	Roanoke
Det. 1, Headquarters	Pulaski
Company A (-)	Bedford

Det. 1, Company A	Roanoke
Company B (-)	Christiansburg
Det 1, Company B	Radford
Company C	Clifton Forge
Second Battalion	
Headquarters	Lynchburg
Company A	Charlottesville
Company B (-)	Altavista
Det. 1, Company B	Rocky Mount
Company C	Lynchburg
Third Battalion	
Headquarters	Winchester
Company A (-)	Lexington
Det. 1, Company A	Staunton
Company B	Winchester
Company C	Harrisonburg

Company A of the Third Battalion added a detachment in Staunton after initial reorganization. In 1992, the DISCOM, located in Maryland, broke out the forward support battalions to improve the effectiveness of support in the brigades of the Division. The following organization was added to the Stonewall Brigade.

429ᵗʰ Forward Support Battalion

Headquarters and Company A (Sup)	Staunton
Company B (Med)	Charlottesville
Company C (Maint)	Richmond

The return of the 29ᵗʰ Division brought with it new equipment and improved readiness. The first High Mobility Multi-Purpose Wheeled Vehicle (HUMMWV) was issued to the Stonewall Brigade, and soldiers began to draw Battle Dress Uniforms (BDUs) for the first time. After the "Rights of Passage" that all soldiers of a Light Division were required to complete, combat arms soldiers were moved into more intensive training to earn the title of "Light Fighters." The training focus was clearly on building from the bottom up, with emphasis on mastering individual soldier skills before moving into the challenges of collective training. Members of the National Guard would soon become eligible for the Montgomery GI Bill, similar to the GI Bill for active duty soldiers, to assist in continuing their education. Named for Congressman G. V. "Sonny" Montgomery of Mississippi, a National Guardsman, the bill would make reservists eligible for up to $5,040 in educational benefits. Congress was recognizing the value of its National Guard.

One of the worst floods in Virginia's history took place in 1985, and many members of the Stonewall Brigade found themselves on active duty as the Valley Rivers swelled beyond their banks. In Roanoke, the National Guard Armory had to be evacuated as the Roanoke River rose. The 1/116th Headquarters and company vehicles and equipment were moved to higher ground or secured in other nearby Guard compounds. Major Buddy Faulconer, 2/116th Operations Officer wrote, "The battalion responded to numerous sites along the James River, none worse than near Buena Vista where the Maury River flows into the James. The Governor authorized the distribution of live ammunition to soldiers standing watch over the homes destroyed by the flooding. Looting was a serious concern." Sergeant George Anthony of B Company, 2/116th, was seriously injured in a vehicle accident while serving in the Eagle Rock area. Tragically, he would never recover from his injuries and became one of the few Virginia Guard members to ever die as a result of State Active Duty.

The scene was not much better along the Shenandoah River to the north, where the 3/116th was deployed to protect the property damaged by the flooding. As the waters began to recede, looters attempted to enter the stricken area by floating down the river and coming on shore to take whatever they could. The 3/116th was also authorized live ammunition to protect themselves in the event the looters decided to use weapons to force their way into the deserted property along the Shenandoah River. As always, the 116th worked closely with the Virginia State Police and local authorities while they served in this state mission. State active duty was a "labor of love," because the Commonwealth authorized only thirty dollars of pay per day and meals to members of the National Guard during state emergency service.

After becoming Light Fighters and Light Leaders, training in the 29th Division was elevated to squad level, then platoon level, and company level. The goal was to build up to battalion level training and, eventually, successfully execute force-on-force exercises. Training year 1986 brought many new challenges to the 29th Division's First Brigade. One highlight, however, was the 2/116th's B Company, having been identified as the Brigade's "best company sized unit," rewarded with an overseas opportunity. The unit, commanded by First Lieutenant Mike Harris, would participate in "Exercise Blue Fox" in Norway, a part of the much larger NATO (North Atlantic Treaty Organization) Exercise, "Northern Atlas." The unit mobilized at Fort A. P. Hill before being deployed on an Air Force C-141 on 1 September to Heistadmoen, Norway, just west of Oslo. The unit moved by truck to a field location, struggling to adjust to the six hour time difference and the extreme cold Scandinavian weather. Just five hundred miles south of the Artic Circle, the company had small wood burning stoves to heat its pup tents at night. After two weeks, the end of the tactical exercise permitted the Stonewallers to move to much larger, warmer tents, and even enjoy a day trip to Oslo, Norway's capital. After three weeks, B Company returned home from its challenging three week annual training experience in Scandinavia, having completed the National Guard experience of a lifetime.

Another significant highlight for the Stonewall Brigade in 1986 was the selection of its First Battalion as the Milton A. Reckord Award winner for TY-86. The award, named for the former 29th Division Commander from 1934-41 and an Adjutant General of Maryland, recognized the top battalion sized unit in the First United States Army. Battalion Commander, Lieutenant Colonel Steve Arey, a long-serving Stonewaller and former Operations Officer of the 116th Separate Brigade, was pleased with his unit's effort. *"This is a Stonewall Brigade first and I'm certainly proud to be a part of it, but the credit goes to the outstanding soldiers of this battalion."* The trophy presentation would be made during the 109th General Conference of the National Guard Association of the United States meeting in Portland, Oregon, in September of the following year.

In 1986, the National Guard Bureau announced funding for a new initiative, the Family Support Group (FSG). The family was a critical element in every soldier's decision to re-enlist, and, finally, there was recognition of the need to formalize the effort to make the family feel a part of its soldier's unit. Previously, there were "Holiday Meals" once each year at either Thanksgiving or Christmas, where families could come to the local armory to share a special lunch meal with their soldiers, and some units also conducted annual family picnics. The FSG, though, would be a continuous effort to keep the families of each soldier informed and involved in the unit's activities. The program would pay tremendous dividends in retention, particularly with the challenging deployments to come.

A number of changes became visible at the start of 1987. BDUs were now the standard uniform of the Stonewallers, and Jungle boots were finally authorized for wear again. HUMMVs were beginning to trickle into the system, but the standard mode of wheeled travel remained the jeep. A Virginia Defense Force (VADF) was organized, and retired Major General Albert R. Morris of Richmond selected as its first commander. Comprised initially of 2,000 volunteers, the VADF became known as the George Washington Division and prepared to backfill Virginia National Guard units called to active duty. The stay-behind-force would assume responsibility for the armory and any property the deploying unit would not need. VADF units, comprised of former Guard members and patriotic citizens, began to spring up throughout the Shenandoah Valley. Members train for a minimum of six hours each month, wear distinctive uniforms, and serve in an organization similar to the Light Division structure. In 1987, soldiers of the Stonewall Brigade again responded to civil emergencies in the Shenandoah Valley, to include heavy snow, flooding, and forest fires.

July 18-30, 1987, found the First Brigade conducting its annual training along with the other units of the 29th Division, in West Virginia. Designated "Operation Mountain State," the Stonewallers found themselves at Camp Dawson and training in the surrounding Monogahela National Forrest, located in West Virginia's northern mountainous coal region. An opposing force enemy from their Capstone partner, the 82nd Airborne Division, provided a challenging training experience for the leaders and soldiers of the Blue and Gray Division. Moving straight to the field, the Brigade successfully operated under continuous combat conditions in a mountain environment. Vehicle support was very limited since the "Light" concept provided little mobility at Brigade level, and the difficult terrain further restricted movement. The soldiers injured in the remote mountain area had to be evacuated to the University of West Virginia Medical Center in Morgantown. It was quite a challenging exercise for the Stonewallers, as well as the other units of the 29th Division that participated.

Problems with MREs had Stonewall Brigade units using boxed meals for much of the mid-80s, but by Operation Mountain State a new ration was available, the tray pack. The "T-Packs" were fully cooked meals which just needed to be heated and served. Staff Sergeant Phillip Diehl from Harrisonburg's C Company, 3/116th, indicated, *"All we need is a couple of spoons and a bunch of hungry soldiers and we're in business."* The meals could be heated and delivered to the units in less than ninety minutes. T-Packs were perfect for the Light Infantryman, and when MREs were finally approved for use again, the logisticians and food service personnel of the 29th Division were elated with their food service options.

The Brigade's highlight in 1988 was the deployment of the 2/116th Infantry Battalion to the Jungle Operations Training Center (JOTC) at Fort Sherman in Panama. The three week training came as the United States began exerting pressure on the Panamanian dictator, Manuel Noriega, to step down and allow for democratic elections. The Battalion was focused on learning jungle operations and survival techniques, but it could not help noticing nearby exercises by the Army's elite Delta Force. This activity was in preparation for the American invasion of Panama which lay ahead. Despite the stressful jungle conditions, the battalion training successfully moved from individual to platoon level under the leadership of LTC Ed Wray, the Battalion Commander, and Operations Officer Major Buddy Faulconer.

The year 1988 found the National Guard moving to a new finance system known as Sure-Pay. There would be no more checks mailed out two months after drill. Instead, the new automated pay system would make a direct deposit into a soldier's bank account, often just weeks after their monthly drill or annual training. Medical requirements were increased, and screening for the Human Immunosuppressive Virus (AIDS), plus dental x-rays or Panorexs, were required of all soldiers as a result of the tragic "Gander Crash," which took the lives of members of the 101st Airborne Division returning from peacekeeping duty in the Sinai. Over forty screening was also now required to insure older Guard members were in strong enough physical condition to participate in the challenging training required to be a Light Infantryman.

The loss of any soldier of the Brigade, or a member of its family, was always difficult, but the death of First Sergeant Jerry Hines on February 20, 1989, of Lexington's Alpha 3/116 came as a huge shock. He had been instrumental in the organization of the new unit in his local community when the 29th Division had been reactivated several years earlier, and was a father figure for the young soldiers enlisting in the company. His own son had joined and was a private in A Company when First Sergeant Hines, a Virginia State Trooper, was shot to death during a routine traffic stop on Interstate 81, just a short distance from the new Lexington Armory. Governor Douglas Wilder was present when the Lexington Armory was dedicated as the First Sergeant Jerry Hines Memorial Armory.Training year 1989 would find the battalions of the Stonewall Brigade moving to a variety of locations from Fort Pickett in Virginia to Camp Dawson in West Virginia. Sergeant Larry Cromer of the Brigade's Headquarters Company would be killed in a vehicle accident while that unit was conducting annual training at Fort A. P. Hill. It was a very sad day when Sergeant Cromer's body was brought to the Staunton Armory for a memorial service preceding a burial with full military honors. The Brigade always had an exceptional safety record; training accidents were rare and fatal accidents practically unheard of. One of the history rooms in the Staunton Armory is dedicated to the memory of this excellent soldier.

The 1st Battalion of the First Brigade was selected to participate in the rigorous evaluation and training program at the Army's new Joint Readiness Training Center (JRTC) located at Fort Chaffee, Arkansas. Lieutenant Colonel Bob Ryder was selected to take the command to this challenging two week annual training period in late May and early June, along with many of the Brigade's most experienced Light Leaders and Light Fighters. The First Battalion operated in the most realistic combat environment the Army could offer. The soldiers honed their skills on everything from land navigation to combat life saving. They successfully fought a "World Class" Opposing Force (OPFOR) from the Soviet-backed country of Atlantica, which had infiltrated our Central American ally of Cortina, all completely fictitious locations, but representing realistic scenarios. The evaluation was conducted under the most difficult continuous combat conditions imaginable--in wooded, hilly, rugged, "tick infested" terrain. It was quite an experience for these Stonewallers. Lieutenant Colonel Ryder recalled that this rotation was one of the last conducted at Fort Chaffee, before JRTC was moved to its current location at Fort Polk, Louisiana.

The level of training intensified leading up to a 29th Division AT scheduled for August 4-18, 1990, at Camp McCall, part of Fort Bragg, North Carolina. Colonel James D. Holden, a veteran Aviator with Viet Nam combat service, had become the new commander of the First Brigade and had focused the organization on operating in a continuous field environment. The Stonewall Brigade arrived in North Carolina amidst news reports of Iraq's invasion of Kuwait. The Stonewallers were welcomed to Fort Bragg by 1-504th PIR, who would be their host and provide support throughout the annual training period. 1-504th had just returned from Panama, but it was the "ready brigade" of the All America Division, and its equipment was positioned at Pope Air Force base, which adjoins Fort Bragg in the event of a call-up. Lieutenant Colonel Theodore Shuey, commanding the 3rd Battalion of the 116th, remembered that during a tactical move on Sunday evening, August 6, the pager being worn by his battalion commander counter-part from the 82nd buzzed. *"Any chance you guys may be getting called in to go to Kuwait?"* he asked. *"No way"* came the reply, *"we've still not recovered from the Panama deployment, but I better go check this out. We are part of the ready brigade!"* That night, all of the members of the 1-504 were recalled to main post, and by the next day they were going through the mobilization line at Pope Air Force Base and headed to Saudi Arabia. As was usually the case, the 82nd Airborne would be first in, as another conflict loomed on the horizon.

As AT-90 progressed, more and more units of the 82nd were deployed, leaving a void at Fort Bragg. Major General Thomas T. Thompson, commanding the 29th Division, seized upon this opportunity to request the Blue and Gray, the only light division in the reserve component structure, remain at Fort Bragg and train-up in case they would be needed in what would become known as the Gulf War. News of the offer soon reached the media and the families of the Stonewall Brigade, the 29th Division unit closest to Fort Bragg and Fayetteville, North Carolina. When the offer was not accepted by the Army, the Stonewallers headed home as their AT ended and were met at the Virginia state line by family members still concerned that they would be stuck at Fort Bragg. It was quite a scene as the Brigade convoy rolled north up Virginia Highway 29, named the *"29th Division Highway,"* past cheering members of family and community. It was not to be like December of 1941.

Combined Armed Services Training (CAST) was initiated in the First Brigade training plans and the event scheduled annually during a five period Multiple Unit Training Assembly (MUTA). That meant training started on Friday evening, with a deployment to Fort A. P. Hill, and concluded on Sunday morning, followed by the unit's movement back to Home Station. CAST brought together the "Slice" elements assigned to the First Brigade, which included Engineers, Artillery, Air Defense, and Chemical support. This new concept was helpful in preparing the Brigade units for the collective training challenges presented during future annual training periods.

The fall of 1990 found soldiers and equipment from the 116th Infantry in Albemarle County at Miller School for the production of the movie *Toy Soldiers*. The Stonewallers remember the star, Louis Gossett, Jr., was a pleasure to work with and it was interesting to see their unit HUMMVs and 2½ ton trucks used in a major movie. *Toy Soldiers*, depicting terrorists taking over a private military boarding school, was released in May, 1991, with appropriate credit and appreciation for the support from America's Stonewall Brigade.

Training in 1991 found the units of the 116th back in the field at Fort A. P. Hill, conducting additional Light Leader and Light Fighter training. Most of the other units of the 29th Division, including the Division Headquarters, were also at "the Hill" testing the command and control relationships. Commander of the Stonewall Brigade was now Colonel Lloyd McDaniel of Waynesboro, Virginia. Colonel McDaniel had many years of experience in the 116th dating back to his enlistment, command of the Headquarters Company, and command of the 3/116th Infantry Battalion.

In the summer of 1992, the Third Battalion, comprised primarily of the Shenandoah Valley units, would conduct its annual training at the National Training Center (NTC), Fort Irwin, California, serving as Infantry for the Opposing Force Regiment comprised of two Mechanized active duty battalions. The 3/116th was commanded by Lieutenant Colonel Ted Shuey who was commissioned a Second Lieutenant in the Stonewall Brigade Headquarters exactly twenty years earlier. The unit shipped its equipment by rail, but the soldiers flew into Las Vegas, before being bused to Fort Irwin for the difficult three week annual training. The battalion deployed at over 100 percent strength. They would have one company serve as Task Force Destroyer, a mounted operation, one become Task Force Angel, an airmobile force, and the third company serving as Task Force Avenger in an anti-armor role. This was the first time a unit of the Stonewall Brigade had gone to the NTC, but the other battalions of the 116th would have this same training opportunity in the years ahead. During these three weeks in the Mohave Desert, the Stonewallers experienced harsh conditions which many were destined to experience again.

The Third Battalion's readiness and combat effectiveness resulted in an outstanding effort, and the battalion would be recognized by the Army with a Superior Unit Award in 1994. Training years 1992, 1993, and 1994 would also see the 3rd Battalion recognized as the best battalion sized unit in the First U.S. Army. The unit also was awarded the Walter T. Kerwin Award as the best battalion in the entire National Guard. One of the keys to the 3rd Battalion's success was its ability to exceed the recruiting and retention standard for an Infantry battalion. It achieved and maintained strength of 110 percent during this period.

During 1993, the First Brigade was back together at Fort A. P. Hill in exercises with support units of the 29th Division. The Army had instituted "Bold Shift," which was a new program to evaluate the readiness of Army National Guard units. Previous to this time, the Army would conduct Inspector General (IG) visits to the Guard units, but now an Operational Readiness Exercise (ORE) inspection would take the place of IG visits and would evaluate not only unit administration, but insure intensive training was being conducted to insure the unit's readiness.

In the summer of 1994, Colonel Steve Arey assumed command of the Brigade during ceremonies held at Fort A. P. Hill. He was an attorney from Tazewell, Virginia, a drive of over two hours from the Brigade Headquarters in Staunton, but his dedication to the historic unit easily overcame the sacrifice of getting to regular command meetings and training weekends. Colonel Arey was a tremendous mentor to the officers of the Brigade and, using his previous experience as Brigade S-3, he developed an exceptional training program. Lieutenant Colonel Bob Ryder, now commanding the 2/116th Infantry Battalion, took the unit to three weeks of annual training in 1994 as part of the OPFOR Task Force at the National Training Center, Fort Irwin. It was quite an experience for these young Stonewallers, as the desert heat often reached 120 degrees during the day. Their performance on "the whale" and in "the valley of death" set a high standard for future National Guard Infantry Battalions to strive for.

In 1995, selected members of the Stonewall Brigade found themselves in the

15-2: Desert Panther pictures: Desert Panther coin, top left; and Virginia Adjutant General MG Carroll Thackston visiting Stonewallers in the Sinai in 1995.

harsh environment of Iceland, participating in a "Northern Viking" exercise. In addition, a volunteer company was formed in 1994 to serve in the United Nation's peacekeeping effort in the Sinai, keeping watch on the border between Israel and Egypt. One hundred plus soldiers of the First Brigade stepped up to become "Desert Panthers" and serve as part of the "Multinational Force and Observers (MFO)" organization of the Task Force 4-505th Parachute Infantry Regiment, deployed from the 82nd Airborne Division based at Fort Bragg. The Stonewallers were displeased to learn that while serving in the Sinai, they would have to take off their 29th Division patch and place the "All American" Division patch of the 82nd on their left shoulder, but they were undeterred in their eagerness to serve in the peacekeeping force. CPT George Roller from Augusta County was one of the volunteers, and remembers well manning the observer outposts spread throughout the Sinai desert. The active duty experience was invaluable for the Brigade's soldiers, and they learned a lot about the challenges of a desert environment. Task Force 4-505 returned to Fort Bragg in early summer and was deactivated on July 28.

In 1996, reorganization would again affect the structure of the Stonewall Brigade. Department of Defense (DOD) force reductions following the Gulf War resulted in three National Guard Divisions being deactivated. One of these, the 26th Division headquartered in Massachusetts would join the 29th Division as a brigade, replacing Virginia's Second Brigade which had struggled to meet its strength objectives. This move resulted in the 3rd Battalion of the 116th gaining a company in Leesburg and another in Manassas, and releasing its Harrisonburg and Lexington companies to the 2nd Battalion. The move clearly improved the demographics of the First Brigade, restoring the communities surrounding these armories to their lineage in the Stonewall Brigade. The move also increased the 3rd Battalion's Woodstock unit to a full company, which would need the new armory, dedicated there on November 17, 1997. This facility was dedicated as the John O. Marsh, Jr. Armory, to honor the former Stonewaller, Secretary of the Army, and Congressman from the lower Valley.

The reorganization of Virginia's Army National Guard units was very positive for the First Brigade as strength soared with the addition of units and soldiers from the old Second Brigade. The 3/116th Infantry was now centered in the lower Valley, with the 2/116th in the upper Valley's and across the Blue Ridge Mountains and into the Piedmont. The 1/116th remained centered in the Roanoke Valley. During the annual training period of 1996, the 1/116th Infantry, commanded by LTC Jim Harmon, would serve with the OPFOR Regiment at the National Training Center. The newly designated "Red Dragons" of this historic unit performed exceptionally well throughout their three week deployment to the California high desert. Another highlight was the deployment of elements of the First Brigade's 429th Forward Support Battalion to the Combat Maneuver Training Center (CMTC) in Hohenfels, Germany. These Stonewallers, predominantly maintenance personnel, turned wrenches to keep the wheeled vehicles of the CMTC rolling while taking advantage of opportunities to serve as OPFOR for units rotating through the center. The annual training in Germany, the Stonewall Brigade's first since the end of World War II, was an exceptional experience for the soldiers of the 429th FSB.

In the fall of 1996, the 116th Infantry Foundation, Inc. was formed with a charter to establish a museum to preserve the history of the 116th Infantry. Its first President

15-3: Freedom Isn't Free - C Company's Leesburg Armory by artist James Dietz

and creator, Colonel (Ret.) Herbert C. Turner, worked tirelessly to capture the history of the unit and develop a museum worthy of its history. America's Stonewall Brigade deserved nothing less and Colonel Turner, a former Stonewaller, was committed to creating a facility worthy of the unit's history.

In the summer of 1997, Command of the Brigade passed to Colonel Theodore G. Shuey, Jr. At the same time, the Stonewall Brigade was selected to provide a rifle company for peacekeeping duty in Bosnia-Hertsogovenia. The initiative was part of "Operation Joint Guard," to determine the readiness of National Guard units to assist the active Army in its peacekeeping role. This was the first activation of a unit of the Brigade for overseas duty since World War II. C Company of the Third Battalion from Leesburg was selected for the honor. Captain Mike Patterson was chosen to command the unit, with Sergeant First Class Bennie Dancy, a Viet Nam War veteran, selected as First Sergeant. The unit was officially mobilized on September 3, 1997, and departed its community and families with great fanfare. Immediately, the Virginia Defense Force, which had always been in the background supporting the Stonewall Brigade units, moved into the Leesburg Armory and took over responsibility for the facility as they had been trained to do. This would be the first of many times the VADF would play an important role in supporting the units of the Brigade called to active duty.

The deployment also brought home the importance of the Employer Support for the Guard and Reserve (ESGR) program, established to assist part time soldiers and airmen with employment rights. This volunteer group of professionals had supported the National Guard for years with job related issues, but now an entire company of soldiers faced critical re-employment and pay problems. Some employers recognized the lower pay most of the soldiers would be receiving on active duty and agreed to continue their civilian salary or make up any difference. Other employers were not prepared to support the unit deployment and threatened to replace the activated soldier or not hold an equivalent job open for his return. The ESGR Committee masterfully worked to assist the deploying soldiers with their employment issues. Their efforts provided valuable experience which would be needed in the future mobilizations.

The activation of C-3/116th was a high visibility event. The Army sent multiple teams to begin their evaluation during the unit's annual training in July at Fort A. P. Hill. C Company was clearly under the microscope as evaluators from the First United States Army, some days almost one for every three soldiers, worked to insure the unit could "integrate" into the active force. There was tremendous emphasis on physical readiness and weapons qualification. Finally, having achieved initial First Army approval, the unit was moved to Fort Polk, Louisiana, for additional evaluation at the Joint Readiness Training Center and then to Fort Benning, Georgia for final validation and theatre specific training. Its mission would be to replace a unit from the Army's 10th Mountain Division and secure the vital bridge over the Sava River connecting Bosnia with Hungary. The one hundred and forty-seven C Company sol-

Illustration 15-4: MG Thackston, along with Division and Brigade leaders, welcome 1SG Dancy and C Company back to Fort Benning.

diers were proud to have the mission and become the first National Guard company-sized unit to be mobilized for foreign duty since 1968. Having been put through their paces, they departed for overseas duty on October 19.

Reaching Bosnia, C Company assumed responsibility for the security of the strategic Sava River Bridge. One memorable event was the arrival of the new year of 1998. The Bosnian citizens welcomed the New Year by firing a variety of weapons into the air and a shower of bullets began falling onto the surface of the bridge. The Stonewallers had to take cover in their defensive positions to avoid the falling lead. During its entire deployment, a history making event, C Company, upheld the highest traditions of the Stonewall Brigade, returning to Fort. Benning on April 22, 1998, to a heroes' welcome. Touching down at Hunter Army Airfield, they were greeted by Major General Carroll Thackston, the Adjutant General of Virginia and former Stonewaller, and other leaders from the 29th Division and 116th Infantry Brigade. An independent review of C Company's efforts recorded by Science Applications International Corporation (SAIC) concluded: "The Company performed the mission well and also executed other tasks, such as weapons site inspection, for which its soldiers had not been trained."

The year of 1997 was also historic as the hard work of the National D-Day Memorial Foundation finally resulted in a groundbreaking ceremony to capture the sacrifices of June 6, 1944. The future site was just off of Route 460 outside Bedford, Virginia, the home of A Company, 116th, the tiny community that had suffered the highest per capita loss on D-Day. The cool fall morning of November 11, 1997, found representatives from all D-Day participants, including representatives of France and the United Kingdom, assembled atop a hill with a panoramic view of the Roanoke Valley. Virginia's United States Senators Charles Robb and John Warner, Governor

George Allen, and numerous other dignitaries spoke, attempting to describe the pride Virginia felt in the heroic service of the 116th Infantry and the opportunity to provide this permanent memorial commemorating the events of D-Day. It was another great day for America's Stonewall Brigade and especially its World War II veterans.

Annual Training for the Stonewall Brigade July 18-25, 1998, was focused on taking the lead for a Division Maneuver Exercise (DMX), organized and led by the 29th Division staff. The event was the vision of Major General Carroll Childers, the Division Commander and former member of the Stonewall Brigade, having commanded the 3/116th Infantry Battalion. A history lover, Major General Childers named the exercise "Operation Chindit" in honor of the Chindit guerrillas who served in Burma during World War II as part of Merrill's Marauders. The First Brigade was tasked to initially seize and hold terrain in the Division's Area of Operation (AO), located in the vicinity of Blackstone, Virginia. As Brigade units arrived, the area was widened, becoming a lodgment and allowing other units of the Division to be flown in. The two weeks of continuous field training challenged all of the units of the Division, especially the support elements. In addition to the 116th or First Brigade, the training included the units of the Division's "26th Brigade," comprised of units from Massachusetts and Connecticut, who had completed their Rites of Passage and Light Fighter training and were ready for a coordinated exercise.

Annual Training for the 3/116th consisted of serving as OPFOR for the Florida Army National Guard's 53rd Enhanced Brigade Separate (ESB) training at Camp Blanding, Florida for their upcoming rotation at the JRTC. Commanded by Lieutenant Colonel Bill Phillips, 3/116 was well prepared for the assignment, having previously served as an opposing force at the National Training Center. This exercise would be centered around the MOUT site at Camp Blanding and include day and night operations. The trip to Florida was the Stonewall Brigade's first since their training there, prior to departing for England in 1942. In setting the conditions for the training, Lieutenant General George A. Fisher commanding the First United States Army, emphasized the need for training in "force protection." His challenge would be prophetic and no doubt save lives as the 53rd ESB would find itself in combat just a few years later.

1999 saw another 29th Division Warfighter (WFX), and key members of the Brigade began preparation at the Division Headquarters at Fort Belvoir. Later in June, the Division team spent a week of Annual Training at Fort Dix, New Jersey, to conclude its final preparation. The remaining members of the 116th conducted their 1999 Annual Training at Fort A. P. Hill. The Division War fighters deployed to Fort Leavenworth, Kansas, in July to fight "Operation Other Clay," named in honor of the World War II book by Major Charles Cawthon of the 2/116th Infantry. The name, of course, was chosen by Major General Childers. The First Brigade played a critical part of this Warfighter which was based on a Korean peninsula scenario.

The new commander of the 29th Division, after AT-99, Major General H. Steven Blum, also loved history and had a special appreciation for the World War II

Stonewallers. Shortly after taking command, he organized a Staff Ride to Normandy, September 7-11. He included senior leaders of the Division, but also many soldiers and, of course, World War II veterans. The trip also included members of the 35th Division, which had served along side the 29th Division as it moved toward St. Lo. Another important participant was historian Joe Balkoski. This was quite a memorable event for the Stonewallers, past and present, as they walked Omaha Beach together and moved through the hedgerows. Each town visited in Normandy turned out great numbers of citizens, everyone from survivors of the German occupation to young elementary school students, waving American flags and signs to welcome home the former and current members of these two great National Guard Divisions.

In the fall of 1999, the First Brigade was selected to augment the 1st Cavalry Division in its War Fighting Exercise, "Phantom Menace." This rare opportunity for a National Guard brigade to integrate into an active duty division and its war fighter would prove to be an invaluable experience for the participants from the First Brigade. The initial seminar was held a Fort Leavenworth, Kansas, in November, but the ramp up and command post exercises were all conducted at the home of the 1st Cav, Fort Hood, Texas, also the base housing the 4th Infantry Division and III Corps. Under the mentorship of recently retired General Tommy Franks, the Division's Commander, Major General David McKiernan, built an effective war fighting team. The Stonewall Brigade participants learned to work with a heavy division and gained tremendous insight into advanced war fighting procedures, to include the successful conduct of deep operations throughout the train up and WFX conducted March 1-5, 2000. There were new terms like BUBS (Battle Update Briefings), leader huddles, and cross talking. It was a "graduate level" exercise with the Chief of Staff of the Army, General Eric K. Shinseki conducting the final After Action Review (AAR).

In March, 2000, C Company, 429th Forward Support Battalion deployed to Belize as part of Operation "New Horizons," to provide medical assistance to the citizens of that under-privileged country. Flying into the capital of Belize City, the Medical Company visited schools, administering physicals and providing inoculations for children throughout the city during their service as part of Task Force Pelican. It was a truly humanitarian effort and an annual training period which the soldiers of C Company will never forget.

On April 7, 2000, during ceremonies at the Hyatt Regency Hotel in Chicago, Illinois, the 429th Forward Support Battalion was awarded the Department of Defense Phillip A. Connelly Award for having the best food service program in the National Guard. The Excellence in Food Service award was the battalion's highest accomplishment to date, but the 429th had been a tremendous credit to the Stonewall Brigade since joining its ranks. The battalion was consistently recognized by the Army as having the National Guard's best maintenance program and supply system. These successes reflect great credit on the unit's former commanders; Lieutenant Colonels Kent Carter, Oliver Norrell, Pete Combee, Tim Williams, Janice Igou, and Tim Mantz.

-Sixteen-

Peacekeeping, 9-11, & the War on Terrorism

As a new century approached, the Stonewall Brigade, like most military units was alerted for potential emergencies which might result from computers not accepting the change to the New Year of 2000. Armories were manned, but fortunately the passage into the Twenty-First Century occurred without issue. Annual Training that year was focused on training at battalion level, and the 1/116th again found itself headed to the National Training Center at Fort Irwin, California, now commanded by Lieutenant Colonel Mike Harris. The battalion performed well, and it was recognized by the OPFOR Regiment as being an "outstanding Infantry unit" and having contributed greatly to the success of NTC Rotation 00-07. On Veteran's Day weekend in November, preceding the Annual Muster of the 116th Infantry Regiment, the command of the Stonewall Brigade changed to Colonel Ronnie Young, who had enlisted in the headquarters almost exactly thirty-one years earlier.

The new millennium also brought the transition from "soft caps" to black berets as the standard headdress for the United States Army, and, of course, the National Guard. The 29th Division's First Brigade also found itself organizing a new unit in Staunton. The 222nd Arid Water Detachment took shape as part of the 429th Forward Support Battalion, with twenty members falling into first formation in February, 1998. The unit would soon reach 100 percent strength under the leadership of Sergeant First Class Gerald Johnson. The small unit quickly became a great credit to the First Brigade. A new century also brought new challenges as the Operational Tempo (OPTEMPO) of the Stonewall Brigade was about to rise to new heights.

In the summer of 2001, annual training for the 116th brought the organization together at Fort Pickett. It seemed like business as usual as the Labor Day weekend passed, with the 29th Division Headquarters leaving Fort Belvoir for a tour in Bosnia to become Stabilization Force 10 (SFOR 10), to insure the ongoing peace in the region formerly known as Yugoslavia. No one would have predicted what would occur just a few days later, on the morning of September 11, 2001. Immediately, the Brigade was alerted and soldiers moved to their armories to prepare for what might happen next and await orders from Governor Jim Gilmore. The attack on the Pentagon was in the area of responsibility of the Stonewall Brigade, now that the headquarters of the 29th Division, along with Major General Blum, the Division's senior leadership and over 2,000 Twenty-Niners, were on active duty at Fort Dix, New Jersey, awaiting deployment.

During the next few days, the activities within the Brigade returned to normal. Then, on September 26, President George W. Bush announced that he was mobilizing the National Guard to provide additional security at America's airports. Immediately, the members of the Stonewall Brigade responded to the President's call, and the Adjutant General of Virginia, Major General Claude Williams, was overwhelmed by the number of volunteers for this new mission. Hundreds of Stonewallers moved to Fort Pickett, Virginia, to mobilize and prepare to establish a presence in the Commonwealth's nine commercial airports. In addition, Virginia was asked to assist with security at the National Guard Bureau and the Army National Guard Headquarters in Arlington. The evolving security mission tasked to the National Guard would become known as Noble Eagle I, commanded by Colonel Ted Shuey, who had been selected as the "stay behind" leader for Virginia's soldiers of the 29th Division who were not deploying to Bosnia.

Following training by the Federal Aviation Administration at Fort Pickett and normal mobilization events, members of the Stonewall Brigade began their deployment to provide security at Virginia's airports. The 3/116th Infantry Battalion set up a headquarters at its Leesburg Armory and took responsibility for Dulles International Airport. The 2/116th Infantry, working from its headquarters in Lynchburg, provided security at Lynchburg and Charlottesville airports, while the 1/116th Infantry, working from its headquarters in Roanoke was responsible for the Roanoke Valley airport. The Headquarters of the Stonewall Brigade assumed responsibility for the Shenandoah Valley Airport in Weyers Cave, Virginia, and set up an office at the Staunton Armory to provide oversight on the five subordinate locations. In addition, the security for the National Guard facilities in Arlington was managed from Staunton headquarters. The headquarters for Virginia Noble Eagle was located at Fort Pickett and was comprised almost exclusively of senior officers and NCOs from the First Brigade. In all, some eight hundred members of the Stonewall Brigade responded to the initial call-up of Operation Virginia Noble Eagle I.

In November, the National Guard Bureau alerted Colonel Young and the Stonewall Brigade for possible overseas deployment. A number of mobilization scenarios were developed, but in the end, the missions were passed to other units not as involved in the airport security mission. In February, 2002, members of the Brigade were sent to Salt Lake City, Utah, to assist in providing security for the XIX Winter Olympics. Requests for support from the Virginia National Guard came from numerous federal agencies housed in Virginia and several private companies involved in

Photograph 16-1: Noble Eagle - Airport Duty: Far Right Standing-CPT Patrick Combs, Commander of HHC 116th Infantry Brigade, and Stonewallers

the defense industry. Also, there were short-term missions which required, for example, providing additional perimeter security at the North Anna and Surry Nuclear Power Plants. In all, Noble Eagle was the most extensive utilization of the First Brigade in a Title 32 role in history. March, 2002, saw command of the Brigade change to Colonel Bob Simpson, an experienced Infantryman whose service began with the 82nd Airborne Division after his graduation from the Virginia Military Institute.

Noble Eagle duty was certainly challenging to the soldiers, their families, and employers, and would be a sign of things to come. The support for the Brigade, however, was exceptional. The events of what became known as 9-11, brought the residents of the Shenandoah Valley and Central Virginia, in fact all of America, to the realization of a new threat to their security and again, the National Guard was there. For the soldiers, the duty was often difficult and demanding. There were difficult commutes to duty, long shifts, and exposure to unexpected events. Each airport experienced a number of security challenges as the duty was extended into the summer of 2002. When the Transportation Security Administration began to become a reality, the need for the National Guard in the airports was lessened and by late summer, the only Stonewallers on duty were providing security at the Guard facilities in Arlington and the Virginia National Guard Headquarters at Fort Pickett. Now a new call to duty was about to occur.

In the summer of 2002, the 2/116th Infantry Battalion was alerted for security duty at the Guantanamo Bay Naval Base on the south eastern coast of Cuba. This would be the first Infantry battalion to deploy to Cuba since the end of the Spanish American War in 1898. It was also the first call-up of a battalion sized unit of the 29th Division to serve outside of the United States since World War II. The unit was initially mobilized at Fort Pickett, before moving to Fort Bragg in early November, 2006, for mission specific training. The unit departed for the Guantanamo (GTMO) mission on December 6. During its tour, the Battalion, led by Lieutenant Colonel Tom Wilkinson, provided external security on the facility that had been constructed to house al Qaeda, Taliban, and terrorist prisoners for interrogation and internment.

While there, the battalion organized enhanced training to include multiple live fire exercises, conducted advanced Infantry training, and even administered testing for the coveted Expert Infantryman's Badge (EIB). The unit re-deployed to Fort Bragg on September 22, 2003, and to its home stations a week later. It was another "job well done" for a Stonewall Brigade unit, and the battalion would later be recognized as the top battalion in the National Guard, earning the Milton A. Reckord and the Walter T. Kerwin Awards and the Chief of Staff of the Army's Deployment Excellence award. During deployment, 2LT Theodore G. Shuey III was a platoon leader.

Throughout 2003, units of the 429th Support Battalion were called to active duty to perform security duty as part of Operation Noble Eagle II. The primary location

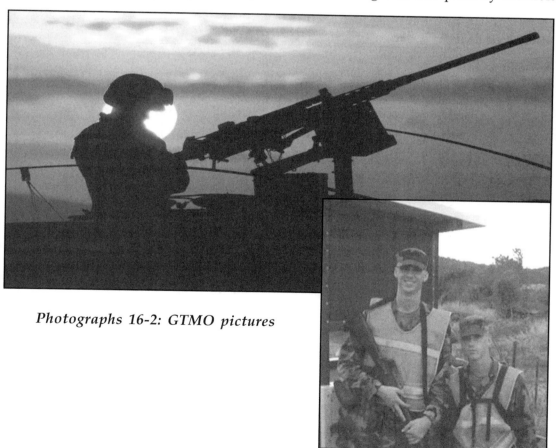

Photographs 16-2: GTMO pictures

was Fort Meade, Maryland, and after mobilization at Fort Pickett, these Stonewallers found themselves securing the vehicle and pedestrian access to this major installation. It was a site not new to the 116th Infantry Brigade, and many of the buildings where the Stonewallers housed after their mobilization in February, 1941, still remained.

Early in 2004, 3/116th Battalion was alerted for possible duty in Operation Enduring Freedom in Afghanistan. Commander LTC Blake Ortner immediately began preparing the battalion for mobilization, and on March 1, 2004, the rumor became a reality. Five hundred and seventy members of the 3/116th were officially called to active duty, later moving to Fort Pickett to conduct final mobilization events prior to their departure to Fort Bragg for theater specific training and validation. The battalion deployed to Afghanistan in July, initially providing perimeter security at Bagram Air Base. Quick reaction forces were identified and readied in the event of a Taliban assault on the facility. Soon "Task Force Normandy" began security patrols as the Afghan Presidential elections approached.

Tragically, on August 7, a motorized patrol was struck by an Improvised Explosive Device (IED) which took the lives of Staff Sergeant Craig Cherry from the hometown of 3/116th, Winchester, and Sergeant Bobby Beasley from Inwood, West Virginia. The incident occurred near Ghazikel, Afghanistan, but news of the tragedy soon spread throughout the Shenandoah Valley and the Commonwealth of Virginia. Two experienced Stonewallers had lost their lives in combat, the first such loss in almost sixty years. The entire Brigade and

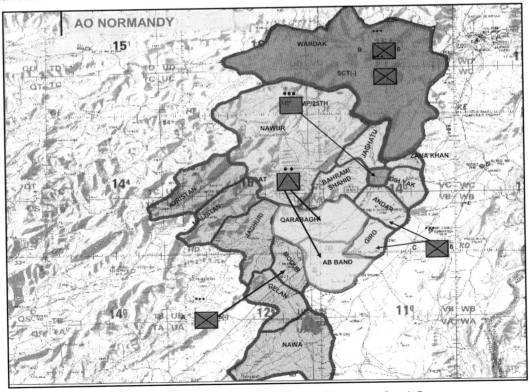

Illustration 16-3: Task Force Normandy AO

Photograph 16-4: On Patrol – Task Force Normandy painting by James Dietz

Valley were shocked and saddened by their deaths, bringing home the reality of risks of Operation Enduring Freedom (OEF) and the Global War on Terrorism (GWOT).

Throughout its tour, TF Normandy, the historic 3/116th performed a magnificent service to the people of Afghanistan. It took part in many humanitarian operations and overcame cultural differences to nurture a friendship with the people of this war torn country. The battalion used this relationship to locate and destroy numerous caches of weapons and munitions in the theater. This, plus its very successful "turn-in" program, helped the 3/116th Infantry Battalion achieve a record number of weapons collected and destroyed.

In May, another tragedy struck TF Normandy with the death of Specialist Kyle Hemanuer, age twenty-one, of Chilton, Wisconsin. Despite being a student at Newport News Apprentice, like so many other young Americans he had responded to the events of 9-11 and volunteered to serve in the Global War on Terrorism. The First Brigade was blessed with young volunteers from another generation stepping up to join the historic Stonewall Brigade and willing to do whatever was necessary to protect their country. After its full year overseas, the 3/116th re-deployed to Fort Bragg in July, 2005. Soon the soldiers were home, having written another chapter in the historic service of America's Stonewall Brigade. After a well deserved break, the unit mustered again in January of 2006 for a "Freedom Salute." This event brings soldiers and families together, along with their community and friends, in recognition of service in the Global War on Terrorism. The Headquarters and C Company gathered in the auditorium of Shenandoah University in Winchester, while A and B Company assembled at Prince William High School in Manassas. The soldiers were glad to be home, their tour complete, but a short two years later they would again receive their country's call.

In the fall of 2006, the 1/116th Infantry Battalion was alerted for possible

Photographs 16-5: Task Force Normandy returns home: In photo at right, TF Normandy Adjutant, CPT Jim Tierney, is welcomed home by CW4 (Ret.) Charles Lillis, one of the Stonewall Brigade's remaining WWII veterans.

mobilization to serve as part of Task Force Falcon (TFF) under the command of the 29th Division. The Task Force would be a part of the Balkans 8 Rotation being deployed to Kosovo, to insure the continuing peace in that region. The unit revised its Training Year (TY) 2006 schedules to begin preparation for its first overseas duty since World War II. Train-up complete, the battalion was mobilized on July 17, 2006 and following initial home station work, they moved to their mobilization site at Camp Atterbury, Indiana, for mission specific training. Time at Camp Atterbury passed quickly, and the battalion successfully validated its readiness, deploying as a part of TFF Balkans

8 in November. For the next year, the battalion was located at Camp Bonsteel, serving with other 29ᵗʰ Division units insuring the peace and security of Kosovo. After a successful one year tour, the "Red Dragons" of the 1ˢᵗ Battalion returned home in time for Thanksgiving 2007. The battalion was commanded by LTC Lapthe Flora.

Photograph 16-6: The 1/116th Red Dragons accept the Transfer of Authority (TOA) for responsibility as part of TF Falcon in December 2006.

During this period the Army was undergoing a transformation which would result in another reorganization of the 116ᵗʰ Stonewall Brigade. The new structure would resemble the old separate brigade organization and allow brigade sized units to be self sufficient. There would, of course, be a brigade commander, but he would be assisted by a deputy brigade commander, also holding the rank of full Colonel. The brigade would have its own organic field artillery battalion, brigade troop's battalion with organic support in place of a "slice" provided from the 29ᵗʰ Division. The existing 2ⁿᵈ Battalion was integrated into the 1ˢᵗ and 3ʳᵈ Battalions, and replaced by what was initially known as a Reconnaissance, Surveillance, and Target Acquisition (RSTA) Battalion, which would become the 2/183ʳᵈ Cavalry. The new organization incorporated a number of Virginia units from the central and tidewater regions of Virginia. The new 116ᵗʰ Infantry Brigade Combat Team (IBCT) broadened the demographics of the Stonewall Brigade, and soon this new organization, under its new commander, Colonel Mike Harris, would reach its authorized strength of 3,448.

The 116th IBCT, today's "Stonewall Brigade"

Headquarters	Staunton
Brigade Special Troops Battalion	
Headquarters	Fredericksburg
Company A	Fredericksburg
Company B	Alexandria
Company C	Hampton
1/116th Infantry	
Headquarters	Lynchburg
Company A(-)	Bedford
Det. 1 CO A	Farmville
Company B (-)	Lexington
Det. 1 CO B	Clifton Forge
Company C (-)	Christiansburg
Det. 1 CO C	Radford
Company D (-)	Pulaski
Det. 1 CO D	Martinsville
2/183rd Cavalry	
Headquarters Troop	Portsmouth
Troop A	Norfolk
Troop B	Suffolk
Troop C	Virginia Beach
3/116th Infantry	
Headquarters	Winchester
A Company (-)	Charlottesville
Det. 1 CO A	Harrisonburg
B Company (-)	Woodstock
Det. 1 CO B	Warrenton
C Company (-)	Leesburg
Det. 1 CO C	Manassas
D Company	Fredericksburg
111th Fires Battalion	
Headquarters Battery	Norfolk
Battery A	Sandston
Battery B	Richmond
Battery C	Norfolk

429th Support Battalion

Headquarters	Danville
Company A (-)	South Boston
Det. 1 CO A	Bowling Green
Det. 2 CO A	Chatham
B Company (-)	Richmond
C Company	Charlottesville
D Company (-)	Portsmouth
Det. 1 CO D	Franklin
Company E	Roanoke
Company F (-)	Fredericksburg
Det. 1 CO F	Winchester
Company G	Norfolk

The Stonewall Brigade was in the midst of reorganization when Hurricane Katrina, America's single worst natural disaster, hit the Gulf Coast of Mississippi and the city of New Orleans, Louisiana, on August 29, 2005. As is always the case, the National Guard quickly stepped up to respond to this tragedy. Under Emergency Management Assistance Compacts (EMACs) which allow National Guard assets from one state to assist in disasters in another state, Guard equipment was put in motion quickly. On September 3 at eight a.m., the 2/116th Infantry Battalion and its commander, Lieutenant Colonel John Epperly, were alerted for possible deployment to the Gulf region. The next day, Sunday, September 4, 250 soldiers reported to the Lynchburg armory, the battalion headquarters, to begin preparations for their relief effort under Title 32 orders. There would be an airlift into Jackson, Mississippi, and a ground convoy of thirty-four vehicles and radios prepared for the 1,300 mile trip to Camp Shelby, Mississippi, the site designated as the battalion's deployment headquarters. The emergency response was in motion on September 6.

The morning of September 8, found Task Force Stonewall in place and providing security, humanitarian relief, and recovery assistance to the Mississippi communities of Biloxi, in the east, to Pass Christian, in the west, with Gulf Port and Long Beach in between, all connected by what remained of Highway 90. The Area of Operations (AO), twenty-two miles wide and ten miles deep, was only a few feet above sea level, and the damage throughout the area was very severe. Within hours, fifty-four checkpoints were manned, and mounted and dismounted patrols were providing security throughout the AO. Despite the unusual heat and humidity, the Stonewallers performed magnificently in all the challenging facets of the operation. As additional units deployed and rotated into Task Force Stonewall's AO, the battalion's duty ended in late September, and the soldiers returned home on October 1. They had witnessed first hand the tragedy along the Mississippi Gulf Coast and took pride in their immediate and effective response. They returned home with vivid memories of the devastation, but positive feelings about

Photographs 16-7: Hurricane Katrina relief efforts: At left, MG Claude Williams, the Adjutant General of Virginia, briefs deploying Stonewallers, while at right, Stonewallers man a checkpoint on the Mississippi Gulf Coast.

their efforts, particularly the humanitarian relief and distributing water, food, and clothing to the survivors of Hurricane Katrina.

In June, 2006, President Bush announced an initiative to help secure America's Southern Border and reduce the stream of illegal aliens and drugs flowing into the United States. The resulting "Operation Jump Start" alerted the 116th Infantry Brigade Combat Team, and 420 Stonewallers and volunteers from Virginia's Air National Guard were mobilized on June 26. After brief processing at Fort Pickett, the Joint Task Force (JTF) "Stonewall" would deploy quickly to Arizona to provide security on the United States border with Mexico. Brigade Commander, Colonel Mike Harris, a retired law enforcement officer, was able to put together an excellent team of experienced citizen soldiers to assist the U.S. Customs and Border Patrol in tightening the southwest border security. On duty, Task Force Stonewall was responsible for one hundred and twenty miles of desert border, with hubs in the towns of Nogales, Sasabe, and Ajo, Arizona. During its service, the Task Force was responsible for the capture of nine hundred detainees and the seizure of over one thousand pounds of marijuana. The Task Force redeployed to Virginia on September 25, 2006, another successful mission accomplished.

Early in 2007, the Headquarters of the Stonewall Brigade and two maneuver battalions were alerted for duty in Operation Iraqi Freedom (OIF). The Headquarters element of 149 citizen soldiers was mobilized on May 1, 2007, led by their new Commander, Colonel Bill Phillips. Citizens of the city of Staunton, Augusta County, and the surrounding communities turned out to send the unit to Camp Shelby, Mississippi, for its final training before departing for Iraq. E Company, 429th Support Battalion, commanded by Captain Tim Eppele, and 180 strong, mobilized ten days later and joined the Headquarters. This mobilization was followed on 8 June by the 2/183rd Cavalry Battalion, commanded by Lieutenant Colonel Walt Mercer, and on 23 June by the 3/116th Infantry Battalion now commanded by Lieutenant Colonel Epperly. The maneuver battalions also deployed

Photographs 16-8: Task Force Stonewall On Duty (photo at left) – From left to right: unknown pilot (CPT) from AZ National Guard, 1LT Jeremy Weiss, CPT Brian Watson, COL Mike Harris, and MAJ Mike Martin. Bottom photo, MAJ Mike Martin with a USCBP agent while on patrol in the Ajo region of Arizona during operation JUMPSTART.

to Camp Shelby, Mississippi, for their training for duty in Operation Iraqi Freedom. After validating their readiness, these two battalions of the 116th IBCT joined the 1st Battalion, still serving on active duty in KFOR, bringing the total number of deployed members of the Stonewall Brigade to 1,952.

As this book goes to press, Colonel Phillips and the 116th Infantry Brigade Combat Team Headquarters are serving as part of the Joint Area Support Group in Bagdad, Iraq. E Company of the 429th is operating from Camp Arifjan, Kuwait, and being utilized as a line-haul transportation company supporting the Army's efforts in southern Iraq. 2/183rd Cavalry is currently conducting security force operations from bases in Kuwait, while 3/116th Infantry, based in southern Kuwait has three companies providing force protection in northwestern Iraq. Colonel Harris has returned as the "stay behind" commander to work with the 116th units that are not deployed and to continue the successful recruiting effort necessary to sustain the Brigade strength and readiness. EVER FORWARD!

Pictures 16-9: The 116th IBCT in training maneuvers at Camp Shelby (top left photo). The 116th IBCT boarding the plane for Kuwait and points beyond.

Picture 16-10: Employed by the author in civilian life, SSG Amy Wenger, who volunteered to serve with the 116th IBCT with which her husband Scott was deploying, is welcomed to Baghdad by Multi-National Force Commander, GEN David Petraus in Baghdad in 2007.

GLOBAL WAR ON TERRORISM

AFGHANISTAN

IRAQ

Battle streamers earned: Global War on Terrorism, Afghanistan, Iraq

Picture 16-11: HQ 116th IBCT JASG-C Command Directorate group picture in front of Saddam Hussein's palace in Baghdad's Green Zone.

TO BE CONTINUED...

Abbreviations, Code Names, and Glossary

AAR – After Action Report. A report that is written after an incident has taken place.

ACU – Army Combat Uniform. For more information see www.globalsecurity.org/military/systems/ground/acu.htm

AEF – American Expeditionary Force

AGR – Active Guard and Reserve

AO – area of operation

APFT – Army Physical Fitness Test

BAR – Browning Automatic Rifle. For more information see www.sproe.com/b/bar.html.

BDU – Battle Dress Uniform. For more information see www.globalsecurity.org/military/systems/ground/bdu.htm.

BUBs – Battle Update Briefings.

C Ration – An individual daily combat meal. Complete meal containing a canned entrée, a package of cheese and crackers and candy, a canned dessert, and an accessory pack with powdered beverage mix, salt and sugar packets, plastic ware, chewing gum, four cigarettes, a p-38 (can opener), and toilet tissue. Used from WWII to the early 1980s and replaced with the MREs. For additional information see www.qmfound.com/army_subsistence_history.htm.

CAST – Combined Armed Services Training

CMTC – Combat Maneuver Training Center. For more information see www.jmrc.hqjmtc.army.mil/JMRC/index.htm.

CARS – Combined Arms Regimental System

CO – Commanding Officer

D-Day – The day a combat attack or operation is to be initiated. The D in D-day represents a variable, designating the day that a significant event will occur.

DDT - dichlorodiphenyl-trichloroethane. Used during WWII as a dusting powder to kill body lice and other biting insects, For more information see www.21stcenturysciencetech.com/articles/Fall02/Mosquitoes.html

DoD – Department of Defense. For more information see www.defenselink.mil/pubs/dod101/index.html.

DMX - Division Maneuver Exercise

Dog Red – Subsector of Omaha Beach on Normandy Shore

Dog White – Subsector of Omaha Beach on Normandy Shore

DPs – Displaced Civilian Personnel

DRAGON - The DRAGON is a medium-range, wire-guided antitank missile that is light enough to be carried and fired by a single infantryman. For additional information see www.redstone.army.mil/history/missile/missiler.html.

deuce-and-a-half – A M-35 series military vehicle, (truck) that weighs 2-1/2 tons; all purpose truck that can carry equipment and/or personnel.

DUKW - an amphibious version of the 2.5 ton General Motors cargo truck. See http:/

/www.transchool.eustis.army.mil/Museum/DUKW.htm for more information.

Easy – nickname for "E" Company

Easy Green – Subsector of Omaha Beach on Normandy Shore

EIB – Expert Infantryman's Badge.

EMAC – Emergency Management Assistance Compacts, for more information see www.emacweb.org/

ESGR – Employer Support for the Guard and Reserve, for more Information see www.esgr.org/

FORSCOM – U.S. Army Forces Command - U.S. Army Forces Command trains, mobilizes, deploys, sustains, transforms, and reconstitutes conventional forces — providing relevant and ready land power to Combatant Commanders worldwide in defense of the Nation both at home and abroad. For more information see www.forscom.army.mil.

Fox – nickname for "F" Company

FSB – Forward Support Battalion

FSG – Family Support Group

GI – Government Issue

George – nickname for "G" Company

GWOT – Global War on Terrorism

GTMO – pronounced "Git' mo." Guantanamo Bay, for more information see www.globalsecurity.org/military/facility/guantanamo-bay.htm

H-Hour - The hour a combat attack or operation is to be initiated. The H in H-Hour represents a variable, designating the hour that a significant event will occur.

IBCT – Infantry Brigade Combat Team

IG – Inspector General; Army IGs inspect, audit, investigate, train, and perform those duties necessary to support the Army in achieving its mission. For more information see www.first.army.mil/ig/ighistory.htm.

JOTC – Jungle Operations Training Center. For more information see junglefighter.panamanow.net/.

JRTC – Joint Readiness Training Center. The Army's training center for light infantry and special operations units. For more information see www.jrtc-polk.army.mil/.

JTF – Joint Task Force. A JTF is formed, executes a mission that has a definite and limited objective, and then is disestablished. A JTF is composed of one or more service components. The JTF organizational structure capitalizes on the unique capabilities of each service and provides the flexibility to tailor the size and makeup of a military force to accomplish specific tasks in peace, crisis, or war.

KFOR – Kosovo Force. For more information see www.nato.int/KFOR/.

KPUP – Key Personnel Upgrade Program

K Ration – The K ration was developed for the soldier who was constantly moving to keep up with the mobile enemy. The C ration was considered too bulky for the individual soldier to carry several days' worth of rations. For more information see www.qmfound.com/army_subsistence_history.htm.

LAW - Light Anti-tank Weapon is a shoulder-fired, man-portable, light anti-tank rocket. For more information see www.inetres.com/gp/military/infantry/antiarmor/M72.html.

LCI – Landing Craft, Infantry

LCVP – Landing Craft Vehicle – Personnel

MILES - The Multiple Integrated Laser Engagement System is a training system that provides a realistic battlefield environment for soldiers involved in training exercises. For additional information see www.fas.org/man/dod-101/sys/land/miles.htm.

MOUT – Military Operations on Urbanized Terrain. For more information see www.globalsecurity.org/military/library/policy/army/fm/90-10/90-10ch1.htm.

MRE – meals ready to eat.

MUTA – Multiple Unit Training Assembly

NATO – North Atlantic Treaty Organization. An alliance of twenty-six countries from North America and Europe committed to fulfilling the goals of the North Atlantic Treaty signed on 4 April 1949. For more information see www.nato.int/.

NCO – Non Commissioned Officer

NTC – The National Training Center is the training center for America's Soldiers, known for its excellent desert environment. For more information see www.irwin.army.mil/channels.

OCS – Officer Candidate School

OEF – Operation Enduring Freedom. For more information see www.globalsecurity.org/military/ops/enduring-freedom.htm.

OIF – Operation Iraqi Freedom

ORE – Operation Readiness Exercise

OPFOR – Opposing Force

OPTEMPO - a measure of the pace of an operation or operations in terms of equipment usage, time spent, miles traversed

POW – Prisoners of War

PX – Post Exchange – much like a department store in its merchandise. In many cases the prices are less than what they are in the civilian stores.

NTC – The National Training Center

RA – Regular Army

ROOP – Reconnaissance, Observation, Operation and Position

S2 – Intelligence Officer – Battalion Level

S3 – Operations Officer – Battalion Level

SFOR – Stabilization Force

TOW – The Tactical Optical Weapon is a Tube-launched, Optically-tracked, Wire-guided missile that is a crew-portable, vehicle-mounted, heavy anti-armor weapon system consisting of a launcher and one of five versions of the TOW missile. For more information see www.redstone.army.mil/history/missile/missiler.html.

T-Pack – See T-Ration

TRADOC – Training and Doctrine Command recruits, trains and educates the Army's Soldiers; develops leaders; supports training in units; develops doctrine; establishes standards; and builds the future Army. TRADOC is the architect of the Army and "thinks for the Army" to meet the demands of a nation at war while simultaneously anticipating solutions to the challenges of tomorrow. For more information see www.tradoc.army.mil.

T-Rations – Type of ration that is an individual item packaged in a tray, e.g. lasagna or cake. It requires no refrigeration and minimal preparation, usually just warming. For more information see www.qmfound.com/army_subsistence_history.htm.

Tray-Pack – see T-Ration

TY – Training Year

USCBP – United States Customs and Border Patrol

UTA – Unit Training Assembly is one training day consisting of four hours.

VADF – Virginia Defense Force.

XO – Executive Officer.

Word Glossary

Allegheny Mountains – Allegheny is an Indian word possibly meaning "the place of the footprint" in reference to the long period the mountains were covered with snow. A chain of mountains that runs from southwest to northeast, starting in southwest Virginia to north-central Pennsylvania. It includes West Virginia and Maryland. In Virginia the Allegheny Mountains are the western range enclosing the Shenandoah Valley.

Appalachian Mountains – Derived from an Indian word meaning "the endless mountains" this series of ranges runs from Newfoundland, Canada, to Alabama, USA. In Virginia, the Blue Ridge and the Alleghenies are both part of the Appalachian Mountains.

Bangalore torpedo – an explosive device in a long tube used to destroy mines and barbed wire barriers. See http://www.sproe.com/b/bangalore.html for more information.

Blitzkrieg – German word for "lightening war." For more information see http://www.2worldwar2.com/blitzkrieg.htm.

Blue Ridge Mountains – Chain of mountains, running southwest to north-central from Fannin County, Georgia, to south-central Pennsylvania including South Carolina, North Carolina, Tennessee, Virginia, and Maryland. In Virginia the Blue Ridge separates the Piedmont from the Shenandoah Valley. The mountains are covered with deciduous and evergreen trees that give the range an aura of being blue.

cache - a hiding place especially for concealing and preserving provisions, weapons, and ammunition

Bocage – French word meaning grove. See pages 191, 192 & 193.

Camp Union – see Fort Savannah

cantonment area – a camp where soldiers train; winter quarters for soldiers

Chesapeake Bay – Indian word meaning "Great Shellfish Bay." The bay at its smallest is three-and-a-half miles wide and thirty-five miles wide at its widest and stretches from Havre de Grace, Maryland, to Virginia Beach, Virginia, about two hundred miles. It is the largest estuary in the United States.

Civilian Conservation Corps (CCC) – The election of Franklin Delano Roosevelt in 1932 was by a landslide vote from a nation that was desperate for an end to high unemployment and economic turmoil. The Emergency Conservation Work (ECW)

Act was passed in 1933, and the largest national employment by the government put thousands of young unemployed men to work on projects to save our natural resources. The CCC operated until 1942 and gave work to three million young men. There was not a state in the country that did not have some project accomplished. The great experiment of the New Deal was a total success and 3,470 fire towers were erected, 97,000 miles of fire roads built, and more than three billion trees planted. To find out more about the CCC, go to www.cccalumni.org.

Commissary – The commissary is the military version of a grocery store. In many cases the prices in the commissary are less than they are in the civilian grocery store.

commonwealth vs. state – Commonwealth is an old term for state that means "an organized political community in which the supreme power is held by the people." Kentucky, Massachusetts, Pennsylvania, and Virginia all took *commonwealth* instead of *state* when they became a part of the United States.

Delaware – Name originated in the early 1600s when Samuel Argall was blown off course and sailed into a bay which he named in honor of his governor, Lord De La Warr. The Delaware Indians were originally called the Lenni-Lenape.

Donnally's Fort – ten miles north of the present site of Lewisburg, West Virginia.

Fall Line – An imaginary line running north to south, in Virginia, where the rivers change from deep water to areas of rapids and waterfalls. This line separates the Coastal Plain (Tidewater area) from the Piedmont area. The soil is characteristic of a floodplain being fine sand and silt loam.

Fincastle – This fort was located at present-day Wheeling, West Virginia. In 1776, Patrick Henry became the first governor of the new Commonwealth of Virginia and in his honor, the fort at Wheeling changed its name to Fort Henry.

force protection – Security measures taken to protect a force from harm by non-military entities, e.g. suicide bombers. For more information see www.globalsecurity.org/military/library/policy/army/fm/90-10/90-10ch1.htm.

Fort Henry – see Fincastle

Fort Randolph – fort at Point Pleasant, West Virginia

Fort Savannah – near Lewisburg, West Virginia, later known as Camp Union

Fort Seybert – twelve miles northeast of present day Franklin, West Virginia

House of Burgesses – The House of Burgesses was modeled after British Parliament. The upper house consisted of the Governor and the council he appointed. The House of Burgesses were the representatives of the people, chosen by the land owners. There were two burgesses from each Virginia county and one burgess from the three towns, Jamestown, Williamsburg, and Norfolk, and one from the College of William and Mary. The last formal meeting of the House of Burgesses was in 1774. See Virginia General Assembly.

Kentucky – The name comes from the Cherokee word *Kentahkeh*. There is some disagreement as to the meaning of the word and its original spelling. One of the definitions is "Great Meadow" and another is "river of blood."

Light Fighters Course – specialized training for soldiers in a Light Division

Light Leaders Course – specialized training for officers and senior NCOs in a Light Division

lodgment - an accumulation or collection deposited in a place or remaining at rest

link up – two parts coming together to merge into one larger entity

militia – A military force comprised of ordinary citizens and used in local communities in emergency situations.

Mulberries - a type of temporary harbor developed in World War II to offload cargo on the beaches during the Allied invasion of Normandy. For more information see http://www.usmm.org/normandy.html.

passage of lines – A tactical enabling operation in which one unit moves through another unit's positions with the intent of moving into or out of enemy contact. For additional information see www.globalsecurity.org/military/library/policy/army/fm/3-90/ch16.htm.

Piedmont – Area, in Virginia, above the fall line, where the land is gently rolling and rises to meet the mountains. The soil ranges from rich black loam to red clay.

pincer attack – A military attack by two coordinated forces that close in on an enemy position from different directions, pinching between two forces.

Potomac – comes from the Algonquian word *Petomeack* meaning "place where people trade."

Rappahannock – comes from an Algonquian word meaning "river of quick rising water," referring to the tides.

rout - a chaotic and disorderly retreat or withdrawal of troops from a battlefield, being chased by their enemy.

Shenandoah – A two-hundred-mile long region in Virginia from Harpers Ferry, W.Va.. to southern Augusta County being the watershed of the Shenandoah River. Shenandoah is supposedly an Indian word meaning "daughter of the stars."

slice element – In a division structure, when a subordinate unit is sent to another location to accomplish a task it may need other pieces of the division to help it complete the mission. A slice of another unit in the division is sent with the task unit to assist in completing the mission, e.g. engineer component or medical component.

validation – As a military term, mission specific training for an overseas deployment. Once the training is done, an evaluation is required before deployment.

Virginia General Assembly – The Virginia Constitution, drawn up in 1776, laid out two branches or houses for the legislative body or General Assembly: the House of Delegates and the Senate of Virginia. Both branches were to be elected by qualified voters. The General Assembly's responsibilities would include formation of public policy, enactment of law of the Commonwealth, and levying of taxes.

-Appendix A-

Official Statement of Lineage & Battle Honors

Status: Active   **Designation: 116th Infantry(Stonewall Brigade)**
Component: NG (Va.) 29th Inf Division

Organized in 1742 as the Augusta County Regiment of Militia, commanded by Colonel James Patton.

- The Virginia Regiment constituted and formed in 1754 from elements of the militia forces of all Virginia counties (Elements of Augusta County Regiment commanded by Captain Andrew Lewis.)
- (Colonel James Patton killed July 1755; Captain Andrew Lewis promoted to Colonel commanding Augusta Regiment.)
- (Three Ranger companies organized in Augusta County, August 1755)
- (Ranger Companies merged with Augusta Regiment, 1758-1759.)
- The Virginia Regiment expanded in March 1758 to form the 2nd Virginia Regiment commanded by Colonel William Byrd, and the First Virginia Regiment commanded by Colonel George Washington.
- 2nd Virginia Regiment mustered out December 1758 (1st Virginia Regiment mustered out at Fort Lewis, Augusta County, in 1762) militiamen returning to their county organizations.
- Virginia Regiment reorganized March 1762; Augusta elements commanded by Colonel Andrew Lewis.
- Disbanded 1763.
- Virginia Regiment (Dunmore Brigade) organized June 1774; Colonel Charles Lewis commanding Augusta County Regiment (Lewis Brigade); General Andrew Lewis commanding Virginia Force. Regiment went out of existence about 1775.
- 2nd Virginia Regiment reconstituted 17 July 1775 in the State Line: Augusta County Regiment furnished two companies for the Regiment; remainder of companies of the Augusta County Regiment guarding frontier of Virginia. (2nd Virginia Regiment commanded by Colonel William Woodford.)
- (2nd Virginia Regiment augmented by assignment of two additional companies from Augusta County, December 1775.)
- (2nd Virginia Regiment organized at Williamsburg, Virginia, in October 1775 and transferred to the Continental Army, 15 February 1776.)
- Colonel Andrew Lewis, former commander of the Augusta County Regiment promoted to Brigadier General in 1776, to command Virginia elements.
- Augusta County Regiment reorganized into three battalions, 16 October 1777.

•Elements of Augusta County Regiment other than those in 2ⁿᵈ Virginia Regiment, Continental Line, ordered into active military service at various times during period 1776-1781.

•(2ⁿᵈ Virginia Regiment, Continental Line formally disbanded 1 January 1783.)

•Augusta County Regiment reorganized about 1785 into a two battalion Regiment.

•Expanded 31 December 1792 to form the 32ⁿᵈ and 93ʳᵈ Regiments, 7ᵗʰ Brigade, Virginia Militia.

•Elements of 32ⁿᵈ Regiment on active military service during periods: July 6-September 6, 1813; January 4-13 April 1814; August 30-November 30, 1814; and July 1814-January 1815.

•Elements of the 93ʳᵈ Regiment on Active military service during periods: March 28-21 August 1813; July 6-28 September 1813; and August 20-30 November 1814.

•Augusta Militia Regiments reorganized into the 32ⁿᵈ, 93ʳᵈ and 160ᵗʰ Regiments, Virginia Militia, about 1833.

•Augusta Company (formed from elements of the 32ⁿᵈ and 160ᵗʰ Regiments) mustered into Federal service 6 January 1847 at Richmond, Va., as Captain Kenton Harper's Light Infantry Company (also known as Augusta Volunteers), 1ˢᵗ Regiment Virginia Volunteers, and mustered out 27 July 1848 at Fort Monroe, Virginia.

•Augusta County Militia Regiments authorized to reorganize as the 5ᵗʰ Virginia Regiment of Volunteers, 27 March 1861.

•5ᵗʰ Regiment Virginia Infantry commanded by Colonel Kenton Harper, organized in State service 7 May 1861, and accepted into Confederate State service 30 June 1861, to include the following Augusta Militia Companies:

> Mountain Guards
> Southern Guards
> Augusta Grays
> West View Infantry
> Staunton Rifles
> Augusta Rifles
> Ready Rifles
> West Augusta Guard

•(5ᵗʰ Regiment became a part of 1ˢᵗ Brigade, Army of the Shenandoah, Confederate States Army, Brigadier General Thomas J. Jackson, commanding; on the field of Manassas the Brigade won for itself and commander the historic name of "Stonewall.")

•Elements of the 32ⁿᵈ, 93ʳᵈ, 106ᵗʰ assigned to 52ⁿᵈ Regiment Virginia Infantry commanded by Colonel John B. Baldwin (former Colonel, 160ᵗʰ Regiment Virginia Militia); organized in state service 19 August 1861 and accepted into Confederate State Service 1 May 1862.

- 5th and 52nd Regiments parolled at Appomattox, Virginia, 9 April 1865.
- Elements reconstituted 1 May 1871 as separate volunteer companies in western (formerly central) Virginia.
- Reorganized during May and June 1881 as 2nd and 3rd Infantry Regiments, Virginia Volunteers.
- Mustered into Federal service at Richmond, Va., as 2nd and 3rd Virginia Volunteer Regiments, 11-26 May 1898 (did not serve outside continental United Sates.)
- 2nd Virginia Volunteer Infantry Regiment mustered out of Federal service 13-20 December 1898; 3rd Virginia Volunteer Infantry Regiment mustered out of service 5 November 1898.
- Disbanded 29 April 1899.
- Elements of 2nd and 3rd Infantry Regiments reorganized and assigned to 70th Infantry Regiment, Virginia Volunteers, 10 October 1900; other elements of the 2nd and 3rd Infantry reorganized and assigned to the 72nd Infantry Regiment, Virginia Volunteers, 26 August 1905.
- 70th and 72nd Infantry Regiments, Virginia Volunteers redesignated 1st and 2nd Infantry Regiments, Virginia Volunteers, 1 September 1908.
- (Virginia Volunteers designated Virginia National Guard, 3 June 1916.)
- 1st and 2nd Infantry Regiments called into Federal service for Mexican order 18 June 1916; mustered in 30 June 1916 at Camp Stewart, Virginia; 1st Infantry mustered out 16 January 1917 at Richmond, 2nd Infantry mustered out 28 February 1917 at Richmond.
- 2nd Infantry Regiment mustered into Federal service 25 March – 3 April 1917; 1st Infantry Regiment mustered into Federal service 25 July – 4 August 1917; drafted into Federal service 5 August 1917.
- Demobilized at Camp Lee, Va., 30 May 1919.
- 2nd Infantry Regiment, Virginia National Guard, reorganized 12 October 1921 in western Virginia.
- Re-designated 116th Infantry Regiment, 9 March 1922; Headquarters Federally recognized 3 April 1922.
- Inducted into Federal service 3 February 1941 as an element of 20th Infantry Division.
- Inactivated at Camp Kilmer, New Jersey, 6 January 1946.
- Reorganized and Federally recognized 24 March 1948, with Headquarters at Staunton, Va.

HOME AREA:
Western Virginia (Headquarters at Staunton.)
CAMPAIGN STREAMERS:

<u>**Revolutionary War**</u>
Virginia 1775
Brandywine
Germantown
Monmouth
Yorktown
South Carolina 1780-1781
North Carolina 1780

<u>**War of 1812**</u>
Maryland 1814

<u>**World War I**</u>
Alsace
Meuse-Argonne

<u>**Civil War**</u> **(Confederate Service)**
Virginia 1861, 1862, 1863
First Manassas
Valley
Peninsula
Second Manassas
Sharpsburg
Fredericksburg
Chancellorsville
Gettysburg
Wilderness
Spotsylvania
Cold Harbor
Maryland 1864
Shenandoah
Petersburg
Appomattox

<u>**World War II**</u>
Normandy(with arrowhead)
North France
Rhineland
Central Europe

DECORATIONS:
•Distinguished Unit Streamer embroidered NORMANDY BEACHHEAD.
•Streamer in the colors of the French Croix de Querre, with palm, embroidered BEACHES OF NORMANDY.

Headquarters Company, 1st Battalion (Roanoke), Headquarters Company, 2nd Battalion (Lynchburg), and Company A (Bedford), H Company (Lynchburg), and Company M (Harrisonburg) are entitled to the following decorations:
•Distinguished Unit Streamer embroidered VIRE.
•Streamer in the colors of the Croix de Querre, with silver-gilt star, embroidered VIRE.
Service Company (Roanoke) entitled to:
• Meritorious Unit Streamer embroidered EUROPEAN THEATER.

-Appendix B-

Commanders of the Regiment

The Augusta County Regiment of Militia 1742-1792
Indian Wars, French and Indian War
Dunmore's War, Revolutionary War

Colonel James Patton 1742-1755 — Killed by Indians at Draper's Meadow, VA. July 30, 1755. Indian Wars, French and Indian War.

Colonel John Buchanan 1755 — Indian Wars, French and Indian War.

Colonel Andrew Lewis 1755-1767 — Indian Wars, French and Indian War, Dunmore's War, Revolutionary War. Captain Augusta County Regiment. Captain and Major Virginia Regiment, County-Lieutenant and Colonel Augusta County Regiment. Brigadier General Virginia Militia, Brigadier General Continental Army. Died in service 1781

Colonel Abraham Smith 1767-1774 — Indian Wars, French and Indian War, Revolutionary War.

Colonel Charles Lewis 1774 — Indian Wars, French and Indian War, Dunmore's War. Killed at Battle of Point Pleasant, October 10, 1774.

Colonel Abraham Smith 1774-1778 — Second time.

Colonel Sampson Mathews 1778-1781 — Indian Wars, French and Indian War, Dunmore's War, Revolutionary War.

Colonel George Moffett 1781-1783 — Indian Wars, French and Indian War, Dunmore's War, Revolutionary War.

Major Alexander Robertson 1783- 1785 — Revolutionary War

Colonel George Moffett 1785-1787 — Second time.

Colonel Alexander Robertson 1787-1788 — Second time.

Colonel William Bowyer 1788-1789

Colonel Alexander Robertson 1789-1790 — Third time.

Colonel William Boyer 1790-1792 — Second time.

Colonel Andrew Anderson, Sr. 1792-1794

(All from Augusta County, VA)

32ⁿᵈ Regiment Virginia Militia, of Augusta County, 7ᵗʰ Brigade 1794-1865
Whiskey Insurrection War, 1812 War with Mexico, War of Secession

Colonel Andrew Anderson, Sr. 1794 — Elected to General Assembly of Virginia, 1794.

Colonel Andrew Anderson, Jr. 1794-1809

Colonel James Allen 1809-1811 — War of 1812 Commander

Note: From 1811-1836 the records of the Regimental Commanders are missing, but the records of Battalions and Companies and their officers were found, covering the period and showing the continuity of the Regiment in service, from 1812 to 1836.

Colonel Franklin McCue 1836-1838
Colonel George McCulloc 1838-1844
Colonel Nathaniel Kerr 1844-1846
Colonel Franklin McCue 1846-1847   Second time
Colonel George Baylor 1847-1849
Colonel Samuel A. Crawford 1849-1858
Colonel Samuel McCune 1858-1861   Resigned to accept Captaincy of Co. G,
                                                    52nd Virginia Infantry, C.S.A.
Major William M. Wilson 1861-1865   Civil War Commander
                    (All from Augusta County, VA)

5th Virginia Infantry, Stonewall Brigade, C.S.A. 1861-1865

Colonel Kenton Harper 1861   War with Mexico, Civil War
                                                    Lt. Col. Comn'dg. Augusta County
                                                    Home Guard Regiment (1862-1865)
Colonel William H. Harman-May 1861- Feb. 1862   Trans. to Staff of Gen. Edward Johnson
                                                    In 1862. Mexican War. Killed at Battle
                                                    of Waynesboro, Va., Comn'dg. Reserves
                                                    from Shenandoah, Rockingham and
                                                    Augusta Counties.
Colonel William S. H. Baylor Feb. 1862-Aug. 29, 1862   Killed at Battle of 2nd. Manassas, Aug.
                                                    29, 1862, Comn'dg. Stonewall Brigade.
Colonel J. H. S. Funk Aug. 29, 1862- Sep. 19, 1864 Killed at 3rd Battle of Winchester, Sept.
                                                    10, 1864, Comn'dg. Stonewall Brigade.
                                                    His Commission of Brigadier General
                                                    found on his body.
Colonel Hazel W. Williams 1864-1865   Last commanding officer of the 5th Vir
                                                    ginia Infantry. Paroled at Appomattox,
                                                    April 9, 1865.

2nd Infantry Virginia Volunteers 1881-1899

Colonel William Bumgardner 1881-1886
Lt. Colonel James C. Baker 1889-1893
Colonel James C. Baker 1893-1898   Spanish- American War Commander

70th Infantry, Virginia Volunteers 1900-1908.
Consolidation of 6 companies from the 2nd and
6 companies form the 3rd to form the 70th Infantry.
Both regiments saw service in the Spanish- American War.

Colonel George W. Anderson 1900-1906   Headquarters Richmond, VA
Colonel William J. Perry 1906-1908   Headquarters Staunton, VA

Spanish- American War
1st Infantry Virginia Volunteers 1908-1917
70th Infantry redesignated 1st Virginia Infantry
Sept. 1, 1908. Mexican Border Service 1916-1917.

Colonel William J. Perry 1908-1917

Headquarters Staunton, VA
116th Infantry Virginia National Guard
29th Division 1917-1919.

Consolidation of the 1st, 2nd, 4th Virginia Infantry Regiments
1st Virginia Brigade at Camp McClellen, AL Oct. 4, 1917

World War I

Colonel William J. Perry 1917-1918	Camp McClellan Period
Colonel Robert L. Leedy 1918	Camp McClellan Period
Colonel Hansford L. Threlkeld, R. A. 1918	Camp McClellan Period
Lt. Colonel Hobard B. Brown 1918	Alsace, France Period
Colonel Hansford L. Threlkeld 1918	Alsace, France Period (second time)
Colonel Reginal Kelley, R.A. 1918	Meuse- Argonne Period
Lt. Colonel C. B. Findley, Jr. R.A. 1918	Meuse- Argonne Period
Lt. Colonel Charles C. Bankhead R.A. 1918	Meuse- Argonne Period
Colonel George W. Ball 1918-1919	Armistice Period
Colonel Fitzhugh L. Minnigerode R.A. 1919	Armistice Period

Note: Colonel Minnigerode brought the regiment home for demobilization at Camp Lee, VA, May 30, 1919.

2nd Infantry Virginia National Guard 1921-1922

Colonel Hierome L. Opie 1921-1922

Headquarters Staunton, VA

116th Infantry Virginia National Guard

Colonel Hierome L. Opie 1921-1933 Staunton	Regimental Commander
Colonel George M. Alexander 1933-1940 Lynchburg	Regimental Commander

World War II

Colonel Evarts W. Opie 1940-1942 Staunton	Regimental Commander
Lt. Colonel Morris T. Warner 1942-1943	Regimental Commander
Colonel C.D.W. Canham, R.A. 1943-1944	England-Normandy Period
Colonel Phillip R. Dwyer, R.A. 1944	Brittany Period
Lt. Colonel Harold A. Cassell, R.A. 1944	Germany
Colonel Sidney B. Bingham, Jr. 1944-1945	Germany
Lt. Colonel Harold A. Cassell, R.A. 1945-1946	Second time

116th Infantry Virginia National Guard 1946-1968
Reorganized and Federally Recognized at Roanoke, Va. On Nov. 29, 1946. Headquarters moved to Staunton, Va. and Federally Recognized on March 24, 1948. Companies from Western Virginia.

Colonel Arthur T. Sheppe, 1946-1952
Colonel Archibald A. Sproul, 1952-59
Colonel Mifflin R. Clowe, Jr. 1959-63
Colonel Cecil T. Runkle, 1963-65
Colonel John C. Steck, 1965-68

116th Brigade
28 Infantry Division
Reorganized and Federally Recognized at Staunton, Va. On 1 February 1968 was transferred to the 28th Infantry Division

Colonel Vernon T. Eastes, 1968-71
Colonel Robert J. Bradshaw, 1971-75

116th Brigade (Separate)
Reorganized and Federally Recognized at Staunton, Va. on 1 April 1975

Colonel Julian R. Bradshaw, 1975-77
Brigadier General John G. Castles, 1977-80
Brigadier General James T. Baber, 1980-83
Brigadier General Gilbert J. Sullivan, 1983-85
Brigadier General Wendell R. Seldon, 1985-86

First Brigade
29th Infantry Division (Light)
Reorganized and Federally Recognized at Staunton, Va., on 30 September 1986

Colonel Rodney W. McNeil, 1986-89
Colonel James D. Holden, 1989-92
Colonel Lloyd D. McDaniel, 1992-95
Colonel Stephen E. Arey, 1995-97
Colonel Theodore G. Shuey, Jr., 1997-2000
Colonel Ronald D. Young, 2000-02
Colonel Robert H. Simpson, 2002-05

116th Infantry Brigade Combat Team (IBCT)
Reorganized and Federally Recognized at Staunton, Va. on 30 September 2005

Colonel James M. Harris, 2005-06
Colonel William R. Phillips, 2007

-Appendix C-

Works cited

Adams, Charles S., **Roadside Markers in West Virginia**. Shepherdstown, West Virginia: Charles S. Adams, 1998.

Alberts, Robert C., **A Charming Field for an Encounter: The Story of George Washington's Fort Necessity.** Washington, DC: National Park Service—Division of Publications, 1975.

Alderman, Pat, **One Heroic Hour at King's Mountain—Battle of King's Mountain-October 7, 1780.** Johnson City, Tennessee: The Overmountain Press, 1990.

Allan, William, **History of the Campaign of Gen. T. J. (Stonewall) Jackson in the Shenandoah Valley of Virginia—from November 4, 1861 to June 17, 1862.** Dayton, Ohio: Morningside House, Inc., 1987.

Allen, Randall and Keith S. Bohannon, Editors. **Campaigning with "Old Stonewall"—Confederate Captain Ujanirtus Allen's Letters to His Wife.** Baton Rouge, Louisiana: Louisiana State University Press, 1998.

Anderson, Niles, **The Battle of Bushy Run**. Harrisburg, Pennsylvania: Commonwealth of Pennsylvania, Pennsylvania Historical and Museum Commission. 1991.

Ansel, David M., Jr., **Frontier Forts Along the Potomac and its Tributaries.** Parsons, West Virginia: McClain Printing Company, 1984.

Babits, Lawrence E. Babits, **A Devil of a Whipping—The Battle of Cowpens**. Chapel Hill, North Carolina: The University of North Carolina Press, 1998.

Babits, Lawrence E., American History Series: **The American Revolution—Southern Campaigns**. Washington, DC: National Parks-Eastern National, 2002.

Bailey, Kenneth P., Ph.D., **The Ohio Company of Virginia and the Westward Movement 1748-1792—A Chapter in the History of the Colonial Frontier.** Lewisburg, Pennsylvania: Wennawoods Publishing, 2000.

Baker-Crothers, Hayes, Ph.D., **Virginia and The French and Indian War**. Bowie, Maryland: Heritage Books, Inc., 1998.

Balkoski, Joseph, **Beyond the Beachhead – The 29th Infantry Division in Normandy**. Mechanicsburg, Pennsylvania: Stackpole Books, 1999.

Balkoski, Joseph, **Omaha Beach – D-Day June 6, 1944.** Mechanicsburg, Pennsylvania: Stackpole Books, 2004.

Bean, W. G., **The Liberty Hall Volunteers – Stonewall's College Boys**. Charlottesville, Virginia: The University Press of Virginia, 2005.

Bearss, Edwin C., **Battle of Cowpens—A Documented Narrative and Troop Movement Maps**. Johnson City, Tennessee: The Overmountain Press, 1996.

Belue, Ted Franklin, **The Hunters of Kentucky—A Narrative History of**

America's First Far West, 1750-1792. Mechanicsburg, Pennsylvania: Stackpole Books, 2003.

Bernage, Georges, **Omaha Beach**. Chateau de Damigny, France: Editions Heimdal, 2002.

Beyer, George R., **Guide to the State Historical Markers of Pennsylvania**. Harrisburg, Pennsylvania: Pennsylvania Historical and Museum Commission, 2000.

Borneman, Walter R., **1812—The War that Forged a Nation**. New York, New York: Harper Collins Publishing, Inc., 2004.

Borneman, Walter R., **The French and Indian War, Deciding the Fate of North America**. New York, New York: Harper Collins Publishers, 2006.

Britton, Rick. **"'Best Enemy-Fighter in the World' – The Frank Dabney Peregoy Story." Albemarle,** December 1999-January 2000, 62-71.

Buchanan, John, **The Road to Guilford Courthouse—The American Revolution in the Carolinas**. New York, New York: John Wiley & Sons, Inc., 1997.

Burns, David M., **Gateway – Dr. Thomas Walker and the Opening of Kentucky**. Middlesboro, Kentucky: Bell County Historical Society, 2000.

Burton, Brian K., **Extraordinary Circumstances—The Seven Days Battles**. Bloomington, Indiana: Indiana University Press, 2001.

Burton, Patricia, **"250 Years Old. . . The Augusta County Regiment, 1742-1992." Donegal Annual 1992,** no. 44. Donegal, Ireland: Donegal Democrat Ltd., 1992.

Callahan, James Morton, **Semi-Centennial History of West Virginia**. Charleston, West Virginia: Tribune Printing Company Press, 1913.

Casler, John O., **Four Years in the Stonewall Brigade**. Dayton, Ohio: Morningside Bookshop, 1994.

Cawthon, Charles R., **Other Clay—A Remembrance of the World War II Infantry**. Niwot, Colorado: University Press of Colorado, 1990.

Cecere, Michael, **Captain Thomas Posey and the 7th Virginia Regiment**. Westminster, Maryland: Heritage Books, Inc., 2005.

Cecere, Michael, **They Behaved Like Soldiers, Captain John Chilton and the Third Virginia Regiment-1775-1778**. Bowie, Maryland: Heritage Books, Inc., 2004.

Chambers, Lenoir, **Stonewall Jackson,** two volumes. New York, New York: William Morrow & Co., 1959,

Clark, Champ, Editors of Time-Life Books, **The Civil War—Decoying the Yanks—Jackson's Valley Campaign**. Alexandria, Virginia: Time-Life Books, 1984.

Clark, Murtie June, **American Militia in the Frontier Wars, 1790-1796**. Baltimore, Maryland: Genealogical Publishing Company, Inc., 2003.

Clark's Kentucky Almanac and Book of Facts – 2006. Lexington, Kentucky: The Clark Group, 2005.

Clifford, John Garry, **The Citizen Soldiers—The Plattsburg Training Camp Movement, 1913-1920**. Lexington, Kentucky: The University Press of Kentucky, 1972.

Coffman, Ralph, **"My Story as a Member of the Co L, 116th Inf – 1 Oct 1940 – 16 Jun 1945."** Manuscript.

Conover, Rebecca Wilson, **James Harrod—The Man and His Family**. Harrodsburg, Kentucky: The Harrodsburg Herald, 1980.

Cuniffe, Marcus, **George Washington – Man and Monument**. Mount Vernon, Virginia: The Mount Vernon Ladies' Association, 1982.

Cutchins, John A., **Lt. Col., History of the Twenty-Ninth Division-"Blue and Gray"—1917-1919**. Philadelphia, Pennsylvania: MacCalla & Company, Inc., 1921.

Dabney, Virginius, **Virginia-The New Dominion**. New York, New York: Doubleday & Company, Inc., 1971.

Daviess, Maria T., **History of Mercer and Boyle Counties**. Harrodsburg, Kentucky: 1998.

Davis, Arthur Kyle, **Virginians of Distinguished Service of the World War – Publications of the Virginia War History Commission**, Source Vol. 1. Richmond, Virginia: The Executive Committee – State Capitol, 1923.

Davis, Burke, **The Campaign that Won America—The Story of Yorktown**. New York, New York: The Dial Press, 1970.

Davis, Burke, **The Cowpens—Guilford Courthouse Campaign**. Philadelphia, Pennsylvania: University of Pennsylvania Press, 2003.

Davis, George B., Leslie J. Perry, Joseph W. Kirkley, **The Official Military Atlas of the Civil War**. Compiled by Calvin D. Cowles, Capt. 23rd U.S. Infantry. New York, New York: Barnes & Noble Publishing, Inc., 2003.

Deerin, James B., **The Militia in the Revolutionary War**. Edited by Luther L. Walker. Washington, DC: The Historical Society of the Militia and National Guard, 1976.

DeHass, Wills, **History of the Early Settlement and Indian Wars of Western Virginia; Embracing an Account of the Various Expeditions in the West, Previous to 1795**. Parsons, West Virginia: McClain Printing Company, 1960.

Derthick, Martha, **The National Guard In Politics**. Cambridge, Massachusetts: Harvard University Press, 1965.

Doddridge, Joseph, **Notes on the Settlement and Indian Wars**. Parsons, West Virginia: McClain Printing Company, 2000.

Doubler, Michael D., **I Am the Guard: A History of the Army National Guard, 1636-2000**, Department of the Army Pamphlet No. 130-1. Washington, D.C.: U.S. Government Printing Office, 2001.

Doubler, Michael D. and John W. Listman, Jr., **The National Guard—An illustrated History of America's Citizen-Soldiers**. Dulles, Virginia: Brassey's, Inc., 2003.

Douglas, Captain Kyd, **I Rode with Stonewall**. Chapel Hill, North Carolina: University of North Carolina Press, 1940.

Downer, Edward T., **Stonewall Jackson's Shenandoah Valley Campaign-1862**. Lexington, Virginia: Stonewall Jackson Memorial Inc., 1971.

Draper, Lyman C., LL.D, **The Life of Daniel Boone**, Edited by Ted Franklin Belue. Mechanicsburg, Pennsylvania: Stackpole Books, 1998.

Drez, Ronald J., ed., **Voices of D-Day—The Story of the Allied Invasion Told by Those Who Were There**. Baton Rouge, Louisiana: Louisiana State University Press, 1994.

Dupuy, R. Ernest, Colonel, USA, Ret., **The National Guard—A Compact History**. New York, New York: Hawthorn Books, Inc., 1971.

Dutcher, David C. G., **American History Series: Concise History of the American Revolution**. Washington, DC: National Parks—Eastern National, 1999.

Dykeman, Wilma, **The Battle of Kings Mountain 1780—With Fire and Sword**. Washington, DC: U.S. Government Printing Office, 1991.

Ecelbarger, Gary L., **We Are in For It!—The First Battle of Kernstown—March 23, 1862**. Shippensburg, Pennsylvania: The White Maine Publishing Company, Inc., 1997.

Esposito, Vincent J., Brig. Gen., **The West Point Atlas of American Wars, Volume 1, 1689-1900**. New York, New York: Henry Holt and Company, Inc., 1995.

Esposito, Vincent J., Brig. Gen., ed., **The West Point Atlas of War, World War II: European Theater**, New York, New York: Black Dog & Leventhal Publishers, Inc., 1995.

Ewing, Joseph H., **29 Let's Go! A History of the 29th Infantry Division in World War II**. Washington, DC: Infantry Journal Inc., 1948.

Foster, Emily, ed., **The Ohio Frontier—An Anthology of Early Writings**. Lexington, Kentucky: The University Press of Kentucky, 1996.

Fort Ligonier Association, **Bushy Run Battlefield, Fort Necessity National Battlefield and Fort Pitt Museum, War for Empire in Western Pennsylvania.** Pennsylvania: Fort Ligonier Association, 1993.

Freeman, Douglas Southall, **Lee's Lieutenants, Volume II: Comprising the Early Life, Public Services and Companions in Arms.** Kessinger Publishing Co., 2007.

Furbee, Mary R., **Shawnee Captive—The Story of Mary Draper Ingles**. Charleston, West Virginia: Pictorial Histories Distribution, 2001.

Furneaux, Rupert, **The Pictorial History of the American Revolution—As told by Eyewitnesses and Participants**. Edited by Thomas C. Jones. Chicago, Illinois: J. G. Ferguson Publishing Company, 1973.

Frye, Dennis E., **2nd Virginia Infantry: The Virginia Regimental Histories Series.** Lynchburg, Virginia: H. E. Howard, Inc. 1984.

Gallagher, Gary W., ed., **The Richmond Campaign of 1862**. Chapel Hill, North Carolina: The University of North Carolina Press, 2000.

Gallagher, Gary W., ed., **The Shenandoah Valley Campaign of 1862**. Chapel Hill, North Carolina: The University of North Carolina Press, 2003.

Gallagher, Gary W., ed., **The Spotsylvania Campaign—Military Campaigns of the Civil War.** Chapel Hill, North Carolina: The University of North Carolina Press, 1998.

Gallup, Andrew, **A Sketch of the Virginia Soldier in the Revolution**. Bowie, Maryland: Heritage Books, Inc., 1999.

Garbarino, William, **Indian Wars Along the Upper Ohio—A History of the Indian Wars and related Events Along the Upper Ohio and Its Tributaries (1745-1795)**. Midway, Pennsylvania: Midway Publishing, 2001.

Golway, Terry, **Washington's General—Nathanael Greene and the Triumph of the American Revolution**. New York, New York: Henry Holt and Company, LLC, 2005.

Goolrick, William K., **The Civil War—Rebels Resurgent—Fredericksburg to Chancellorsville**. Edited by Time-Life Books. Alexandria, Virginia: Time-Life Books Inc., 1985.

Graham, James, **The Life of General Daniel Morgan, of the Virginia Line of the Army of the United States**. Bloomingburg, New York: Zebrowski Historical Services Publishing Company, 1993.

Grant, Bruce, **American Forts—Yesterday and Today**. New York, New York: E.P. Dutton & Company, Inc., 1970.

Griffith, Paddy, **Battle in the Civil War—Generalship and Tactics in America 1861-65**. Fieldbooks, 1986.

Grubert, Reese T., **"Line of Senior Ancestor Regiments of the 116th Infantry."** Manuscript.

Grubert, Reese T., **"The Augusta County Regiment of Militia – Under the Colony: 1742-1755, Under the Commonwealth: 1776-1792."** Manuscript.

Hale, John P., **Trans-Allegheny Pioneers**. Edited by Harold J. Dudley. Radford, Virginia: Roberta Ingles Steele, 1971.

Hammon, Neal, Richard Taylor. **Virginia's Western War 1775-1786**. Mechanicsburg, Pennsylvania: Stackpole Books, 2002.

Hardesty's Historical and Geographical Encyclopedia, Including **Mason County, West Virginia**. Unknown.

Harrison, J. Houston, **Settlers by the Long Grey Trail**. Harrisonburg, Virginia: C.J. Carrier Company. 1998.

Harwell, Richard, **Washington, An abridgment in one volume of the seven-volume George Washington by Douglas Southall Freeman**. New York, New York: Charles Scribner's Sons, 1957.

Hastings, Max, **Overlord—D-Day and the Battle for Normandy**. New York, New York: Simon and Schuster, Inc., 1984.

Henderson, G. F. R., Lieut.-Col., **Stonewall Jackson and the American Civil War—The Definitive Biography of the Great Confederate General**, two volumes. Seacaucus, New Jersey: The Blue and Grey Press, 1989.

Hendriques, Peter R., PH.D, George Mason University, **America's First President - George Washington, National Park Famous American Series**. Washington, DC: Eastern National, 2002.

Hennessy, John J., **Return to Bull Run—The Campaign and Battle of Second Manassas**. Norman, Oklahoma: University of Oklahoma Press, 1999.

Higginibotham, Don, **Daniel Morgan—Revolutionary Rifleman**. Chapel Hill, North Carolina: University of North Carolina Press, 1961.

Hill, Jim Dan, Ph.D., D.Litt., **The Minute Man in Peace and War—A History of The National Guard**. Harrisburg, Pennsylvania: The Stackpole Company, 1964.

Hitsman, J. Mackay, Updated by Donald E. Graves, **The Incredible War of 1812—A Military History**. Toronto, Canada: Robin Brass Studio, 1999.

Hofstra, Warren R., ed., **George Washington and the Virginia Backcountry**. Madison, Wisconsin: Madison House Publications, Inc., 1998.

Holton, Woody, **Forced Founders, Indians, Debtors, Slaves, and the Making of the American Revolution in Virginia**. Chapel Hill, North Carolina: University of North Carolina Press, 1999.

Jackson, Mary Anna, **Memoirs of Stonewall Jackson**. Dayton, Ohio: Morningside Bookshop, 1976.

Johns, Glover S., Jr., **The Clay Pigeons of St. Lô**. Mechanicsburg, Pennsylvania: Stackpole Books, 2002.

Kennedy, Billy, **The Scotts-Irish in the Shenandoah Valley**. Greenville, South Carolina: Emerald House Group, Inc., 1996.

Kercheval, Samuel, **A History of the Valley of Virginia**. Woodstock, Virginia: W. N. Grabill, 1902.

Kershaw, Alex, **The Bedford Boys – One American Town's Ultimate D-Day Sacrifice**. Cambridge, Massachusetts: Da Capo Press, 2003.

Koontz, Louis K., Ph.D., **The Virginia Frontier – 1765-1763**. Baltimore, Maryland: The Johns Hopkins Press, 1925.

Krick, Robert K., **Conquering the Valley—Stonewall Jackson at Port Republic**. New York, New York: William Morrow and Company, 1996.

Lawrence, Joseph Douglas, **Fighting Soldier – The AEF in 1918**, ed. Robert H. Ferrell. Boulder, Colorado: Colorado Associated University Press, 1985.

LeCouturier, Yves, **The Beaches of the D-Day Landings**. Rennes, France: Edilarge S. A., 1999.

Leepson, Marc, **Desperate Engagement—How a Little-Known Civil War Battle Saved Washington, D.C., and Changed the Course of American History**. New York, New York: Thomas Dunne Books, St. Martin's Press, 2007.

Lewis, Thomas A., **For King and Country, George Washington-the early years**. New York, New York: John Wiley & Sons, Inc, 1993.

Lewis, Thomas A., **For King and Country – The Maturing of George Washington—1748-1760**. Edison, New Jersey: Castle Books, 2006.

Lewis, Virgil A., **History and Government of West Virginia**. Chicagoand New York, New York: Werner School Book Company, 1896.

Lewis, Virgil A., **Life and Times of Ann Bailey—The Pioneer Heroine of the Great Kanawha Valley**. Point Pleasant, West Virginia: Discovery Press, 1998.

Listman, John W., Jr., Robert K. Wright Jr., and Bruce D. Hardcastle, Editors, **The Tradition Continues—A History of the Virginia National Guard—1607-1985**. Richmond, Virginia: Taylor Publishing Company, 1987.

Mahon, John K., **History of the Militia and the National Guard**. Edited by Louis Morton. New York, New York: Macmillan Publishing Company, 1983.

Margin, David G., **Jackson's Valley Campaign, November 1861-June 1862**. New York, New York: Gallery Books, W.H. Smith Publishers, Inc., 1988.

Martin, David G., **The Second Bull Run Campaign—July-August 1862— Great Campaign Series**. Conshohocken, Pennsylvania: Combined Bookes, Inc., 1997.

Mason, David, **BREAKOUT: Drive to the Seine, Campaign Book No 4**. New York, New York: Ballantine Books, 1968.

McAllister, J. T., **Virginia Militia in the Revolutionary War**. Hot Springs, Virginia: McAllister Publishing Company, 1989.

McCullough, David, **1776**. New York, New York: Simon & Schuster, 2005.

McDonald, JoAnna M., **We Shall Meet Again—The First Battle of Manassas (Bull Run), July 18-21, 1861**. Shippensburg, Pennsylvania: This White Mane Publishing Company, Inc., 1999.

McDonald, William N., Captain, **Laurel Brigade–Originally Ashby's Cavalry**, ed. Bushrod C. Washington. Arlington, Virginia: R. W. Beatty, Ltd, 1969.

Messenger, Charles, **The D-Day Atlas—Anatomy of the Normandy Campaign**. New York, New York: Thames & Hudson, Inc., 2004.

Morton, Richard L., M.A., Ph.D, **History of Virginia, Volume III, Virginia Since 1861**. New York, New York: The American Historical Society, 1924.

Miller, William J., **Mapping for Stonewall—The Civil War Service of Jed Hotchkiss**. Washington, DC: Elliott & Clark Publishing, 1993.

Morehead, David A., **A Place Grown Quiet—300 Years of West Virginia History**. Parsons, West Virginia: McClain Printing Company, 1984.

Netherton, Ross, **Braddock's Campaign and the Potomac Route to the West**. Falls Church, Virginia: Higher Education Publications, Inc.

Newland, Samuel J., Major, **U.S. Army War College, Strategic Studies Institute—The Militia's Role in National Defense: A Historical Perspective-Final Report**. Carlisle Barracks, Pennsylvania: U.S. Army War College, 1987.

Newland, Samuel J., Ph.D., **The Pennsylvania Militia: The Early Years, 1669-1792**. Annville, Pennsylvania: Department of Military and Veterans Affairs, 1997.

Official National Park Handbook 135, Fleming, Thomas J., **Cowpens—"Downright Fighting"—The Story of Cowpens**. Washington, D.C.: National Park Service, Division of Publications, 1988.

Payne, Dale, Indian **Warfare and Massacres—On the Virginia Frontier-Part III**. North Kansas City, Missouri: Technical Communication Services, 2002.

Peyser, Joseph L., **Ambush and Revenge: George Washington's Adversaries in 1754, Ensign Joseph Coulon de Jumonville and Captain Louis Coulon de Villiers.** Dunbar, Pennsylvania: Stefano's Printing. 1999.

Peyton, J. Lewis, **History of Augusta County**. Harrisonburg, Virginia: C.J. Carrier Company. 1985.

Pitch, Anthony S., **The Burning of Washington—The British Invasion of 1814**. Annapolis, Maryland: Naval Institute Press. 2000.

Powell, Allan, **Fort Frederick: Potomac Outpost**. Parsons, West Virginia: McClain Printing Company, 1988.

Powell, Allan, **Maryland and the French and Indian War – 1756**. Baltimore: Gateway Press, 1998.

Prewitt, Don M., Major, **US Army Command and General Staff College—Combat Studies Institute, Citizen Soldiers: A History of the Army National Guard.** Fort Leavenworth, Kansas: US Army Command and General Staff College, 1987

Quarles, Garland R., "George Washington and Winchester, Virginia— 1748-1758," **Winchester-Frederick County Historical Society Papers, Vol. VIII**. Winchester, Virginia: Winchester-Frederick County Historical Society, 1974.

Reidenbaugh, Lowell, **33rd Virginia Infantry: The Virginia Regimental Histories Series**. Lynchburg, Virginia: H. E. Howard, Inc. 1987.

Rhea, Gordon C., **The Battle of the Wilderness—May 5-6, 1864**. Baton Rouge, Louisiana: Louisiana State University Press, 1994.

Rice, Otis K., **A History of Greenbrier County**. Parsons, West Virginia: McClain Printing Company, 1986.

Rice, Otis K., Stephen W. Brown, **West Virginia A History**. Lexington, Kentucky: The University Press of Kentucky, 1993

Robertson, James I., Dr., **4th Virginia Infantry: The Virginia Regimental Histories Series**. 2d ed. Lynchburg, Virginia: H. E. Howard, Inc., 1982.

Robertson, James I., **The Stonewall Brigade**. Baton Rouge, Louisiana: Louisiana State University Press, 1987.

Robertson, Jr., James I., **Stonewall Jackson – The Man, The Soldier, The Legend.** New York, New York: MacMillan Publishing, 1997.

Roosevelt, Theodore, **The Winning of the West, Vol. 1.** Kessinger Publishing Company, 2004

Russell, David Lee, **The American Revolution in the Southern Colonies**. Jefferson, North Carolina: McFarland & Company, Inc., 2000.

Ryan, Cornelius, **The Longest Day—June 6, 1944**. New York, New York: Simon and Schuster, 1959.

Salmon, John S., compiled., **A Guidebook to Virginia's Historical Markers**. Charlottesville, Virginia: University Press of Virginia, 1996.

Schildt, John W., **The Long Line of Splendor**, 1742-1992. Chewsville, Maryland: Antietam Publications, 1993.

Schwartz, Seymour I., **The French and Indian War, 1754—1763: the imperial struggle for North America.** Edison, New Jersey: Castle Books, 1994.

Seal, Henry F., Jr., compiled & revised. **History of the 116th U.S. Infantry Regiment, 29th Division organized from the 1st, 2nd and 4th Regiments, Virginia National Guard—1917-1919.** Richmond, Virginia: Adjutant General of Virginia, 1953.

Simkins, Francis Butler, Spotswood Hunnicutt Jones, Sidman P. Poole, **Virginia: History—Government—Geography**, Revised Edition. New York, New York: Charles Scribner's Sons, 1964.

Skeen, C. Edward, **Citizen Soldiers in the War of 1812.** Lexington, Kentucky: The University Press of Kentucky, 1999.

Slaughter, John Robert, **Omaha Beach and Beyond—The Long March of Sergeant Bob Slaughter.** St. Paul, Minnesota: Zenith Press, MBI Publishing Company LLC, 2007.

Smith, James Power, Captain and A.D.C., **With Stonewall Jackson in the Army of Northern Virginia.** Gaithersburg, Maryland: Zullo and VanSickle Book, 1982.

Spruille, Matt, III and Matt Spruill, IV, **Echoes of Thunder—A Guide to the Seven Days Battles.** Knoxville, Tennessee: The University of Tennessee Press, 2006.

Swartz, John C., **George Washington—The Making of a Young Leader.** Medina, Ohio: Harbor Bend Publishing, 1995.

Symonds, Craig L., **A Battlefield Atlas of the American Revolution.** Mount Pleasant, South Carolina: The Nautical & Aviation Publishing Company of America, Inc., 1986.

The Militia-Man—1740. Schenectady, New York, New York: United States Historical Research Service, 1995.

Thom, James Alexander, **Follow the River.** New York, New York: The Ballantine Publishing Group, 1981.

Thomas, William H. B., **Patriots of the Upcountry, Orange County, Virginia in the Revolution.** Orange, Virginia: Green Publishers, Inc., 1976.

Time-Life Books, Editors., **Echoes of Glory—Illustrated Atlas of The Civil War.** Alexandria, Virginia: Time-Life Inc., 1991.

vanWyck Mason, F., **The Fighting American—A War-Chest of Stories of American Soldiers from the French and Indian Wars through the First World War.** New York, New York: Reynal & Hitchcock, Inc., 1943.

Waddell, Joseph A., **Annals of Augusta County, Virginia—From 1726 to 1871.** Harrisonburg, Virginia: C. J. Carrier Company, 1986.

Waddell, Joseph A., **Historical Atlas of Augusta County, Virginia.** Verona, Virginia: Mid Valley Press, 1991.

Wallace, Lee A., Jr., **5th Virginia Infantry: The Virginia Regimental Histories Series.** Lynchburg, Virginia: H. E. Howard, Inc. 1988.

Wayland, John W., **The German Element of the Shenandoah Valley of Virginia**. Harrisonburg, Virginia, 1989.

Webb, James, **Born Fighting—How the Scots-Irish Shaped America**. New York, New York: Broadway Books, A Division of Random House, Inc., 2005.

Whitehouse, Patrick & Thomas, David St. John, **LMS 150 – The London Midland & Scottish Railway – A Century and a Half of Progress**. London, England: David & Charles Book, 2002.

Withers, Alexander Scott, **Chronicles of Border Warfare, or, A History of the Settlement by the Whites, of North-Western Virginia, and of the Indian Wars and Massacres in the section of the State with Reflections, Anecdotes, &c.**, edited by Reugen Gold Thwaites. Parsons, West Virginia: McClain Printing Company, 2001.

Wood, W. J., LTC U.S.A. (Ret.), **Battles of the Revolutionary War—1775-1781**. Edited by John S. D. Eisenhower. Chapel Hill, North Carolina: DaCapo Press, 2003.

Wright, Robert K., Jr., **Army Lineage Series: The Continental Army**. Washington, D.C.: U.S. Government Printing Office, 2000.

Wright, Robert K., Jr., Captain, **A Brief History of The Militia and the National Guard**. Washington, D.C.: National Guard Bureau, 1986.

Index

Symbols

"29 Let's Go"   175, 221, 229
"Stony of the Pony"   233
9-11   258, 261
38th Parallel   224
222nd Arid Water Detachment   256
246 Coast Artillery   158
330th Infantry   215
506th Fighter-Bomber Squadron   200
183rd Cavalry   235
212th Signal Detachment   235
222nd Arid Water Detachment   256
237th Engineer Company   235
246th Field Artillery   235
429th Forward Support Battalion   243
616th Ordinance Detachment   235

Battalions

1/116 Battalion   190, 205
2/116 Battalion   190, 205
3/116 Battalion   190
2nd Ranger Battalion   178
5th Ranger Battalion   207
116th Armored Battalion   228
352nd Battalion   182, 196
429th Forward Support Battalion   243, 251,
    255, 256, 259
747th Tank Battalion   190, 196-198, 215
Fincastle Battalion   40
Second Battalion   234, 243

Brigades

1st Virginia Volunteer Infantry (Mexican
    War)   73
2nd Wisconsin Brigade   85-86, 115-116
53rd Enhanced Brigade (Separate)   254
54th Artillery Brigade   148
57th Brigade   148
58th Brigade   147-148
93rd Brigade 77
116th Infantry Brigade   204, 206-207, 210,
    214-215, 217, 219-220, 222, 224, 227,
    229, 240
116th Infantry Brigade Combat Team (IBCT) 201
116th Infantry Brigade (Separate)   234-235
First Brigade   77-80, 82, 84-91, 93-98, 102,
    106-107, 110, 112, 114-116, 122, 124,
    126, 242-243, 255

Second Brigade   80
Third Brigade   80
Fourth Brigade   80
Seventh Brigade   70-72
Iron Brigade   See 2nd Wisconsin Regiment
Louisiana Brigade   101, 134
Loring's Brigade   93
Taylor's Brigade   102
Terry's Brigade   137-138, 140

Corps

III Corps   255
V Corps   140, 174, 177, 194, 196-197
VII Corps   145, 194
XIII Corps   219
XVI Corps   217, 219
XVIII Corps   206, 235, 239
XIX Corps   194, 196, 209-210, 212, 214
Second Corps   122, 125-126, 128-129, 138-
    139
Twelfth Corps   129

Divisions

1st Cavalry Division (All American Divi-
    sion)   250
1st Division   140, 165, 173, 178, 190
2nd Division   196, 203, 209, 210, 212, 214
2nd Panzer Division   203
2nd Parachute Division   206
3rd Armored Division   206
3rd Fallschirmjager (German)   196, 198
4th Division   190, 255
7th Infantry Division   231
8th Division   199, 207
18th Division 150
26th Infantry Division 163
28th Infantry Division   231
29th Division   147-148, 150, 154, 159-160,
    163, 165-166, 173, 174, 190-191, 194,
    196, 199, 200-201, 241, 206-220, 224,
    227-229, 231, 242, 248, 250, 254-259
30th Division   209, 210
35th Division   196, 201, 231
38th Division   197
82nd Airborne Division   209, 235, 237,
    239-240, 246, 248, 250
101st Airborne Division   190, 209
325th Infantry Division   239

George Washington Division   245
V-2 Rocket Division   219

Regiments
1ˢᵗ Maryland Regiment (Confederate) 102
1ˢᵗ Maryland Regiment (Union) 102
1ˢᵗ Virginia Regiment 16, 34, 78, 147
2ⁿᵈ Virginia Regiment   50, 55, 78-79, 82, 84,
    86, 94-96, 98-99, 102, 104, 106, 109-110,
    112, 114-116, 122, 124, 126-127, 129,
    131-136, 138, 140, 143-147, 156
3ʳᵈ Virginia Regiment 146
4ᵗʰ Virginia Regiment   78-79, 84, 86, 94-96,
    114-115, 122, 124, 126, 131-138, 140, 147
5ᵗʰ Ohio Regiment   96
5ᵗʰ Regiment Band   98
5ᵗʰ Virginia Regiment   77-78, 80-82,84-86,
    92, 94-96, 98, 102, 104, 106, 109, 112, 114-
    115, 124, 126-127, 132-136, 138, 140
7ᵗʰ Virginia Regiment   54
8ᵗʰ Virginia Regiment   58
10ᵗʰ Virginia Regiment   55
11ᵗʰ Virginia Regiment   55
12ᵗʰ Virginia Regiment   55
13ᵗʰ Virginia Regiment   55
18ᵗʰ North Carolina Regiment   125
23ʳᵈ Virginia Regiment   94
27ᵗʰ Virginia Regiment   78-79, 84, 86, 94-
    96, 98, 102, 106, 109, 112, 114-116, 124,
    126, 132-136, 138, 140
32ⁿᵈ Regiment   70, 72
33ʳᵈ Virginia Regiment   82, 86-87, 94, 98,
    102, 106, 109, 112, 114-115, 124, 126,
    132-136, 138, 140
37ᵗʰ Virginia Regiment   94
38ᵗʰ Infangry Regiment   196
44ᵗʰ Regiment (British)   26
48ᵗʰ Regiment (British)   26
51ˢᵗ Highlanders Regiment   236-237
62ⁿᵈ Ohio Regiment   96
66ᵗʰ Armored Regiment   203, 211
93ʳᵈ Regiment   70, 72
72ⁿᵈ Virginia Infantry 146
116th Infantry Foundation, Inc.   251
116th Infantry Regiment, formation   147
116th Regiment   148, 150, 154, 156-167,
    189-190, 196-198, 203
116th Regiment Memorial Museum
    Association   237
120th Infantry Regiment   211
160ᵗʰ Regiment   71, 72

175ᵗʰ Regiment   166, 190, 198, 203-204,
    215-216
352ⁿᵈ Regiment (German)   190
505ᵗʰ Parachute Infantry Regiment   250
726ᵗʰ Regiment (German)   182
Augusta Regiment   40, 7,0, 71
Botetourt Regiment 39, 40
First Virginia Regiment 19, 21-22, 24, 28, 34
Irish Regiment 26

A
A Company 181, 189
Abrams, Creighton Jr. (General) 232
Acts:
    Army Appropriations Act (of 1867) 143
    Conscription (of 1862) (Confederate)   97
    Dick (of 1903) 145-146
    National Defense (of 1916)   146
    National Defense (of 1920)   154-155
    National Security (of 1947)   223
    Selective Service (of 1940)   160
    Service Extension (of 1941)   163
    Stamp (of 1765) 50
    Townshend (of 1767)   50
    Uniform Militia Reform (of 1792) 69-70,
        79, 77, 145
Adjusted Service Rating 220
Afghanistan 260
African-Americans 233
airport security 257
Alamo 72
Alexandria 26
All American Division 250
"all volunteer" Army 233
Allegheny Light Infantry 78
Allegheny Rifles 79
Allen
    James W. (Colonel) 96, 98, 110, 115,
    George (Senator) (Governor)   254
    Hugh (Lieutenant) 48
Alsace Campaign   150
American Expeditionary Forces   148
Anderson
    George (Captain) 16
    R.S. (Brigadier General) 90
Annual Muster   229
Annual Training   239, 240, 242, 254
Anthony, George (Sergeant)   244
Antietam, Battle   (See Battles)
Appomattox Surrender 140

Arbuckle, Mathew (Captain) 55
Arey, Stephen E. (Lieutenant Colonel) 245,
       (Colonel) 249
armories   160, 223
    John D. Howie
    John O. Marsh   251
    Leesburg   251
Armory Commission   223
Armstrong, Thomas (Captain)   32
Army Appropriations Act   (See Acts)
Army of the Potomac   126
Army of the Shenandoah   76
Arnold, Benedict (General)   52, 58
Articles of Confederation   69
Ashalecoans   34
Ashby
    Turner (Captain) 80, (Colonel) 90, 94, 97,
       (General) 104
    Woodrow 159
Atlas Force One   235
Augusta County (See Counties)
Augusta County Court House   32
Augusta Militia,   12, 14-19, 22, 24-25, 28-32,
       34-36, 39, 48, 51, 53-56, 61, 63-65, 67,
       69-75, 77, 88, 149, 156
Augusta, Princess of Saxe-Gotha   11
Augusta Guards   72
Augusta Rifles   78
Augusta Volunteers   73
Auslander, Joseph   200

B
Back Creek (See Creeks)
Bagram Air Base   260
Balcony Falls   16-17
Balkans 8 Rotation   262
Baltimore and Ohio Railroad   119
Bangalore torpedo   188
Banks, Nathaniel (General)   94, 98-99, 101,
       113, 115
Barbour, James (Governor)   71
Bartow, Francis S. (Brigadier General)   80, 84
basic training   162
battle cry   175
battle dress uniforms   243
Battles
    Alsace   149, 151
    Antietam (Sharpsburg) 119-122
    Appomattox   139-140
    Bloody Angle (See Spotsylvania Court House)
    Blue Licks   67

Brest   208
Britain (of)   189
Bulge (of the)   214
Cedar Creek   138-139
Cedar Mountain   113-115
Chancellorsville   124-127
Chantilly   119
Chapultepec   73
Cold Harbor   109-112
Cowpens   58
Cross Keys   104-105
Dam #5   90-91
Dortmund   217-218
Fallen Timbers   68
Falling Waters   81-82
Fisher's Hill   138
Five Forks   140
Fort Stedman   139
Fort Stevens   137
Fredericksburg   123-124
Front Royal   102
Gettysburg   129-130
Great Bridge   52
Groveton   115-117
Guilford Court House   61-62
Harpers Ferry   119
Hatcher's Run   139
Julich   216-218
Kernstown   94-96
Kings Mountain   57, 64
McDowell   99-100
Malvern Hill   112
Manassas, First   83-87
Manassas, Second   116-119
Mine Run   131-132
Monocacy Junction   137
Meuse-Argonne   148, 151-152
New Market   138
Point Pleasant   43-46
Port Republic   105-107
Romney Expedition   92-93
Roer River   212-215
Savage Station   111-112
    Sharpsburg See Antietam)
Spotsylvania Court House (Bloody Angle)
    135-136
St. Lô   197
Vise   210
Wilderness   133-134
Winchester, First   102-104
Winchester, Third   137-138
Yorktown   64

Batts, Thomas 5
Baumgarten, Harold (Private) 176
Baylor
   George 76
   William S. H. (Captain) 74-75, (Colonel)
   115, 118-119, 122, 137
beach assault training 175
Beasley, Bobby (Sergeant) 260
Beauregard, P.G.T. (General) 83
Bedford 161, 222
Bedford Boys 161, 181, 190
Bedford County Riflemen 40
Bedford, Thomas (Captain) 40
Bee, Bernard E. (General) 80, 84-85
Belize 255
Bell, James (Captain) 65
Bellefonte 11-12, 17, 35, 63
Benjamin, J.P. (Confederate Secretary of War) 93
Berkeley Border Guards 78
Berkeley
   Norborne 39
   William, Sir (Governor) 4
Berlin 218, 224, 227
Betsy Bell 12
Beverley Manor 7, 9, 11-12, 24
Beverley, William 7, 11, 14-15 (County
      Lieutenant) 16
Beverley's Mill Place 13, 17, 24
"Big Sandy" Expedition 30-31, 46
Big Sandy River 31
Bingham, Sidney V. (Major) 177, 197-199
(Lieutenant Colonel) 203, (Colonel) 213
Black Hat Brigade (See 2nd Wisconsin Regiment)
Bladensburg Races 71
Blenker, Louis (Brigadier General) 96
Bloody Ban 58
Bloody Tarlton 57
blockhouses 9
Bloody Angle 95, 136
Bloody Bucket 231
Bloody Ford 37
Bloody Sevens 55
Blue and Gray Division 148, 242
Blue Jacket (See Indian Chiefs)
Blue Licks Battle 67
Blue Ridge Mountains 2, 7
Blum, H. Steven (Major General) 254, 257
Bocage (See hedgerow)
Bold Shift 249
Bolivar Heights 104, 119
Boone, Daniel (Captain) 50, 56, 63, 67

Boonesborough 56
Booth, Paul (Major General) 227
Borden, Benjamin 12
border duty 146, 266
Bosnia 252, 253, 256
Botetourt County (See Counties)
Botler's Ford 120-121
Botts Greys 78
Botts, Lawson (Lieutenant Colonel) 116
Bouquet, Henry (Colonel) 34, 37, 44
Braddock, Edward (Brigadier General) 24,
      (Major General) 26-30, 34
Braddock Expedition 29
Braddock Road 26, 27
Bradley, Omar (General) 177, 182, 196, 231
Bradshaw, Julian R. (General) 231, 233, 235
Breckenridge, Robert (Captain) 32
Brest 206
Brown
   John 73-74
   John (Captain) 16, (Major) 32
Brown's Gap (See Gaps)
Browning, (Lieutenant General) (British) 209
Buchanan
   John (Captain) 14, 15, (Colonel) 16, 18, 32
   Patrick (Captain) 65
Bulge, Battle of (See Battles)
Bull Pasture Mountain 99
Bull Run 83, 86
Bullitt, Thomas (Captain) 34
Bumgardner, James Jr. (Lieutenant) 75
Burke, Thomas J. (Lieutenant) 75
Burnside, Ambrose (General) 124
Bush, George W. (President) 257, 266

C
calvados 192, 206
Cameron, George (Lieutenant) 48
Camps
   A.P. Hill 162, 163, 166-168, 232
   Arifjan 267
   Atterbury 262
   Blair 46
   Blanding 167-168, 254
   Bonsteel 263
   Charlotte 46-47
   Dawson 245
   Drum 159, 168, 232
   Harman 87
   Indiantown Gap 168
   Kilmer 167-168, 221

Lee 145, 153
Livingston 231
Maggot 87
McCall 247
McClellan 147, 148, 149, 161
Pablo Beach 145
Paxton 127
Pendleton 144
Randolph 131
Shelby 265, 266-268
Stephenson 88
Stonewall 129
Stonewall Jackson 131
Stuart 146
Union 40, 47
Winder 124
Campbell, William (Captain) 52, 56-57
Canham, Charles D. (Colonel) 167, 176, 170,
    178, 184, 188, 190, 196, 199, (Briga-
    dier General) 208
Capstone 232, 235, 240, 246
Cape Henry 165
Carentan 190
Carr, Wilson R. (Sergeant) 207
Carter, Kent (Lieutenant Colonel) 255
Casler, John O. 90
Cassel, Harold A. (Lieutenant Colonel) 178,
    204, 212, 221
Castles, John G. (Brigadier General) 235-236,
    (Major General)241
Cathray, James (Captain) 14, 15
Cawthon, Charles R. (Lieutenant) 140, 161,
    175-176, 180, (Major) 203, 254
Cedar Creek (See Battles)
Chamberlain, Joshua (General) 140
Chancellorsville (See Battles)
Chantilly (See Battles)
Chapultepec 73
Charles II (King) 5
Charlottesville 73, 160, 191, 224, 236, 239
Chase City 222
Chatham, Earl of 35
Cherokees 35, 55
Cherry, Craig (Staff Sergant) 260
Chief of Staff of the Army's Deployment
    Excellence 259
Childers, Carroll (Major General) 254
Christian
    Israel (Captain) 32
    John (Captain) 14-15
    William (Colonel) 32, 40, 46

William (Captain) 32, 55
Churchill, Winston, Sir 189
Civilian Conservation Corps (CCC) 156
citizen-soldier 13
Civil War centennial 227
Clark, George Rogers (Major) 51, 56, 69
Clarke Riflemen 78
Clinch River 7, 32
Clinton, Henry Sir (General) 56, 62-64
Clowe, Mifflin (Colonel) 227
Cochran, Henry King Sir (Lieutenant) 75
Coffman, Ralph (Private) 159, 175, (Sergeant)
    213, 220
Cold Harbor (See Battles)
Cold War 224
Colleville-Sur-Mer Cemetery 193, 195, 201
Colston, Raleigh (Lieutenant Colonel) 110, 131
Combat Arms Regimental System (CARS)
    226, 229
Combat Maneuver Training Center (CMTC) 251
Combee, Pete (Lieutenant Colonel) 255
Combined Armed Services Training (CAST) 248
Combs, Patrick (Captain) 258
Conrad's Store 98
Continental Army 51, 54, 58
Continental Congress 37, 51
Continental Line 51-52, 56,
Continental Morgan Guards 78
Corlett, Charles (Major General) 194
Cornstalk See Indian Chiefs
Cornwallis, Charles Sir Lord (General) 56-58,
    61, 63, 61-65
Cota, Norman (General) 174, 184-186, 188,
    200, 206,231
Coulon de Villiers, Louis (Captain) 23-24
Coulon de Villiers de Jumonville, Joseph
    (Ensign) 22, 24, 32
Counties
    Albemarle 56
    Augusta 11-17, 19, 22, 28-29, 34-35, 37-39,
        41, 54-56, 65, 67, 70, 77, 127
    Bedford 40
    Botetourt 38-41
    Culpeper 40
    Dunmore 52, 40
    Essex 10
    Fincastle 38
    Frederick 11
    Giles 5
    Greenbrier 54
    Kentucky 38, 56

Monongahela 54
Ohio 54
Orange 11
Pittsylvania County 157
Rockbridge 2, 16, 54
Rockingham 54
Shenandoah 52
Spotsylvania 10
Youghiogheny 54
court-martial 15-16, 52
Couvains 193
Cowpens (See Battles)
Craig, John (Reverand) 30
Craney Island 71
Crawford, Alexander 36

Creeks
Back 36
Beaverdam 111
Cedar 139
Crooked 45-46
Kerr's 36
Lewis 11
Turtle 27-29
Wills 20-21, 24, 26-27

Crockett, Davy 72
Croghan, George 20
Cromer, Larry (Sergeant) 247
Cross Keys (See Battles)
Cuba 145, 258
Cuff, Robert (Sergeant) 174
Culp, John Wesley 129
Culpeper Militia 53
Culp's Hill 129-130
Culton, Joseph (Captain) 32
Cumberland Gap 18
Cumberland, Maryland 26
Cummings, Arthur (Colonel) 85

D
D-Day 177, 179
Dallas, Tom (Lieutenant Colonel) 204
Dam No. 5 90-91
dams, capture of 215
Dan River Cotton Mills 156-158
Dancy, Bennie (Sergeant First Class) 252 (1st Sergeant) 253
Davis
Jefferson (Confederate President) 86, 127

John B. (Lieutenant) 96
de Beaujeu, Daniel (Captain) 28
De Grasse, François Joseph Paul (Admiral) 63
Dellinger, John 36
DePuy, William E. (General) 184
Desert Panthers 250
Dick Act (See Acts)
Dick, Charles (Major General/Congressman) 145
Dickenson, John (Lieutenant Colonel) 55
Dickinson, John (Captain) 36
Dickinson's Fort 32
"dining-in" 237
Diehl, Phillip (Staff Sergeant) 246
Dinwiddie, Robert (Governor) 18-26, 28-32
disasters, response to 224, 228, 237, 244, 265
Distinguished Unit Citation 189
District of West Augusta 54-55
Division Maneuver Exercise (DMX) 254
Division Support Command (DISCOM) 241
Division Warfighter 254
Department of Defense (DOD) 250
Doubleday, Abner (General) 120
Douglas, Henry Kyd (Captain) 87, 96
Dragoons (British) 59-61
Draper
John (Captain) 30
Lyman C. (Doctor) 30
Draper's Meadows 29-30
drilling 16
Dunbar, Thomas (Colonel) 26, 28
Dunker Church 119, 121
Dunkirk Pocket 158
Dunlap, Alex (Captain) 16, 33
Dunmore County Vounteers 40
Dunmore, Robert (Governor) 39, 41, 46, 50-53
Dunmore's War 37, 39
Duquesne de Meneval, Marquis 21
Dusseldorf 215
Dwyer, Philip R. (Colonel) 199, 212

E
E Company 181
Early, Jubal (Lieutenant Colonel) 138
Eisenhower, Dwight D. (General) 177, 179, 180, 206, 212, 225
Elbe River 219
Elk River 40
Emerald Guards 82
Emergency Management Assistance Compacts 265

Employer Support (Guard and Reserve program ESGR) 252
England, WW II 173
Eppele, Tim (Captain) 266
Epperly, John (Lieutenant Colonel) 265-266
equipment
  D-Day 180
  eighteenth century 15
Estill family 36
Evans, William (Lieutenant) 14
Ever Forward 151, 153, 178, 267
Ewell, Richard S. (Major General) 97, 99, 101-102, 104, 106, 113, 116, 127
Exercises
  Blue Fox 244
  Hanover 174
Expert Infantry Badge (EIB) 259

F
F Company 181
Fairfax, Thomas (Lord) 7
Fairfax Line 11
Falaise Pocket 206
Fallam, Robert 5
Fallen Timbers, Battle (See Battles)
Falling Waters (See Battles)
Fallschirmjager Division 198
Family Support Group (1986) 245
Faulconer, Charles B. Jr. [Colonel] (Captain) 237, (Major) 244, 246
Fellers, Taylor (Captain) 181
females, in the military 233
Ferguson, Patrick (Major) 56-57
Field, John (Colonel) 40, 48
Fifth Regiment Armory 166
Fincastle County (See Counties)
Finlay, William (Captain) 65
First Battle Group 226
First Carolina Maneuvers 163, 168
First United States Army 150, 263
Fisher, George A. (Lieutenant General) 254
Five Forks (See Battles)
Five Nations 35
Fleming, William (Colonel) 39, 41, 42, 44, 46
Flora, Lapthe, (Lieutenant Colonel) 263
Floyd Guard 78
Forbes, John (General) 34
Forbes Road 34
Ford, Gerald (President) 238
Forgyce, Captain 52
Forks, The 20-21

Fort 10
Forts
  A. P. Hill 229, 237, 239, 242, 244, 247-249, 252, 254
  Ashby 33
  Bedford 35
  Belvoir 242, 254, 256
  Benning 242, 252-253
  Blair 55
  Boonsboro 68
  Bowman 33
  Bragg 163, 239, 247-248, 259, 261
  Breckenridge's 33
  Campbell's 33
  Chaffee 247
  Chiswell 33
  Clendenin (Charleston, W.Va.) 55
  Cumberland 26-28, 33-35
  Delaware 135
  Detroit 68
  Dickenson 32-33
  Dinwiddie 32-33
  Dix 254, 257
  Dunlap 32
  Duquesne 21, 23, 25, 27, 28, 34-35
  Edwards 33
  Frederick 30, 33
  Germanna 6
  Harper's 33
  Harrison's 33
  Henry (Petersburg, Va.) 5, (Wheeling, W.Va.) 55, 68
  Holston 68
  Hood 255
  Hugh Mann's 32-33
  Hupp's 33
  Irwin 249, 256
  Jefferson 68
  John's Creek 33
  Kaskaskia 68
  Kuykendall 33
  Le Boeuf 19, 20
  Leavenworth 254, 255
  Lee (Charleston, W.Va.) 55, 68
  Lewis (Staunton, Va.) 12, (Salem, Va.) 24
  Ligonier 35
  line of forts 32-33
  Loudoun (Tenn.) 32, 33, 35 (Maryland) 37
  Maidstone 33
  McClellan 68
  McClelland 55-56

McHenry   71-72
McNeil's   33
Mason's Fort (John)   32-33
Meade   160-162, 164-168, 260
Miller's   33
Monroe   73, 165
Montbarey   207
Nelson   68
Necessity   23, 24, 28
Ohio   33
Paul's   33
Pearsall   33
Peterson's   33
Pickett   193, 229, 232, 236-238, 242, 256,
    257, 258-260
Pitt (Pittsburgh, Pa.)   34, 39, 41, 68 (Wheel-
    ing, W.Va.)   55-56
Pleasant   33
Polk   247, 252
Prince George   20
Randolph   55
Recovery   68
Savannah   33, 40-41
Seybert   32-33
Sherman   246
Stedman   140
Stevens   138
Sumter   74
Trial   33
Trout Rock   33
Upper Tract   32, 33
Vause   33
Vincennes   56, 68
Washington   68
Watuga   68
Wayne   68
William   32-33
Wolfe   33, 36
Woodstock   33
Young   32-33
Fort Lewis Volunteers   78
France, liberation   206, 209
Franklin, Benjamin   26, 37
Franks, Tommy (General)   255
Frazier's Farm   111
Fredendall, Lloyd R. (Major General)   163
Frederick, Prince of Wales   11
Fredericksburg   124
Freedom Salute   261
Frémont, John C.   99. 104-105, 107
French and Indian War   19, 26, 35

French Croix de Guerre   222
Frogg, John (Lieutenant)   48
Front Royal   101, 102
Front Royal, Battle   (See Battles)
Frontier Indian War of 1763-64   35
frontier unrest   18
Frye, Joshua (Colonel)   22
Fulkerson, Samuel (Colonel)   94, 102
Funk, H.S.   126
Fusiliers   60, 236

G
G Company   181
Gaines Mill   111
Gaps
    Ashby   83
    Brown's   98, 104, 106-110, 138
    Buffalo   36
    Chester   127
    Cumberland   18
    Massanutten   99-101
    Rockfish   12, 65
    Swift Run   6
    Thoroughfare   83, 115-116

Garnett, Richard B. (Brigadier General) 90, 92,
    94, 96-97, 106, 113
Gates, Horatio (General)   58
Gay
    Samuel (Captain)   14, 15
    Samuel R. (Brigadier General) 231
General Orders
    No. 7   144
    No. 13   154, 165
George III (King)   6, 11, 46
geography, Virginia   1
Gerhardt, Charles H. (Major General)   174,
    176-177, 190, 198, 199, 206-207, 211
German defenses   184
German Roer River defense   214
Germana Ford   125
Germany 251; invasion of   211
Gerow, Leonard T. (Major General)   165-167,
    170, 174, 177, 188, 194
Gettysburg, Battle   (See Battles)
Gibbon, John (Brigadier General)   116
Gibson, George (Captain)   52
Gilham, William (Colonel)   90
Gill, James (Captain)   15
Gilmore, Jim (Governor)   257
Gist, Christopher   20, 22

Global War on Terrorism   261
Godwin, Mills (Governor)   229
Gooch, William, Sir (Governor)   7, 9, 12, 14
Gordon, John B. (Lieutenant General)   137, 140
Gordonsville   109, 113, 124
Gossett, Louis, Jr.   248
Grandcamp   190, 191, 195, 220
Grant
    James (Major) (British)   34
    Ulysses (General)   73, 133, 135, 138-139
Grave Bridge   209
Graves, Thomas (Admiral)   63, 65
Grayson Dare Devils   78
Great Bridge, Battle   52
Great Depression   156, 162
Great Knives   34
Great Meadows   20, 22, 24-25, 27
Great Road   8, 12, 18
Great Snowball Battle   133
Great Warrior Path   4-5
Greenbrier Land Company   18
Greenbrier Rifles   79
Greenbrier River   4
Greene, Nathanael (General)   58, 61-62
Greenock Harbor   170-171
Greenville Greys   77
Gregory, Earle (Sergeant)   150
Grigsby, Andrew Jackson (Colonel)   98, 116,
    118-119, 121, 122
Grover, Bruce [Brigadier General] (Colonel) 233
Grubert, Reese T. (Major)   30, 58
Guantanamo Bay Naval Base   258-259
Guilford Court House, Battle   (See Battles)
Guiney's Station   124, 126
Gulf War   248
Gwynn's Island   52
Gypsy Hill Park   160

H
H Company   161
H-Hour   181
Haig, Douglas Sir (Field Marshall)   153
Halkett, Peter (Colonel Sir)   26
Halkett's Irish Regiment   27
Hamilton's Crossing   124
Hamtranck Guards   78
Harman, John (Major)   87 (Colonel)   98
Harmon, Jim (Captain)   236, (Lieutenant
    Colonel)   251
Harper, Kenton (Captain)   73, (Colonel)   92
Harpers Ferry   73, 74, 76, 80

Harris, James M. (First Lieutenant)   244,
    (Lieutenant Colonel) 256, 264, (Colonel)
    266-267
Harrisburg, Pennsylvania   231
Harrison, Benjamin (Governor)   69; Daniel
    (Captain)   16
Harrison's Landing   111-112
Harrod, James (Captain)   40
Hatcher's Run   139
Haute Marne Sector   150
Headquarters   242
hedgerows   191
Hedgesville Blues   78
Hemanuer, Kyle (Specialist)   261
Henderson, G. F. R. (Lieutenant Colonel)   96
Henry House Hill   85-86, 115-116, 158
Henry, Patrick (Colonel)   50, (Governor) 55, 58
Heubner, Clarence (Major General)   178
High Mobility Multi-Purpose Wheeled
Vehicle   243
Highlanders   60
Hills
    Hill 122   192-197, 199
    Hill 203   206
    Hill 219   205
    Hill 251   206
Hill
    A.P. (Major General)   113-114
    D.H. (Major General)   112
Hillsboro plane crash   224
Hines, Jerry (1st Sergeant)   246
Hines Memorial Armory (First Sergeant Jerry)
    246-247
Hitler, Adolph   158, 219
HMS (ships):
    Curacao   169
    Dunmore   52
    Empire Javelin   177, 181
    Fowey   50
    Leopard   70
    Magdalen   50
    Queen Mary   167, 169
Hocking River   41
Holden, James D. (Colonel)   247
Holt, James (Major)   239
Homan, George   170, 191
Hooker, Joseph (General)   124, 126
Hotchkiss, Jedediah (Major)   101, 114
House of Burgesses   11, 13, 50
Howard, Terry (SFC)   189
Howie, Thomas D. (Major)   160, 178, 196,
    198-202, 223

Huebner, Clarence (Major General) 178
Hugart, Thomas (Colonel) 65
Hughey, Joseph 43
Hull, Peter Captain) 65
HUMMWV 243, 245, 258
Hunter, David (General) 138
Hurricanes:
    Agnes 228
    Camille 228
    Hazel 224
    Katrina 265-266

I
Iceland 250
Igou, Janice (Lieutenant Colonel) 255
Illingworth, Gordon (Captain – Navy) 169
Independent Greys 82
Individual Explosive Device (IED) 260
Indian Chiefs
    Blue Jacket 43
    Cornstalk 43, 44, 46
    Logan 39
    White Eyes 46
Indian Nations 3, 17-18,35
Indian Tribes
    Algonquin 4
    Catawbas 4, 16
    Cayugas 3, 14, 39
    Cherokees 3-4, 32, 35-37, 55
    Chicasaw 4
    Chippewas 68
    Delaware 3-4, 6-7, 16, 37, 67-68
    Huron 4
    Illini 4
    Iroquois 4, 35
    Kickapoo 4
    Meherrin 6
    Menominee 4
    Miamis 3, 67-68
    Mingos 67
    Mohawks 3-4
    Onandagas 3-4
    Oneidas 3-4
    Ottawa 4
    Piankashaw 4
    Pottawatomies 68
    Senecas 3-4
    Shawnees 3, 32, 35-37, 43, 55, 67-68
    Susquehannock 4
    Tawas 68

Tuscaroras 3-4
Winnebago 4
Wyadots 3, 67-68

Infantry Brigade Combat Team 263-265
Ingles
    George 29
    Mary Draper 29-31
    Thomas 29
    William 29
Inspector General (IG) 249
Iraq 266
Iron Brigade See 2nd Wisconsin Brigade
Iron Curtain 224

J
Jackson,
    Andrew 72
    Thomas J. "Stonewall" 73-74 (Major) 75, (Colonel) 76, 80 (Brigadier General) 84-86 (Major General) 87-88, 90, 93, 96, 99, 119, 126
Jay's Treaty (See Treaties)
Jefferson Guards 78
Jefferson, Thomas (Governor) 58, 62, 160
Johnson
    Albert Sidney (General) 109, 131
    Edward (General) 99, 127
    Gerald (Sergeant First Class) 256
    Lyndon B. (President) 228;
Johnston
    Joseph E. (General) 80-84, 93, 127, 140
    Zachariah (Captain) 65
Joint Area Support Group 267
Joint Readiness Training Center 247
Jones, Frank (Major) 110
Jouett, John "Jack" Jr. (Captain) 63
Julich 215
Jumonville, Coulon de See Coulon de Villiers
Jumonville Glen 24-25
Jungle Operations Training Center 246

K
K Company 160
Kearneysville 122
Keigh-Tugh-Qua (Cornstalk) (See Indian Chiefs)
Kennedy, John F. (President) 227
Kenton, Simon 56
Kentucky 30, 67
Kentucky County (See Counties)
Kentucky Militia 40

Kernstown   94
Kernstown, Battle (See Battles)
Kerr's Creek (See Creeks)
Key Personnel Upgrade Program (KPUP)   238
Keystone Division   231
Kincaid, Captain   55
King, Rufus (Major General)   116
Kings Mountain, Battle (See Battles)
Knights of the Golden Horseshoe   6
Korean War   224
Koslar   213
Kosovo   262

L
La Force, Captain (French)   20
Lafayette, Marquis de (General – French) 63, 160
Landing Craft   180, 182, 185
landing exercises   172
Lederer, John   4
Lee
    Fitzhugh   145
    Henry   55
    Richard Henry   96
    Robert E. (Colonel)   73, 75 (General) 79,
        82, 98, 113, 119, 124, 129, 133, 135, 138
    Thomas   16
Leesburg Armory   257
Les Moulins Draw   181, 184, 186, 188
Letcher, John (Governor)   68, 74, 76, 87
Letcher Riflemen   78
Lewis
    Andrew   12 (Captain) 15, 18, 21, 22, 24, 30,
        (Colonel) 34, 37 (General) 39, 43-44, 51, 52
    Charles 12, 18 (Captain) 36 (Colonel) 39,
        41, 44, 48
    John   6, 8-9, 11 (Colonel)12,-14, 16,
        (Colonel) 18, 35
    Samuel   12, (Colonel) 63
    Thomas   12
    Virgil   63
    William   12
    William Irvine   72
Lewis family   69
Lewisburg, West Virginia   18
Liberty Hall Volunteers   78
Light Division   242
Light Fighters   243-244, 248
Light Leaders   242, 244, 248
Lillis, Charles (CW4)   262
Lincoln, Abraham (President)   74, 131, 133
Lockart, James (Captain)   32

Lockridge, Captain   55
London, Midland and Scottish Railroad 170, 171
Logan, Chief   39
Logstown   20
Long, Francis (Captain)   65
Long Knives   15, 46
Longstreet, James (Lieutenant General) 73, 84,
        116, 119, 123
Loring, William W. (Brigadier General) 90,
        (Major General) 93
Loyal Company   18
Loyalists   55
Lyle, John (Captain)   55

M
Madison, James (President)   71, 129
Major of St. Lô 202
Major, Stanley P. (Private)   164
Malvern Hill   111-112
Manassas (First), Battle (See Battles)
Manassas (Second), Battle (See Battles)
Manassas Maneuvers   146, 158
Mantz, Tim (Lieutenant Colonel)   255
Marion Rifles   77
Marsh, John O. Jr. (The Honorable) (Lieuten-
        ant Colonel) 237-238, 241, 251
Marshall, George C. (General)   24
Martin
    Mike (Major)   267
    Patrick (Captain)   32
Martinsburg. West Virginia   81
Martinsville, Virginia   161
Martinville Ridge   198, 199
Mary Gray   12
Mason, Captain   55
Mathews, Captain   46
McCabe, E.R. Warner (Brigadier General) 193
McCaddin, William J. (Major General)   232
McClanahan, John (Captain)   36
McClellan, George   73, 96, 104, 108, 113
McClelland, John   56
McClennahan, Robert (Captain)   48
McCutchen, William (Captain)   56, 65
McDaniel, Lloyd D. [Brigadier General]
        (Colonel) 248
McDowell, Battle (See Battles)
McDowell burial ground   16-17
McDowell
    Ephraim   12
    Irvin (General/Doctor)   82, 96, 103, 113
    John (Captain)   15, 16

McGuire, Hunter Holmes (Doctor) 93
McKiernan, David D. (General) 255
McKinley, William (President) 145
McLain, Raymond S. (Major General) 212
McNair
   Daniel (Captain) 16
   Leslie (Lieutenant General) 172
McNamara, Robert S. (Secretary of Defense) 228
McNeil, Rodney W. (Brigadier General) 242
Meade, (General) 131
Mechum's River Station 98, 109
Meeks, Lawrence (Lieutenant Colonel) 178, 198
Mercer, Walt (Lieutenant Colonel) 266
Metcalfe, John (Lieutenant Colonel) 177
Meuse River 150
Meuse-Argonne Campaign 151
Mexican War 72-73
Michel, Franz 5
Middlebrook Rifles 72
MILES system 239
Military Code of Virginia 157-158
militia
   description 15, 69
   origin 13
   structure 13, 15-16, 69
Miller, George 36
Miller School 248
Milroy, Robert H. (General) 99
Milton A. Reckord Award 244, 259
Mine Run, Battle (See Battles)
Minuteman 13, 53
mobilization 257
Moffett
   George (Captain) 36
   John (Lieutenant) 14
Mohave Desert 249
Monongahela River 20, 21, 28
Monroe Guards 79
Montgomery Fencibles 78
Montgomery, G.V "Sonny" (Major General/
   Congressman) 243
Montgomery GI Bill 243
Montgomery Highlanders 78
Montgomery Mountain Boys 78
Monticello Guard 160-161, 230, 236
Mooney, James 43
Moore House 64
Moorefield Grays 82
Morgan, Daniel (Colonel) 51, 52, (Brigadier
   General) 58-59, 60-61

Morris
   Albert R. (Major General) 245
   Jim (Major) 209
Mount Jackson Rifles 82
Mountain Guards 77
Mountain Rangers 80, 82
Mountain Sax Horn Band 98
Muhlenberg, Peter (Lutheran Minister)
   (General) 58
Mule Shoe 135
Mullins, Thomas C. (Lieutenant Colonel) 185
Multinational Force and Observers (MFO) 250
Multiple Unit Training Assembly (MUTA) 248
Munchen-Gladbach 216
Murray, John (Captain) 48
muster 15

N
Nance, Ray (Lieutenant) 222
National D-Day Memorial Foundation 253
National Defense Act (See Acts)
National Encampment 144
National Guard Association of the United
   States 143-145
National Guard Memorial 188
National Road 20
National Security Act of 1947 (See Acts)
National Training Center (NTC) 248, 249,
   251, 256
Navy Task Force 219
Neff, John Francis (Colonel) 88, 98, 107, 116,
   119
Nelson Guards 78
Nelson, Thomas (Governor) 63
New Horizons 255
New Market, Battle (See Battles)
Nichichuk, Eddie 221
Nijmegen bridge 209
Ninth Army Reserve 216
Noble Eagle I 257
Noble Eagle II 259
Noriega, Manuel 246
Norrell, Oliver (Lieutenant Colonel) 255
North Atlantic Treaty Organization (NATO) 244
North, Lord (Britsh Prime Minister) 37
North Resolution 37
Northern Viking exercise 250
Northwest Territory 68
Norway 244
nuclear power plant security 258

O

Ogle, Joseph (Captain) 55
O'Hara, Charles (Brigadier – Navy) 64
Ohio Company 18
Ohio River 20, 27, 46, 67
Ohio River Valley 4, 18, 21, 26
Olympics, XIX Winter 257
Olympics security 257
Omaha Beach 178, 181-187, 190, 194-196
Operations
  Chindit 254
  Cobra 200, 203,
  Duck 176
  Enduring Freedom 260-261
  Iraqi Freedom 266
  Joint Guard 252
  Jump Start 266
  Market Garden 209
  Mountain State 246
  Nobler Eagle I 257
  Noble Eagle II 259
  Other Clay 254
  Overlord 176, 179
Operational Readiness Exercise (ORE) 249
Operational Tempo (OPTEMPO) 256
Opie
  E. Walton (Colonel) 161, 167, (Major
    General) 229
  Hierome (Colonel) 157, 161, 167, (Briga-
    dier General)
Orange Court House 113
Ord, J. G., (Major General) 231
Ortner, Blake (Lieutenant Colonel) 260
Over Mountain Militia 57

P

Page Greys 82
Panama 246
Patterson
  Mike (Captain) 252
  Robert (Major General) 80, 83
Patton
  George (General) 200, 203, 206, 214
  James (Lieutenant Colonel) 7, 14-16, 18,
    19, 21, 25, 29-30
Pattonsville 18
Paxton, Frank (Colonel) 122, 126-127, 137
Payne's Farm 131-132
peacekeeping efforts 250
Pearl Harbor 164
Pender, Dorsey (Brigadier General) 118

Pendleton, William Nelson (Reverend
    Doctor) (Captain) 79, (Brigadier
    General) 144
Peninsula Campaign 113
pentomic structure 226
Peregoy, Frank (Sergeant) 160-161, (Corporal)
    164, (Serpeant) 190-191, 193-194
Pershing, John J. "Blackjack" (General) 148,
    150, 153
Petersburg Siege 139
Petersburg 5
Phantom Menace 255
Phillip A. Connelly Award 255
Phillips, William R. (Lieutenant Colonel)
    254, (Colonel) 266, 269
Physical Fitness Test 235
Pickett, (General) George 137
Pickett's Charge 137
pillbox 185
Pisgah Church 131
Pitt, William (Sir, Earl of Chatham) 34, 37
Pittsburgh 20, 21
Point du Hoc 178,190, 195
Point Pleasant 39, 42-46
Point State Park 21
Polk, James (President) 73
Pollard, John (Governor) 157
Polyniak, John (Sergeant) 185, 188-189
Pope Air Force Base 248
Pope, John (Major General) 113, 115-116, 118
Port Republic 105
Port Republic, Battle (See Battles)
Posey, Thomas (Captain) 52-53
Potomac Guards 82
Presidential Unit Citation 222
Proclamation Line of 1763 67
Provision Forces of Virginia 88
Pulaski Guards 78, 127
Puntenney, William (Captain) 200

Q

Queen Mary See HMS
Queens Own Highlanders 236

R

Raggett, Eugene (Lieutenant) 203
Ramcke, Hermann (Major General) 206
Randolph,
  John (Virginia Stateman) 53
  William (Colonel) 134
Ranger Stockades 32

Rapidan River   6
Ready Rifles   78
Reckord, Milton A. (Major General) 159, 165-
    166, 244, 259
Red Dragons   251, 265
Regimental Crest   153
reorganization   250, 263
Reorganization Objectives Army Division
    (ROAD)   228
Revolutionary War   47, 52, 55
Revolutionary War service   52
Reynolds, John (General)   110
Rhine River bridge   209
Roach, George (Private)   182
Roads family   37
Robb, Charles S. (Governor)   253
Robertson, James   43-44
Robinson, George (Captain)   15
Rochambeau, Jean-Batiste (General)   63
Rockbridge Artillery   79, 113, 122, 144
Rockbridge County   (See Counties)
Rockbridge Grays   78
Rockbridge Rifles   72, 77, 79
Rockingham Confederates   82
Rockingham Grays   72
Roller, George (Captain)   250
Romney Expedition   92
Ronald, Charles (Colonel)   98, 114
Roosevelt, Franklin D. (President)   158
Root, Elihu (Secretary of War)   145
Rude's Hill   97
Ruhr Pocket   217
Ryder, Robert (Lieutenant Colonel)   247, 249

S
Saint Croix Church   200
Salisbury Plain   170
Sampson Mathew's Ordinary   39
Scales, Robert   182
Schenck, Robert (Brigadier General)   99
Scholl, Peter (Captain)   15
Scioto River Valley   46
Scott
    Charles (General)   68
    Robert (Captain)   32
Seal of Virginia   153
Second Carolina Maneuvers   166, 168
Second Indian War   19, 26
Seldon, Wendell R. (Brigadier General)   242
Selective Service Act   (See Acts)
Selective Service System   233

Sennybridge Training Area (Wales)   236
September 11, 2001   256
Service Extension Act   163
Seven Days Campaign 109, 112-113
Seven Years War   28
Sevier
    John (Colonel)   56, 57
    Joseph   57
    Valentine (Colonel)   43-44
Stabilization Force 10 (SFOR 10)   256
Sheetz, Daniel 131
Shelby
    Isaac (Captain)   46
    James   43
Shenandoah Riflemen   82
Shenandoah River   2
Shenandoah Valley   2-3, 6, 16-17, 30, 51, 69-
    70, 76, 83, 88, 103, 139, 143, 146, 159, 259
Shepherdstown, West Virginia   27
Sheridan, Philip A. (General)   138
Sherman, William T. (General)   73
Shields, James (General)   94, 104, 105, 107
Shinseki, Eric K.   255
Ships
    British (HMS)
        Curacao   169
        Dunmore   52
        Empire Javelin   177, 181
        Fowey   50
        Leopard   70
        Magdalen   50
        Queen Mary   167, 169-170, 231
    American (USS)
        Aroostook   112
        Charles Carroll   178
        Chesapeake   70
        Finland   150
        Galena   112
        Maine   145
        Matsonia   153
        Texas   181
        Thomas Jefferson   178, 181

Shriver Grays   79
Shuey
    Benjamin Franklin (Lieutenant)   85
    George Washington (Captain)   73
    Theodore G. III (Lieutenant)   259
    Theodore G. Jr. [Brigadier General] (Lieuten-
    ant Colonel)   247, 249, (Colonel) 189, 252, 257
Siegfried Line   210

Simpson, Robert (Colonel) 258
Sinai 250
Six Nations 3
Slapton Sands 176, 179
Slaughter at Waxhaws 57
Slaughter
    Bob (Sergeant) 184
    Thomas (Captain) 40
Smith
    Abraham (Colonel) 55
    John (Captain) 14, 15
    Kirby (Brigadier General) 80-84
    Thomas (Captain) 55, 65
    Thompson (Lieutenant Colonel) 24
Smyth Blues 78
South Wales 236
Southampton 220
Southern Army (Continental) 58
Southern Guard 77
Southern Military District of Virginia 19
Spanish American War 145
Special Orders 129 (Confederate) 127
Spotswood, Alexander (Governor) 5-6
Spotsylvania Court House, Battle 135
Sproul, Archibald (Major General) 192, 227, 229
St. Clair-sur-l'Elle 192
St. Laurent Draw 188
St. Lô 192-193, 195, 197-203
Stabilization Force 10 256
Stalnicker, Samuel (Captain) 32
Stamp Act (See Acts)
State Military Reservation (SMR) 144, 235
Staunton 13-14, 16, 24, 36, 63, 73, 146, 229
Staunton Military Academy 160, 201, 223
Staunton Rifles 78
Stephen, Adam (Captain) 21
Stephenson, Daniel (Captain) 51
Stephenson's Depot 102
Steuart (General) 136
Stewart, David (Colonel) 32
Stobo, Robert (Captain) 22
stockades 10
Stonewall Brigade 86, 90, 107, 127, 131, 133, 140-144, 231, 242, 156
Stonewall Brigade Band 98, 140
Stonewall Brigade, Civil War veterans
        muster 1 44
Stonewall Jackson Hotel 160
strike relief 146, 157
Stuart
    Captain 46

Henry Carter (Governor) 146
J. E. B. (Lieutenant) 74 (Lieutenant Colonel) 79, (Colonel) 81-82, 97 (General) 126
John (Colonel) 4 7
Sullivan, Gilbert J. (Brigadier General) 239
summer camp 158, 232
Superior Unit Award 249
Support Battalion 235
Sure-Pay 246
Swift Run Gap   (See Gaps)

T
Taliaferro, William B. (Colonel) 90, (General) 116
Tarleton, Banastre (Colonel – British) 57, 61, 57-62
Tarleton's Quarter 57, 61
Task Forces
    4-505 255
    C 200
    Falcon 262-263
    Normandy 260-262
    Pelican 255
    Stonewall 265-266
Tate, William (Captain) 65
Taylor
    Richard (Brigadier General) 101
    Zachary (General) 72-73
Tennessee River 32
Terry, William (Colonel) 131, 133, (General) 137-140
Thackston, Carroll (Major General) 250, 253
The Total Force Policy 232
Third Army 203
Thomas D. Howie Memorial Armory 223, 237
Thomas, Mrs. 36
Thompson
    Alex (Colonel) 55
    Captain 56
    Hugh (Captain) 15
    Thomas T. (Major General) 248
Tidworth Barracks 170, 171-173
Tierney, Jim (Captain) 262
Title 32 225, 258
Todd, John (Colonel) 67
Todd's Tavern 46, 125
Toms Brook Guards 82
Total Force Policy 232
Toy Soldiers 248
Training and Doctrine Command (TRADOC) 239

Treaties
　Camp Charlotte　46
　Ghent　72
　Greenville　68
　Jay's　68
　Lancaster　17-18
　Paris　35-36, 65
　with Mexico　73
trench warfare　148
Trent, William (Captain)　20
Trimble, John　36
Trinity Episcopal Church　63
Truman, Harry S. (President)　222, 231
Tu-Endie-Wei Park　48
Turner
　Augustus J. (Professor)　98
　Herbert C. (Colonel)　252
Turner's Silver Coronet Band　98
Turtle Creek (See Creeks)

U
Ulio, James (Major)　148
Unger, Washington　92
Unger's Store　92
Uniform Militia Act (See Acts)
uniforms　167, 238, 245, 256
Uniontown, Pennsylvania　24
United States Ford　125-126
United States Customs and Border Patrol　266
Utah Beach　182, 190, 194

V
Valley Campaign　108
Valley District Army　94
Valley of Virginia　2
Vanmeter, Isaac　9
Vencil, Clarence, Jr. (Sergeant)　236
Verdun, France　150
Victory Europe　219
Vierville　181, 195
Vierville Church　181
Vierville Draw　185-186, 188
Viet Nam War　228
Villa, Pancho　146
Vire　203
Virginia Central Rail Road　98, 113
Virginia Convention　52, 74
Virginia Defense Force　245
Virginia General Assembly　50, 54, 62-63, 67, 70
Virginia Guardsman　156

Virginia Military Institute　74, 99, 138
Virginia Militia　48, 51, 56, 58, 70-71
Virginia National Guard　146
Virginia Noble Eagle　257
Virginia Regiment　19, 21, 28
Virginia Riflemen　78
von Steuben, Friedrich Wilhelm, Baron
　(General)　63

W
Walker
　James (General)　127, 129,131, 133, 135-137
　Thomas (Doctor)　6, 7
Walter T. Kerwin Award　249, 259
War Department (Confederate)　127
War of 1812　70, 72
Warfighter　254-255
Ward, Edward (Ensign)　20
Warner, John W. (U.S. Senator)　253
Washington
　George 18, (Major)19, 21 (Lieutenant
　Colonel) 22, 24, 26-28, 32 (Colonel) 34
　(General) 51, 56, 58, 63 (President) 69, 70
　Lawrence　18
Washington's Expedition　21
Water, J.H. (Lieutenant)　75
Watson
　Brian (Captain)　267
　Leroy H. (Colonel)　206
Wayne, Anthony (General)　68
weapon types　237
Weinberger, Casper (Secretary of Defense)　241
Wenger, Amy (Staff Sergeant)　268
West Augusta　54
West Augusta Guards　72, 74, 78
West Augusta Militia　75
West View Infantry　77
Western District　56
Whiskey Rebellion　70
White
　Charles　56
　Hugh (Captain)　118
　Robert (Major)　36
White Eyes (See Indian Chiefs)
White Oak Swamp　111-112
Wilder, Douglas (Governor)　247
Wilderness, Battle (See Battles)
Wilderness Tavern　125
Wilkes, John (Master Sergeant)　167
Wilkinson, Tom (Lieutenant Colonel)　259

Williams
    Claude (Major General)   257, 266
    Tim (Lieutenant Colonel)   255
Wills Creek 24 (See Creeks)
Willson, John (Captain)   15
Wilson
    Samuel (Captain)   48
    Woodrow (President)   146-147, 153
Winchester   26, 102
Winchester, First Battle (See Battles)
Winchester, Third Battle (See Battles)
Winchester Riflemen 78
Winder, Charles S. (Brigadier General) 97, 109,
        102, 115, 137
Wingate, George W. (Brigadier General) 144

winter quarters 124
Wood, Abraham (Colonel) 4-5
Wray, Ed (Lieutenant Colonel) 246
Wright, William (Lieutenant) 25
Wythe Grays 78

Y
Yorktown Siege 63
Yorktown Surrender 65
Young, D. S.
    (Colonel) 36
    Ronald D. (Brigadier General) 256-257
    Thomas 36

About the author

Theodore G. Shuey, Jr., Brigadier General, is retired after serving close to thirty-eight years in the Army National Guard, most of it in the Stonewall Brigade as a commander at all levels. He is the natural choice to write this history of the 116th Infantry Regiment, tracing the evolution of the Guard. His extensive experience with this remarkable unit, in both active and non-active duty, gives him a rare insight into all aspects of its modern operation through Vietnam and Iraq. And, like Stonewall Jackson before him, he had the rare opportunity to lead and learn from this highly decorated and historic unit.

Shuey's background as a history major at Bridgewater College and a history teacher with a masters of education from the University of Virginia in public school administration has enabled him to carry out the historical research on this unit that stretches back to the Augusta Militia and its formation even before the French and Indian War. His love of history, especially that of his native Augusta County, shines through in the pages of this account.

Shuey is a graduate of the U.S. Army Command and General Staff College in residence and the Army War College. His awards and decorations include a Legion of Merit, Commendation Medal, the Army Achievement Medal, the National Defense Service Medal, the Global War on Terrorism Service Medal, the Humanitarian Service Medal, and the Armed Forces Reserve Medal. In his last assignment, he served on the Joint Staff of the National Guard Bureau in Arlington, Va. He was selected to serve as the Honorary Colonel of the Regiment upon his retirement in July, 2007.

On the civilian side of his life, he is President of the TGS Group, Inc., in Staunton, Va., an administrative and marketing company that provides financial services and products for military and government personnel and families throughout the United States and its territories.

Shuey has two children, Ellen and Tad, and he and his wife, Elizabeth, reside in Staunton while continuing to operate the family farm in Augusta County. *Ever Forward!* is Shuey's first foray into the publishing world, but it is probably not his last. A historical novel with a military story line is already well underway.